British History in Per

General Editor: Je~

continued overleaf

A.J. Pollard *The Wars of the Roses (2nd edn)*
David Powell *British Politics and the Labour Question, 1868–1990*
David Powell *The Edwardian Crisis: Britain, 1901–1914*
Richard Rex *Henry VIII and the English Reformation (2nd edn)*
Matthew Roberts *Political Movements in Urban England, 1832–1914*
David Scott *Politics and War in the Three Stuart Kingdoms, 1637–49*
G.R. Searle *The Liberal Party: Triumph and Disintegration, 1886–1929 (2nd edn)*
George Southcombe & Grant Tapsell *Restoration Politics, Religion and Culture:*
Britain and Ireland, 1600–1714
John Stuart Shaw *The Political History of Eighteenth-Century Scotland*
W.M. Spellman *John Locke*
William Stafford *John Stuart Mill*
Robert Stewart *Party and Politics 1830–1852*
Alan Sykes *The Radical Right in Britain*
Bruce Webster *Medieval Scotland*
Ann Williams *Kingship and Government in Pre-Conquest England*
Ian S. Wood *Churchill*
John W. Young *Britain and European Unity, 1945–99 (2nd edn)*
Michael B. Young *Charles I*
Paul Ziegler *Palmerston*

Please note that a sister series, Social History in Perspective, is available
covering the key topics in social and cultural history.

British History in Perspective
Series Standing Order: ISBN 0–333–71356–7 hardcover/ISBN 0–333–69331–0 paperback
You can receive future titles in this series as they are published by placing a standing
order. Please contact your bookseller or, in case of difficulty, write to the address
below with your name and address, the title of the series and the ISBN quoted above.

Customer Services Department, Macmillan Distribution Ltd
Houndmills, Basingstoke, Hampshire RG21 6XS, England

KINGSHIP AND GOVERNMENT IN PRE-CONQUEST ENGLAND C. 500–1066

ANN WILLIAMS

palgrave
macmillan

First published in Great Britain 1999 by
MACMILLAN PRESS LTD
Houndmills, Basingstoke, Hampshire RG21 6XS and London
Companies and representatives throughout the world

A catalogue record for this book is available from the British Library.

ISBN 10: 0-333-56797-8 hardcover
ISBN 10: 0-333-56798-6 paperback
ISBN 13: 978-0-333-56797-5 hardcover
ISBN 13: 978-0-333-56798-2 paperback

First published in the United States of America 1999 by
ST. MARTIN'S PRESS, INC.,
Scholarly and Reference Division,
175 Fifth Avenue, New York, N.Y. 10010

ISBN 0-312-22090-1

Library of Congress Cataloging-in-Publication Data
Williams, Ann, 1937–
Kingship and government in pre-conquest England, c. 500–1066 / Ann
Williams.
    p. cm. — (British history in perspective)
Includes bibliographical references and index.
ISBN 0-312-22090-1 (cloth)
1. Great Britain—Politics and government—449–1066.   2. Monarchy-
-England—History—To 1500.   3. Anglo-Saxons—Kings and rulers.
I. Title. II. Series.
DA152.W545   1999
942.01—DC21   98–46258
                                                          CIP

This book is printed on paper suitable for recycling and made from fully managed and
sustained forest sources. Logging, pulping and manufacturing processes are expected to
conform to the environmental regulations of the country of origin

Printed in Great Britain by the MPG Books Group, Bodmin and King's Lynn

To the generations of students at the Polytechnic of North London who, between 1965 and 1988, attended my classes on pre-conquest history, and (in some cases) were kind enough to say that they enjoyed the experience, this book is dedicated in love and gratitude.

'The people must know how well I govern them. How would they know, if we didn't tell them?'

(Frank Herbert, *Dune*)

CONTENTS

PREFACE

This book is a study of the exercise of royal authority before the Norman Conquest. Six centuries separate the *adventus Saxonum* from the battle of Hastings; the same length of time which separates the late twentieth century from the age of Chaucer. During those long years, the English kings changed from warlords who exacted submission by force into law-givers to whom obedience was a moral duty. In the process, they created many of the administrative institutions which continued to serve their successors. They also created England; the united kingdom of the English people.

To write the history even of a few aspects of such a lengthy process is not easy, and this book has been long in the making; much perforce has been omitted. It could not have been done at all without the support and encouragement of friends, especially Stephen Church, who cheered me with help and advice over many difficult times. I should like to thank all those who, over the years, have sent me papers which I might otherwise have missed or had difficulty finding, especially Simon Keynes, Susan Reynolds, David Roffe, Pamela Taylor, Patrick Wormald and Barbara Yorke. I am particularly grateful to Dr Keynes for a copy of his privately-published *Atlas of Attestations in Anglo-Saxon Charters*; the frequency of its appearance in the footnotes will show the labour it has saved me. For similar reasons I must thank Susan Kelly for the interim update of P. H. Sawyer's *Anglo-Saxon Charters*, on a new edition of which she is currently engaged. Many debts are acknowledged in the bibliography and the endnotes, but not all the assistance I received was in published form, and I should like to mention a few who helped me with discussion of particular problems; Tom Cain, Marios Costambeys, David Dumville, Guy Halsall, Michael Hare and Sally Harvey. I also owe much to those who participated in the now-defunct seminars on English Diplomatic at the Institute of Historical Research, London, notably Paul Fouracre, Wendy Davies, Diana Greenway, Alex Rumble, T. A. Heslop and Janet Nelson. And I must record a

special debt to the late John Brand, from whom I derive whatever under-
standing I possess of the mysteries of numismatics. All errors, omissions
and misunderstandings are, of course, my own.

Wanstead   ANN WILLIAMS

Acknowledgements

The author and publishers wish to thank Routledge for permission to
use copyright material from the table 'Regnal list of the West Saxons'
(p. xxvii), from Barbara Yorke, *Kings and Kingdoms of Early Anglo-Saxon
England* (1997), p. 133. Every effort has been made to trace all the copy-
right-holders, but if any have been inadvertently overlooked the publishers will be pleased to make the necessary arrangement at the first
opportunity.

LIST OF ABBREVIATIONS

Æthelweard, *Chron*	A. Campbell (ed.), *The Chronicle of Æthelweard* (London, 1962).
Anon Life	Anonymous *life of St Cuthbert*, in *Two Lives*.
ANS	*Anglo-Norman Studies*.
ASC	Dorothy Whitelock, David C. Douglas and Susie I. Tucker (eds), *The Anglo-Saxon Chronicle: a revised translation*, 2nd edn (London, 1965).
ASE	*Anglo-Saxon England*.
ASSAH	*Anglo-Saxon Studies in Archaeology and History* (vols 1–3 published by BAR; subsequent volumes by Oxford Committee for Archaeology and History).
Asser	'Asser's Life of King Alfred', Simon Keynes and Michael Lapidge, *Alfred the Great* (Harmondsworth, 1983) pp. 66–110.
BAR	British Archaeological Reports.
Bede, *Letter to Ecgbert*	*Epistola Bede ad Ecgbertum episcopum*, in Charles Plummer (ed.), *Venerabilis Baedae Opera Historica* (Oxford, 1896) pp. 405–23.
Bede, *Prose Life*	Bede's *Prose life of Cuthbert*, in *Two Lives*.
BNJ	*British Numismatic Journal*.
CBA	Council for British Archaeology.
Chron Abingdon	Joseph Stevenson (ed.), *Chronicon Monasterii de Abingdon*, Rolls Series (London, 1858).
Chron Evesham	W. Dunn Macray (ed.), *Chronicon Abbatiae de Evesham*, Rolls Series (London, 1863).
Chron Ramsey	W. Dunn Macray (ed.), *Chronicon Abbatiae Rameseiensis*, Rolls Series (London, 1886).
Domesday Book iv	*Domesday Book seu Liber Censualis Willelmi Primi Regis Angliae*, vol iv *Additamenta* (London, 1816).

ECEE	C. R. Hart, *The Early Charters of Eastern England* (Leicester, 1966).
ECNENM	C. R. Hart, *The Early Charters of Northern England and the North Midlands* (Leicester, 1975).
ECW	H. P. R. Finberg, *The Early Charters of Wessex* (Leicester, 1964).
ECWM	H. P. R. Finberg, *The Early Charters of the West Midlands* (Leicester, 1961).
EHD i	Dorothey Whitelock (ed.), *English Historical Documents*, i, *c*. 500–1042 (London, 1955).
EHR	*English Historical Review*.
Exon Domesday	*Liber Exoniensis* (printed in *Domesday Book* iv).
GDB	R. W. H. Erskine (ed.), *Great Domesday: facsimile*, Alecto Historical Editions (London, 1986).
GP	N. E. S. A. Hamilton (ed.), *William of Malmesbury, De gestis pontificum Anglorum*, Rolls Series (London, 1870).
GR	W. Stubbs (ed.), *William of Malmesbury, De gestis regum Anglorum*, Rolls Series (London, 1887).
HA	*Historia Abbatum auctore Baedae*, in Charles Plummer (ed.), *Venerabilis Baedae Opera Omnia* (Oxford, 1896) pp. 364–87; translation in D. H. Farmer (ed.), *The Age of Bede* (Harmondsworth, 1983).
HAA	Anonymous Life of Ceolfrid, *Historia Abbatum auctore anonymo*, in Charles Plummer (ed.), *Venerabilis Baedae Opera Historica* (Oxford, 1896).
HB	*Historia Brittonum*, in John Morris (ed.), *Nennius: British History and the Welsh Annals* (Chichester, 1980).
HC	Hemming's Cartulary, Thomas Hearne (ed.), *Hemingi Chartularium Wigornensis* (Oxford, 1723).
HE	Bertram Colgrave and R. A. B. Mynors (eds), *Bede's Ecclesiastical History of the English People* (Oxford, 1969).
HR	*Historia Regum*, in Thomas Arnold (ed.), *Symeonis monachi Opera Omnia*, Rolls Series (London, 1882–5) ii, pp. 3–283.
J. Med. Hist.	*Journal of Medieval History*.
JnW	P. McGurk and R. R. Darlington (eds), *The Chronicle of John of Worcester* (Oxford 1995).

LDB	Little Domesday, Abraham Farley (ed.), *Domesday Book, seu Liber Censualis Willelmi Primi Regis Anglie* ii, Record Commission (London, 1783).
Origins	Steven Bassett (ed.), *The Origins of Anglo-Saxon Kingdoms* (Leicester, 1989).
P&P	*Past and Present.*
S.	P. H. Sawyer, *Anglo-Saxon Charters: an Annotated List and Bibliography*, Royal Historical Society (London, 1968).
Stenton, *ASE*	F. M. Stenton, *Anglo-Saxon England*, 3rd edn (Oxford, 1971).
TRHS	*Transactions of the Royal Historical Society.*
Two Chronicles	Thomas Earle and Charles Plummer (eds), *Two of the Saxon Chronicles parallel* (Oxford, 1952).
Two Lives	Bertram Colgrave (ed.), *Two Lives of Saint Cuthbert* (Cambridge, 1940).
VCH	*Victoria History of the Counties of England.*
VG	Bertram Colgrave (ed.), *Felix's Life of Saint Guthlac* (Cambridge, 1985).
VW	Bertram Colgrave (ed.), *The Life of Bishop Wilfrid by Eddius Stephanus* (Cambridge, 1985).
Wallace-Hadrill, Commentary	J. M. Wallace-Hadrill, *Bede's Ecclesiastical History of the English people: a Historical Commentary* (Oxford, 1988).
WG	Bertram Colgrave (ed.), *The Earliest Life of Gregory the Great* (Cambridge, 1985).

CHRONOLOGY

658	Mercians throw off Northumbrian rule.
658–75	Wulfhere king of Mercia.
664	Synod of Whitby (Northumbria).
664–709/10	Wilfrid bishop of York.
668–90	Archiepiscopate of Theodore.
670–85	Ecgfrith king of Bernicia; Ælfwine king of Deira.
672	First synod of the whole English Church at Hertford.
673–c. 685	Laws of Hlothhere and Wihtred of Kent.
c. 674	Wulfhere defeated by Ecgfrith.
675–704	Æthelred king of Mercia.
679	Battle of the River Trent: Ecgfrith defeated by Æthelred; death of Ælfwine of Deira.
685	Battle of Nechtanesmere (Dunnichen Moss): Ecgfrith killed by Bruide, king of the Picts.
685–7	Cædwalla king of Wessex.
685–705	Aldfrith king of Northumbria.
688–726	Ine king of Wessex.
688–94	Laws of Ine.
690–726	Wihtred king of Kent.
695	Laws of Wihtred.
716–57	Æthelbald king of Mercia.
731	Bede completes the Historia Ecclesiastica.
735	Death of Bede; York becomes an archbishopric.
736	Ismere charter; Æthelbald called 'king of Britain'.
757	Murder of Æthelbald; Beornred and Offa fight for Mercia.
757–86	Cynewulf king of Wessex.
758–96	Offa king of Mercia.
765–92	Jænberht archbishop of Canterbury.
768	Charlemagne king of the Franks.
786	Papal legation to England; murder of Cynewulf.
786–802	Beorhtric king of Wessex; Ecgberht in exile in Frankia.
787	Synod of Chelsea: Lichfield an archbishopric. Ecgfrith, Offa's son, consecrated king of the Mercians.
789	Beorhtric marries Offa's daughter, Eadburh; viking raid on Portland, Dorset.
793	Vikings sack Lindisfarne.
796	Deaths of Offa and Ecgfrith; Eardwulf consecrated king of Northumbria.
796–821	Coenwulf king of Mercia.
800	Charlemagne crowned emperor.

802-39	Ecgberht king of Wessex.
803	Synod of *Clofesho*: Lichfield demoted to a bishopric.
814	Death of Charlemagne.
814-40	Louis the Pious emperor and king of the Franks.
821-3	Ceolwulf I king of Mercia.
823	Ceolwulf deposed.
823-6	Beornwulf king of Mercia.
825	Battle of *Ellendun* (Wroughton): Ecgberht defeats Beornwulf.
826	Beornwulf killed in East Anglia.
826-7	West Saxon conquest of south-east England; Æthelwulf son of Ecgberht king of Kent.
827	Ludeca, king of Mercia, killed in East Anglia.
827-*c*. 838	Wiglaf king of Mercia.
829-30	Wiglaf temporarily expelled by Ecgberht.
838	Battle of Hingston Down: Ecgberht defeats the Britons of Dumnonia and their viking allies.
839-58	Æthelwulf king of Wessex.
839-*c*. 852	Athelstan, son of Æthelwulf, king of Kent.
840-52	Beorhtwulf king of Mercia.
843-77	Charles the Bald king of the Franks.
849	Murder of Wigstan, grandson of Wiglaf and Ceolwulf I; cult develops at Repton.
852-74	Burgred king of Mercia.
853	Burgred marries Æthelswith, daughter of Æthelwulf.
855-6	Æthelwulf's pilgrimage to Rome.
856	Æthelwulf marries Judith, daughter of Charles the Bald.
858-60	Æthelbald king of Wessex.
860-65	Æthelberht king of Wessex.
865-71	Æthelred I king of Wessex.
865	Arrival of the 'Great Army' of Ivar the Boneless.
867	Great Army attacks York.
869	Great Army attacks Mercia.
870	Great Army attacks East Anglia; martyrdom of King Edmund of East Anglia.
871	Great Army attacks Wessex; battles of Ashdown and Basing; death of Æthelred I; arrival of 'Summer Army' of Guthrum.
871-99	Alfred king of Wessex.

874	Vikings occupy Repton; Burgred flees to Rome.
874–878/9	Ceolwulf II king of Mercia.
876	Vikings settle southern Northumbria; Danish kingdom of York established.
877	Ceolwulf partitions Mercia with Guthrum.
878	Guthrum occupies Chippenham; Alfred takes refuge at Athelney; battle of Edington: Alfred defeats Guthrum.
880–90	Guthrum king of East Anglia.
883	Æthelred lord of Mercia.
886	Alfred takes London from the Danes; ?marriage of Æthelred and Æthelflæd, Alfred's daughter.
889/99	Æthelred and Æthelflæd fortify Worcester.
898	Alfred fortifies London.
899–924	Edward the Elder king of Wessex.
910	Battle of Tettenhall: West Saxons and Mercians defeat Danes of York.
911	Death of Æthelred lord of Mercia.
911–18	Æthelflæd Lady of the Mercians.
918	Death of Æthelflæd; Edward takes over Mercia.
920	Sigtrygg Caech king of York.
924–39	Athelstan king of the English.
926	Sigtrygg Caech marries Eadgyth, sister of Athelstan.
927	Sigtrygg dies; Athelstan seizes York; meeting of Athelstan with Constantine II, king of Scots, at *Eamot*.
934	Athelstan campaigns in Scotland.
937	Battle of *Brunanburh*: Athelstan defeats coalition of Scots and Vikings.
939	Death of Athelstan; Olaf Gothfrithsson seizes York.
940–6	Edmund king of the English.
940	Olaf Gothfrithsson sacks Tamworth and seizes the 'Five Boroughs'.
943	Edmund recovers the 'Five Boroughs'.
946–55	Eadred king of the English.
954	Eric Bloodaxe, last viking king of York, killed on Stainmore.
955–9	Eadwig king of the English.
957	Edgar king of the Mercians.
958–87	Harald Bluetooth, son of Gorm the Old, king of Denmark.
959–75	Edgar king of the English.

973	Coronation of Edgar at Bath; meeting with the Scots and British kings at Chester.
975–8	Edward the Martyr king of the English.
978	Edward murdered at Corfe, Dorset.
978–1016	Æthelred II king of the English.
979	Æthelred crowned at Kingston.
986	Harald driven from Denmark by his son Swein Forkbeard.
987–1014	Swein Forkbeard king of Denmark.
991	Battle of Maldon: Vikings defeat and kill Byrhtnoth, ealdorman of Essex.
994	Treaty of Æthelred with Olaf Tryggvasson.
995–9	Olaf Tryggvasson king of Norway.
1002	Marriage of Æthelred with Emma, daughter of Richard I of Normandy.
1002–23	Wulfstan *lupus* bishop of Worcester and archbishop of York.
1007–17	Eadric Streona ealdorman of Mercia.
1009–12	Thorkell the Tall's army in England.
1012	Martyrdom of Archbishop Ælfheah (St Alphege).
1013–14	Swein Forkbeard king of the English; Æthelred flees to Normandy; ?marriage of Cnut, Swein's son, with Ælfgifu of Northampton.
1014	Death of Swein; return of Æthelred; Cnut returns to Denmark.
1014–19	Harald, Swein's son, king of Norway.
1015	Murder of Sigeferth and Morcar, thegns of the 'Seven Boroughs' (Northumbria); Edmund ætheling, son of Æthelred married Sigeferth's widow.
1016	Death of Æthelred; Edmund Ironside king of the English. Cnut defeats Edmund at *Assandune*; death of Edmund on 30 November.
1016–35	Cnut king of the English.
1017	Coronation of Cnut; marries Emma, widow of Æthelred.
1018	Agreement of Oxford; Cnut's law-code of 1018.
1019	Harald dies; Cnut king of Denmark.
c. 1023	Godwine earl of Wessex.
1023/32	Leofric earl of Mercia.
1027	Cnut's pilgrimage to Rome.
1028–30	Norway conquered by Danes.

1033	Siward earl of Northumbria.
1035–47	Magnus king of Norway.
1035–42	Harthacnut king of Denmark.
1035–40	Harold I Harefoot king of the English.
1036	Murder of Alfred ætheling.
1038–46	Lyfing bishop of Worcester.
1040–2	Harthacnut king of the English.
1042	Magnus invades Denmark; opposed by Swein Estrithson.
1042–66	Edward the Confessor king of the English.
1043	Swein Godwineson an earl; Stigand bishop of East Anglia.
1044	Robert of Jumieges bishop of London.
1045	Marriage of Edward with Edith, Godwine's daughter; Harold Godwineson earl of East Anglia.
1046–60	Ealdred bishop of Worcester.
1047	Stigand translated from East Anglia to Winchester.
1050	Ralph, King Edward's nephew, made an earl; Robert of Jumieges becomes archbishop of Canterbury.
1051–2	Edward expels Earl Godwine and his family.
1052	Return and reinstatement of Earl Godwine; Stigand archbishop of Canterbury.
1053	Death of Godwine.
1053–66	Harold Godwineson earl of Wessex.
1055	Death of Earl Siward of Northumbria.
1055–65	Tostig Godwineson earl of Northumbria.
1057	Deaths of Ralph, earl of Hereford, and Leofric of Mercia.
1057–?1062	Ælfgar, Leofric's son, earl of Mercia.
1060–69	Ealdred archbishop of York.
1062–95	Wulfstan bishop of Worcester.
?1062–70	Edwin, son of Earl Ælfgar, earl of Mercia.
1063	Harold and Tostig conquer North Wales; ?marriage of Harold and Edwin's sister Ealdgyth.
1065	Northumbrian revolt; Tostig exiled; Morcar, son of Earl Ælfgar, earl of Northumbria.
1066	Edward dies, 5 January; Harold II Godwineson crowned, 6 January. Battle of Stamfordbridge, 25 September; battle of Hastings, 14 October: Harold II killed. William of Normandy becomes king of the English.

GENEALOGICAL TABLES

Table 1 Northumbrian kings of the seventh century

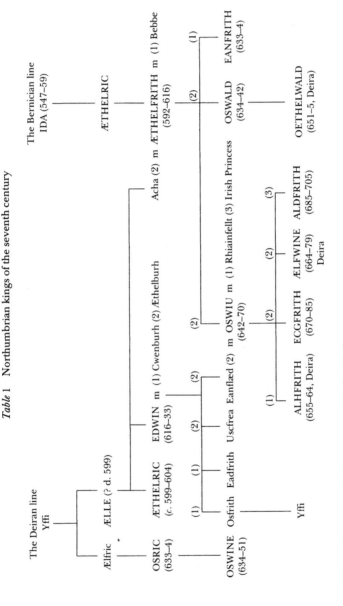

Note: Kings in capitals; m= married; d= died.

Table 2 Mercian kings

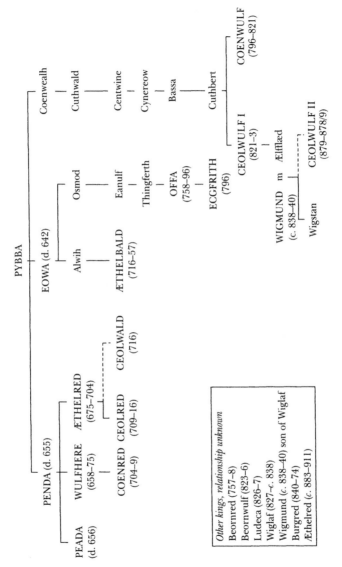

PYBBA

EOWA (d. 642)

PENDA (d. 655)

PEADA (d. 656)

WULFHERE (658–75) ÆTHELRED (675–704)

COENRED (704–9) CEOLRED (709–16) CEOLWALD (716)

Alwih Osmod

ÆTHELBALD (716–57) Eanulf

Thingferth

OFFA (758–96)

ECGFRITH (796)

Coenwealh

Cuthwald

Centwine

Cynereow

Bassa

Cuthbert

CEOLWULF I (821–3) Ælfflæd

WIGMUND (c. 838–40) m

Wigstan

CEOLWULF II (879–878/9)

COENWULF (796–821)

Other kings, relationship unknown
Beornred (757–8)
Beornwulf (823–6)
Ludeca (826–7)
Wiglaf (827–c. 838)
Wigmund (c. 838–40) son of Wiglaf
Burgred (840–74)
Æthelred (c. 883–911)

Table 3 The West Saxon kings of the ninth century (simplified)

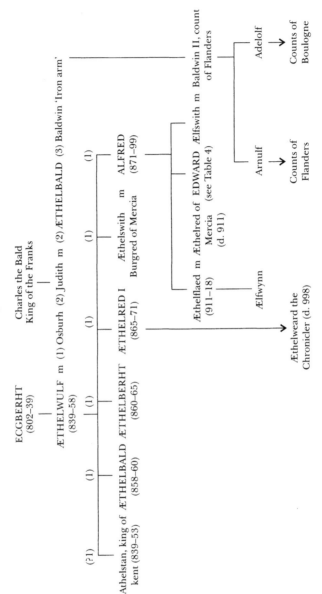

Table 4 The West Saxon kings (i)Edward to Æthelred II (simplified)

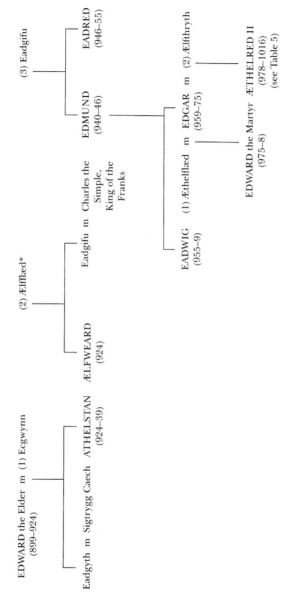

EDWARD the Elder m (1) Ecgwynn
(899–924)

Eadgyth m Sigtrygg Caech   ATHELSTAN
(924–39)

(2) Ælfflæd*

ÆLFWEARD
(924)

Eadgifu m Charles the
Simple,
King of the
Franks

(3) Eadgifu

EDMUND
(940–46)

EADRED
(946–55)

EADWIG
(955–9)

(1) Æthelflæd m EDGAR m (2) Ælfthryth
(959–75)

EDWARD the Martyr   ÆTHELRED II
(975–8)   (978–1016)
              (see Table 5)

Note: *Other children of this marriage include:
Edith (Eadgyth) m Otto I, the Great, Emperor
Eadhild m Hugh the Great, duke of the Franks.

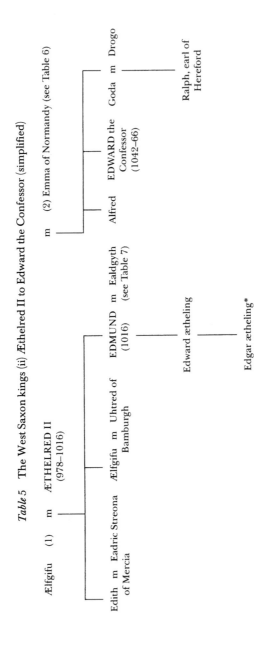

Table 5 The West Saxon kings (ii) Æthelred II to Edward the Confessor (simplified)

Note: *His sister, Margaret of Scotland, m Malcolm III Canmore; their daughter, Edith/Matilda, m Henry I (1100–35).

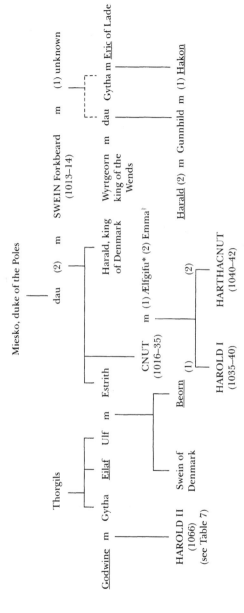

Table 6 The Danish Kings (simplified)

Note: *See Table 7; †See table 5. *Earls* in England underlined.

Table 7 The earls of Mercia and the family of Ælfgifu of Northampton

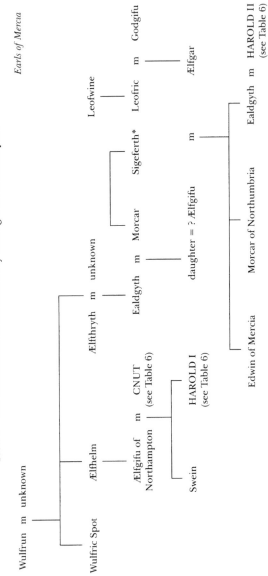

Note: *His widow m EDMUND Ironside (see Table 5).

Table 8   Regnal list of the West Saxons

Cerdic 538–554

Cynric 554–581

Ceawlin 581–588

Ceol 588–594

Ceolwulf 594–611

Cynegils 611–642

Cenwalh 642–673

Seaxburh 673–674

Æscwine 674–676

Centwine 676–685/6

Cædwalla 685/6–688

Ine 688–726

Æthelheard 726–740

Cuthred 740–756

Sigebert 756–757

Cynewulf 757–786

Beorhtric 786–802

Egbert 802–839

Æthelwulf 839–855(8)

Æthelbald 855–860

Æthelbert 860–866

Æthelred 866–871

Alfred 871–899

Source: Reproduced by kind permission of Routledge, from Barbara Yorke (1997) *Kings and Kingdoms of Early Anglo-Saxon England.*

1

THROUGH A GLASS DARKLY: THE ORIGINS OF ENGLISH KINGSHIP

Now when the Saxons subjected the land to themselves, they established seven kings, and imposed names of their own choice on the kingdoms.

(Henry of Huntingdon)[1]

The origins of English kingship lie in the fitfully-lit, if no longer pitch-dark years of the fifth and sixth centuries; the age of the *adventus Saxonum* and the English settlements, where archaeologists tread warily and historians venture at their peril.[2] Sources for these centuries are not completely lacking, but they are fragmentary, partial and ambiguous. Continental writers of the fifth and sixth centuries occasionally refer to events and people in Britain, but indigenous sources are few and mostly composed much later than the events they describe. We must wait until 731 for Bede's *Ecclesiastical History of the English People*, and the *Anglo-Saxon Chronicle* was not put together until the reign of Alfred (871-99).[3] The *Historia Brittonum*, attributed to the Welsh scholar Nennius, was assembled earlier in the ninth century, and the *Annales Cambriae* may be contemporary for the seventh and eighth centuries, but not for the fifth and sixth.[4] *The Ruin of Britain* (*De Excidio Britonum*) was written in the middle of the sixth century by the British monk and priest Gildas, but its usefulness is vitiated by uncertainty as to precisely where Gildas lived, and by the fact that he was not (and did not claim to be) an historian; the work is a polemic

1

on the abuses of contemporary British kings and churchmen, and moral concerns colour its historical content.[5] Moreover Gildas had little interest in the English except in their role as the instrument of God's punishment upon the sinful British. The archaeological record for the fifth and sixth centuries is scarcely more tractable. Numerous modern accounts have been constructed upon these materials, many of them plausible, some mutually exclusive; but in general it is hard to disagree with the conclusion of J. M. Kemble that 'the genuine details of the German conquests in England [are] irrevocably lost to us'.[6]

Sources and Problems

The *Chronicle* places the origins of three kingdoms, Kent, Sussex and Wessex, in the late fifth century. Kent is said to originate in Hengest's defeat of the British king Vortigern in 455, after which 'Hengest and his son Æsc succeeded to the kingdom'. The kingdom of Sussex begins with the landing of Ælle and his three sons, Cymen, Wlencing and Cissa, at *Cymenes ora* in 477. As for Wessex, the *Chronicle* gives two versions of its origin: Cerdic and his son Cynric 'came with five ships to Britain at the place which is called *Cerdices ora*' in 495, and 'succeeded to the kingdom' in 519; alternatively, the West Saxons came to Britain in 514 in three ships, apparently under the leadership of Stuf and Wihtgar, later described as kinsmen of Cerdic and Cynric.

This simple and elegant picture of the origins of the English kingdoms is profoundly untrustworthy.[7] The account of the English settlement in the early sections of the *Chronicle* is not only internally inconsistent, but is also at variance with the archaeological record.[8] The discrepancies are such that it has been argued that its traditions about the *adventus Saxonum* and the English settlements are largely worthless as history, representing only 'a southern English view of the English conquest of southern Britain'.[9] In so far as its account of the fifth and sixth century is concerned, the *Chronicle* has more to do with the politics of the late ninth century than the events of the English *adventus*.[10]

Bede's account of the fifth and sixth centuries is no more reliable than that of the *Chronicle*.[11] Apart from Gildas, he had little material on which to work, most of it traditional tales of the kind which underlie the *Chronicle*'s account. He has a version of the story of Hengest, for whom he provides a genealogy, in which his son Æsc is identified with 'Oeric, surnamed Oisc', founder of the Kentish royal dynasty, the Oiscingas.[12] Seventh-century

Kent was an amalgam of two originally separate regions; East Kent (the 'Jutish' province) was probably not united with West Kent until the mid-sixth century, in the time of Iurminric (Eormenric), father of Bede's hero, Æthelberht, under whom the Kentishmen became Christian.[13] The Kentish genealogy recorded by Bede may have been concocted 'to show Æthelberht's purported ancestors operating in West Kent and in the vicinity of London so as to justify his claim to that half of the kingdom'.[14] Most of the surviving royal genealogies were composed in the eighth and ninth centuries. Though they purport to trace the ancestry of contemporary rulers back through the *adventus* to the pre-Migration period, they are more concerned with the politics and ideologies of their own day than with the veracity of the history they relate.[15] Their earlier sections have been manipulated to legitimize the powers and territories claimed by eighth- and ninth-century kings, and there is no necessary institutional or biological connection between them and their alleged ancestors. In each case, the names above those of the dynastic founder (not necessarily identified with the first to hold the kingship) are mostly 'borrowings from heroic legend'.[16] Thus the Mercian genealogy traces the descent of Offa (758–96) back to his namesake, Offa, king of Angeln before the Migration, but it is no longer possible to agree with Sir Frank Stenton that 'an historical basis underlies this genealogy'.[17] The names of the alleged ancestors of Hengest and Horsa, Uihtgisl, Uitta and Uecta, are clearly related to the place-name Wight (Latin *Vecta/Vectis*, Old English *Uiht*), and their appearance in the Kentish genealogy may record a Kentish claim to overlordship of the island.[18] King-lists, whose purpose seems to have been to establish chronology, may be more reliable, but only if they can be checked against other contemporary sources; in cases where this has been done, the conclusion seems to be that they are as likely as genealogies to have been manipulated for political purposes.[19]

If the written sources will not provide us with credible information on the earliest English kingdoms, we must turn to the archaeological record. At first sight, this appears encouraging. Kent is the only English kingdom attested in any contemporary sixth-century source. Gregory of Tours, writing in or before 581, says that the daughter of the Merovingian King Charibert (561–67) married 'a man from Kent', subsequently described as 'the son of a king in Kent'. The lady is usually identified as Bertha, wife of Æthelberht son of Iurminric, king of Kent; he came to power some time between 580 and 593, and died between 616 and 618.[20] The Merovingian kings of Frankish Gaul seem to have exercised some degree of overlordship in southern England, and Æthelberht's family may already have had Frankish connections; the first element in the name of his father Iurminric is more commonly found among the Franks than among the English.[21] Archaeological investigation has confirmed these connections between Kent and Frankia, expressed in luxury goods of Frankish type and origin deposited in rich Kentish graves.[22]

Frankish influence also appears in East Anglia.[23] Rædwald, a contemporary of Æthelberht of Kent, is the first East Anglian king of whom more than the name is known, but neither the date of his accession to the kingship, nor that of his death can be fixed with certainty. Bede says that his father Tytilus was a son of Wuffa 'from whom the kings of the East Angles are called Wuffingas', and the genealogy of King Ælfwald (713–49) is traced to Eni son of Tyttla son of Wuffa, presumed to be a brother of Rædwald.[24] The Wuffingas have been associated with the barrow-burials at Sutton Hoo, Suffolk; indeed the great ship-burial in Mound 1 has been claimed as the monument of Rædwald himself.[25] If Sutton Hoo is indeed the dynastic cemetery of the Wuffingas, then their ascendancy may have been of recent date in Rædwald's time, for the burials date from the late sixth to the eighth centuries. The Wuffingas, like the Kentish Oiscingas, seem to have established their kingship at the turn of the sixth and seventh centuries.

The grave-field at Sutton Hoo has implications beyond East Anglia. Analysis of the grave-goods deposited in fifth- and sixth-century cemeteries suggests the emergence of 'a class of male burial which has a number of distinctive characteristics and is substantially richer than the average warrior burial'; this trend culminates in 'burial under mounds . . . with a rich array and variety of grave-goods'.[26] Such burials have been categorized as *Fürstengräber* (princely graves). It is suggested that, as the fifth century passed into the sixth and the sixth into the seventh, there was an increase not in the number of ranks in society, but in the comparative wealth of the elite *vis-à-vis* the rest.[27] Thus (it is argued) increasing inequalities of access to resources led both to stratification within individual societies, and to competition between the elites of neighbouring societies. In the course of such struggles, successful leaders absorbed the territories of their rivals and created larger territories – kingdoms – for themselves: 'the development of ranked societies . . . forms part of a transition period culminating in the formation of states'.[28]

The suggestion that 'princely graves' indicate the establishment of stable kingships is an attractive one. The earliest are dated to the last quarter of the sixth and the first quarter of the seventh centuries, and some can plausibly be associated with the ruling dynasties of historically-attested kingdoms.[29] Moreover this form of royal or quasi-royal burial appears to coincide with the 'superior limit of credibility ... somewhere in the second half of the sixth century' which has been detected in the later sections of the royal genealogies; just at the time when the genealogies seem to record historical kings, we have the graves in which those kings were buried. But problems still remain. If the genealogies were first composed in the early seventh century, the mid-sixth-century horizon may represent merely the limit of human memory at that time.[30] There may have been earlier kings of whom the royal genealogists knew nothing (hence they had to invent them), and the dynasties which the genealogies record may be older than the sixth century, even if no accurate descents can now be established. As to the 'princely graves', they themselves may represent not a recent enhancement of the status of certain families, but a new means of indicating a status which those families already possessed.[31] Moreover, the whole concept of a 'rebuilding' of hierarchies after the collapse of Roman provincial administration has itself been criticized on the grounds that both the English and the post-Roman British were already hierarchical in their social structure: 'we are not dealing with the long-term development of hierarchical societies, but a short-term consolidation of power within such societies'.[32]

The Idea of the 'Seven Kingdoms'

Bede, in his account of the origins of the English, names the Jutes as the ancestors not only of the people (*gens*) of Kent (the *Cantuarii*), but also of the people (*gens*) of the *Uictuarii* (the Isle of Wight) and 'those opposite the Isle of Wight, that part of the kingdom of Wessex which is still today called the nation (*natio*) of the Jutes'. The East, South and West Saxons came from 'the *regio* now known as Old Saxony', while the East and Middle Angles, the Mercians and 'all the Northumbrian race' (*progenies*), as well as 'the other Anglian peoples' (*Anglorum populi*), came from the *patria* of *Angulus*, between the kingdom of the Jutes and that of the Saxons; as a result *Angulus* (Angeln, in Denmark) 'is said to have remained deserted from that day to this'.[33] Bede's terminology is worthy of note. He speaks of 'peoples' (*gentes, nationes, populi*) in preference to 'kingdoms', a reminder that in the early middle ages kings ruled over people, not places, though of course in any settled society 'authority over people must imply authority over land'.[34] Here and throughout the *Historia Ecclesiastica* Bede uses the word *provincia* (province) for the English kingdoms, rather than *regnum*, which is used to denote royal authority; *regio* usually means a sub-division within a *provincia*.[35]

This passage should also be compared with the final chapter of the *Historia Ecclesiastica*, where Bede lists the bishops holding office in 731 and the peoples and places over which they ruled: Kent; the *provinciae* of the East Saxons, East Angles, West Saxons, and Mercians; 'the people (*populi*) who dwell west of the River Severn'; the *provinciae* of the Hwicce and the *Lindisfare*; the Isle of Wight; the South Saxon *provincia*; and the *provinciae* of the Northumbrians. Bede also mentions but does not name the 'other southern kingdoms' (*provinciae ceterae…australes*), which, like the named kingdoms south of the Humber, were subject to the authority of Æthelbald, king of the Mercians.[36]

It is clear that Bede's lists reflect the reorganization of the English Church in the late seventh century, and the political divisions of the early eighth century, rather than the kingdoms of the settlement period. The traditional 'seven kingdoms' of the Heptarchy, first popularized by Henry of Huntingdon, are clearly recognizable: Kent, Essex, Sussex, Wessex, East Anglia, Mercia and Northumbria.[37] Side by side with them, however, appear other peoples (*gentes*) and kingdoms (*provinciae*): the *gens* of the *Uictuarii* in the Isle of Wight, a Jutish *natio* in what is now south Hampshire, the Middle Angles, 'the people (*populi*) who dwell west of the river Severn', the kingdom of the Hwicce (with its see at Worcester) and the kingdom of the *Lindisfarorum*.[38] Nor is this list exhaustive, for the 'other Anglian *populi*', whom Bede mentions but does not name in his first list are presumably included among the 'other southern kingdoms' of his second.[39]

Bede's account may also be compared with the list of peoples in the *Tribal Hidage*. Though the earliest surviving text dates only from the eleventh century, the *Tribal Hidage* was probably first compiled in the seventh century.[40] Thirty-four peoples are named and assessed, including the Mercians and the East Angles (30000 hides each), the Kentishmen (15000 hides), the South and East Saxons (7000 hides each) and the West Saxons (100000 hides).[41] The *Hwinca* of the *Tribal Hidage* can be identified as Bede's Hwicce and the *Lindesfarona* are the *Lindisfare*, the men of Lindsey; the *Westerna* are probably 'the people who dwell west of the River Severn' (that is, the Magonsæte, with their see at Hereford).[42] They are assessed at 7000 hides each, as are the *W[r]ocensætna* (the dwellers in the Wrekin), whom Bede does not record. Not all the lesser peoples, whose assessments vary between 300 and 4000 hides, can be identified, but most of them seem to inhabit the east midlands.[43] A few are mentioned by Bede elsewhere in the *Historia Ecclesiastica*; for instance, he gives the name of

Tondberht, *princeps* of the South *Gyrwe*, who appear in the *Tribal Hidage* alongside the North *Gyrwe*, assessed at 600 hides apiece. Bede adds that the monastery of *Medeshamstede* (Peterborough) lay in the territory of this people.[44] Bede also mentions territories which the *Tribal Hidage* does not record: the *regio* of Ely, assessed at 600 hides; the *provincia* of Oundle; and the *regio* of *Loidis* (Leeds). It is clear that some of these were by Bede's time subordinate to the larger kingdoms; Ely, for instance, lay in the kingdom (*provincia*) of the East Angles.[45]

These lesser peoples are the clue to the origins of the English kingdoms. The *Tribal Hidage* gives no indication of a single kingdom in the east midlands, the area later known as Middle Anglia. The Middle Angles, as a group, seem to originate during the dynastic power struggles of the mid-seventh century between the kings of Mercia, East Anglia and Northumbria. They first appear in 653, when Penda of Mercia raised his son Peada to 'the *regnum* of that people'.[46] Penda was killed in 655 and Peada in 656, and no further kings of the Middle Angles are known. Peada's short-lived kingdom was made up of the smaller settlements established between the lands of the East Anglians and those of the Mercians; hence its name, Middle Anglia.[47] The region had preserved into the seventh century a pattern which had once been characteristic of all the English settlements: 'the larger units seen in the *Tribal Hidage*, in other seventh-century sources and in Bede's works would, in an earlier century, have appeared as many minor ones'.[48] They 'had grown through absorbing smaller principalities'.[49]

In this context, it may be instructive to consider what was happening in those parts of Britain still in the control of the indigenous inhabitants. When the Roman administration collapsed at the beginning of the fifth century, the province of Britannia fragmented.[50] In the north and west, there seems to have been a resurgence of tribal kingships. Some appear in the work of Gildas, who addresses by name five of the more important kings of his own day: Constantine of Dumnonia (the Cornish peninsula, including Devon); Aurelius Caninus; Vortipor 'tyrant of the Demetae', also named on a memorial stone; Cuneglasus, usually located in North Wales; and the 'dragon of the island', Maglocunus (Maelgwyn) of Gwynedd. It is clear that some, if not all, were well-established by the middle of the sixth century, for Vortipor (Gwrthefyr of Dyfed) is presented both as an old man and as the 'bad son of a good king'.[51]

Gildas' kingdoms were beyond the limits of the English settlements, but there had been British kingdoms in areas conquered by the English. The kingdoms of Elmet and Rheged survived into the seventh century before they were overrun by the Northumbrian kings, and Celtic Dumnonia was not finally incorporated into Wessex until the ninth century. Some English kingdoms have British names, suggesting appropriation of some pre-existing polity.[52] There may have been many more small kingdoms and principalities which sank without trace as the English established political control over eastern and southern Britain.

The north British kingdoms may represent a re-emergence of tribal groupings suppressed under Roman rule, but in the more Romanized south the *civitates* themselves perhaps survived for a time as regional centres of power; this has been argued for Wroxeter in the west and for Chichester in Sussex.[53] In Somerset the emergence of post-Roman lordships has been connected with the re-occupation of hilltop settlements, of which the best-known is the Iron-Age hill-fort at South Cadbury.[54] In the east, territories under British control are less easy to identify, but St Albans (*Verulamium*) was in British hands until the later sixth century, and Wighton (Norfolk), Burgh Castle (Suffolk) and Great Chesterford (Essex) have all been suggested as centres of British power in the subRoman period.[55] Both developments produced a series of minor princedoms, at war with each other and, sooner or later, with the English.

Given the intractability of much of the evidence, both historical and archaeological, identification of even a few British kingdoms and lordships must raise questions about those which may once have existed but of which we know nothing. It has been difficult to identify the British in the archaeological record, a problem also found with regard to the Gallo-Roman population of Frankish Gaul. In both cases, the likeliest explanation of their archaeological invisibility is that they adapted to the material culture of their political masters.[56] It is not necessary to assume that 'Germanic' artifacts indicate 'Germanic' people.[57] Indeed, for any remaining members of the British elites, identification with the new rulers would be a necessity of survival. One of the main differences between England and Frankia is the absence in an English context of any group corresponding to the educated Gallo-Roman elite, whose members, lay and ecclesiastical, played a decisive part in shaping the emergent Frankish kingdom.[58] Yet the survival of some Romano-British aristocrats is suggested by the British names in the genealogies of some English royal dynasties, which imply intermarriage with the British elite.[59]

The presence of British survivors was not necessarily negligible, though their influence probably varied from place to place.[60] It has been plausibly argued that the conversion of the English settlers in the west midlands was the work of surviving Christian British communities.[61] That such communities survived even in the south and east, the areas which saw the earliest and heaviest of the English settlements, suggests that even here, people of Romano-British origin formed a substantial part of the population.[62] How substantial depends on the view taken of the numbers of English who settled in Britain in the fifth and sixth centuries. Estimates have varied from a tiny elite aristocracy which seized political power to a mass migration, caused by economic collapse in the Germanic homelands. Both cases can be argued, though rarely with profit.[63] All that can be said is that though warriors with their warbands figure prominently in the surviving sources, some of the settlers seem to have been impoverished refugees rather than aristocratic warlords.[64] It must remain likely that people of British descent formed the majority of the population within the English kingdoms.

Unity in Diversity? The Emergence of 'Englishness'

For Gildas all the invaders were 'Saxons', a usage preserved among the Welsh and Scots, to whom the English are still *saesneg* (*sais*) and *sassenach*. Bede claimed that they came 'from three very powerful tribes, the Saxons, Angles and Jutes', and archaeological investigation appears to bear him out, at least in general terms.[65] When the invaders settled in Britain, their origins, though not forgotten, seem to have become submerged in identification with their new homelands. The Jutes of Kent became the *Cantware*, 'dwellers in Kent' (*Cantium*), taking their name from the place where they settled, not the region from which they had come.[66] Their cousins in the Isle of Wight were known to Bede as the *Wihtware* (from *Vectis*, the Romano–British name for the island), though this may not have been their 'original' name.[67] Some of the Jutes who settled in south Hampshire were later known as the *Meanuare* (from the name of the River Meon) but place-names like *Ytedene*, 'valley of the Jutes', suggest an early 'Jutish' name for this *provincia*.[68]

Of the Anglian settlements north of the Thames, only one kingdom, East Anglia, preserved an ethnic name. The Mercians seem never to have been known as the 'West Angles'; their name, 'boundary-folk' (*mearc*, boundary, mark, march) derives from the position of their earliest English homeland, on the borders with the north Welsh. We have already seen how the numerous peoples who lived in the regions between the Mercians

and the East Angles came to be called the Middle Angles. The northern
Angles were defined by reference to the Humber. The *Humbrenses* may
once have included people dwelling south of the Humber, but by the late
seventh century it was a boundary between the Northumbrians and
the 'southern English'.[69] Yet Northumbrian identity may itself have
emerged only during the dynastic struggles of the seventh century.[70]
The first kingdoms of the northern Angles, like those of the Jutes, had
British, not English names, though whether this implies an appropriation
by English dynasties of pre-existing British kingdoms is debateable.[71]
The etymologies of Bernicia (the land to the north of the Tees) and Deira
(which centred on York) are obscure, but Lindsey's name derives from
that of the Roman *colonia* at *Lindum* (Lincoln), and its people were known
as the *Lindissi*.[72]

The Saxons present something of a contrast to the Jutes and Angles in
their nomenclature, but it is doubtful whether Bede's classification of
them as East, West and South Saxons would have been recognized by the
early seventh-century kings and their peoples. He himself says that the
West Saxons were once known as the *Gewisse*, which seems to be 'a self-
conferred nickname', meaning something like 'the ones we can trust'
(*gewis*, 'sure, reliable').[73] Bede associates the *Gewisse* with the valley of the
upper Thames, and only after this region was lost to the Mercians in the
660s does he regularly call them West Saxons.[74] They seem to have
regarded themselves simply as Saxons. When the first West Saxon charters appear, the king's normal regnal style is *rex Saxonum*; the title 'king of
the *West* Saxons' is used only from the mid eighth century.[75] A late seventh-
century charter applies the style *rex Saxonum* to Sighere of the East
Saxons.[76]

It seems to be only in the late seventh century that West Saxons are regularly distinguished from South and East Saxons, and East from Middle
Angles.[77] The precipitating factor may have been the tidy mind of Theodore, archbishop of Canterbury (668–90), who reorganized the chaotic
diocesan structure of the English Church and tied the sees more firmly to
regions rather than peoples. The geographical modifiers may first have
indicated the spheres of the bishops; at the council of Hertford in 672, Bisi
is described as bishop of the East Angles and Leuthere as bishop of the
West Saxons.[78] By the time of the council of Hatfield (679 or 680) they
had been applied to kingdoms, for its canons are dated *inter alia* by the
regnal year of Aldwulf of the East Angles.[79] As Professor Kirby has pointed
out, the underlying symmetry of the names represents southern England viewed from Canterbury.[80]

Although politically divided, the English soon developed a sense of common identity; even Saxons came to define themselves (and their language) as 'English'. Attempts have been made to trace this perception back to a domination established by the continental Angles over their Saxon neighbours, or to the influence of Roman imperial ideas transmitted through the surviving Britons. Sir Frank Stenton saw the origins of English unity in the sequence of kings named by Bede as exercising *imperium* over the English kingdoms south of the Humber; in the ninth century, these kings are described as *Bretwaldas*, or *Brytenwaldas*.[81] The first was Ælle of Sussex, placed in the late fifth century by the *Chronicle* (though Bede gives no indication of his *floreat*), followed by Ceawlin of Wessex (late sixth century), Æthelberht of Kent, who died between 616 and 618, and Rædwald of East Anglia, who was dead by *c.* 627; then come the three Northumbrian kings, Edwin (616–33), Oswald (634–42) and Oswiu (642–70).

Bede lists no successors to Oswiu, and the next *Bretwalda* in the *Chronicle* is Ecgberht of Wessex (802–39). It is clear, however, that the Mercian kings of the eighth century were acknowledged, from time to time, as overlords by at least some of the southern English kings. Bede says that in 731 the 'southern kingdoms' were subject to Æthelbald of Mercia (716–57), who, in a charter of 736, is variously described as 'by the gift of God king not only of the Mercians but also of all provinces which are called by the general name "South English"'; 'king of Britain' (*rex Britanniae*); and (in an endorsement) 'king of the South English'.[82] Similar styles appear in other charters, though this is the only one in which the 'South English' and 'British' titles are combined; indeed any which incorporate the latter are of dubious authenticity.[83] Even more suspicious are those charters which employ the title *rex Anglorum* and variants thereof, for most of them are copies or forgeries written in the tenth and eleventh centuries, when such titles were applied to contemporary West Saxon kings.[84]

Stenton saw in the rule of Æthelbald's successor, Offa (758–96), a step towards a united kingdom of the English.[85] It is difficult to gain any idea of Offa's own conception of his authority, but the Mercian royal genealogy may contain a clue.[86] The significant name is that of Offa son of Wærmund, who (if he existed) must have flourished in the pre-migration period. In the Old English poem *Widsith*, he appears as Offa, king of Angeln, who 'with one sword . . . marked the boundary of the Myrgings at *Fifeldore* (the River Eider)', and he is described in *Beowulf* as 'the best of all mankind between the seas'.[87] The appearance in Offa's genealogy of a celebrated namesake who was (allegedly) king of all the continental Angles may suggest ambitions to rule all those Angles, Mercians and others, who had settled in Southumbrian Britain.[88] This may be the context for the title *rex Anglorum* found on some of Offa's coins, which need not mean 'king of [all] the English', but simply 'king of the Angles'.[89] It must be remembered, however, that the Mercians were themselves an Anglian people; *rex Anglorum* is used in the *Life* of St Guthlac with reference to Æthelred of Mercia, and also on the coinage of the ninth-century kings of East Anglia, but in neither case does it imply 'overlordship' even of all the Angles, let alone all the English.[90] The title most commonly used, both by Æthelbald and by Offa, was 'king of the Mercians' (*rex Merciorum*).[91]

Much has been written about the influence of the *Bretwalda* on the development of a single kingdom of the English, but on close examination the *Bretwalda*'s alleged powers seem to be based on little more than military might and the ability of individual warlords to exact obedience by force. More convincing is the hypothesis that the sense of English unity arose not from the fluctuating fortunes of competing overlords but from the idea of an *ecclesia Anglicana*, going back to Gregory the Great: 'our apostolic saint' as the Whitby *Life of Gregory* calls him, who will lead the *gens Anglorum* into God's presence on the Day of Judgement.[92] It was perhaps at Canterbury, where Gregory's emissary, Augustine, established his archiepiscopal see, that the concept of a single English kingdom was fostered, based upon the ideal of a single English (indeed a single British) church.[93]

The details of the English settlement remain a matter of debate, but some general themes emerge. The earliest English communities were established within and upon a network of pre-existing Romano-British princedoms and lordships, sometimes by conquest, sometimes perhaps by gradual infiltration or mutual agreement. It may be that the incoming English took over not only political power but even some administrative expedients from their British predecessors, but the multiplicity of independent communities among both the indigenous Britons and the invaders themselves must have affected any transmission of cultural and political influence from one to the other.[94] Each region of what became England probably experienced its own *adventus Saxonum*, at different times and in different circumstances, and the seventh-century kingdoms represent local hegemonies established by the most successful dynasties.[95] In this respect the English settlements differ from contemporary movements on the continent, for there was no one dynasty powerful enough, like the Merovingians in Gaul, to impose a permanent authority over the rest. With the conversion, however, came a sense of common identity overriding political divisions, given enduring form in Bede's influential history of the religious life of the *gens Anglorum*: the *English* people.

2

THE TIME OF THE WARLORDS

Every lord that was mighty of men made him strong, and many weened to have been king.

(Thomas Malory, *Le Morte d'Arthur*)

In contrast to the fifth and sixth centuries, our sources for the seventh century are relatively abundant. Chief among them is Bede's *Historia Ecclesiastica*, completed in 731. Indeed we see the seventh century very largely through Bede's eyes, which has drawbacks as well as advantages. Bede was an historian of genius, but he had little interest in secular affairs as such. He betrays extreme reluctance to divulge any scandal or unpleasantness, though he cannot quite conceal the sheer thuggery often practised not only by secular, but also ecclesiastical magnates.[1] An antidote to Bede's sweetness and light is provided by the *Life* of Wilfrid, bishop of York, composed by Eddius Stephanus within ten years of Wilfrid's death in 709. Wilfrid's episcopal office brought him closer than the cloistered monk to the violence and treachery of seventh-century politics and, though ostensibly a saint's life, Eddius's work differs from the usual hagiographies in advancing a polemical justification for his hero's stormy career.[2]

What emerges both from Bede and Eddius is an impression of a struggle for supremacy between the more successful of the English royal dynasties, particularly those of Wessex, Mercia and Northumbria. All were creations of the seventh century. Wessex was an amalgam of the *Gewisse*, associated with the middle-Thames region, and other early settlements in the Hampshire and Wiltshire areas.[3] The critical period was the reign of Cædwalla (685–7), whom Bede describes as 'a young man of the royal race of the *Gewisse*, exceptionally gifted as a warrior (*strenuissimus*)'.[4] He spent some of his early years in exile; Eddius describes him 'wandering in the desert places of Chiltern and the Weald ... until he was powerful enough to overcome his enemies and get the kingdom (*regnum*) [by] slaying or subduing his foes' (*occisis et superatis inimicis eius*).[5] His immediate predecessor, Centwine, retired to a monastery, though whether this was the result or the occasion of Cædwalla's coup is unclear.[6] It was during his exile that Cædwalla killed Æthelwealh king of the South Saxons, and when he became king of the *Gewisse* he slew one of Æthelwealh's successors, Berhthun, and reduced west Sussex to a 'state of slavery'.[7] He went on to overwhelm the Jutish settlements in south Hampshire and the Isle of Wight, an event which, for Bede, seems to mark the transformation of the *Gewisse* into West Saxons.[8] The *Chronicle* links this conquest with a campaign into Kent itself.[9] The centre of West Saxon power was shifting southwards; the episcopal see, originally at Dorchester-on-Thames, had been transferred to Winchester by the mid-660s, and the trading-centre of Hamwic (Southampton) was founded within the formerly Jutish province soon after Cædwalla's conquest.[10] Cædwalla and his successor Ine (688–726), may be regarded as the founders of the West Saxon kingdom.

Cædwalla's aggression towards the south and south-east was a response to the loss of the Thames Valley settlements to the Mercians.[11] Like Wessex, the historic kingdom of Mercia had grown by absorbing its neighbours. In the early seventh century the Mercians were merely one of a large number of Anglian peoples established north of the Thames and south of the Humber. Bede locates them in the region of the middle Trent, which was settled in the sixth rather than the fifth century.[12] The twelfth-century historian Henry of Huntingdon couples the Mercian settlements with those in East Anglia, adding that 'many chiefs contended for the occupation of districts ... but these chiefs, because they were many, are not known by name'.[13] By the eighth century, the Mercian kings were known as the Iclingas, but since the Mercians themselves preserved no stories about their origins (or at least none which have survived) their deeds are lost even to legend. Their later dynastic centres lay at Lichfield, Breedon-on-the-Hill, Repton and Tamworth, all within the territory of the *Tomsæte*, 'the dwellers by the River Tame', and the Iclingas perhaps began as the leaders of this people.[14]

The first Mercian king mentioned by Bede is Cearl, but he has no place in the Mercian royal genealogy, and all subsequent kings trace their descent either from Cearl's successor Penda (d. 655) or from one of his brothers.[15] Penda's career is hard to reconstruct (even the date at which he became king is unclear). This is unfortunate, for he occupies a place in the history of Mercia comparable to that of Cædwalla in Wessex; indeed Bede introduces us to him in terms almost identical to those he uses of Cædwalla, 'a man of the royal stock of the Mercians, exceptionally gifted as a warrior'.[16] His military abilities are well to the fore in Bede's account of him. By 655 his power had grown to such an extent that he could marshal a coalition of all the Anglian rulers and several British kings against King Oswiu of Northumbria.

How Penda achieved this position is irrecoverable. He was lord of the east midlands by 653, when (according to Bede) he made his son Peada, 'a most noble youth, worthy both of the name and office', king of the Middle Angles.[17] In the west midlands, we do not know when, let alone how the land of the *Pecsæte* (the Derbyshire Peak) passed into the control of the Mercian kings.[18] The *Wreocensæte* of north Shropshire may once have been part of the North Welsh kingdom of Powys; Welsh legend, of dubious authenticity, remembers the loss of land in this area to Mercia in the time of Penda.[19] South Shropshire and Herefordshire were occupied by the Magonsæte, whose first recorded king, Merewalh, is said to have been a son of Penda.[20]

Better recorded are the southern neighbours of the Magonsæte, the Hwicce of Worcestershire and Gloucestershire. Bede has a good deal to say about them, and charters of the Hwiccian kings survive from the last quarter of the seventh until the end of the eighth century, but despite this relatively abundant evidence, it is no easier to chart the beginnings of Mercian lordship over the Hwicce than it is for the other west midlands peoples. It has been assumed that the Hwicce were subordinate to Penda.[21] The first definite sign of Mercian influence in the area comes, however, from the reign of his son, Wulfhere.[22] Since it was Wulfhere who drove the West Saxons out of the old Gewissan lands in the upper Thames valley, the Hwicce may originally have been dependents not of the Mercians but of the West Saxons.[23]

Bede's interest in Penda stems from the latter's lifelong struggle with the Northumbrian kings; he participated in Cadwallon of Gwynedd's victory over Edwin at Hatfield Chase in 633, and himself killed Edwin's eventual successor Oswald at *Maserfeld* in 642.[24] Edwin and Oswald came from different kindreds, Edwin from the ruling house of Deira, Oswald from that of Bernicia.[25] Deira seems the older of the two, but its first recorded king is Edwin's father, Ælle.[26] Bernicia was settled rather later, in the late fifth and early sixth centuries; its ruling line is traced to Ida, who allegedly united the various peoples north of the Tees and built his fortress at *Dinguoaray* (Bamburgh).[27] In 604 Ida's grandson Æthelfrith of Bernicia expelled Ælle's line from Deira, taking Ælle's daughter Acha as his second wife.[28] Edwin spent the next ten years or so in exile, first in Mercia, then Rheged, and finally with Rædwald of East Anglia. When, with Rædwald's help, he regained power in 616, it was the turn of Æthelfrith's sons to flee to Pictland and Dal Riata.

It was under Edwin that the Northumbrians first accepted Christianity. He married Æthelburh, sister of Eadbald, king of Kent, a Christian who brought with her, as a condition of her marriage, the Italian missionary Paulinus. He was consecrated as bishop of York in 626, and after some hesitation Edwin was baptized on Easter Day (12 April) 628.[29] Paulinus' evangelization of Northumbria reveals the extent of Edwin's authority; not only did he work both in Deira and Bernicia but also extended his campaign to Lindsey.[30]

Bede presents Edwin as the fifth king to exercise supremacy (*imperium*) over the southern English, though he specifically excepts Kent from the kingdoms under Edwin's domination.[31] By 626, Edwin's power was clearly regarded as threatening by at least some southern kings, for an attempt was made to have him assassinated. Bede describes it in detail: the assassin Eomer, sent by the West Saxon king Cwichelm, came to Edwin's hall by the Derwent in the guise of a messenger. His attempt to stab the king with a poisoned sword was thwarted by the faithful thegn Lilla, who, not having a shield to hand, flung himself between the weapon and his lord and took the blow, which killed him and wounded Edwin. The king's retainers then fell upon Eomer and cut him down, but not before he had killed another of their number, called Forthhere. When Edwin had recovered from his wound he led his host to Wessex and 'either slew all whom he discovered to have plotted his death or forced them to surrender'.[32]

On Edwin's death in 633, Deira passed to his cousin Osric, the son of Ælfric, Ælle's brother, but in Bernicia the line of Æthelfrith returned, in the person of his eldest son Eanfrith.[33] Within the year both had been killed, and Cadwallon himself fell at the battle of 'Heavenfield', near Hexham.[34] The victor was Oswald, Eanfrith's half-brother, who rebuilt the Northumbrian hegemony which had collapsed on Edwin's death.[35] Bede's attitude to Oswald is coloured by his posthumous status as a martyr-saint, but it is clear that he was as ruthless in his own way as his father Æthelfrith.[36] It took a miracle to persuade the monks of Bardney, in the kingdom of Lindsey, to admit Oswald's remains into their church 'because he belonged to another kingdom and had conquered them' and therefore 'they pursued him even when dead with their former hatred'.[37]

Even Bede admits that it was for fear of Oswald's influence over her brother King Eadbald that Queen Æthelburh sent the Deiran æthelings for safe-keeping in Frankia, where both died in childhood.[38]

It was Penda of Mercia who caused Oswald's downfall and death at the battle of *Maserfeld* in 642.[39] The kingship of Bernicia passed to Oswald's brother Oswiu, then 30 years of age, who ruled 'for twenty-eight troubled years'.[40] It may have taken him some time to establish himself; it was a year before he was able to retrieve his brother's dismembered remains from the battlefield.[41] Meanwhile the Deiran ætheling Oswine took power in Deira.[42] The resurgence of the Deiran line must have been a factor in Oswiu's choice of Eanflæd, Edwin's daughter, as his second wife.[43] The marriage was solemnized by 644 but not until *c.* 650 did Oswiu feel strong enough to challenge Oswine directly.[44] Bede describes how, after seven years of peaceful rule, dissension broke out between them, until at length they gathered their forces. Oswine, 'realizing that he could not fight against an enemy with far greater resources', disbanded his army and took refuge in the house of one of his noblemen at Gilling; but the man betrayed him to Oswiu, who had him murdered on 20 August 651, in the ninth year of his reign.[45] Queen Eanflæd later prevailed upon her husband to endow a monastic community at Gilling in memory of her slaughtered kinsman; its first abbot, Trumhere, was also a near kinsman of Oswine.[46]

Deira passed to the Bernician Oethelwald, son of King Oswald, but there is no indication that he was Oswiu's man; indeed Bede includes him in his list of Oswiu's enemies.[47] Nevertheless Oswiu's power was growing in the 650s. He seems to have been at peace with his northern neighbours, the Strathclyde Britons and the Scots of Dal Riata, and in 653 his nephew Talorcan, son of Eanfrith, became king of the Picts.[48] He may have had allies in Ireland, for it was perhaps *c.* 650 that Aldfrith, his son by an Ui Neill princess, was born.[49] Oswiu also had influence in south-east England. Sigeberht Sanctus, king of the East Saxons, used regularly to visit Oswiu's court. Indeed it was Oswiu who persuaded him to become a Christian; he was baptized at Wallbottle by Finan, bishop of Northumbria, and a mission was sent to evangelize the East Saxons.[50]

In 653, Peada, king of the Middle Angles, married Oswiu's daughter Alhflæd. The price, as usual, was conversion, and Peada was baptized (like Sigeberht) at Wallbottle by Bishop Finan. Bede says that he was influenced in his decision by Oswiu's son Alhfrith, who was already married to Penda's daughter Cyneburh.[51] Peada took back to his kingdom four missionary priests, Cedd, Adda, Betti and Diuma.[52] Bede's account of this mission is revealing. He says that Penda did not forbid the preaching of the Word, even in his own Mercian kingdom, if any wished to hear it. But he hated and despised those who, after they had accepted the Christian faith, were clearly lacking in the works of faith. He said that they were despicable and wretched creatures who scorned to obey the God in whom they believed.

One may suspect some element of polemic here, but Penda's attitude is not dissimilar to that of Rædwald before him.[53] The significant fact is that he himself did not accept conversion, presumably because to do so under Oswiu's auspices would imply an acknowledgement of dependence which he was unwilling to give. Indeed Oswiu was not able to have a bishop appointed to the Middle Angles until after Penda's death.

Penda had reason to be alarmed at the growth of Oswiu's influence in the early 650s. He had already besieged Bamburgh before the death of St Aidan in 651, and he launched a second raid, again reaching up to the walls of Bamburgh, after Aidan's death.[54] The *Historia Brittonum* recounts a campaign in which Penda and his British allies besieged Oswiu in a city (*urbs*) called *Iudeu*, perhaps to be identified as Stirling.[55] Oswiu was forced to yield up 'all the riches that he had in the city into the hand of Penda', who distributed them amongst his British allies; this is described as the *atbret Iudeu*, 'restitution of *Iudeu*', which implies that Oswiu had previously seized treasure from (or levied tribute on) the British kings. Oswiu subsequently killed Penda and the British kings who followed him at the field (*campus*) of Gai, except for Cadafael of Gwynedd, who escaped with his army 'by rising up in the night' and thereby earned himself the opprobrious epithet of *catguommed*, 'battle-dodger'.[56]

In his account of what appears to be the same campaign, Bede does not mention the British princes, any more than the *Historia Brittonum* mentions Penda's English allies.[57] He says that Penda commanded 30 legions of battle-hardened troops, led by *duces regii*, 'royal military commanders'.[58] This figure may be symbolic, but the *Tribal Hidage* records some 30 minor peoples likely to have been tributary to the Mercian king at this time.[59] Bede records the presence in Penda's entourage of Æthelhere, king of East Anglia, and Oswiu's nephew, Oethelwald of Deira; the latter, like Cadafael, 'withdrew in the hour of battle and awaited the outcome in a place of safety'.[60] As for the 'restitution of *Iudeu*', though Bede does not mention it by this name, he does record that Oswiu promised Penda 'an incalculable and incredible store of royal treasures and gifts as the price of peace'. He also reveals the fact that Oswiu's young son Ecgfrith was a hostage in Mercia, in the keeping of Penda's queen, Cynewise.[61]

Mercians and Northumbrians met at the River *Winwæd* (the 'field of Gai' of the *Historia Brittonum*), probably to be identified as the Went, a tributary of the Don, for Bede says the battle was fought in the *regio* of Leeds.[62] It was the fifteenth of November, and the stream was swollen with the autumn rains so that more perished by drowning in the flood-waters than were slain in the battle; the dead included Æthelhere of the East Angles, and Penda himself. The battle of the *Winwæd* established Oswiu's dominance among the English kings. He is the seventh (and last) in Bede's list of those who had *imperium* over the southern English, and Bede specifically claims that he ruled not only Mercia but also 'the rest of the southern peoples'. He certainly governed Mercia directly for the next three years, appointing both its bishops and its lay governors.[63] At first Peada was allowed to hold the territory of the South Mercians, which perhaps included the familial lands of his dynasty, but he was murdered in the spring of 656 'by the treachery, or so it is said, of his wife during the very time of the Easter festival'.[64]

Oswiu's dominance was very brief. In 658 'the *duces* of the Mercian peo-ple, Immin and Eafa and Eadberht, rebelled against King Oswiu and set up as their king Wulfhere, Penda's young son, whom they had kept con-cealed; and having driven out the *principes* of the foreign king, they boldly recovered their lands and their liberty at the same time'.[65] By the 650s, the area of London was in Wulfhere's control, for he sold the see to Bishop Wine.[66] Ten years later, Essex itself was falling under Mercian influence; Æthelwald of East Anglia had sponsored the baptism of King Swithelm, successor of Sigeberht Sanctus, but when, on Swithelm's death *c.* 664, the East Saxons apostatized, it was Wulfhere who organized the reconversion.[67]

Wulfhere was also pushing into Kentish territory. He married a Ken-tish princess, Eormenhild, daughter of King Eorcenberht (640–64); her brother Ecgberht, who succeeded their father, died in 673. At about this time, Frithuwold, described as a *subregulus* of Wulfhere, granted a huge estate at Chertsey to the monastery which Ecgberht had established there, and Wulfhere himself confirmed Frithuwold's charter from his royal manor at Thame, Oxon.[68] The charter describes Frithuwold as 'of the province of the men of Surrey', but his kingdom seems to have extended north of the Thames into south Buckinghamshire. He is likely to have come from a Mercian family, for Frithuric, who is the first witness to his charter, was probably a kinsman and the donor of Breedon-on-the-Hill, Leics, and Repton, Derbys, to the monastery of *Medeshamstede* (Peter-borough).[69] Frithuwold may indeed have been married to Wulfhere's sister Wilburh.[70]

Marriage brought the South Saxons too into the Mercian orbit. Æthelwealh of Sussex took the Hwiccian princess Eafe as his wife, which probably led to his baptism 'at the suggestion and in the presence of Wulfhere', who not only stood godfather to him but also 'as a token of his adoption . . . gave him two *provinciae*, namely the Isle of Wight and the *provincia* of the *Meanuare*' (the Meon Valley in South Hampshire).[71] Wulfhere's expansion to the south-east brought him into conflict with the West Saxons. The *Chronicle* records that he 'harried on Ashdown' in 661, and this is an area which it associates with the West Saxon royal house; in 648, Cenwealh is said to have given 3000 hides of land near Ashdown to his kinsman Cuthred son of Cwichelm, who died in the year of Wulfhere's harrying.[72] It seems to have been about this time that the West Saxons abandoned Dorchester-on-Thames in favour of a new centre of power at Winchester.[73]

In the north, Wulfhere began the process of attrition which eventually brought Lindsey into Mercian hands.[74] Already when Oswiu had appointed Diuma as bishop for the Mercians and Middle Angles, he had added the *Lindesfare*, and later bishops of Mercia continued to administer the province of Lindsey as well. The Mercian see was established at Lichfield by Chad, appointed in 669, who received from Wulfhere land at Barrow, in Lindsey, on which he founded a monastery; Wulfhere's ability to grant this estate demonstrates his control of the province.[75]

In Northumbria itself, the *Winwæd* marks the final absorption of Deira into Bernicia. Oethelwald is not heard of after 655 and his treachery probably cost him his kingdom. For a while Deira was ruled by members of the Bernician ruling house, first by Oswiu's son Alhfrith, and, after he fell out with his father, by his half-brother Ecgfrith, Queen Eanflæd's son.[76] When Ecgfrith succeeded Oswiu as king of Bernicia in 670, Deira passed to his younger brother Ælfwine, who was killed at the battle of the Trent in 679; thereafter Deira was ruled directly from Bernicia.[77]

It was at this time also that the northern frontiers of Northumbria reached their greatest limits. In fact Ecgfrith, who succeeded Oswiu in 670, overreached himself; he was killed in 685 by the Pictish king Bruide (his cousin) at the battle of *Nechtanesmere* (Dunnichen Moss, near Forfar).[78] Ecgfrith's successor was his half-Irish half-brother Aldfrith (685–704), who ruled a smaller though still powerful Northumbria. The kingdom entered upon a period of cultural and artistic brilliance (the 'Northumbrian renaissance') which lasted, despite dynastic upheavals, until the end of the eighth century.[79] South of the Humber the lesser kingdoms were falling, to a greater or lesser extent, under the shadow of Mercia.

3

THE SHADOW OF MERCIA

You are the glory of Britain, the trumpet of proclamation, the sword against foes, the shield against enemies.

(Alcuin, Letter to Offa, king of the Mercians)

After Bede's death in 735, the narrative sources diminish. For Wessex there is the *Anglo-Saxon Chronicle*, though that is not contemporary until the end of the ninth century, and for Northumbria the annals added to Bede's *Historia Ecclesiastica* (the *Continuations*), and those which now form part of the *Historia Regum*, once attributed to Symeon of Durham.[1] There is also a poem on the Church of York by the Northumbrian scholar Alcuin, which carries its story down to the death of Archbishop Ælberht (780).[2] It is unfortunate that no Mercian religious house produced an historian to chronicle the deeds of its eighth-century kings, though the *Life* of St Guthlac, composed in the reign of King Ælfwald of East Anglia (713–49), contains some material on the early career of King Æthelbald (716–57).[3] Much information can be gleaned from the correspondence of the West Saxon missionary saint, Boniface, and from that of Alcuin.[4] There is an increasing number of royal charters, from Kent, Sussex, Wessex, Mercia and the kingdom of the Hwicce.[5] Though much of the detail is inevitably lacking, it is still possible to gain a general idea of how the Mercian kings achieved and maintained their hold over much of southern England.

The foundations of Mercian power were laid by Wulfhere (658–75). He is not included in Bede's list of rulers exercising *imperium*, but by the early 670s he commanded the allegiance of 'all the southern nations' (*australes populos*), and it is perhaps to the later years of his reign that the compilation of the *Tribal Hidage* should be assigned.[6] Like that of Oswiu, Wulfhere's supremacy was brief. About 674 he led his whole strength against Ecgfrith of Northumbria, but it was the Northumbrians who had the victory.[7] As a result of this defeat Lindsey reverted to Northumbrian control and Wulfhere's standing in the south seems to have been compromised. The *Chronicle* records that in 675 Æscwine of Wessex fought against Wulfhere at *Biedanheafde*, and that Wulfhere died soon afterwards.[8]

Wulfhere's brother Æthelred (675–704) recovered Lindsey after defeating Ecgfrith at the battle of the Trent in 679. He and his Northumbrian wife Osthryth founded a monastery at Bardney in Lindsey, to which Æthelred eventually retired, as abbot, in 704.[9] Æthelred made some attempt to perpetuate Mercian influence in the south-east with a punitive raid on Kent in 676, but the resurgence of Wessex under Cædwalla effectively put paid to his efforts. He did maintain Mercian pressure on northern Wessex, for his nephew Beorhtwald had some authority in the area of north Wiltshire and south Gloucestershire. Northumbrian influence on Mercia is demonstrated when Beorhtwald attempted to befriend Bishop Wilfrid, who fell out with Ecgfrith in 681, for Æthelred forbade it, in order 'to flatter King Ecgfrith'.[10] The murder of Æthelred's wife, Queen Osthryth (the sister of Ecgfrith), 'by her own Mercian nobles' (*a suis, id est Merciorum, primatibus*) in 697 may have been a reaction against Northumbrian dominance.[11]

The direct line of Penda failed in the early eighth century. In 704 Æthelred retired into his monastery at Bardney, leaving the kingship to Wulfhere's son Coenred, who abdicated in 709; his cousin Ceolred, Æthelred's son, died in 716. Ceolred's immediate successor, Ceolwald, may have been a brother, but before the end of the year he had been displaced by a more remote kinsman, Æthelbald (716–57), who claimed descent from Penda's brother Eowa.[12] He had been in exile during the reign of Ceolred, possibly in East Anglia, for the *Life* of his kinsman St Guthlac shows him being consoled at Crowland, where the saint prophesied his future eminence.[13] Æthelbald's charters show him promoting his own kinsmen and friends to positions of power. His faithful companion Oba, who had shared his exile, attests between 716 and 748, once as *patricius*, which may imply that he was in charge of the royal household, and between *c.* 730 and 757 Æthelbald's brother Heardberht attests in a position which suggests that he was one of the king's chief advisors.[14] Another favoured kinsman in Æthelbald's earlier years was Eanulf, probably his cousin, and grandfather of his eventual successor, Offa (758–96).[15]

Both Æthelbald and Offa were acknowledged from time to time as overlords by at least some of the southern English kings.[16] Æthelbald had some connection with East Anglia, demonstrated by the popularity there of the cult of his kinsman Guthlac, but shortage of information makes his relationship with King Ælfwald (d. 749) difficult to determine. Æthelbald's influence on the borders of Essex is demonstrated by his ability to grant exemptions from toll at London in the 730s, but there is no indication of Mercian activity within Essex itself.[17] The East Saxon kings of the eighth century are shadowy figures, but the continuance of the dynasty suggests that they maintained a degree of independence, though perhaps under Mercian suzerainty.[18]

Mercian control of London must have affected the kingdom of Kent. The long and peaceful reign of Wihtred, who came to power in 691 or 692, ended in 725. He was succeeded by his three sons, though Alric, who was probably the youngest, is not heard of again.[19] The evidence of their charters suggests that the elder sons partitioned the kingdom, Æthelberht II, the senior, taking East Kent, and Eadberht I (who is said to have died in 748) controlling West Kent.[20] There is no indication that either king acknowledged Æthelbald's authority, but the succession of Mercian priests elected to the archbishopric of Canterbury in the 730s and 740s is suggestive of Mercian influence.[21]

Wihtred's contemporary, Ine of Wessex, abdicated in 726 and departed to spend the remainder of his life in Rome. He had established a considerable power-base in the south-east. Bede says that he oppressed the South Saxons and at least one of their kings, Nothelm or Nunna, was in Ine's following, and may even have been related to him by marriage.[22] Ine seems also to have had designs on London and Essex. In the preamble to his law-code, he described Eorcenwald, bishop of the East Saxon see of London, as 'my bishop', and in 704–5 Eorcenwald's successor Wealdhere wrote to Brihtwold, archbishop of Canterbury, of the difficulties he experienced because of the 'disputes and discords…between the king of the West Saxons and the rulers of our country'.[23]

Ine's departure probably enabled Æthelbald to intervene in the south-east and also weakened his own kingdom. He left behind a succession dispute between his kinsman Æthelheard and an ætheling called Oswald, which was not resolved, in the former's favour, until 730. Such disturbances are a common theme of the eighth-century *Chronicle*, which in this period 'pays particular attention to disputes within the royal house' of Wessex.[24] It was perhaps the strife between Æthelheard and Oswald that allowed Æthelbald to seize Somerton, Somerset, in 733.[25] Both Æthelheard (726–39) and his kinsman and successor Cuthred (740–56) fought under Æthelbald's command, a clear sign of dependency, and Æthelbald himself disposed of lands in Somerset, Wiltshire and Berkshire.[26] Yet towards the end of his reign, Cuthred defeated Æthelbald at the battle of *Beorhford* (unidentified), an act which the northern annals present as an insurrection.[27]

In 757 Æthelbald was murdered at Seckington, near Tamworth. The northern annals say that he 'was treacherously killed by his own household', a fate which befell more than one Northumbrian king in the late eighth century.[28] The same source records civil war in Mercia between Beornred, of whom nothing is known for certain beyond his name, and Æthelbald's kinsman, Offa, which ended when Offa expelled Beornred, probably in 758.[29] It was presumably Offa who presided over the burial of Æthelbald, in considerable state, at Repton, the house wherein his kinsman and helper St Guthlac had first received the tonsure. Recent excavation there has uncovered a fragment from the upper part of a great cross-shaft, one face of which shows an armed rider in a pose closely related to the equestrian portraits of the late Roman period. It has been interpreted as a representation of Æthelbald himself, as *rex Britanniae*.[30]

The disturbances attending Æthelbald's violent death seem not to have affected the Mercian kingdom itself, but Offa had to rebuild his wider hegemony. His ability to mint coins at Canterbury indicates his control of Kent.[31] The death of King Æthelberht II in 762 seems to have been followed by three years of political instability, in which the direct line of the Oiscingas came to an end.[32] Æthelberht's immediate successor in East Kent was Eadberht II, probably his son, but West Kent passed to a certain Sigered, whose name suggests he belonged to the East Saxon royal house. By 765, Sigered and Eadberht II had been replaced, respectively, by Ecgberht II and Eanmund, of whose antecedents nothing is known.

The instability argued by this rapid turnover of kings probably allowed Offa to extend his power into the south-east. In 764 he appears at Canterbury granting land to Rochester; not only is this the first occasion on which a Mercian king disposed of land in Kent in his own name, but the estate concerned was one originally given by Sigered.[33] Moreover Offa's charter is attested by King Heahberht, presumably the Heahberht who had attested another of Sigered's grants to Rochester in 762.[34] He was perhaps a Kentish magnate raised to the kingship with Mercian aid. In 765, Offa and Heahberht jointly confirmed a charter to Rochester of Ecgberht II.[35] It was at Offa's court too that Jænberht, archbishop-elect of Canterbury, was consecrated, on 2 February in the same year.[36]

The next Kentish charters, which date from the 770s, are in the name of Ecgberht II, and make no acknowledgement of Mercian permission. In 776, according to the *Chronicle*, 'the Mercians and the people of Kent fought at Otford'; the outcome is not recorded but Stenton argued that it was in 776 that the Kentishmen threw off Mercian domination.[37] The death of Ecgberht, the probable victor of Otford, allowed Offa to regain control of Kent. In 784 Ealhmund, Ecgberht's successor, gave land in East Kent to the church of Reculver.[38] He is not heard of again, and from 785 Offa was disposing of lands in Kent in his own name and without reference to any Kentish king. Ealhmund was probably driven out by Offa; if he was indeed, as later tradition claims, the West Saxon ætheling who fathered King Ecgberht (802–39), he may have fled to the court of his kinsman, Cynewulf of Wessex.[39] Ecgberht himself is known to have been exiled in Frankia in Offa's time, as was a certain priest called Odberht, who has been plausibly identified with Eadberht *Præn*, leader of an unsuccessful Kentish revolt after Offa's death in 796.[40]

The hiatus in Mercian control of Kent between 776 and 785 may be the background to Offa's establishment of a Mercian archbishopric at Lichfield. It is possible that Archbishop Jænberht, himself a Kentishman and former abbot of St Augustine's, had been involved in the Kentish uprising against Mercian control, for he was a kinsman of one of King Ecgberht's reeves, and a close friend of the king.[41] In 787, according to the *Chronicle*, 'there was a contentious synod at Chelsea, and Archbishop Jænberht lost a certain part of his province'. The new province of Lichfield seems to have included the Mercian sees of Worcester, Leicester, Lindsey and Hereford, and the East Anglian sees of *Domnoc* and Elmham, leaving Jænberht with Rochester in Kent, and the 'Saxon' sees of London, Selsey, Winchester and Sherborne. It was later believed, at least by some, that Offa had acted out of 'the enmity he had formed against the venerable Jænberht and the people of Kent'.[42]

Evidence for the other south-eastern kingdoms is lacking, but Sussex may have fallen under Offa's control in the 770s; it was in 771 that, according to the northern annals, he 'subdued the people of Hastings by force of arms'.[43] Nothing is known of the East Saxons beyond the names of their kings, but Offa's control of London and its region is shown by his ability to mint coins there; indeed London may have become his principal mint.[44] The situation in East Anglia is unclear. On the death of Ælfwald in 749, the kingdom is said to have divided between three kings and one of them, Beonna, was sufficiently independent to issue coins, which seem to have circulated in the 750s and 760s; some of his moneyers subsequently worked for Offa. The date of Beonna's death is not recorded, but his successor may have been Æthelred, whose son, St Æthelberht, is said to have succeeded in 779. Æthelberht's coinage featured a she-wolf and her twins, which not only refers to the Romulus and Remus legend but also to the name of the East Anglian royal house, the Wuffingas. He may have become too independent, for Offa had him murdered in 794.[45] The East Angles may have thrown off Mercian control after the deaths of Offa and Ecgfrith in 796, for at about that time a certain Eadwald was issuing coins in East Anglia. He seems not to have lasted long, and the East Anglian moneyers soon resumed minting in the name of Offa's eventual successor Coenwulf.[46]

There is no indication that Cynewulf of Wessex (755–87) ever acknowledged Offa as overlord.[47] He attests what was probably Æthelbald's last charter, a grant of Tockenham, Wilts, to Malmesbury in 757, but the murder of the Mercian king in the same year allowed him to restore West Saxon control in the valley of the upper Thames.[48] The weather-vane which shows how the political winds were blowing in this debateable land is the minster at Cookham, Berks.[49] In Æthelbald's time the region was in Mercian hands, for it was he who granted the minster to Christ Church, Canterbury. After the death of the Mercian archbishop Cuthbert in 760, however, two priests of Christ Church, Dægheah and Osberht, stole the title-deeds and delivered them to Cynewulf, who seized both the church and its lands. Archbishop Cuthbert's successor Bregowine (761–4) appealed to Offa in vain, and it was only in the time of Archbishop Jænberht (765–92) that Offa regained Cookham 'and many other *urbes* and brought them under Mercian rule'. No date is given for the event, but it is probably to be associated with Offa's capture of Bensington (Oxon) from Cynewulf in 779.[50] Offa did not restore Cookham to Christ Church, but kept it in his own hands and passed it to his heirs; only in 798 was the community recompensed for the loss by Abbess Cynethryth, who is probably to be identified as Offa's widow.

Offa's treatment of Cookham may be compared with his dealings with Bath, which, like Cookham, lay on the frontiers of Wessex and Mercia. By the later eighth century the minster had come into the hands of the bishops of Worcester, but it was still patronized by the West Saxon kings; in 758 Cynewulf gave to the community five hides in North Stoke, a grant confirmed by Offa.[51] The estate encompassed the Iron Age promontory fort of Little Down Camp, a site with 'obvious military potential', and once relations between the kings had worsened, Offa had a clear motive for exercising direct control over the minster of Bath and its lands.[52] A memorandum drawn up for Bishop Heathored of Worcester describes how, at the Synod of Brentford in 781, he was compelled to relinquish the minster of Bath to Offa and his heirs, along with '30 hides nearby on the south side of the river which is called Avon, which land we bought for a proper price from Cynewulf, king of the West Saxons'.[53] Offa was clearly strengthening his frontier against encroachment from the south.

It is noteworthy that the papal legation which visited England in 786 was received in an assembly over which both Cynewulf and Offa presided, and it was only after Cynewulf's murder in the same year that Mercian influence was extended into Wessex itself.[54] Cynewulf's slayer, the ætheling Cyneheard, was himself killed by the king's army, and power passed to Beorhtric, whose relationship to the main line of Wessex is (like Cynewulf's) unknown. In 789 he married Eadburh, a daughter of Offa and (to judge by her later reputation in West Saxon circles) 'an active representative of Mercian interests at the West Saxon court'.[55] It was Offa who assisted Beorhtric to expel his chief rival, Ecgberht son of Ealhmund, from Wessex.[56]

In the late 780s Offa was at the height of his power, and he began to take thought for the succession. His own path to the kingship had not been smooth and it was perhaps for this reason that he had his son Ecgfrith consecrated (*gehalgod*) as king in 787.[57] The ceremony took place after the 'contentious' synod at Chelsea, where Archbishop Jænberht lost the Anglian sees to the new archbishopric at Lichfield. It may be that Offa had intended to have his son blessed by Jænberht, but that the latter refused, and that the division of the province of Canterbury was Offa's riposte to the snub. All that we know is that the ceremony was performed by Hygebald, archbishop of Lichfield, and that Ecgfrith's title, like that of his father, was *rex Merciorum* (king of the Mercians).[58]

It seems clear that there was opposition within Mercia to Ecgfrith's advancement. In a letter written to a Mercian magnate after the deaths of both Offa and his son, Alcuin laments that

> this most noble young man has not died for his own sins, but the vengeance for the blood shed by the father has reached the son. For you know how much blood the father shed to secure the kingdom on his son.[59]

A little earlier, Charlemagne wrote to Archbishop Æthelheard, Jænberht's successor, asking him to intercede for some Mercian exiles whom he had harboured in Frankia, and who now wished to return home, since their lord, Hringstan, was dead:

It seemed to us that he would have been faithful to his lord, if he had been allowed to remain in his own country. But to shun the danger of death, as he was wont to say, he fled to us; and was ever ready to purge himself with oath from all disloyalty. We kept him with us for some little time, for the sake of reconciliation, not from enmity.[60]

How far Offa's purge of the Mercian royal stock went we do not, of course, know, but when Ecgfrith followed his father to the grave in 796, it was a remote cousin who succeeded to the kingship.[61] Coenwulf (796–821) and his brother Ceolwulf I (821–3) traced their descent from Coenwalh, allegedly a brother of Penda and Eowa. No such person appears in the earlier sources (which is not necessarily significant) but Penda and Eowa did have a brother-in-law of this name, Cenwealh of Wessex, who married and repudiated their sister. In view of the enmity of the West Saxons and Mercians in the early ninth century, it would be ironic indeed if Coenwulf and Ceolwulf were descended from a West Saxon king.[62]

The change of dynasty produced a change in policy and outlook.[63] Coenwulf was confronted with a revolt in Kent, where Eadberht Præn established himself as king, probably with Frankish help. He overreached himself, however, by expelling the Mercian archbishop, Æthelheard, and perhaps even sacking his cathedral church. Æthelheard, supported by Coenwulf, appealed to Pope Leo III, who excommunicated Eadberht and sanctioned the use of force to remove him. In 798, 'Coenwulf, king of the Mercians, ravaged the people of Kent and of the Marsh [Romney Marsh], and they seized Præn their king and brought him in fetters into Mercia'.[64]

Eadberht had no successor; the next king of Kent was Coenwulf's brother Cuthred (798–807), after which Coenwulf himself was king of Kent as well as Mercia.[65] Both before and after 807, Coenwulf seems to have governed Kent from a distance. One of his rare visits was in 801, when he and Cuthred endowed the Kentish nobleman Swithhun with land at Bromhey 'on this condition, that he remain a faithful thegn and an unshakeable friend to us and to our *optimates*'.[66] Unshakeable friends among the Kentish lay aristocracy were precisely what Coenwulf and his brother needed, but there is little or no evidence that any of those nobles played a role in Mercia itself, nor for the appointment of Mercian officials within Kent. The two kingdoms, though subject to one king, seem to have had completely separate hierarchies, who 'moved in strikingly different orbits'.[67]

The Mercian seizure of Kent probably brought the whole of the south-east into their hands; the kingdoms of Kent, Sussex, Surrey and Essex are said to have been 'wrongfully forced away' from the kinsmen of Ecgberht of Wessex, among whom Eadberht Præn may have been numbered.[68] Sigered, king of Essex, attests some of the Kentish charters of Coenwulf, though 'with a rapid demotion of title' from *rex* to *subregulus*.[69] His Mercian associations can be seen from the fact that when the Mercian supremacy collapsed after 825, he was expelled by Ecgberht of Wessex.[70]

In a charter of 799, Coenwulf is styled *rector et imperator Merciorum regni*, a title not unbefitting for the authority which he exercised.[71] His hegemony differed in some respects from that of Offa. He had to acquiesce in the demotion of Lichfield to a bishopric in 803, and the consequent restoration of the province of Canterbury; his attempts to get the archiepiscopal see transferred to the Mercian city of London were unsuccessful.[72] The relations of Coenwulf and Ceolwulf I with Archbishop Wulfred (805–32), who succeeded Æthelheard, were noticeably strained.[73] It was not until almost a year after his accession that Ceolwulf I secured consecration from Wulfred, on 17 February 822, and the Canterbury moneyers seem to have been uncertain whom to support; neither the royal nor the archiepiscopal coinages bear the names of king or archbishop, and in fact only two Canterbury moneyers ever struck coins for Ceolwulf.[74]

Northumbria too was moving away from Mercian involvement. Æthelred, who had married Offa's daughter Ælfflæd in 792, was murdered in 796.[75] His successor Eardwulf had been in exile during the reign of Æthelred, who had attempted (unsuccessfully) to have him murdered.[76] Coenwulf, it seems, was prepared to shelter Eardwulf's enemies in Mercia.[77] The northern annals record a good deal of opposition to Eardwulf within Northumbria, and he was expelled in 806, but was reinstated two years later, with papal and Frankish help. One of the agents was perhaps Aldwulf, an English priest in papal service, who, while returning to Rome from Northumbria in 809, was captured by Vikings, and ransomed by Coenwulf himself.[78] How long Eardwulf continued in power is uncertain, but he succeeded in establishing a stable, though perhaps impoverished dynasty, carried on in turn by his son, Eanred and his grandson Æthelred.[79]

Coenwulf did not enjoy the good relations which Offa had with Charlemagne, who was crowned Emperor on Christmas Day 800. In the ninth century, Carolingian diplomacy was directed away from Mercia, not only towards Northumbria, but also Wessex; Ecgberht son of Ealhmund was being harboured in Frankia.[80] Developments in Wessex were, in the long run, the most serious for the Mercian hegemony. Coenwulf and Beorhtric seem to have become estranged after Offa's death, for a charter of 799 refers to a treaty of peace made between the kings in the same year.[81] In 802 Beorhtric died, and Ecgberht son of Ealhmund returned from his Frankish exile to claim the kingship, probably with Carolingian support.[82] On the very day on which he was acclaimed king, the Mercian ealdorman Æthelmund led the forces of the Hwicce into Wessex, meeting the men of Wiltshire under their ealdorman, Weohstan, at Kempsford. In the ensuing battle, both ealdormen were killed, but the men of Wiltshire had the victory.[83]

Coenwulf maintained Mercian control over south-east England, but his death in 821 was followed by 'much discord and innumerable disagreements…between various kings, nobles, bishops and ministers of the Church of God, on very many matters of secular business'.[84] The last surviving charter of his brother, Ceolwulf I, is dated May 823 and he was deposed later that year.[85] Beornwulf, possibly a descendant of the Beornred who had opposed Offa, became king of Mercia and Kent was ruled by Baldred, perhaps a kinsman, who is best known from the coinage struck in his name.[86] Beornwulf was an able and determined king, who was probably responsible for the Mercian conquest of Powys in 822 or 823, but when he invaded Wessex in 825, he was defeated by Ecgberht at the battle of *Ellendun* (Wroughton), Wiltshire. In the following year Beornwulf was killed while invading East Anglia, and in 827 his successor Ludeca met the same fate 'and his five ealdormen with him'. At about the same time Baldred was driven from Kent by Ecgberht's son Æthelwulf, and the whole region passed into the West Saxon hegemony.[87]

The battle of *Ellendun* marks the effective end of the Mercian supremacy. King Wiglaf, who succeeded Ludeca, may have been a scion of the Mercian royal house, but the fact that his son Wigmund married Ælfflæd, daughter and heir of Ceolwulf I, suggests a need to acquire legitimacy, and his descendants disputed the Mercian kingship with the kinsmen of Beornwulf for the next half-century.[88] In 829 Ecgberht succeeded in driving Wiglaf from Mercia itself; and though he was restored in 830, Mercian dominance in southern England had come to an end.

4

STRATEGIES OF POWER

[He] became great under the skies, prospered in honour, until every one of those who lived about him . . . had to pay him tribute. That was a good king.

(*Beowulf*)[1]

In the seventh and eighth centuries successful kings gained power by conquest, but their hard-won confederations were rarely stable; what was welded together in one generation dissolved in the next, to be reassembled in other equally short-lived hegemonies. The real problem was not to acquire but to maintain control. Lordship was based upon rewarding faithful service, and kings especially were expected to be generous: both kings and queens 'must first of all be free with gifts'.[2] Bede praises Oswine of Deira because he was not merely 'tall and handsome, pleasant of speech, courteous in manners' but also 'bountiful to nobles and commoners alike', and the Bernician King Oswald had at his court an official specifically charged to distribute alms to the poor.[3]

A major source of the largesse which kings distributed was the spoils of war. Successful kings gathered treasure and ensured further success by distributing it among their followers, who would then serve them in future wars to acquire more treasure: 'a kind of beneficent circle which was bound in the end to break'.[4] The penitential code of Archbishop Theodore requires that anyone who, at the king's command, has taken part in the plunder of another's land shall give a third of the goods (*pecunia*) thus acquired to the church or to the poor; that this was sometimes observed is suggested by the *Life* of St Guthlac, which praises its hero for having, as a young man, returned to his defeated enemies a third of the treasures seized from them by his victorious warband.[5]

Tribute and Tax

The spoils of war were not the only source of treasure. The defeated kingdoms could also be laid under tribute, to be levied year by year as long as the victorious overlord could compel obedience. Bede describes how Oswiu of Northumbria 'made tributary even the tribes of the Picts and Irish', who recovered their liberty only after the defeat of Oswiu's son Ecgfrith at *Nechtanesmere* in 685.[6] Eddius is even more specific about the nature of such transactions; Wulfhere of Mercia, he says, was 'intent not merely on fighting [the Northumbrians] but on compelling them to pay tribute in a slavish spirit'. In the event Wulfhere was defeated by Ecgfrith and it was the Mercians who were 'laid under tribute'.[7] The bitterness which such levies could arouse is suggested by Bede's story of the initial refusal of the monks of Bardney, in Lindsey, to receive the bones of Oswald of Northumbria: 'they knew that Oswald was a saint but, nevertheless, because he belonged to another kingdom and had once conquered them, they pursued him even when dead with their former hatred'.[8]

There is little evidence for the form in which such tribute was paid, though cattle and other livestock seem to have been a significant element among both the Celtic and the continental neighbours of the English.[9] The means of levying tribute are clearer. Bede's statements about assessment are often linked with the conquest and subordination of the peoples and lands assessed. Thus the assessments of the Isle of Man (300 hides) and Anglesey (960 hides) are mentioned in the context of their conquest by Edwin of Northumbria; that of the North and South Mercians (7000 hides and 5000 hides respectively) in the context of Oswiu of Northumbria's defeat of Penda of Mercia in 655; that of Sussex (7000 hides) in the context of the Mercian overlordship; and that of the Isle of Wight (1200 hides) in the context of its conquest by Cædwalla of Wessex in 685.[10] It was on such assessments, presumably, that the overlords levied their tribute.

Bede's unit of assessment is the 'land of one household' (*terra unius familiae*), which translates Old English *hid*, 'hide'. Though Bede says that the hide or household was the English method of reckoning, it was in fact common to both the Germanic and the Celtic peoples (but not to the Roman administration).[11] Whether the English took over measurement in hides from their Romano-British forebears, or whether it was simply 'a common inheritance from a European past' is debateable.[12] In either case, the notion of the hide looks back to the extended family, the clan, whose coherence was defined as descent from a common ancestor, real or imagined. The lands of such clans were allocated among their adult male members according to rank, the hide being the land which would support one free man, his family and household. Above the free men were the nobles, ranked according to the number of free households they could command, and beneath the free men were the dependents, who relied on the landholders, free or noble, for their sustenance. Among the Irish of Dal Riata, the lowest grade of nobles commanded five free households, the next had ten and the highest fifteen.[13] Traces of a similar system are found in the early English law-codes.[14] The code of Ine of Wessex (between 688 and 694) distinguishes three types of nobleman (*gesiðcund mon*), with 20 hides, 10 hides and three hides respectively, and that of Æthelberht of Kent (before 616/8) reveals that ordinary free men (*ceorlas*) might have dependants (*hlafætas*).[15]

Such real or notional 'families' are perhaps remembered in some of the English place-names consisting of a personal name with the old genitive suffix -*ingas* ('belonging to' or perhaps even 'sons of'); Hastings, Reading, Godalming and the like. Names like these denote not specific settlements but districts or regions.[16] Though once associated with the earliest phase of the English settlements, they are now thought more likely to be coinages of the sixth century, when (it seems) the earliest kingdoms were forming.[17] Of course not all the *Hæstingas* (for example) need literally be descended from a real ancestor named Hæsta; indeed they need not all have been from the same ethnic group. Their cohesion, though validated by appeal to the past, derived from a voluntary or enforced obedience to a present authority, who was in all probability seen as and called a king. How old such territorial units were is a contentious matter. They have been claimed as Romano-British, Roman and even pre-Roman and perhaps some were of considerable antiquity even in the sixth century; others may have been created by the amalgamation of English and British in the process of settlement itself.[18]

By the beginning of the eighth century these smaller princedoms had been swallowed up by their larger neighbours. Some vanished without trace; it is, for instance, no longer possible to determine locations for the *Noxgaga* and the *Ohtgaga*, even though they were among the more substantial peoples listed in the *Tribal Hidage*, assessed at 5000 and 2000 hides respectively.[19] Others were taken over as functioning and already assessed units, and continued in existence as distinctive districts, which influenced future structures of local administration.

For the overlords, lasting power depended upon making these tribute-paying client-kingdoms into provinces of their wider realms. So far as the Mercian dependencies are concerned, this transformation was achieved by the middle of the eighth century; no king of the Magonsæte is heard of after 740, and though the Hwiccian rulers retained power, it was as subordinates of the Mercian kings. The history of the Middle Angles is largely a blank, but the emergence of Repton, Derbyshire, as a cult centre of the Mercian kings suggests that, in this area at least, any lesser royalties had been demoted or eliminated.[20]

The *Tribal Hidage* is part of the same process. It marks a stage in the transformation of the hide from a measure of social status within a clan into a unit of assessment for the exactions of a king. It is usually interpreted as a tribute list compiled for one of the early overlords, but much about it is still enigmatic. The earliest text survives in a manuscript of the early eleventh century, but the lost original is assumed to date from the seventh century. If the tribute-taking overlord was, as most current opinion supposes, a Mercian king, then the reign of Wulfhere (658–75) provides a plausible context; since both the East Saxons and the people of Lindsey are included, the date would fall between the early 660s, when Wulfhere was intervening in East Saxon affairs, and the early 670s, when he suffered his disastrous defeat at the hands of Ecgfrith of Northumbria.[21] However, the very reasons for assigning the *Tribal Hidage* to a Mercian overlord – the omission of the Northumbrians of Deira and Bernicia – may indicate rather that the tribute was being paid to a Northumbrian king. The imposition of a crushing tribute by a Northumbrian overlord on a conquered people might account for the figure of 30000 hides applied to the 'Mercian lands' themselves, far in excess of Bede's 12000 hides for the North and South Mercians. The tribute-taker might be Oswald (634–42), his brother Oswiu, who dominated Mercia between 655 and 658, or Oswiu's son Ecgfrith, between *c*. 674 and 679.[22]

Nor is it certain that the *Tribal Hidage* is a tribute-list at all. It may be no more than a tract by 'an unknown Mercian scholar [who] was moved to compile a list of the constituent territories of Southumbrian England' at an unknown date, and for reasons now irrecoverable.[23] The *Tribal Hidage* itself is no help in determining its purpose for it gives no information beyond the names of the various peoples and their respective hidages. Very little survives with which to compare it. The only near-contemporary texts are two assessment-lists relating to the Dal Riata, the Irish settlers in Argyll, preserved in the *Senchus fer nAlban* ('History of the men of Alba'). Like the *Tribal Hidage* itself, this survives only in a later (tenth-century) transcript, but is assumed to date from the later seventh century. The *Senchus* assesses the three clans of the Dal Riata in terms of house-holds ('houses'), equivalent to the hides of the *Tribal Hidage*. It differs in being quite specific about what is being assessed: the 'fighting-strength' of the respective clans, reckoned both in numbers of men, and, if the expedi-tion is by sea, by ships ('two seven-thwart ships from every twenty houses').[24]

Military Service

The existence of the *Senchus* reminds us that the *Tribal Hidage* may not be assessing tribute alone (or indeed at all). That English overlords expected military service from their client-kings is suggested by Bede's statement that even while Æthelberht of Kent (580/93–616/8) held the *imperium*, the East Anglian King Rædwald 'acted as the military leader (*ducatum praebe-bat*) of his own people'; that is, he did not, in this respect, behave as a trib-utary of Æthelberht.[25] Conversely the 30 *duces regii* ('royal military commanders') who followed Penda of Mercia to the fateful battle of the *Winwæd* (655) were most probably the kings of those peoples whom Penda had subordinated to his rule as overlord.[26] Sea-power too was important, at least to the Northumbrian kings; without a fleet Edwin could scarcely have subdued Anglesey and the Isle of Man, nor could Ecgfrith have invaded Ireland.[27]

There is a subtle difference between the exaction of tribute and the imposition of military obligation, for whereas the first can, at a pinch, be extracted by force from an unwilling population, the latter, to be of any use, requires some goodwill on the part of those imposed upon.[28] Mil-itary service, then, suggests a rather different relationship between a people and their overlord than merely that of conquered to conqueror.

Kings were of course entitled to military service from their own as well as from tributary peoples. In the seventh century, this entailed participa-tion in the king's host, what the law-code of Ine of Wessex calls the *fyrd* (literally 'a [military] expedition').[29] Ine lays down the penalties for various categories of people who do not attend such expeditions:

> If a nobleman (*gesiðcund mon*) who holds land neglects military service, he shall pay 120s and forfeit his land; he who holds no land shall pay

60s; a non-noble man (*cierlisc mon*) shall pay 30s as a penalty for neglecting the fyrd (*to fierdwite*).

It is by no means clear that the duty of attending the king's hosting was obligatory on all West Saxons.[30] Other men than the king had military retinues, bound to their lords by ties of loyalty, even when those lords fell out with the king. St Aldhelm, bishop of Sherborne in Ine's time, reproached those clerical followers of St Wilfrid who did not accompany him into exile:

> Now then, if worldly men, exiles from divine teaching, were to desert a devoted master, whom they embraced in prosperity, but once the opulence of good times began to diminish and the adversity of bad fortune began its onslaught, they preferred the secure peace of their dear country to the burdens of a banished master, are they not deemed worthy of the scorn of scathing laughter, and the noise of mockery from all?[31]

The gesiths, landed and unlanded, and *cierlisc men* of Ine's Code may have been the king's personal following, rather than the whole body of free West Saxons.

Bede is almost the sole source for the military organization of Northumbria. Particularly illuminating is his description of the aftermath of the battle of the Trent in 679, where the Northumbrians were defeated by the Mercians.[32] Among those killed was Ælfwine, king of Deira and brother of King Ecgfrith of Northumbria. His retinue (*militia*) was slain with him, but one of its members, called Imma, though left for dead, recovered from his wounds and was captured by 'men (*milites*) of the enemy army' (the Mercians). They took him to their lord (*dominus*), who is unnamed, but described as a *comes* of King Æthelred of Mercia. Imma 'was afraid to admit that he was a *miles*' (because to do so would be to incur the blood-feud).[33] He claimed, therefore,

> that he was a poor peasant (*rusticum ... pauperem*) and married; and he declared that he had come to the army in company with other peasants to bring food to the *milites*.

As a result his life was spared, but he was imprisoned in the residence of his captor, where, after a while, 'those who watched him closely realized by his appearance, his bearing and his speech that he was not of the common stock (*de paupere vulgo*) but of noble birth (*de nobilibus*)'. Under a guarantee of his safety, Imma finally admitted this, and the *comes*, instead of killing him, sold him to a Frisian trader in London. Through the good offices of King Hlothhere of Kent, Imma was able to raise his ransom, for he had formerly been in the service of Hlothhere's aunt, St Æthelthryth, the first wife of King Ecgfrith; and at last he returned to Northumbria.

For Bede, Imma's story was an example of the efficacy of prayer, for Imma's brother, Abbot Tunna, believing him dead, was celebrating masses for the repose of his soul; since Imma was in fact alive, these had the result of freeing him from earthly captivity. But like many such stories, that of Imma provides a glimpse of contemporary social conditions. Like the young Wilfrid before him, Imma had begun his career in the household of a Northumbrian queen, and had then entered the military retinue of the ætheling Ælfwine.[34] Though of noble family, Imma had no resources of his own, and presumably hoped to gain treasure and eventually land in return for his loyal service.[35] He was, as Bede describes him, a *iuvenis* (translating *geoguð*, 'youth'); one of the 'young, unmarried warriors who, having as yet no land of their own, resided with their lord, accompanying him as he progressed through his estates'.[36] Imma's story, combined with other scraps of information, suggests that seventh-century armies were composed of such warbands, led by and owing allegiance to their lords, who in turn followed the king. It is significant, for instance, that when the Mercian *milites* found the wounded Imma wandering among the slain, it was not to King Æthelred that they took him, but to their own lord.

The unnamed Mercian *comes* is a very different figure. He has men (*milites*) of his own, and his own landed property, where Imma was imprisoned; he also has connections with the Frisian merchants of London. Bede consistently opposes *comites* to *milites*. In his account of the murder of Oswine of Deira in 651, he distinguishes the king's faithful companion Tondhere (who was killed with him) as a *miles*, whereas the treacherous Hunwald, who betrayed Oswine to Oswiu of Northumbria, is a *comes*; like the Mercian *comes*, he was a landed noble, in whose house Oswine vainly sought refuge.[37] In the Old English translation of Bede's *Historia Ecclesiastica*, commissioned by King Alfred, *miles* is rendered as thegn ('boy, young man, servant') and *comes* as *gesið*, the word used for 'nobleman' in Ine's Code; both *comes* and *gesið* mean 'companion'. The *comites* were, it seems, men who had passed through a lord's warband and received their reward in land on which to settle, marry and collect followings of their own. But they remained liable to serve their lords, bringing with them the men of their own retinues. They are the proven warriors (*veterani*, *milites emeriti*, or in Old English, the *duguð*), the equivalents (one might suppose) of Ine's landholding gesiths, whereas the *milites*, the 'young men' (*iuvenes*, *geoguð*) correspond to the gesiths who have (as yet) no land.[38] Together they made up the *comitatus*, the personal following of the early kings and chieftains.[39]

The most contentious part of Imma's story, so far as modern scholars have been concerned, is its implications for the military service of non-nobles. For Stenton, the *ceorl*, 'the free peasant landholder ... by no means negligible as a fighting man', was the backbone of early English society.[40] Others have argued from Imma's story that only the nobles fought and bore arms, whereas the military service of the *ceorlas* (peasants) consisted of provisioning the army of noblemen. Most recently it has been proposed that Imma's false description of himself as 'a poor peasant and married' refers to 'a particular sort of *cierlisc mon*', and that a young, unmarried *ceorl*, or a 'more prosperous husbandman' might well bear arms.[41] This would assume among the English a ranking of society into nobles, free men and semi-servile dependents, resembling that of their Celtic and continental neighbours (a not unreasonable proposition).[42] Only the first two categories would bear arms and owe military service to their lords; the third group, the dependent peasantry (the *pauper vulgus*, in Bede's phrase) would owe the less honourable, but nevertheless essential service of supplying provisions.

Hospitality

Kings were entitled to other dues as well as military service, including, so far as noble landowners were concerned, the duties of entertaining and feeding the king and his household. In the Anonymous *Life* of Ceolfrith, abbot of Monkwearmouth/Jarrow, Ceolfrith's father, who 'held a most noble office in the king's personal retinue (*comitatus*)', prepared 'a very magnificent banquet for the king's entertainment', but since the king was prevented from coming by 'the unexpected exigency of war', Ceolfrith's father invited 'the poor, the strangers and the sick' instead.[43] The father of St Wilfrid, perhaps of lesser rank than Ceolfrith's, was accustomed to entertain the king's companions rather than the king.[44] A charter of Ceolwulf I of Mercia, dated 822, grants freedom from the entertainment of king, bishop, ealdormen (*principes*), reeves (*praefecti*), taxgatherers (*exactores*), keepers of dogs, horses or hawks, and 'the feeding or support of all those who are called *fæstingmen*'.[45]

All medieval kings constantly perambulated their kingdoms in a more or less regular circuit, as a visible reminder of their personal authority, putting up at noblemen's residences or monasteries. Æthelberht's Code doubles the normal penalty for any offence committed 'while the king is drinking at a man's home', and Eddius describes how Ecgfrith and his second wife Iurminburg, while 'making their progress with worldly pomp and daily rejoicings and feastings' arrived at the abbey of Coldingham, where they were entertained by Abbess Æbbe, the king's paternal aunt.[46] Coldingham had something of a reputation for luxury, in strong contrast to Lindisfarne, at least in its early days.[47] Bede describes the austere life there under Bishop Colman, who left the island after the Synod of Whitby in 664, adding that when the king visited he brought only five or six companions and 'if they happened to take a meal there, they were content with the simple daily fare of the brothers and asked for nothing more'.[48] The bishop of Lindisfarne was able to compel restraint, but Eangyth, an eighth-century Kentish abbess, complained to St Boniface that the *servitium* which she owed to the king was one of her greatest trials.[49] In the late eighth century, King Offa of Mercia freed the bishopric of Worcester from 'the provision of food in the form of six dinners over three years', presumably representing the entertainment the king could expect when he and his court stayed at Worcester.[50] Onerous though such hospitality might have been, it did provide for regular contact with the king, and access to the patronage he dispensed.

The Kings' Lands

Kings did not depend entirely on others for their sustenance and that of their household. Their itineraries included their own lands, the 'royal vills' (*villae regia, vici regis*) often mentioned in the pages of Bede, *cynges tunas* ('Kingstons') in the vernacular version. To call them 'estates' is tempting but misleading, for, unlike continental *villae* (which were often based upon late Roman villa-estates), 'an English *villa regis* was not a great estate in the sense of a discrete block of land owned and exploited in special ways [but] the centre of a fairly wide area all or most of whose people owed something to it'.[51] What they owed was *feorm*, a rent in kind, whose purpose was to feed the itinerant household of the king. Ine's Code specified the food-rent from ten hides as '10 vats of honey, 300 loaves, 12 ambers of Welsh ale, 30 of clear ale, 2 full-grown cows or 10 wethers, 10 geese, 20 hens, 10 cheeses, an amber full of butter, 5 salmon, 10 pounds of fodder and 100 eels'.[52] Similar dues were required from Mercian estates. The *feorm* of Westbury-on-Trym, Gloucs, assessed at 60 hides, is specified in a charter of the 790s as 'two tuns full of pure ale and a coomb full of mild ale and a coomb full of Welsh ale, and seven oxen and six wethers and 40 cheeses . . . and 30 ambers of unground corn and four ambers of meal'; all to be rendered annually to 'the royal estate', presumably the royal vill in whose territory Westbury lay.[53]

By the eighth century, the kings of Wessex, Mercia and Northumbria are unlikely to have perambulated the whole of their extended kingdoms on anything like a regular basis. In the more rarely visited regions, the *feorm* must have been paid in a simpler form, perhaps even in cash. However it was paid, royal vills could act as the collecting-points for renders due from very wide areas, to which modern scholars, following Bede's usage, have given the name of *regiones*.[54] In 794, Beorhtric of Wessex freed an estate from 'all matters of royal taxes and service and everything which is due to the royal vill' (*omnium fiscalium negotiorum et operum regalium et omnium rerum quas ad villam regiam pertinent*).[55] The reeves (*gerefan*) who managed the vills and collected the various renders and dues were as much fiscal officials as estate managers.[56]

The structure of royal vills is revealed when they are given away. Bede records that Æthelwealh of Sussex (d. 685) gave the exiled Bishop Wilfrid 87 hides of land at Selsey for the foundation of a monastery, 'with all the stock on it, along with the fields and the men', among whom were 250 male and female slaves. He describes the estate as 'the adjacent lands and dependent settlements (*possessiunculi*)' of the monastery.[57] If Æthelwealh issued a charter in respect of the estate (and Bede's words might suggest that he did) it has not survived, but Winchester Cathedral preserved an abbreviated copy of the charter whereby Cædwalla of Wessex (685–87) granted 'the land whose name is Farnham [Surrey]' for the construction of a monastery; it consisted of

> 60 hides, of which 10 are in Bindon, 2 in Churt, and the rest are assigned to their own names and places, that is *Cusanweoh* [the rest of the names were omitted by the copyist], with everything belonging to them, fields, woods, meadows, pastures, fisheries, rivers, springs.[58]

The Farnham grant reveals the structure of the estate; a central vill, to which were attached dependent settlements in other places, owing dues and services.[59] In this case, the name of the central vill was applied to the whole complex, but in others the name of the area (or a derivative of it) became that of the central vill; Ely and Leeds, for instance, were once the names of districts dependent upon the settlements to which they are now applied. Some idea of what the central vills looked like is suggested by the excavations at Yeavering, Northumberland, Bede's *villa regia* of *Adgefrin*. Here, in the reign of King Edwin, the missionary Paulinus spent 36 days preaching to the people who 'flocked to him from every village and district (*de cunctis viculis ac locis*)' and baptizing them in the River Glen.[60] Yeavering was deserted after the mid-seventh century, and the site was never re-used, so that its archaeological record (nothing of which remains above ground) was undisturbed. The excavations revealed a series of timber halls and outbuildings, including a possible church, perhaps converted from a pagan temple, adjacent to a huge enclosure, perhaps for the corralling of cattle rendered as tribute. The most striking structure was the 'grandstand', which resembled a segment of a Roman amphitheatre, focused upon a raised platform; at its largest extent, it could have held 300 people.[61] This structure, clearly intended for formal meetings, 'gives a kind of reality to Bede's description of Edwin consulting his *amici*, *principes* and *consiliarii* (friends or relations, great men and counsellors) on the adoption of Christianity'.[62]

All the known functions of the later royal vill, as residence, as collecting-point for royal tax or tribute, and as meeting-place for public assemblies, are foreshadowed in the structures at Yeavering. It is possible that Cowdery's Down, Hants, and Foxley, Wilts, where elaborate sequences of timber halls set within fenced enclosures have recently been excavated, were also royal vills, this time of the West Saxon kings.[63] Work on royal halls and other buildings was one of the common duties imposed on their subjects by the Mercian kings of the eighth century; indeed St Boniface complained, in 747, that King Æthelbald and his officials had even compelled monks to labour on such works.[64]

What Yeavering conspicuously lacked was any form of defence. Given the endemic warfare of the seventh century, this is something of a surprise, but the consensus seems to be that this was true of most, if not all, Northumbrian royal vills of the period.[65] Parts of the Roman walls of York may have been repaired in the seventh century, but this is exceptional.[66] The walls of Carlisle were allowed to fall into disrepair, though they continued to be a mark of status, for the king's reeve, Waga, conducted St Cuthbert and Queen Iurminburg on a tour which included both the walls and a Roman fountain.[67]

References to defensible sites are rare, but Eddius' description of the royal centre of *Inbroninis* (probably Fenwick, Northumberland), where Wilfrid was imprisoned in 680, suggests the presence of some kind of stronghold.[68] The name of Bamburgh, the chief royal residence of the Bernician kings, means 'the fortified place of [Queen] Bebbe' (*Bebban-burh*), and both Bede and Eddius describe it as an *urbs*, which seems to translate the English placename element *-burh*, 'a fortified place'.[69] In placenames, *-burh* can denote a variety of features, and does not necessarily imply a current fortification, but Bamburgh was certainly defended, for it was unsuccessfully besieged by Penda between 635 and 651 and again between 651 and 655.[70] Some of the royal vills in Wessex had defences, for Ine's Code lays down the fines for the offence of *burhbryce*, breaking into the fortified residences of the king and other magnates, ecclesiastical and lay.[71] In 786, the West Saxon ætheling Cyneheard killed King Cynewulf at the *burh* of *Meretun* (perhaps Martin, Dorset), and was himself besieged and eventually killed there by the king's army.[72] But only in the ninth century does the construction of fortresses become of major significance.[73]

Towns and Trade

The towns which grew up in seventh- and eighth-century England could be seen as royal vills of a particular kind. Specifically urban life, characterized by manufacture and trade, did not survive the collapse of the late-Roman economy in fifth-century Britain. Trading in itself did not cease, for no agrarian settlement, however large and varied, could produce everything which its inhabitants required. Salt in particular, an absolute necessity for a society with few other techniques for preserving food, was to be obtained only in coastal areas (by extraction from sea-water), or from natural brine-springs. A charter of Æthelbald of Mercia (716–57) records an exchange of salthouses and furnaces on the River Salwarp, Worcs, between the king and the bishop of Worcester.[74] Both Droitwich, Worcs, and Nantwich, Cheshire, had probably been continuously exploited since the Roman period.[75]

Such local commerce could have been conducted by travelling traders. Ine's Code requires a trader (*cepemann*, 'chapman') who 'buys among the people in the countryside' to transact his business before witnesses, and provides for the eventuality that stolen goods may be found in such a trader's possession.[76] Traders, like all men who travelled, moved out of the protection of their own lords and kinsfolk into an often hostile world. The Anonymous *Life* of Cuthbert relates a story of the saint's journey into Teviotdale, with a young companion. As they walked, Cuthbert asked the boy where he thought they would find their midday meal: the boy replied 'that he knew of none of their kindred along that way, and he did not hope for any sort of kindness from unknown strangers'.[77] Travellers' suspicions of their hosts were returned in full. In both the laws of Ine and the contemporary Kentish code of Wihtred, a stranger who wanders off the beaten track 'and neither shouts nor blows a horn' may be killed as a thief.[78] Yet some provision was made for travellers. The Kentish laws of Hlothhere and Eadric, which date from 673–85, require those who harbour strangers in their own homes for three nights to bear responsibility if an offence is committed by such a stranger, whether he is 'a trader (*cepemann*) or any other man who has come across the frontier'.[79] More commercial arrangements are suggested by Bede's story of the man whose horse was cured of colic at *Maserfeld*, by rolling on the spot where the Northumbrian king, St Oswald, had been killed in 642.[80] Its master told his story at the inn (*hospitium*) whither he was bound.[81] The word *hospitium* could be used of a monastic guesthouse; St Cuthbert, when guest-master (*prepositus hospitium*) at Melrose, entertained an angel unaware.[82] The *hospitium* near *Maserfeld*, however, belonged to a layman (*paterfamilias*), whose sick niece was also cured when the household (*familiares domus*) carried her in a cart to the site of Oswald's martyrdom and laid her down upon it.

Foreigners, including traders, might have royal protection. Ine's Code divides the wergeld (blood-price) of a slain foreigner between the king and the dead man's kinsmen; if he had no family, the kinsmen's share was to go to the West Saxon lord, whether a gesith, or an abbot or abbess, under whose temporary protection he had been.[83] This provision hints that, as in later centuries, monasteries were accustomed to hold fairs on the feast-days of their saints, though there is no direct evidence.[84] The public assemblies which regulated local affairs and resolved disputes would also provide opportunities for trading, for they met regularly, at central places (often, perhaps, at royal vills), and were protected for their duration by special arrangements for keeping the peace.[85]

Protection could easily become control, as seems to have happened with the more permanent trading centres, the *emporia*.[86] They are found all over north-western Europe between the sixth and the ninth centuries, lying either in coastal regions or on navigable rivers. They dealt not merely with local produce, but with long-distance trade, especially in luxury goods, like amber, garnet or walrus-ivory. Such materials, and the ornaments which could be made from them, were of particular interest to aspiring kings as treasure which they could dispense to signify and perpetuate their power. Treasure could be acquired by gift, but acceptance without reciprocity implied subordination.[87] The political dominance of the Kentish and East Anglian kings in the late sixth and early seventh centuries may be connected with the close ties of both with the treasure-dispensing kings of Merovingian Gaul, but it entailed some recognition of Frankish hegemony.[88] The need for kings to give lavishly explains the close watch which they kept on the long-distance trading-centres.[89]

Several *emporia* have been identified in the English kingdoms. Hlothhere's Code regulates the procedures for Kentishmen buying goods in London: the buyer must have the witness of 'two or three honest free men (*ceorlas*) or the king's town-reeve (*wicgerefa*)' and if any dispute should subsequently arise, the matter must be dealt with 'at the king's hall (*cyninges sele*) in that *wic*'.[90] One of the meanings of *wic* is 'a trading-settlement', and a charter of Hlothhere's contemporary, Frithuwold, who governed a cross-Thames principality under Wulfhere of Mercia, includes a reference to 'the port of London, where ships come to land'.[91] Bede, writing in 731, when London had come under Mercian control, describes the city as 'an *emporium* for many nations who come to it by land and sea', implying the presence not merely of local traders but also of foreign merchants engaged in long-distance trade, including (presumably) the Frisian who bought Imma from his Mercian captors.[92]

Excavation has shown little post-Roman settlement within the Roman walls of London, until the foundation of the episcopal church of St Paul by Æthelberht of Kent and Sæberht of Essex. Hlothhere's hall too may have been within the walls, perhaps on the site of the Roman fort at Cripplegate.[93] But *Lundenwic*, the trading-centre, lay outside the Roman city, around the Strand and the area still known as the Aldwych ('the old *wic*').[94] A similar picture is emerging at York (*Eoforwic*). The Roman legionary headquarters (the *principia*), now partly under York Minster, may have been re-used both as a palace-site and for the earliest church founded by Paulinus, but *Eoforwic* itself seems to have been outside the walls, in the Fishergate area.[95]

At Canterbury, too, the Roman town fell into decay and was largely abandoned, but by the turn of the sixth and seventh centuries, the Kentish kings had a royal residence within the walls and perhaps another in the area of St Martin's church. The dominant building in the town was the old Roman theatre, and it has been suggested, on the analogy of the Roman-style 'grandstand' at Yeavering, that it was re-used for public assemblies: 'here the kings of Kent may have met their folk, the *Cantware*'.[96] As at York and London, Canterbury also became an ecclesiastical centre, the site of the archiepiscopal church established by St Augustine. Once again, however, the trading-*wic* grew up outside the walls.[97] It may originally have occupied the whole area between the walls and the upper tidal limits of the River Stour, but eventually crystallized around Fordwich in the east, and the extra-mural monastery of St Augustine's in the west. In the early middle ages the Stour flowed into the Wantsum channel which separated Thanet from the Kentish mainland, affording an excellent harbour for shipping, and another early *wic*, Sandwich, was established at the Wantsum's south-eastern end.[98]

The *emporium* of the East Anglian kings lay at Ipswich, controlled perhaps from a royal *villa* to the north of the *wic*.[99] That of the West Saxons was at Hamwic (Southampton); 'the *wic* on the *hamm*', *hamm* signifying the strip of land between the Itchen and the Test where the earliest settlement lay. In the late eighth-century *Life* of St Willibald, Hamwic is called a *mercimonium* ('[place for] the exchange of merchandise').[100] Excavations indicate traffic in foreign as well as local goods and its main function was probably to act as the port for the royal palace at Winchester. Hamwic was also a centre for manufacture. It seems to have been established in the early eighth century, and both its date and its site have prompted the suggestion that it was founded by Ine to control the former Jutish territories in south Hampshire.[101]

The emergence of these *emporia* marks a important stage in royal control of trade. Not only did they ensure a regular supply of the luxury goods required by kings and (increasingly) churches, but the protection which the kings offered to merchants and the places where they operated allowed them to levy tolls and other charges in return.[102] In 808, the Danish king, Godfred, carried off merchants from the Slavonic trading-town of Reric, on the Baltic, to his town at Hedeby, because of the tolls he could levy on them.[103] Æthelbald of Mercia (716–57) had toll-collectors (*thelonarii*) to gather his dues at London, and perhaps elsewhere in the Mercian kingdom. In the 730s and 740s he issued a series of charters granting exemptions from toll to the abbess of Minster-in-Thanet, the bishop of Rochester, the bishop of London, and the bishop of Worcester. By the 760s, the kings of Kent were collecting tolls at Fordwich, Sarre and possibly Reculver. Once again exemptions were granted, to the churches at Minster-in-Thanet and Reculver, both of which were well-placed to exploit trade passing through the Wantsum Channel; Minster was operating at least three ships in the area. Such toll-exemptions appear only during a limited period; Offa, Æthelbald's successor, confirmed the privileges of Minster, but made no new concessions, perhaps because he was 'unwilling to compromise an important source of income'.[104]

A letter of 796, from Charlemagne king of the Franks (768–814) to Offa of Mercia (758–96), may contain the earliest recorded trade agreement in English history:

> You have written about merchants and by our mandate we allow that they shall have protection and support in our kingdom, according to the ancient custom of trading. And if in any place they are afflicted by wrongful oppression, they may appeal to us or to our judges, and we then order true justice to be done. Similarly our men, if they suffer any injustice in your dominion, are to appeal to the judgement of your equity, lest any disturbance should arise anywhere between us.[105]

Charlemagne goes on to specify some of the goods exchanged:

> As for the black stones which your reverence begged to be sent to you, let a messenger come and consider what kind you have in mind, and we will willingly order them to be given, wherever they are found, and will help in their transport. But as you have intimated your wishes concerning the size of the stones, so our people make a demand about the size of the cloaks, that you may order them to be such as used to come to us in former times.

What the 'black stones' were is still conjectural. They may have been lava millstones; a mill was part of the royal *tun* of the Mercian kings at Tamworth, Staffs.[106] An alternative explanation is that they were luxury goods, blocks or columns of Mayen lava originating from Egypt and Turkey, looted by the Franks from Rome or Ravenna for prestigious building projects.[107] It is interesting that the main English export, as in later centuries, was woollen cloth. Noteworthy too are the implied 'trading-standards', which are also the responsibility of the king who protects, and profits from the activities of the international merchants.

The importance of this cross-Channel trade is demonstrated in 790. In this year, Frankish ambassadors arrived in Mercia, requesting one of Offa's daughters as a bride for one of Charlemagne's sons. Offa agreed, but only on a *quid pro quo* basis; a daughter of Charlemagne for his own son,

Ecgfrith. Charlemagne was extremely touchy on the subject of his daughters and diplomatic relations were temporarily broken off.[108] Trade between England and Frankia was suspended, as Charlemagne forbade English merchants to be received. Matters were patched up through the agency of Gervold, abbot of Saint-Wandrille in what was to become Normandy, and one of the royal agents in charge of the customs posts in the Channel ports of Frankia.[109]

The period which saw the development of the *emporia* also witnessed the appearance of a true currency, the silver *denarii* or pennies (*sceattas*). They replaced the gold *thrymsas*, so-called from the late Roman and Frankish *tremissis* which they imitated, which were being minted from *c*. 620, notably at Canterbury and London. By the 670s the gold coinage of Merovingian Frankia had petered out and the English issues were heavily adulterated with silver.[110] The minting of silver pennies is associated with the centres of power and commerce in the English kingdoms, but as well as facilitating trade the pennies may also have enabled rents and renders to be paid in cash, for the *thrymsa* was too valuable an object to be used as an ordinary means of exchange.[111]

The acceptability of minted coinage rested on the authority of the king who licensed its issue. Æthelbald of Mercia seems to have had a minting-centre in the Upper Thames region, but Offa is the first Mercian king whose name appears upon the coins minted for him.[112] In the 790s his moneyers introduced a new penny, broader, thinner and heavier, modelled on the coinage introduced on the other side of the Channel by Pepin I of Frankia (755–78).[113] These reforms were presumably intended to facilitate trade between England and Frankia, and the new coinage circulated mainly in southern and eastern England; the centres of its production (Canterbury, East Anglia and London) demonstrate the intimate connection between coined silver and long-distance trade.

5

ALL THE KING'S MEN

Historians who write about kings tell us that ancient kings in former times considered how they might alleviate their burdens, because a single man cannot be everywhere and sustain all things at once, though he might have sole authority. Then the kings appointed ealdormen under them, as supports for themselves.

(Ælfric the Homilist)

The early kings of the English appear before us surrounded by their advisors, councillors and servants. Bede gives us a vivid picture of Oswine of Deira, about to dine with Bishop Aidan, 'warming himself by the fire with his *ministri*' (literally 'servants'); the members of his household (*hired*), who dwelt with him and accompanied him on his journeys.[1] Such progresses could be full of pomp, as another Bedan vignette, this time concerning Oswine's kinsman, Edwin of Northumbria, shows:

> So great was his majesty in his realm that not only were banners carried before him in battle, but even in time of peace, as he rode about among his cities, estates and kingdoms (*civitates siue uillas aut provincias*) with his *ministri*, he always used to be preceded by a standard-bearer (*signifer*).[2]

It was one of Edwin's household who saved his lord's life from an assassin sent by Cwichelm of Wessex, by taking in his own body the blow meant for the king.[3]

Other and more eminent councillors might meet from time to time to discuss matters of particular moment. In the preamble to his law-code,

Ine of Wessex acknowledges 'the advice and instruction' of his father Cenred, Bishop Hædda of Winchester and Bishop Eorcenwald of London who have come 'along with all my ealdormen and the chief councillors (*ieldstan witum*) of my people, and also a great assembly of the servants of God' to establish 'true law and true statutes'.[4] Wihtred of Kent, when issuing his decrees, 'assembled a deliberative council of the leading men', including Archbishop Beorhtwald and Bishop Gefmund of Rochester, to advise him.[5] These assemblies are *witenagemotan* ('meetings of the wise'), consisting of the *witan* ('wise men'), whose right and duty it was to help and advise the king. The Northumbrian witan appears in Bede's account of the conversion, debated by the *sapientibus consilio* ('council of the wise', witenagemot), composed of 'all the leading men whom [King Edwin] knew to be the wiser' (*primatibus quos sapientiores noverat*).[6]

The King's Household

There is little information on the structure of the king's household in the early English period, and perhaps such households were in fact unstructured, their members serving both as warriors and in other capacities, from time to time, as occasion demanded. A few men with specified duties are recorded. Edwin, as we have seen, had a standard-bearer (*signifer*) and his successor Oswald had a *minister* 'whose duty it was to relieve the needy' (*cui suscipiendorum inopum erat cura deligata*), perhaps a sort of king's almoner.[7] There may have been officials to receive more affluent guests. In *Beowulf*, the hero is welcomed to King Hrothgar's court by Wulfgar, described as *ar ond ambiht* (messenger and herald), who conducts him to the king's presence; such functionaries were later known as *hostiarii*, 'ushers'.[8] *Nuntii* (messengers) are also mentioned; Eomer, the assassin sent by Cwichelm of Wessex to kill Edwin, posed as a *nuntius*.[9] The *fæstingmen* who, in later charters, were entitled to hospitality from the king's subjects were perhaps royal messengers.[10]

Some of the witnesses who attest royal charters of the eighth and ninth centuries are probably members of the king's household, but they are rarely distinguished by any specific title. In Mercian charters of the early ninth century some men attest as *pedes sessor* or *pedisecus* (literally, 'one who sits at the feet').[11] In the tenth century the title is applied to men of rank who were in the king's confidence and entrusted with important missions, but it is impossible to say whether this was the case in the ninth century, or whether the title is 'simply a pedantic translation of thegn'.[12]

Queens' households were separate from that of the king.[13] The household of St Æthelthryth, first wife of King Ecgfrith, was under the direction of Owine, described as 'the leading *minister* and chief of the household' (*primus ministrorum et princeps domus*).[14] Like his royal lady, Owine abandoned his worldly career to enter religion; he became a monk at Lastingham, arriving there 'dressed only in a plain garment and carrying an axe and an adze' to show his willingness to undertake manual work.[15] In eighth-century Northumbria, the head of the king's household was sometimes styled *patricius*, a title used also of the Frankish mayors of the palace, the chief ministers (and eventually the supplanters) of the Merovingian kings.[16] Some Northumbrian *patricii* also succeeded in ousting the kings whom they ostensibly served; Æthelwald Moll, *patricius* of King Oswulf, became king after Oswulf was murdered by his own household in 759, a crime in which Æthelwald may well have been involved.[17]

The title *patricius* was also used in Wessex and Mercia, though perhaps without the same connotations; Brorda, who seems to have been the leading magnate at Offa's court in the 780s and 790s, is occasionally styled *patricius*, but more often *princeps* or *dux*.[18] One of the major problems in the pre-viking period is to marry up the Latin titles used in charters and narrative sources with the English usages of the *Chronicle* and the law-codes. Later translations are of little help in determining the English equivalents, since they reflect the customs of their own time rather than those of the seventh and eighth centuries, and an ealdorman, for instance, of the time of Alfred (when Bede's *Historia Ecclesiastica* was translated) may not have had the same powers and functions as his eighth-century counterpart.[19]

The Reeve

One of the most troublesome Latin titles is *praefectus*, translated as *gerefa* (reeve) in the Old English Bede. Both *gerefa* and *praefectus* had a wide range of meanings, from St Wilfrid's *praefectus*, Hocca, reeve of the unidentified vill *on Tiddanufri*, to high-ranking royal officers.[20] Northumbrian *praefecti* seem to have a particular connection with royal towns and vills. In the time of Edwin, Blæcca, *praefectus* of Lincoln, had his own household (*domus*) and was rich enough to build a stone church 'of remarkable workmanship' in the city.[21] Two of King Ecgfrith's reeves are mentioned in the *Life* of Wilfrid, Osfrith *praefectus* of *Inbroninis* (possibly

Fenwick), and Tydlin *praefectus* of Dunbar; Osfrith, like Blæcca, was a married man with his own household.[22] Waga, who conducted St Cuthbert and Queen Iurminburg on a tour of Carlisle, was probably another such official, but he is described not as *praefectus* but as *praepositus*, which can also be used to translate *gerefa*.[23]

As in Northumbria, Kentish *praefecti* may have been especially associated with royal estates, urban and rural, and the regions dependent upon them. The laws of Hlothhere and Eadric describe the duties of the king's *wicgerefa* ('town-reeve') at London in whose presence buying and selling must take place, and who (presumably) presided over the king's hall in the city.[24] The *praefectus* Rædfrith, sent to Frankia to conduct Archbishop Theodore to England, may have been reeve of Canterbury, Theodore's episcopal city.[25] Ealdhun, a later *praefectus* of Canterbury, was a kinsman of Archbishop Jænberht (765–92).[26] Æthelnoth *praefectus* is described in his will as *gerefa* of Eastry, a royal manor and the administrative centre of the *regio* of Eastry.[27] Another Kentish reeve (*gerefa*), Abba, made a will in the late 830s, but his area of office is not specified.[28]

Æthelnoth and his wife Gænburg made their will because they were about to undertake the pilgrimage to Rome, as did the *praefectus* Ealdhun of Canterbury. Royal reeves could be influential men and their office enabled them to amass wealth.[29] Indeed it was frequently alleged that their prosperity was based on abuse of their power and their activities were subject to much criticism. St Boniface complained to Æthelbald of Mercia that 'his reeves and gesiths (*prefecti et comites*) had imposed greater violence and servitude on monks and priests than any other Christian kings before'.[30] Freedom from the exactions of reeves is sometimes specified in charters.[31]

The Ealdorman

Some *praefecti* seem to have had commands more wide-ranging than a single vill. Beorhtfrith *praefectus*, who led a Northumbrian expedition against the Picts in 711, is probably identical with the Beorhtfrith whom Eddius describes as a *princeps* 'next only to the king' (*secundus a rege*). After the death of King Aldfrith in 704 he supported Aldfrith's son, Osred, against his rival Eadwulf.[32] Beorhtfrith was perhaps a son of Beorhtred, the *dux regius* sent by Ecgfrith against the Irish in 684, who was killed fighting the Picts in 698.[33] This Beorhtred was the son of Beornhæth *subregulus*, who campaigned against the Picts in the early years of Ecgfrith's reign.[34]

The members of this family may have occupied a position in the Northumbrian court resembling that of the Frankish mayors of the palace, though none of them are styled *patricius*.[35] Their associations with northern Bernicia, especially Bamburgh, also suggest that they had some particular responsibility for the region, like later ealdormen over their shires rather than reeves over royal vills. They may be compared with the Mercian *praefectus* Beorhtwald, who was entrusted by his uncle King Æthelred with a *territorium* on the borders of Mercia and Wessex. In 685 he gave land at Somerford Keynes, Gloucs, to Aldhelm, abbot of Malmesbury, and his charter describes him as 'king (*rex*) or *subregulus*'.[36] Similar figures in Wessex (all, like Beorhtwald, related to the ruling king) are Cuthred, to whom, in 648, his paternal uncle Cenwealh entrusted '3000 hides near Ashdown' (that is, north Berkshire); Cenred, Ine's father, who disposed of land in the Dorset region in the 670s; and Baldred *subregulus*, who disposed of land in the area of Wiltshire and north Somerset in the 680s.[37]

Such appointments were part of the process of incorporating the lesser kingdoms into the greater. The successful creation of Northumbria involved the subordination of Deira and the replacement of its dynasty by the sons, brothers and nephews of the dominant Bernician kings.[38] Appointing one's own men to command subjected territories could backfire; when the Mercians threw off Northumbrian control in 658, they drove out the *principes* appointed by King Oswiu.[39] Other subject kingdoms, like the Hwicce, continued for a time under their own rulers, subject to the authority of their overlord.

In the seventh century, such subordinate rulers appear as kings, subkings or 'princes' (*reges, subreguli, principes*). During the eighth century , these quasi-regal titles are replaced by such terms as *praefecti, comites, duces*, and (in the vernacular) ealdormen. This need not in itself imply much diminution in the powers of the subordinate rulers, for most such titles are derived from sources produced by and for the overlords, and reflect their pretensions as well as their actual powers. The reality may have been rather different, and the enlarged kingdoms of the eighth century 'may not have been as fully integrated as they superficially appear'.[40] By the ninth century, however, the process of attrition had succeeded in transforming the dependent *regiones* from client-kingdoms, whose rulers retained some concept of their ancestral rights, into territories governed in the king's name by ealdormen drawn from among his own men; 'an administrative tier between the king ... and the royal vills with their dependent districts'.[41]

Ealdormen first appear in vernacular guise in Ine's laws. In the pre-amble they are coupled with the chief councillors and clergy among those who advise the king.[42] Ealdormen, however, have a special responsibility for enforcement; they are specifically forbidden to pervert the 'true law and true statutes' which have been agreed. The ealdorman is one before whom criminal cases may be brought; indeed it is this judicial function which is stressed in the lawcode, whereas ninth-century ealdormen appear primarily as military commanders.[43] Justice may also be obtained before the *scirman* or other judge (*dema*), but the *scirman* may be the ealdorman himself, for an ealdorman who allows a thief to escape his custody, or conceals knowledge of the theft is to forfeit his *scir*, 'unless the king wishes to pardon him'.[44] The word *scir* had probably not as yet acquired its later meaning of a territory with defined boundaries; 'sphere of jurisdiction' is probably a more accurate (or at least less misleading) translation. It is in this sense that a man may secretly decamp into the *scir* of another lord, thereby depriving his former lord of the service due to him.[45]

The six West Saxon shires certainly existed in the territorial sense by the early ninth century, when each had its own ealdorman. Weohstan of Wiltshire appears in 802, Æthelhelm of Dorset in 840, Eanwulf of Somerset in 845, Ceorl of Devon in 851, and Osric of Hampshire and Æthelwulf of Berkshire in 860.[46] How old they then were it is difficult to say; the only one recorded in an eighth-century context is Hampshire. The three western shires may be based on earlier, British entities; Devon (which included Cornwall) is more or less coterminous with the British kingdom of Dumnonia, and the *Dornsæte* of Dorset take their name from the Romano-British town of *Durnovaria* (Dorchester). Somerset's name comes from the royal vill of Somerton from which it was presumably administered, but the estate encompassed Romano-British Ilchester, which may have been the original centre. The eastern shires seem to have evolved during the creation of Wessex itself. Even if the later shires did exist in embryo in the eighth century, their boundaries are likely to have been considerably modified in later years.[47]

It may be presumed that ninth-century Mercia had a network of *provinciae* analogous to the West Saxon shires, but the West Saxon kings of the tenth century completely reorganized the patterns of local power between the Thames and the Tees, obscuring the original structures. The *Chronicle* says that five Mercian ealdormen were killed in 827, but does not name them, nor their *provinciae*; nor was this the full complement of Mercian ealdormen, for an Ealdorman Mucel attests Mercian charters throughout the period from 814 to the 840s, and cannot therefore have been one of the five who fell in 827.[48]

The Mercian *provinciae* must have included the old kingdom of the Hwicce. By the end of the eighth century the former kings were styled *subreguli* or *duces* by their Mercian overlords, and the Hwiccian commander killed in 802 at the battle of Kempsford is called an ealdorman by the West Saxon *Chronicle*.[49] North and west of the Hwicce, the *provincia* of the Magonsæte likewise lost its kings, but preserved something of its territorial integrity into the tenth century and beyond.[50] In 848 the *Tomsæte* of the Tame valley appear, when their *princeps* Hunberht, under the direction of Beorhtwulf king of the Mercians, freed the church of Breedon-on-the-Hill from 'all the rights (*causae*) which ever belonged heretofore to me or to the *principes* of the Tomsæte'.[51]

These three *provinciae* correspond to the bishoprics of Worcester, Hereford and Lichfield respectively, which suggests that we should look for at least two *provinciae* in the east midlands, corresponding to the bishoprics of London and Leicester. It is here that we find, at the turn of the seventh and eighth centuries, the '*provincia* of the men of Surrey', under the *subregulus* Frithuwold, which extended into what became south Buckinghamshire; another *provincia* in the Leicester region, governed by Frithuwold's putative kinsman, Frithuric; and perhaps a third in the upper Thames valley, held by *Didan*, 'king of Oxford', who may have been another of Frithuwold's kinsmen.[52] The boundaries in this region were probably less stable than in the western *provinciae* and it must be remembered too that the upper Thames was, for much of the eighth and ninth centuries, a disputed land; it was only finally relinquished to Wessex when Burgred of Mercia married Æthelswith, daughter of Æthelwulf of Wessex, in 853. Æthelwulf, ealdorman of Berkshire, who appears as an officer of the West Saxon king in 860, was a Mercian, originally in the service of the Mercian kings.[53]

The only other Mercian *provincia* recorded in a ninth-century context is that of the *Gaini*, whose ealdorman, Æthelred Mucil, was the father of Ealhswith, wife of Alfred of Wessex.[54] The territory of the *Gaini* cannot be identified, but Æthelred Mucil may be the ealdorman Mucel, who attests Mercian royal charters between the 830s and 868.[55] His father may have been Mucel Esne's son, mentioned in a charter of King Wiglaf in 836, in favour of the minster of Hanbury, Worcs. The king remitted to the minster all entertainment (*pastus*) whether due to him or to his *principes* and, in a vernacular addition, two named ealdormen (presumably the *principes* concerned) are compensated for their loss of dues, Mucel Esne's son with land and Sigered with cash.[56] Since Hanbury lay within the *provincia* of the Hwicce, one or other of them was presumably ealdorman of that region.

Whether the ealdormen's rights arose from their position as royal delegates or from the residual rights of a once-independent dynasty probably depended upon the particular circumstances of individual *provinciae*. There is a noticeable difference between the Mercian kings' treatment of the Hwicce, whose princes who continued in power (though increasingly diminished), and that of Kent. When, in 798, Coenwulf of Mercia took over the Kentish kingdom, he appropriated the lands and rights of the Kentish kings.[57] His brother Cuthred (d. 807) became king in Kent, but he was assisted, and eventually replaced by Oswulf, ealdorman from about 805 until his death in or before 820.[58] Oswulf was a Kentish nobleman, who may even have been in the entourage of King Ecgberht II, and his appointment presumably helped to win over the Kentish aristocracy to Mercian rule; but he did not belong to the Kentish royal dynasty, and he owed his position to the favour of the Mercian kings.[59]

By the middle of the ninth century, Mercian ealdormen, like their West Saxon counterparts, were provincial commanders responsible for particular regions from which they received dues and services. They had subordinates to help them in carrying out their judicial and military duties. The Laws of Alfred (which related to Mercia as well as Wessex) mention an official known as the 'ealdorman's junior' (*cyninges ealdormannes gingra*), who could preside over public assemblies, and a Mercian charter of 845 refers to 'ealdormen and their juniors' (*principis vel iuniorum eorum*), from whose entertainment (*pastus*) the land is to be freed.[60] One such was perhaps Badanoth Beotting, a Kentish thegn to whom King Æthelwulf of Wessex granted land near Canterbury in 845, at the request of Ealhhere, ealdorman of East Kent. Badanoth, whose will is also extant, is described as *apparitor*, 'servant, public servant' and thus possibly 'reeve', but Ealdorman Ealhhere's role in the proceedings might imply that Badanoth was an *ealdormannes gingra*, enjoying his lord's patronage.[61]

Church, Law and Literacy

The witenagemot included not only members of the king's household and ealdormen but also the leading churchmen.[62] The fortunes of the Christian Church in England were indissolubly bound up with those of the kings. To convert the king was to convert his people, or at least that section of it which possessed wealth and influence.[63] Kings provided the property on which churches could be established and maintained; it was Ecgfrith of Northumbria and his brother Ælfwine of Deira who gave St Wilfrid land for his monastery at Ripon.[64] They also enforced the payment of ecclesiastical dues (*ciricsceat*, 'churchscot').[65] Many of the early monasteries and minsters were founded on or near royal vills, which must have made collection of such dues easier, and perhaps they provided administrative support for the king's reeve as well.[66] In fact relations could become too close. The early ninth century saw a long struggle between successive kings and archbishops of Canterbury over control of the Kentish churches and their associated *regiones*, made more bitter by the efforts of ecclesiastical reformers to free all such churches from lay control.[67]

The conversion had a profound effect upon the concept of kingship in England. The Italian and Frankish missionaries who converted the southern kingdoms brought with them their own assumptions about the nature of political authority, drawn from the ideology of the later Roman Empire and its continental successor states, especially Merovingian Gaul.[68] The long involvement of the English kingdoms with the Merovingian kings of Frankia and their supplanters, the Carolingians, intensified continental influence on the theory and the practice of English royal government.[69] The earliest recorded consecrations of pre-Conquest kings are those of Ecgfrith, son of Offa of Mercia in 786 and Eardwulf, king of Northumbria, who was consecrated in the archiepiscopal church of York on 26 May 796.[70] Ecgfrith's consecration, which took place while his father was still living, has been seen in the context of the papal anointing of Charlemagne's two sons, Pepin and Louis, in 781, whose purpose was to ensure the succession and to hallow the whole ruling dynasty.[71] That the same idea was in Offa's mind might be suggested by the coinage minted at about this time in the name of his wife, Queen Cynethryth, Ecgfrith's mother, an honour not bestowed on any other Mercian (or indeed English) queen.[72] However, although it is often said that these are the earliest royal consecrations in England, it would be truer to say that they are the first to be recorded; earlier rituals may simply have been taken for granted. The consecration of a later king of the Mercians, Ceolwulf I, on 17 September 822, is recorded only in a charter in favour of Wulfred, archbishop of Canterbury, who performed the ceremony.[73] Nor do we know precisely what rites were observed; in particular there is no direct evidence that either Ecgfrith or Eardwulf was anointed with holy oil, the central rite of the later ceremony.[74] They were certainly not crowned; the first text to prescribe the use of a crown in the king-making rite dates from *c*. 900.[75] The earliest kings wore the ceremonial royal helmet; the coinage attributed to Æthelbald shows him in such a *cynehelm*, carrying two long crosses or, in a related design, a falcon.[76]

One of the products of ecclesiastical expectations was the appearance of written law. The earliest English royal laws are those of Æthelberht of Kent, which, though surviving only in a twelfth-century copy, are described by Bede as 'a code of law after the Roman manner'.[77] Bede's words do not relate to the content of Æthelberht's code (about which there is nothing 'Roman' at all) but to its form; it was in writing down his laws that the English king emulated the Romans. St Augustine and his companions were Italians, accustomed to the long literary traditions of Roman Law, recently codified by the Emperor Justinian, whose *Corpus Iuris Civilis* was completed in 534. They were also, and perhaps more deeply influenced by their study of the Bible and particularly (in this context) the Mosaic Code of the Old Testament. These traditions underlie the production of written lawcodes in all the barbarian successor-kingdoms founded upon the wreckage of the western Empire, even if the content of such codes may owe little to either Roman or specifically Christian ideas.

In promulgating written laws, Æthelberht and the other early kings of Kent and Wessex (the areas most affected by Roman and Frankish traditions) were making an ideological statement; that they were not merely warlords but lawgivers, guarantors of peace and justice. This may be the primary intent of the early codes, which do not have the appearance of texts intended for practical use.[78] Their selectivity and their often illogical arrangement suggest that they were intended as general statements of the issuing king's legitimate authority, and they are often coupled with royal genealogies and king-lists, which had similar aims.[79] They are not worthless as evidence for early English law and society, for the compilers are unlikely to have invented customs which were not observed, but they do not constitute a full description of contemporary legal and social customs.[80]

No legislation is preserved from the eighth century, but Alfred's preamble to his laws, which date from the late 880s or early 890s, acknowledges the legislation of Offa, as well as that of Ine and Æthelberht of Kent, among its sources. Alcuin too, in a letter of 797, mentions 'the good, moderate and chaste customs which Offa of blessed memory established for [the Mercians]'.[81] Offa's laws have long been regarded as lost, but they may be identical with the decrees promulgated in 786 on the occasion of the visit to England of the papal legates, George, bishop of Ostia and Theophylact, bishop of Todi.[82] The legates' remit was to remedy the shortcomings of the English Church. They were provided with papal letters to this effect, which they presented first to Jænberht, archbishop of Canterbury and then to a council held under the joint presidency of Offa and Cynewulf of Wessex. Both promised to obey the pope's commands. Theophylact then set off on a journey through Mercia and Wales, while George went to Northumbria. No account of Theophylact's travels survives, but those of George are described in the report he sent to Pope Hadrian I. He found serious failings in the Northumbrian church and compiled a capitulary 'concerning the various matters'. It was presented to a council held in the presence of King Ælfwald and Eanbald, archbishop of York, 'and all the bishops and abbots of that region and also of the councillors, ealdormen and people of that land' (*senatoribus et ducibus et populo terrae*). Needless to say the capitulary was approved, and the attestations of the leading men present are recorded in George's report.

George returned to Mercia, accompanied by two emissaries of the Northumbrian king, one of whom was Alcuin himself. He brought the decrees approved by the Northumbrians to a Mercian council, presided over by Offa and Archbishop Jænberht, which, like that in Northumbria, included both ecclesiastical and lay magnates. The decrees were expounded first in Latin and then in English (*theodisce*), and all promised to obey them; the attestations of Jænberht, Offa, all the southern bishops, four abbots and four leading laymen are appended.

George's capitulary contained 20 headings, 10 addressed to the Church and 10 to the laity. Even if it does not represent the 'lost' code of Offa, it is still of great interest for the history of English kingship. The twelfth *capitula* is particularly noteworthy, for it includes a prohibition on the killing of any king, because he is the Lord's anointed (*christus Domini*). Any bishop or priest who is involved in such a crime is to be degraded, and anyone involved is to suffer excommunication. Though there are continental parallels, this diktat had particular relevance to English conditions, for both Æthelbald of Mercia and Oswulf of Northumbria had been murdered, as was Cynewulf in Wessex in the very year that the decrees were promulgated. The mutual support of Church and king is clearly demonstrated even if, in this particular case, it was ineffective.[83]

George's report to the pope is in Latin, but the decrees themselves were expounded in the vernacular. All the surviving royal codes are in English, unlike their counterparts on the European continent, which are in Latin. One of the major differences between the English settlements and those of the other Germanic peoples was the linguistic break with the late Empire. In Gaul the Franks eventually abandoned Frankish, their Germanic tongue, in favour of the spoken Latin of the Gallo-Romans, the ancestor of French. In England, on the other hand, Latin ceased to be a spoken language, being displaced by English, and became a foreign tongue which had to be learnt. Conversely, the Italian and Frankish missionaries had either to learn English or employ interpreters.[84] Augustine's interpreters were probably Franks, but presumably English-speaking Franks, for the experiences of the Frankish bishop Agilbert suggest that Frankish and English were not mutually intelligible.[85] Neither were the English and Irish tongues, and one of Bede's most charming vignettes is of King Oswald, who had learnt the Gaelic in exile, translating for St Aidan as he preached to the Northumbrians.[86]

It is sometimes assumed that the pre-Christian English were illiterate, but like all Germanic peoples, they had an alphabet, the runic *futhorc*.[87] Runes were designed to be incised, and could be cut not only on stone or metal, but also on strips of wood or bark, and in this form could be used for ordinary communication.[88] Such fragile items are particularly vulnerable to the ravages of time, but there is no sign that runes were ever used for this purpose in England. There are, however, a few texts on more durable materials, notably the Ruthwell Cross (stone), and the Franks Casket (ivory); in the eighth century, they appear on coins, runic examples of which continue to 'proliferate at an alarming rate'.[89]

It was not, however, the runic *futhorc* but the Roman alphabet which the English adopted for their written vernacular, though certain runic letters were imported for sounds which had no equivalent in Latin; *thorn* (þ) for *th* and *wynn* (ƿ) for *w*.[90] The adaptation of the Roman alphabet to English must have been the work of ecclesiastics, beginning with the first Italian missionaries. It is unlikely that they undertook this labour simply to provide King Æthelberht with a law-code.[91] Their main purpose was probably to produce materials to teach themselves and those who came after them the English tongue, and conversely to instruct English clergy in Latin. Another aim may have been to provide basic texts in the vernacular (the Lord's Prayer and the Creed, for instance) for the use of the laity and the less educated priests.[92] Their efforts, however motivated, provided the English with two written languages; Latin (always dominant) which was primarily associated with ecclesiastical affairs, and English, which, as the early law-codes demonstrate, was always an administrative as well as a literary language.

More directly concerned than the law-codes with ecclesiastical affairs are the Latin charters which provide so much detail on pre-Conquest England. The first authentic survivors date from the late seventh and early eighth centuries; they come from Kent, Essex, Sussex, Wessex, Mercia and the kingdom of the Hwicce.[93] There are none from Northumbria, but this is due to the vicissitudes of time, not least the devastation of the northern religious houses during the viking invasions. The *Vita Wilfridi* is clearly referring to charters when it describes the lands given to Ripon by Kings Ecgfrith and Ælfwine, 'over the signatures of the bishops and all the chief men (*principum*)'.[94] Bede too is clearly speaking of charters in his letter to Ecgberht, archbishop of York, when he complains of laymen who found false monasteries on land purchased from the king and 'have it inscribed for their hereditary enjoyment by royal edicts', these 'documents of their privileges' being confirmed by 'the subscription of bishops, abbots and secular persons'.[95]

The Old English royal charter, or, to give it its technical name, the diploma, is based ultimately on Roman models; not the products of the imperial chancery (the exemplars for contemporary Merovingian royal diplomas) but private deeds. The fact that the earliest authentic charters to survive come from Kent, in the 670s, led Stenton to conclude that the charter was 'one of the innovations which mark Theodore's archbishopric'.[96] The variation in form between the earliest charters suggests, however, that a considerable period of development lies behind them, and it is likely to have been Augustine who introduced the charter to England, even though all those which purport to belong to his time are later forgeries.[97] The surviving examples show a variety of influences, Roman, Frankish and even Celtic, and the form was clearly adapted to suit local needs; in this sense the English diploma can be described as *sui generis*.[98]

The diploma was introduced not only by but for the Church, and all the earliest genuine examples are in favour of ecclesiastical persons or bodies. Churches required for their support not just land, but land held in perpetuity, and the diploma, which creates a perpetual right of free bequest, was intended to fulfil such a need. Land granted by a diploma or, in Old English, a landbook (*landboc*) was said to be 'booked' (*gebocode*) and was known as bookland (*bocland*); it was held 'by ecclesiastical right' (*ius ecclesiasticum*), and disputes concerning bookland could be heard before ecclesiastical synods.[99] Diplomas were also written by ecclesiastics, sometimes the beneficiary, but also by the local bishop (or a scribe in his service). Eorcenwald, bishop of London (675–93) drafted diplomas not only for different beneficiaries, but also for different kings, including the

Mercian sub-king Frithuwold, Oethelred, kinsman of King Sebbi of Essex, and Cædwalla of Wessex.[100]

A rare glimpse into the production of diplomas is provided by a memorandum written in 759 by Cyneheard, bishop of Winchester.[101] It is attached to a grant in the name of Cenred (King Ine's father), giving land at Fontmell, Dorset to Abbot *Bectun* at some time between 670 and 676. Cyneheard explains that *Bectun*'s successor had sold the land at Fontmell to the abbot of Tisbury, Wilts, and had given him a written document recording the transaction. Fontmell had, however, been only one among a number of estates given by Cenred at the same time, and the abbot therefore

> withheld both the charter of the original donation and the subscription of kings, bishops, abbots and leading men, because, since this portion of land [at Fontmell] had been enroled among the other testimonies of their lands, it could not easily be detached, nor can it yet.[102]

As a result, the land at Fontmell was held by Tisbury, but the diploma relating to it remained at *Bectun*'s unnamed house. Much later, *Bectun*'s successors attempted, because they had the charter, to reclaim the land at Fontmell. The case came before the West Saxon witan, and a compromise was arranged; more money changed hands, and Abbot Tidbald, of *Bectun*'s house, agreed that Tisbury should have Fontmell. Therefore, says Cyneheard:

> I have transcribed the present deed (*libellum*, 'little book') and made extracts from that originally given to Abbot *Bectun* . . . and I have given this writing (*scripturam*) to Abbot Ecgwold [of Tisbury] . . . rejecting other writings (*scriptura*) which have been drawn up about this land.

The memorandum warns us that other early texts may have been tampered with without any record being made or preserved. Abbot Ecgwold's title-deed is not a new grant issued in his name by King Cynewulf and his witan, but an emended version of the original grant of Cenred in favour of Abbot *Bectun*.[103] The diploma itself was evidence of possession of the land named in it. If it changed hands, an endorsement to that effect was occasionally added to the original diploma, but the practice is not common.[104] Simple possession of the relevant diplomas was sufficient to claim the estates named in them. The stolen title-deeds of Cookham Minster, Berks, were used by King Cynewulf of Wessex as proof of his ownership of church and lands, despite the fact that he was not the named beneficiary.[105]

The whole question of the role of writing in early English administration is a contentious one, even for the comparatively well-documented tenth and eleventh centuries. Before the reign of Alfred there is little direct evidence; only the Kentish and West Saxon law-codes and the Mercian (if it is Mercian) *Tribal Hidage* survive, and their purposes and uses are ambiguous. Against this, one could set the evidence that some kings and laymen were literate and able to understand the uses of the written word. It must always be remembered that in this period and for some time to come, 'literate' meant being able to comprehend Latin; people described as illiterate might yet be able to read the vernacular.[106] Aldfrith of Northumbria was certainly literate in the medieval sense; he was a great collector of books in the Latin tongue, and was remembered as 'a scholar with great powers of eloquence, of piercing intellect, a king and a teacher at the same time', but he was perhaps exceptional, having been educated in Ireland and possibly for an ecclesiastical career.[107] Not all reached Aldfrith's standards; as we have seen, the *edicta* of Bishop George were expounded to the Mercian council in English (*theodisce*) as well as Latin, presumably for the benefit of the laymen present.

The presence of educated men who could read and interpret the written word could compensate for the illiteracy, however defined, of a lay audience. In 706, a synod was assembled near the River Nidd, to hear the complaints of St Wilfrid touching his bishopric, and the ecclesiastical foundations of which he had been deprived. The papal letters which Wilfrid had obtained in his support were read, whereupon the chief layman present, the *praefectus* Beorhtfrith, asked Archbishop Beorhtwald for a translation; the archbishop replied that 'the judgements of the Apostolic See are expressed in roundabout and enigmatic language' and offered an expository precis.[108] Particularly illuminating are the instructions of Boniface, in 746–7, to the priest Herefrith, who was to deliver a minatory letter to Æthelbald of Mercia. Boniface commands him

> to make known the words of our admonition to Æthelbald, king of the Mercians, *interpreting them and reading them out, and to show them to him*, carefully relating and announcing them in the way and order in which we send them written to you.[109]

The stress on both reading out the words of the letter and showing them to the king may be compared with the strictures of the tenth-century homilist, Ælfric, on the recalcitrant king's thegn, who, when he receives his lord's written instruction (*gewrit*) 'will not hear it nor look at it'.[110]

Boniface took some care with his letter to Æthelbald, sending it first to the archbishop of York, 'that, if any things in it are badly put, you may amend them'.[111] There were dangers for churchmen who became too involved in secular affairs. In a letter written to Beorhtwald, archbishop of Canterbury, in 704 or 705, Wealdhere, bishop of London, puts his finger on their dilemma:

> Indeed I do not think it can have been hidden from your notice how many and what sort of disputes and discords have meanwhile arisen between the king of the West Saxons and the rulers of our country, and, what is still more unfortunate, also *the ecclesiastics on both sides, who share the direction of the government under them, have willy-nilly been involved in this same dissension.*[112]

Wealdhere's immediate problem was that he had been summoned to a meeting between the West Saxon and East Saxon rulers to settle their political dissension. The archbishop, however, had forbidden ecclesiastics to have any dealings with the West Saxons until King Ine obeyed his orders to reorganize the West Saxon church. Whom was Wealdhere to obey; the king on whom he depended for secular patronage, or the archbishop, his spiritual lord? Since we do not have Beorhtwald's reply to his appeal, we do not know how the matter was resolved. Wealdhere's letter demonstrates the price paid for entering into lay politics; but only by such participation could churchmen hope to exercise the moral direction which was their *raison d'être*.

6

OUT OF THE NORTH: THE IMPACT OF THE VIKINGS

And in his days came first three ships of Northmen from Hordaland; and then the reeve rode there and wanted to compel them to go to the king's *tun* because he did not know what they were; and then they killed him.[1]

In the first half of the ninth century, a balance of power was struck in Southumbrian England.[2] Mercian dominance came to an end with the battle of *Ellendun* (825), when Ecgberht of Wessex (802–39) defeated King Beornwulf (823–6). As a result the East Angles threw off Mercian control and retained their independence until they were conquered by the Danes in 880.[3] The south-east passed into the control of the West Saxons; Baldred, the Mercian sub-king of Kent, was driven out by Ecgberht's son, Æthelwulf, probably in 826 or 827.[4] Sigered of Essex was probably expelled from his kingdom at about the same time.[5] The West Saxon conquest of Kent brought with it control of the commercial centres of the south-east, and especially of the minting-centres at Canterbury and Rochester.[6] After the expulsion of Baldred, the moneyers in both towns struck coins in the names of Ecgberht and his son Æthelwulf (839–58); even the London moneyers struck for Ecgberht in the years around 829–30, though they then seem to have ceased operation until *c.* 843, after which their issues carry the name of Beorhtwulf of Mercia (840–52).[7]

Mercia itself fell briefly under West Saxon control in 829 when Wiglaf, who succeeded in 827, was driven out, but he regained his kingdom in 830. His successor Beorhtwulf was perhaps a kinsman of King

Beornwulf, but the line of Wiglaf remained in the person of Wiglaf's grand-son Wigstan (St Wistan), whose mother Ælfflæd was the daughter of King Ceolwulf I (821–3).[8] In 849 Wigstan was murdered by King Beorhtwulf's son Beorhtfrith, allegedly because he had opposed the marriage of Beorhtfrith with his widowed mother. Wigstan was buried beside his father and grandfather at Repton, where he rapidly came to be venerated as a saint. Such relic-cults had political as well as religious significance, and Repton was later to play a key role in the accession to the Mercian kingship of Ceolwulf II, possibly a kinsman of the murdered Wigstan.[9] When Beorhtwulf died, however, he was succeeded by Burgred (852–74) who was arguably one of his kinsmen.

From the 830s to the 870s we hear of cooperation rather than competi-tion among the Southumbrian kingdoms. In 841 Beorhtwulf of Mercia exempted the minster of Breedon-on-the-Hill, Leics, from a number of secular obligations, reserving, however, the duty of entertaining ambas-sadors (*praecones*) from overseas, or from the West Saxons and Northum-brians.[10] Eleven years later, in 853, Burgred of Mercia sought alliance with Æthelwulf of Wessex for a campaign against the Welsh, and subse-quently married Æthelwulf's daughter Æthelswith.[11] It seems to have been at this time that the long-disputed territory of Berkshire passed from Mercian into West Saxon hands, though its Mercian ealdorman Æthelwulf remained in office.[12]

Military Organization in the Eighth Century

Mercian and West Saxon charters give some idea of how the English kings organized their military resources in these years. The personal ser-vice due from the king's own men, whether retained in his household or endowed with temporary grants of land, remained significant through-out the Old English period and beyond, but from the eighth century the basis of military obligation became increasingly territorial.[13] Bookland (land granted by a royal diploma or *landboc*) did not long remain a pre-serve of the church. In 734 Bede complained to Archbishop Ecgberht of the lay nobles who falsely represented their households as monasteries in order to obtain grants of bookland from the king; thus the lands available for the king's military retainers were depleted, and they, balked of their expected rewards, left the country to try their fortunes elsewhere.[14] No Northumbrian charters survive, but by the middle of the eighth century the Southumbrian rulers were granting bookland to their lay nobles.

The earliest surviving charters are Mercian, from the 770s and 780s, but the Kentish kings were making similar grants a decade or so earlier; Dunwald, thegn of King Æthelberht II (d. 762) had his donation of land in Canterbury to St Augustine's inscribed on the diploma whereby it was originally granted to him by his royal lord.[15]

The diploma or *landboc* freed the land concerned from secular services so that the ecclesiastical recipients could devote themselves to the service of God, and the same privilege accompanied grants to laymen. It is unlikely, however, that all secular service was ever remitted, even to ecclesiastics.[16] When specific exemption clauses appear, so do clauses reserving services, including military service, which must still be performed; in 739, King Æthelheard of Wessex granted land at Crediton, Devon, to Bishop Forthhere of Sherborne free from all royal and secular dues except those relating to *expeditio*, fyrd-service.[17]

Mercian royal charters demanded other military services as well as service in the fyrd. In 749 Æthelbald, reacting to the complaints of St Boniface, freed the Mercian churches from all royal and secular exactions, but reserved the building of bridges and fortifications against enemies.[18] In 792 Offa exempted the Kentish churches from all public burdens except 'military service against the roaming fleets of seaborne heathen' (*paganos marinos cum classis migrantibus*), that is, the Vikings; the construction of fortresses and bridges was limited to 'the bounds of the Kentish people', but *expeditio* (service in the fyrd) was to be performed in Sussex as well as Kent.[19] Kentish charters of the early ninth century occasionally specify the destruction of fortresses built within Kent by the Vikings themselves; it was perhaps to one of them that the Northumbrian priest Aldwulf was taken after his capture in 809, for he was ransomed by Coenwulf of Mercia, who controlled Kent at the time.[20]

By the end of the eighth century, bridge- and fortress-building, coupled with service in the fyrd, had become the 'common burdens' which were always reserved, and by the middle of the ninth century, they are regularly found in West Saxon, as well as Mercian charters.[21] Any search for the fortifications produced by the eighth- and ninth-century Mercians is hampered by terminology. The Old English word *burh* is the root of Modern English 'borough', implying an urban settlement, but in origin it meant no more than a defensible place, and in placenames is applied to all manner of sites, including fortified towns, Iron Age hill-forts and defended or fortified manor-houses. Some royal residences were probably defensible; Tamworth had banks and ditches contemporary with the eighth-century watermill which formed part of the residential complex.[22]

More impressive are the pre-Alfredian works at Hereford, where a grid of streets datable to the mid-eighth century was surrounded by walls of eighth- or early-ninth-century date.[23] It has been suggested that Offa's Mercia had a whole network of such fortress-towns.[24]

The purpose of bridgework was to defend strategic river-crossings against the movement of potential enemies. A timber and clay causeway at Oxford, dated either to the later part of Offa's reign or to that of Coenwulf (796–821), may be an example of Mercian bridgework-obligation. Elsewhere we have only the late seventh-century timber causeway linking Mersea Island to the Essex mainland, and the Roman bridge at Rochester, which seems to have been continuously maintained by the men of the surrounding region until the fourteenth century.[25]

One obvious area requiring defences was the border with Wales. One thinks immediately of the work which preserves Offa's name until this day: Offa's Dyke to the English, Clawdd Offa to the Welsh. Stenton saw it as the delineation of an agreed frontier, one which involved the surrender of territory by Mercians and Welsh alike.[26] Later opinion has redefined the Dyke as an instrument of war rather than peace, built to stem Welsh inroads into the westernmost lands of the Mercians.[27] Whatever its purpose, it stands as an impressive testament to the administrative capabilities of the Mercian kings.[28]

The distribution of places named Burton and variants thereof has revealed what may be a significant concentration along the Welsh borders, from Cheshire to Herefordshire. The name (*burh*, 'fortification', *tun*, 'settlement, vill') has various interpretations, among which might be a particular type of defended settlement, and the Mercian *burhtunas* may represent a system of defence-posts on the frontier with Wales.[29] Whether they were produced by a centrally-directed royal policy or by the natural response of local landowners in a particularly vulnerable region is debateable. In the eleventh century, both Norman incomers and native lords built castles and fortified manors in the same areas, but while some of these might be the results of royal direction, others were clearly a matter of private enterprise.[30]

The Viking Raids

The balance of power among the English kingdoms was overturned in the viking wars of the later ninth century. The kings of the late eighth and early ninth centuries were not unprepared for the dangers to come;

warfare was one of the facts of early medieval life. But the Vikings presented particular problems, the most important of which was coordination of resources. The same viking force, moving rapidly in its superior ships, could assail the coastal and riverine settlements of several kingdoms in a short space of time, striking and withdrawing before the victims could organize a defence.[31] In 850, for instance, Ealdorman Ceorl and the men of Devon actually defeated a viking force at *Wicganbeorg* (unidentified), but it moved off to ravage Kent; in fact this was the first viking host to over-winter on Thanet.[32]

Hindsight suggests that the nature of the viking assault changed with the arrival in 865 of what the *Chronicle* describes as 'the Great Army' (*micel here*). The Great Army was not concerned with plunder alone; its members intended to establish permanent settlements for themselves. The dominant commander was the Danish chieftain, Ivar the boneless (*inn beinlausi*). Ivar had already established himself in viking Dublin as the ally of its Norwegian ruler Olaf, and his arrival marks the beginning of the link between the viking settlements in Ireland and those in the north of England which was to last for nearly a century.[33]

The Great Army spent the winter of 865–6 in East Anglia, with the enforced consent of the East Anglians. In the autumn of 866 they crossed the Humber and attacked York, taking advantage of a civil war between rival Northumbrian factions, which prevented the Northumbrians from organizing an effective defence. When the Northumbrians finally mounted an attack on the Danes in York, on Palm Sunday (23 March) 867, the result was a Danish victory; the contending Northumbrian kings were killed, and their successor, Ecgberht, made peace with the Danes. For the next few years the Great Army seems to have been based in York, with Ecgberht's acquiescence, making probing raids into Mercia in 868, and East Anglia in 870.

In 871 the Great Army turned its attention to Wessex. By this time Ivar had returned to Ireland, to establish his rule in Dublin, and the overall commander was his brother Halfdan. During the year, according to the *Chronicle*, 'nine general engagements were fought against the Danish army in the kingdom south of the Thames [that is, Wessex], besides the expeditions which the king's brother Alfred and single ealdormen and king's thegns often rode on, which were not counted'.[34] In the course of these struggles, King Æthelred I died, soon after Easter (15 April) 871, and was succeeded by his brother Alfred. The West Saxons were compelled to make peace, and in 872 the Danes moved to London, where they spent the winter; the Mercians made peace and paid a heavy tribute.[35] The

West Saxons may also have paid tribute, for at some time in the 870s Bishop Ealhferth of Winchester gave King Alfred lands at Chiseldon, Wilts, and Hampton Priors, Hants, on condition that the king paid Winchester's share of the tribute to 'the pagans', since the bishop could not raise the cash.[36]

By this time the Great Army had been joined by a second force, which the *Chronicle* calls 'the great Summer Army' (*mycel sumorlida*).[37] The two armies operated in concert over the next few years, their most successful operations being in Mercia. In 873–4, they over-wintered at Repton, Derbys, after which the reigning monarch, Burgred, fled, and the kingdom passed to Ceolwulf II, who had allied with the Danes.[38] The *Chronicle* describes Ceolwulf as 'a foolish king's thegn', but this represents the view from Wessex, whose king (Alfred) was Burgred's brother-in-law; Ceolwulf was regarded as a legitimate king by the Mercians.[39] His name suggests that he was (or claimed to be) related to King Ceolwulf I, whose murdered grandson, St Wigstan, was venerated at Repton.[40]

In 875 the Danish armies divided; Halfdan returned to York, where in 876 he 'shared out the land of the Northumbrians' among his veteran troops, and 'they began to plough and support themselves'.[41] Such peaceful pursuits were not, it seems, to Halfdan's taste; he departed to Ireland where he was killed in 877 attempting to establish himself as ruler of Dublin.[42] The Summer Army remained in Mercia. The dominant leader was Guthrum, who, it seems, was left with Southumbrian England as his oyster.[43] In 877 he and Ceolwulf II formally divided up the kingdom of Mercia.[44] Æthelweard says that the Danes occupied Gloucester, and the events of 878 suggest that they had bases in western Mercia.[45] Ceolwulf II seems to have retained control in south-eastern Mercia, for the London moneyers continued to issue coinage in his name.[46]

It was in 878 that Guthrum made his decisive move against Wessex:

> in this year, at midwinter, the enemy army came stealthily to Chippenham after Twelfth Night, and occupied the land of the West Saxons, and settled there; and drove a great part of the people across the sea and conquered most of the others; and the people submitted to them, except King Alfred [who] journeyed in difficulties through the woods and fen-fastnesses with a small force.[47]

Alfred's epic defence of Wessex against the 'Summer Army' is celebrated both in the West Saxon *Chronicle* and in the pages of the king's biographer, Asser.[48] From his fortified base on Athelney in the Somerset Marshes, he organized the levies of western Wessex, until he was able to bring Guthrum to battle at Edington, Wilts, and put the Danish host to flight. He pursued the fleeing Vikings to Chippenham and besieged them in the royal *tun*. After a fortnight, Guthrum capitulated. He and his leading followers were baptized, and agreed to leave Wessex in peace. Guthrum retired first to Cirencester, Gloucs, and thence, in 879–80, to East Anglia, where he and his men 'shared out the land'.[49] At some time between 878 and 886, Alfred and Guthrum concluded a formal peace defining the boundary between their spheres of influence.[50] Guthrum ruled East Anglia as king, in his baptismal name of Athelstan, until his death in 890.[51]

The Rise of Wessex

By 880 the Danes had established political control both of East Anglia and of southern Northumbria (Deira). Northern Northumbria (Bernicia) was under English rule, but cut off from direct contact with the southern English; and Mercia was partitioned between English and Danes. Wessex was the only English kingdom in southern England to preserve full independence under its native king.

At this time Wessex included England south of the Thames, plus at least southern and western Essex.[52] Alfred's grandfather, Ecgberht, had completed the conquest of the south-west (Devon and Cornwall) by his defeat of the Cornish and their viking allies at Hingston Down in 838.[53] Kent and the south-east had passed from Mercian into West Saxon control after the battle of *Ellendun*. The West Saxon rulers exercised a more direct authority in Kent than had the Mercian kings, with both Ecgberht and Æthelwulf making regular visits.[54] Æthelwulf, sub-king of Kent under his father, may have married a Kentish woman, for his wife's father Oslac, Æthelwulf's butler (*pincerna*), is said to have been descended from the mythical Jutish princes Stuf and Wihtgar.[55] In 838 the West Saxon kings reached a compromise over the Kentish monasteries, whereby the archbishops were to exercise spiritual authority and the kings to give secular protection.[56] They also went to some pains to win over the Kentish nobility. Whereas only a third of the surviving Kentish grants of Coenwulf and Cuthred are in favour of laymen (six out of 19), under the West Saxons the proportion rises to half (13 out of 27).[57]

Despite the closer relations between the West Saxon kings and the Kentish hierarchy, lay and ecclesiastical, Kent and Wessex were still administered as separate kingdoms.[58] Kent in this period has sometimes been seen as a kind of appanage, reserved for the heir to the West Saxon kingship. Æthelwulf, who was probably king of Kent from the moment of his successful expulsion of the Mercian Baldred, was, of course, Ecgberht's eventual successor.[59] When Æthelwulf himself became king of Wessex in 839, he 'gave his son Athelstan the kingdom of Kent and the kingdom of the East Saxons and of the people of Surrey and of the South Saxons', and Athelstan duly attests his father's Kentish charters as *rex* from 839 to 850.[60] He did not, however, issue charters in his own name (or at least none have survived), nor, unlike their Mercian predecessors, did either Athelstan or Æthelwulf as sub-king issue their own coinage. Between 826/7 and 839 the Canterbury and Rochester moneyers struck coins in Ecgberht's name, not that of Æthelwulf, and between 839 and 851 in that of Æthelwulf, not of Athelstan. Indeed when Æthelwulf became king of the West Saxons in 839, he signalled his new status by a change of design: the obverse of the Canterbury mintage carried the legend *rex Saxoniorum* and that of Rochester *rex Occidentalium Saxoniorum*.[61]

It might be assumed that Æthelwulf had intended Athelstan to succeed him as king of Wessex, as he himself had succeeded his father Ecgberht, but it is far from certain that the West Saxon kings of this time entertained any notion of a designated heir, or indeed a permanently united kingdom. When Æthelwulf undertook the pilgrimage to Rome in 855, he left Wessex proper in the charge of his eldest surviving son, Æthelbald, while the next eldest, Æthelberht, became king of Kent, and this arrangement was ratified on his return to England in 856.[62] It is possible that Æthelberht was intended to be Æthelbald's eventual successor to the whole kingdom (which is what actually happened) but it is equally plausible that the division was originally meant to be permanent.[63] When Æthelbald died in 860, however, Æthelberht came to an arrangement with his surviving brothers, Æthelred and Alfred, whereby he succeeded both to Wessex and to Kent. It is probably significant that no Kentish sub-king was appointed; nor, when Æthelred I succeeded to the combined kingdoms in 865, was Alfred given charge of Kent. It seems that, after 860, Kent was regarded as an integral part of Wessex.[64]

It has sometimes been suggested that the success of the West Saxon kings was due in part to their ability to govern the royal succession so as to avoid the antagonism between collateral lines of heirs such as marked the political history of ninth-century Mercia, and indeed Northumbria.[65] But the apparently orderly succession of West Saxon kings from 802 to 899 was achieved by a series of complex agreements and attended by disputes now only partly visible.[66] It must be remembered that the *Chronicle*, our chief source for the period, is not only a West Saxon text, but one produced close to the court of Alfred, the eventual beneficiary of all this royal manoeuvring; it thus has every reason to present Alfred's succession as the result of a deliberate policy. The resulting contrast between the smooth succession of West Saxon heirs, and the internal disputes within the contemporary Mercian royal house may be more apparent than real.

The Achievement of Alfred

Alfred is one of the best recorded of the pre-Conquest kings. Not only is the *Chronicle* a contemporary text for his reign, but we also have a biography of the king, written during his lifetime by his friend Asser, soon to become bishop of Sherborne.[67] The king's will survives, and the text of his law-code, as well as a number of works from his own pen, including his translations of Boethius' *Consolations of Philosophy*, Gregory the Great's *Pastoral Care* and the *Soliloquies* of St Augustine of Hippo. Other translations were undertaken at the king's direction: Wærferth of Worcester's translation of the *Dialogues* of Gregory the Great, the Old English text of Bede's *Ecclesiastical History* and the West Saxon version of Orosius' *Histories against the pagans*.[68] All this, when added to the usual sources (charters, coins, manuscripts and other artifacts), allows a much deeper insight than is common into the ideas and actions of an early medieval king. It may seem ungracious to look such a gift-horse in the mouth, but one of the major problems in evaluating the achievement of Alfred is the very fact that the sources for his reign were largely produced by and for the royal court, and are therefore concerned to exhibit the king and his deeds in the most favourable light. This factor must be borne in mind in attempting to assess Alfred's achievement.[69]

Alfred's victory at Edington in 878 left him in secure control of the West Saxon kingdom, and in the 880s his authority came to be recognized in English Mercia also. Ceolwulf II died in 878 or 879. By 883, he had been succeeded by Æthelred, who issued a charter in that year with 'the leave and cognisance of King Alfred'.[70] It was in 883, according to the *Chronicle*, that 'the English were encamped against the enemy army at London', and it may be that Æthelred and Alfred were already engaged in the campaign that eventually led to the recapture of the city from the Danes in 886.[71] The city was placed in Æthelred's control and it was perhaps at this time, or a little earlier, that he married Æthelflæd, Alfred's first-born child.

The *Chronicle* claims that it was after Alfred's capture of London that 'all the English people that were not under subjection to the Danes submitted to him'. Alfred's law-code, promulgated in the late 880s or early 890s, drew upon earlier Mercian and Kentish codes as well as the laws of Ine, and was clearly intended to express his authority over all the English peoples.[72] It is in the 890s that his charters begin to use the title 'king of the Angles and Saxons' (*rex Angul-Saxonum* and its variants), signifying his authority over the (Anglian) Mercians as well as his own people.[73] Æthelred, on the other hand, usually appears simply as ealdorman or (more frequently) 'lord of the Mercians', and the *Chronicle* can describe Mercia as 'Alfred's kingdom – that part of it for which Æthelred was responsible'.[74] Its account of the warfare of the 890s shows the 'English army' defending a single realm, to the extent of suppressing the role of Æthelred, and even that of Alfred's own son Edward.[75]

Mercia, however, was not yet a province of Wessex. The late tenth-century chronicler Æthelweard (himself a descendant of the West Saxon royal house) calls Æthelred a king and Mercia his kingdom.[76] The Mercian council (*witan*) was still separate from that of the West Saxons, and Æthelred issued charters in his own name, though usually acknowledging Alfred's consent.[77] Indeed a Mercian charter of 898, albeit not of unquestioned authenticity, describes Æthelred as *subregulus et patricius Merciorum*.[78]

Mercians played an important part at Alfred's court. The charters of his later years draw upon Mercian as well as West Saxon diplomatic practice, suggesting the presence of Mercian and Mercian-trained scribes.[79] Mercians were also prominent among the scholars assembled by Alfred, notably Wærferth, bishop of Worcester (the translator of Gregory's *Dialogues*) and Plegmund, appointed archbishop of Canterbury in 890.[80] Their chief concern was the revival of Latin learning, but the chosen route entailed translation into the vernacular of the 'books most necessary for all men to know', in order to provide prior instruction in written English, both for those who would enter religion, and for laymen.[81] Alfred himself, in his translation of St Augustine's *Soliloquies*, speaks of a lord's 'written message and seal' (*ærendgewrit and hys insegel*), suggesting that he was accustomed, on occasion at least, to communicate with his officials in writing as well as by word of mouth.[82]

The major targets for instruction in vernacular literacy were the ealdormen and reeves who, in addition to their military duties, were required to administer justice.[83] Alfred was the first West Saxon king since Ine to issue a code of laws; indeed Ine's code is appended to his own.[84] Alfred's Laws have a clear ideological purpose but this need not preclude a more practical intention. It is true that there are no recorded cases of any Old English law-code being cited in the course of a legal suit, but it can be argued that those responsible for the administration of justice were required to have some knowledge of the written texts. To take only one example, the earliest law-code of Alfred's son, Edward, commands the king's reeves to 'give such just judgements as you know most right and as it stands in the lawbook (*domboc*)'; this lawbook can scarcely be other than his father's Laws.[85]

The lay officials on whom the king relied are occasionally mentioned, usually when they died or were killed. A list of the 'best king's thegns' who died in the period between 893 and 896 includes three ealdormen, Ceolmund of Kent, Beorhtwulf of Essex and Wulfred of Hampshire; Eadwulf, a king's thegn in Sussex; Beornwulf, town-reeve of Winchester; and Ecgwulf the king's marshal (*horsþegn*). Among the casualties in the abortive sea-battle in 896 were Lucuman the king's reeve, Æthelfrith the king's *geneat*, and three men distinguished simply as 'Frisians', Wulfheard, Æbbe and Æthelhere; another marshal, Wulfric, who was also the 'Welsh-reeve', died in the same year.[86]

Some at least of these men must have been officials of the king's household. The two marshals would have had charge of the royal stables and the transport of the king and his entourage; presumably they also supervised the men in charge of the king's horses, mentioned in Mercian and West Saxon charters of the time.[87] What additional duties were incumbent on the Welsh-reeve is uncertain but he may have supervised the king's 'Welsh horsemen', who carried his messages and commands.[88] Other household officers include Deormod *cellerarius*, Ælfric *thesaurius* and Sigewulf *pincerna*, who attest a charter of 892.[89] These three officers correspond to the vernacular *byrele* (butler), who was responsible for the provision of drink, the *hordere* or *burþegn* (chamberlain), who kept the king's valuables, and the *discþegn* (seneschal, steward), who provisioned his household.[90] The holders of such offices were men of rank: Alfred's mother Osburh was the daughter of King Æthelwulf's butler (*pincerna*), Oslac, allegedly a descendant of Kentish royalty.[91]

The king's household officers were rewarded for their services according to their rank and office. Asser says that Alfred divided his revenues into two parts, one for secular and one for religious purposes; of the secular revenue, one-third was devoted to 'his fighting-men (*bellatores*) and likewise to his noble thegns (*ministri*) who lived at the royal court in turns, serving him in various capacities'. He adds that the thegns were divided into three groups, each of which in turn served for a month at the king's court before returning to their homes.[92] Such men expected reward, but they were far from being a paid bureaucracy. Their service was personal, a consequence of their rank as king's thegns.[93] They took oaths to the king as their lord; the importance of such oaths is underlined in the first clause of Alfred's Laws, on the duty of honouring one's oath and pledge (*að and wedd*).[94]

A second part of Alfred's secular revenue went to his craftsmen (*operatores*), presumably the goldsmiths, masons, carpenters and others who worked on the building programmes and artistic projects of which Asser speaks so glowingly elsewhere.[95] The last portion was reserved 'to foreigners of all races who came to him from places near and far'. In another passage, Asser lists the 'many Franks, Frisians, Gauls, Vikings, Welshmen, Irishmen and Bretons' who flocked to Alfred's court.[96] Presumably he means to include ecclesiastics like himself; but the Frisians killed in the sea-battle of 896 must fall into the same category. Next to the Vikings themselves, the Frisians were the master shipbuilders and seamen of the northern world, and it is presumably in this capacity that they served the king.[97] Much of the effectiveness of viking attacks lay in the speed and manoeuvrability of their ships; if the Vikings could be cut off from their ships, or those ships be captured or destroyed, the assailants might be neutralized and driven off. The English army which stormed the fortified viking camp at Benfleet, Essex, in 893 'either broke up or burned all the ships, or brought them to London or Rochester'.[98] It was presumably after examination of such captured vessels that Alfred ordered his new 'long-ships' in 896:

> they were almost twice as long as the others. Some had sixty oars, some more. They were both swifter and more stable, and also higher, than the others. They were built neither on the Frisian nor on the Danish model, but as it seemed to Alfred himself that they would be most useful.[99]

It has to be said that, despite the *Chronicle*'s lavish praise of the new warships, its own account of their first action, later in the same year, describes a complete disaster.[100]

Asser's mention of Vikings in King Alfred's service is also interesting. One thinks of the Norwegian Ohthere (Ottar) and the Dane Wulfstan, whose accounts of their voyages (around the north coast of Norway and through the Baltic respectively) are among the additions made by the anonymous West Saxon translator to the text of Orosius' *Histories against the pagans*.[101] But such peaceful visitors may not have been the only Scandinavians at Alfred's court. It has become fashionable to distinguish 'raiding' Vikings from 'trading' Vikings, but we may simply be looking at the same people at different times, first acquiring their merchandise (by stealing it, for instance) and then disposing of it by sale in a convenient market.[102] It is conceivable that, as in later times, many of these roving bands of pirates were available for hire, and that not all the non-English seamen on Alfred's ships were Frisians.

The key to Alfred's military successes in the last decade of his reign lay not in sea-power but in fortification. As we have seen, some royal manors had defences even in the eighth century, and these could be strengthened at need. Rochester held out against a Danish assault in 885 and its rampart (*veribracho*) is mentioned in 868.[103] In 878, Alfred built a *geweorc* or stronghold at Athelney, and the *Chronicle* uses the same word for the royal manor of Chippenham, where Alfred successfully besieged Guthrum after the battle of Edington. Iron Age hill-forts could also be re-used; Asser describes how, in the same year, some of the thegns of Devon took refuge in the *arx* (stronghold) of Countisbury and held it against a force of Vikings, despite the fact that it was 'unprepared and altogether unfortified'.[104]

It seems to have been in the 880s that Alfred embarked on a concentrated programme of fortress-building throughout his realms. Fortifications at Exeter, Chichester and Pilton, Devon, are mentioned in the *Chronicle*, and at Lyng, Wareham and Shaftesbury by Asser.[105] A double burh, as yet unidentified, was built on both sides of the Lea in 895, to block the river against a force of Vikings encamped some twenty miles north of London.[106] Such 'double-boroughs' had been used in Frankia, notably at Pont de l'Arche on the Seine, but whether there was any direct Frankish influence on Alfred's burhs is debateable.[107]

These burhs and their garrisons played a key role in the warfare of the 890s. In 893, 'the men who guarded the burhs' helped drive out the viking forces established at Milton Regis and Appledore, in north and south Kent respectively; indeed the ability of the Vikings to fortify Appledore lay in their capture of a half-built English fortress (*geweorc, fæsten*) manned only by a few free men (*ceorlas*).[108] Later in 893, we hear of the king's thegns in the west assembling 'from every borough east of the Parret, both west and east of Selwood, and also north of the Thames and west of the Severn' to intercept and defeat a viking host at Buttington.

Alfred's programme of fortification is revealed in the *Burghal Hidage*, drawn up in the reign of Edward the Elder.[109] It has been described as 'the earliest administrative record of English government that survives'.[110] The most recent examination has concluded that its 'close relationship to actual practice in the West Saxon kingdom' shows it to have been 'a practical document describing a real scheme'.[111] It gives the hidages assigned to the burhs of Wessex, and describes how they relate to the obligations of constructing, maintaining and manning them:

> For the establishment of a wall (*weal-stilling*) of one acre's breadth, and for its defence (*waru*) 16 hides are required. If each hide is represented by one man, then each pole (*gyrd*) [of wall] can be furnished with four men.[112]

Taken literally, the *Burghal Hidage* assigns 27070 men to the construction and defence of the burhs of Wessex alone, but it is not likely that all were called upon to perform such duties in person. *Waru* implies not merely 'defence' in the literal sense of manning the walls, but also fiscal liability, a tax laid on the district for the upkeep of the burh.[113] The *Chronicle*'s description of the campaigns of 893 implies that Alfred's burhs had permanent garrisons, and presumably these could have been maintained, in part, from revenue raised from the surrounding area. A similar levy presumably provisioned the warriors (*bellatores*) serving their turn in the field.[114] As for the physical building and maintenance of the fortifications, this could have been met by the normal obligations of burh-work laid on all estates, including bookland.

The programme of burh-building initiated by Alfred and maintained by his son Edward placed a considerable strain on the available resources.[115] The task required the active cooperation of the local magnates, lay and ecclesiastical, whose men were required to carry it out. The church of Worcester preserved a record of the agreement made between Bishop Wærferth and Ealdorman Æthelred and his wife Æthelflæd, when the city was fortified, in the closing decade of Alfred's reign.[116] It is clear that the bishop's assistance went far beyond the prayers offered daily for the ealdorman and his lady, for he received half the rights belonging to their lordship in the city, including the fines for fighting, theft, dishonest trading, failure to maintain the burh-walls and other emendable offences, that is those which could be redeemed by a cash fine, as opposed to those which required the death and forfeiture of the offender.[117] The agreement suggests that 'the establishment of a burh was not just a military matter [but] also a financial carve-up between the king (or here the ealdorman of the Mercians) and the interested greater lords'.[118]

Similar arrangements may have been made at London. In 898 a meeting was held at Chelsea to discuss the *instauratio* ('laying out') of the city; the area concerned seems to be the grid of streets reaching north from Thames Street to Cheapside. Present were the king, his son Edward, Æthelred and Æthelflæd, Archbishop Plegmund and Bishop Wærferth of Worcester. The two ecclesiastics received lands on the river frontage of the area, at *Ætheredes hid*, later known as Queenhithe, which was presumably held by the lord of Mercia himself.[119]

In the case of towns like Worcester and London, there were economic forces which encouraged the building and upkeep of defences against enemies, but not all the burhs of the *Burghal Hidage* were (or became) towns. Several seem to have been no more than 'emergency forts' built against a present danger, with little to commend them as potential centres of trade or settlement.[120] The 'half-built' fortification on the River Limen, seized by the Vikings in 892, may have been such a one. Asser, writing in 893, complains of 'fortifications commanded by the king which have not yet been begun, or else, having been begun late in the day, have not been brought to completion'.[121] No doubt the arrival of Danish armies concentrated the minds of the recalcitrant, even if belatedly; but once the danger receded, forts with little economic function were presumably neglected.[122]

There are other signs of strain in the later years of Alfred's reign. Asser acknowledges that the king ruled by force as well as persuasion, 'sharply chastising those who were disobedient and...despising popular stupidity and stubbornness'.[123] Nor was he unopposed. His Laws prescribe death and forfeiture for anyone who plots against the king's life, 'either on his own account or by harbouring outlaws', or for any of the king's own men who have incurred his displeasure; similar penalties are laid down for any who commit the like offences against their own lords.[124] One of Alfred's own ealdormen, Wulfhere, forfeited his land 'when he deserted without permission both his lord King Alfred and his country, in spite of the oath which he had sworn to the king and all his leading men (*optimates*)'; as a result, 'by the just judgment of all the councillors (*sapientes*) [that is the witan] of the *Gewisse* and of the Mercians, he lost the control and inheritance of his lands'.[125]

Criticism of Alfred is voiced by Pope John VIII in a letter to Æthelred, archbishop of Canterbury, written in 878 or 879. He urges the archbishop to 'resist strongly not only the king but all who wish to do any wrong' to the Church; he adds that he himself has written a letter of exhortation to the king, which (unfortunately) has not survived.[126] There are other hints of ecclesiastical discontent. The monks of Abingdon remembered Alfred as a despoiler of their land 'for the uses of himself and his men', and he is presumably also among the 'kings up to King Edmund' who retained an estate at Wouldham, Kent, which belonged to the bishopric of Rochester.[127] Tribute to the Danes could place heavy demands on churches' finances, and the same may be true of other royal demands. We do not, of course, have any detailed knowledge of Alfred's finances; indeed he himself remarks, in his will, that he is not sure whether there is money enough to pay his bequests 'though I suspect so'.[128] He had the resources common to all the early kings: the royal estates and his own personal property, the rights to *feorm*, the profits of justice, and of course the tolls levied on trade; land forfeited for any reason would also come into his hands.[129] But Alfred's policies clearly cost money, and this need may underlie the discontents, ecclesiastical and lay, which surface from time to time in his reign.

7

THE MAKING OF ENGLAND

This measure is to be common to all the nation, whether Englishmen, Danes or Britons, in every province of my dominion.[1]

On Alfred's death the frontier between English and Danes was defined, roughly speaking, by the line of Watling Street. To the north and east lay the Danish kingdoms of York and East Anglia. Eastern Mercia was dominated by individual jarls and their warbands, most of them probably under the nominal control either of York or East Anglia.[2] In the far north lay the remnant of Bernicia, still governed by a line of English rulers established at Bamburgh, but under pressure not only from Danish York but also from the ambitious Scottish kings.

By 954 all this territory had fallen to the West Saxon kings in what is often but misleadingly called a 'reconquest'. In the process they created the kingdom of the English, and laid claim, with varying success, to the overlordship of the British rulers of Wales and the north-west, and even the kings of the Scots. Battle and war were their tools, but they also had to govern the lands they acquired, and in the tenth century the foundations were laid which determined the future shape of English central and local administration.

In view of the significance of this achievement, it is unfortunate that the *Chronicle* ceases to be a contemporary record after 920. This narrative dearth is offset by the increasing volume of charters and memoranda and by the law-codes of the West Saxon rulers. For the north we have the *Historia de Sancto Cuthberto*, composed at Chester-le-Street about the middle of the tenth century, with a continuation into the mid-eleventh, and some northern annals covering the years 888–957, preserved in the

Historia Regum.[3] Other, possibly reliable, northern material is incorporated into the *Flores Historiarum* of the thirteenth-century St Albans
chronicler, Roger of Wendover.[4] The surviving Welsh, Scottish and Irish
annals all contain matter of interest.[5] For the later tenth century, the
writings of the Benedictine reformers throw light on individual kings
and their activities, though it should be remembered that they are being
judged according to their zeal (or lack of it) in promoting ecclesiastical
reform.[6] The *Chronicle* of Æthelweard (d. 998), ealdorman of the Western
Shires, and a kinsman of the West Saxon kings, provides another viewpoint.[7]

Making the Kingdom

The conquest of the southern settlements was the work of Edward the Elder
and his sister Æthelflæd, who ruled alone as Lady of the Mercians after
the death of her husband in 911.[8] The first step was to draw the sting
from the Danes of York. In 909 a joint West Saxon and Mercian force
raided Lindsey, provoking a Danish raid into Mercia in 910; they were
brought to battle at Tettenhall, Staffs, and there decisively defeated with
the death of two kings. The way was cleared for the conquest of the southern settlements.[9]

Edward directed his attack towards East Anglia and the south-east
midlands, while Æthelflæd concentrated on the north and north-east.
The means to hand were the fortified burhs developed by their father,
which (like later castles) could be used both to defend and control territory
already held, and to launch fresh attacks into the lands of the enemy. The
Chronicle's account of Edward's advance is marked by the construction of
such fortifications: at Hertford and Witham (Essex) in 912, at Buckingham in 914, at Bedford in 915, at Maldon (Essex) in 916, at Towcester
(Northants) and the unidentified *Wigingamere* in 917.[10] Some were double-
burhs, built to control navigable rivers; at Hertford, the northern burh
lay between the rivers Maran, Beane and Lea, and the southern burh to
the south of the Lea.

The mere construction of such fortresses sometimes ensured the capit-
ulation of the local forces. In 914, for instance, the building of a double
burh at Buckingham brought about the submission of Thurcytel, jarl of
Bedford, and his men 'and also many of those who belonged to
Northampton'.[11] In the following year, Edward occupied Bedford,
building the southern 'English' burh across the Ouse from the viking

encampment, and in 916 Jarl Thurcytel and his men took themselves off to seek their fortunes in Frankia.[12]

In 917, the Danes of Northampton and Leicester with their allies attacked Towcester, but the burh held out until a relieving force arrived. Meanwhile, the Danes of Huntingdon and East Anglia established a burh of their own at Tempsford, whence they unsuccessfully attacked Bedford, while a great force from East Anglia and the east midlands besieged *Wigingamere*, again without success.[13] Edward's army took Tempsford killing the unnamed East Anglian king, with Jarl Toli of Huntingdon, his son and brother, and 'all those who were inside and chose to defend themselves'. Edward rebuilt the walls of Towcester in stone, and there received the submission of Thurferth, jarl of Northampton; the fall of Huntingdon soon followed. Finally Edward refortified Colchester, taken by the English earlier in the year, and received the submission of the East Anglian Danes and the army of Cambridge.

Æthelflæd's campaigns are recorded not in the *Chronicle* but in the *Mercian Register*, probably compiled by someone close to her court.[14] A note of particular pride is sounded in its account of Æthelflæd's fortification of the old Mercian royal centre at Tamworth in 913: 'in this year, by the grace of God, Æthelflæd, lady of the Mercians, went with all the Mercians to Tamworth, and built the burh there in the early summer'. Soon after the battle of Tettenhall, she built a burh at *Bremesbyrig*, probably in the neighbourhood of Bromsgrove.[15] Worcester had been fortified in the 890s and Hereford and Gloucester had defences by 914 at the latest.[16] Bridgnorth and *Sceargeat* (unidentified) were built in 912, the first certainly and the second probably to defend the Severn crossings; a third fortress at Chirbury (915) controlled one of the main routes into central Wales.

It seems that brother and sister were following a mutually-agreed strategy. The fortifications built by Æthelflæd at Tamworth and Stafford in 913 and Warwick in 914 not only defended eastern Mercia, but also put pressure on the Danish armies of the midlands, especially at Bedford, which (as we have seen) capitulated to Edward in 915. Conversely, it was Edward's successful campaign against Northampton which allowed Æthelflæd to seize Derby in 917 and occupy Leicester in 918.[17]

Æthelflæd's fortresses at Eddisbury and Runcorn (Cheshire), built in 914 and 915 respectively, were directed against viking fleets operating in the Irish Sea. Chief among them were the grandsons of Ivar the boneless. They were temporarily expelled from Dublin in 902, and Ragnall, the eldest, may have established himself at York in the immediate aftermath of Tettenhall.[18] By 917 he was rebuilding his family's interests in Dublin, and in his absence Æthelflæd joined, or perhaps organized an alliance against him, including Constantine II king of Scots, Ealdred the English ruler of Northumbria, and even some of the York Danes who in 918 promised 'that they would be under her [Æthelflæd's] direction'.[19]

On 12 June, 918, Æthelflæd died at Tamworth. Edward was at Stamford, receiving the submission of the Danish army there, and building the 'English' burh on the south bank of the Welland.[20] On hearing of his sister's death, he occupied Tamworth, and 'all the nation of the Mercians which had been subject to Æthelflæd submitted to him'.[21] Henceforward the kingdom of the Mercians was to be subsumed into Wessex, and in 919, as the *Mercian Register* bitterly records, Æthelred's daughter Ælfwynn 'was deprived of all authority in Mercia'.[22] The main text of the *Chronicle*, produced in Wessex, has nothing to say of the Mercians' role in the subjugation of the Danish settlements; all the glory is attributed to Edward the Elder.

The death of Æthelflæd allowed Ragnall to re-occupy York in 919. Edward strengthened the defences of northern Mercia by fortifying Thelwall and Manchester, and in 920 he built the southern burh at Nottingham (the northern burh was the viking settlement) and bridged the Trent between them, thus securing the strategic river crossing. In the same year he moved into the Peak district to build a fortification at Bakewell, and there met with Constantine II king of Scots, Constantine's brother Donald king of Strathclyde, Ealdred of Bamburgh and his brother Uhtred, and Ragnall of York. Ealdred and Uhtred may already have been adherents of Edward, but (despite the claims of the *Chronicle*) it is unlikely that either Constantine or Ragnall saw themselves as dependants of the West Saxon king, and the agreement reached between them was probably no more than a mutual definition of their spheres of interest.[23] There was trouble of an unspecified kind at Chester in 924, and it was while dealing with this that Edward died at Farndon on 17 July.[24] Ælfweard, the elder son of his second wife Ælfflæd, died soon afterwards and the kingship passed to Athelstan the child of Ecgwynn, Edward's first wife who was consecrated and crowned at Kingston-on-Thames on 9 September 925.[25]

Kings of the English

Edward left his son an impressive legacy, but most of Athelstan's reign was occupied in transforming his theoretical authority into real power.

Ragnall of York had died in 920, and in 927 Athelstan concluded an alliance with his brother, Sigtrygg *Caech* ('the squinty'), cemented by the marriage of the Danish king with Athelstan's sister.[26] When Sigtrygg died in the following year Athelstan expelled his brother Gothfrith and seized York. With the capture of York Athelstan became the first West Saxon king to rule all the English peoples.[27] This show of power brought him the (temporary) allegiance of Constantine II of Scotland; the two kings met at *Eamot* ('watersmeet'), near Penrith in Cumbria, and there 'established peace with pledge and oaths', along with Owen, king of Cumbria, and Ealdred of Bamburgh.[28] The verse panegyric which records this triumph speaks of *perfecta Saxonia*, 'England [now] made whole', and it is from about this time that Athelstan's coins begin to bear the legend *rex totius Britanniae*, 'king of all Britain', and the image of the crowned king.[29] A similar meeting at Hereford was attended by the Welsh kings, led by Hywel Dda ('the Good') of Deheubarth, and either in the same year or in 928 Athelstan received the submission of the Britons of Cornwall at Exeter.[30]

It was perhaps in the 930s that an anonymous Welsh cleric composed the *Armes Prydein* ('The Prophecy of Britain'), which urges the expulsion of the English ('the scavengers from Thanet') not merely from Wales, but from the whole island of Britain, by a grand alliance of Welshmen, Irishmen, Dublin Norse, Bretons, Scots and men of Strathclyde, united against the 'tax gatherers of Cair Geri (Cirencester)'.[31] This alliance failed to materialize, but in 934, for reasons not specified, Athelstan led an expedition into Scotland. His land-army ravaged as far as Dunnotar (Fordun, Kincaidshire), while his fleet raided the coast up to the Norse settlements in Caithness.[32] The effect was to drive Constantine II still further into the arms of the Dublin Vikings. Gothfrith, whom Constantine had harboured in 928 after his expulsion from York, died in 934, and it took his son, Olaf Gothfrithson, three years to establish his authority in Dublin, but by 937 he was ready to make a bid for York. He and Constantine harried deep into Mercia, until they met with Athelstan's forces at the still unidentified site of *Brunanburh*.[33] The entry for this year in the hitherto laconic *Chronicle* consists of a specially-composed poem, describing how Athelstan and his brother Edmund 'clove the shield-wall, hewed the linden-wood shields with hammered swords' and made 'a greater slaughter of a host by the edge of the sword [than any] since the Angles and Saxons came hither from the east'.[34] Their kinsman Æthelweard, writing towards the end of the tenth century, claims that the engagement 'is still called the great battle by the common people'.[35] Olaf and Constantine escaped, but Constantine's son was killed, along with five kings, including Owen of Cumbria, and seven of Olaf's jarls.[36]

The *Chronicle* has no more to report of Athelstan but his death, on 27 October 939, at the age of about 45. His successor was his half-brother Edmund, elder son of Edward the Elder's third wife and widow, Eadgifu, then in his eighteenth year.[37] Much of his short reign was occupied in the struggle with the viking rulers of York. Athelstan's death allowed Olaf Gothfrithson to seize York itself, before the end of 939. His desire to re-create the York–Dublin axis destroyed by Athelstan is shown by the coinage minted for him, whose designs included the figure of a raven, recalling the 'raven banner' captured by the English from his great-uncle in 878.[38] In 940, Olaf overran the north-east midlands as far as Northampton. Unable to take the burh he turned to Tamworth, which was taken by storm. In order to campaign so far into Mercian territory Olaf must already have captured the old Danish strongholds to the north-east, and indeed it was at Leicester that he was overtaken by Edmund's army. After an inconclusive siege a truce was arranged in which the north-east midlands, so laboriously won, were conceded to Olaf.[39]

On Olaf's death in 941, York was disputed between his brother Ragnall and his cousin Olaf Sigtryggson, called *Cuaran* ('sandal') by the Irish.[40] In 942, Edmund recaptured the lost lands in the north-east; indeed he went further, for he detached Lincoln and Lindsey from the control of the York kings. The *Chronicle* breaks into alliterative verse at this point, celebrating the 'redemption' of the Danes in these regions, hitherto 'subjected by force under the Norsemen', but it was probably composed only in the 950s, and is unlikely to represent contemporary opinion.[41] Edmund expelled both Olaf Sigtryggson and Ragnall Gothfrithson from York in 944. In 945 he ravaged Cumbria and 'granted it all to Malcolm, king of Scots, on condition that he should be his ally both on sea and on land', which presumably means that he acknowledged Malcolm's overlordship of the area in return for some kind of alliance against the Dublin Vikings.[42]

Edmund was murdered on 26 May 946 at the royal manor of Pucklechurch, Gloucs, and the kingship passed to his full brother, Eadred. Like Edmund, Eadred had to fight to maintain his pre-eminence among the rulers of Britain. In the north he was challenged not only by Olaf Sigtryggson but also by the Norwegian prince, Eric Bloodaxe, and the position was complicated by the existence of rival factions within York itself (one of them led by Archbishop Wulfstan), and by rivalry between the Anglo-Scandinavians of York and the English of Northumbria beyond the Tyne, led by Osulf of Bamburgh.[43]

The chronology of Eadred's reign is particularly confused but by 954 at the latest he had succeeded in expelling both Olaf and Eric, and bringing the viking kingdom of York to an end.[44] Eric was killed in 954, ambushed as he attempted to flee across the Pennines by the Stainmore Pass. It is said that he was betrayed to his enemies by Osulf of Bamburgh, whom Eadred chose as the first ealdorman of all Northumbria, including both Bamburgh and York.[45]

Eadred himself died on 23 November 955, leaving the kingdom to his brother's sons Eadwig and Edgar. Estimates of Eadwig, who can have been no more than 20 when he died in 959, vary wildly. For the earliest biographer of St Dunstan, writing between 995 and 1005, Eadwig was a foolish young man 'endowed with little wisdom in government'. This estimate is coloured by Eadwig's poor relations with Dunstan; Dunstan's biographer gives a vivid picture of how, on the night of his coronation feast, Dunstan discovered the young king in bed not merely with his future wife, but also with the lady who subsequently became his mother-in-law. St Æthelwold, who was on better terms with the king, criticizes Eadwig's folly but attributes it to his youth. Only Eadwig's kinsman and brother-in-law, Æthelweard the Chronicler (the only lay commentator), is wholly favourable; Eadwig was named 'All-fair' because of his great beauty, and 'deserved to be loved'.[46]

Much is still obscure about the politics of Eadwig's reign. The year 956 is marked by the issue of an unprecedented number of royal charters which might suggest that the king had to buy support, but too little is known of the background to be sure.[47] In 957, Eadwig's brother Edgar became king of the Mercians. Dunstan's biographer presents this as a coup; Eadwig, because of his foolishness, 'was wholly deserted by the northern people'. Æthelwold, however, says merely that Eadwig 'dispersed his kingdom and divided its unity', whereas Æthelweard claims that 'he held the kingdom continuously for four years'.[48] It is not impossible that the division resulted from a mutual agreement between the brothers nor even that it signalised Eadwig's acceptance of Edgar as his heir. Though Edgar issued his own charters in 958, usually as 'king of the Mercians', Eadwig retained throughout the title 'king of the English'.[49]

Edgar succeeded to the whole kingdom on Eadwig's death on 1 October 959. His patronage of the Benedictine reformers was amply repaid in the favourable portrait of the king which appears in their writings. As a result, we are well-informed on Edgar's ecclesiastical dispositions, but have few

indications of his secular career. The *Chronicle* has little to record apart
from his consecration, on 11 May 973, at Bath, and his meeting immediately afterwards with the rulers of north Britain at Chester. Here Edgar
was rowed on the Dee, 'from the palace to the monastery of St John the
Baptist', by six (or eight) kings, including Kenneth II, king of Scots, Malcolm of Cumbria and Iago, king of Gwynedd.[50]

The ramifications of Edgar's consecration at Bath have been much discussed.[51] It has been seen as an 'imperial' coronation of Edgar as lord of
Britain, the culmination of previous West Saxon claims to overlordship
of all other British rulers. No doubt it seemed very different to the British
and especially to the Scots. Kenneth II had his own reasons for allying
with Edgar, notably to secure Edgar's acceptance of Scottish control in
Lothian, which had once been part of Bernicia, but it is unlikely that he
saw himself as in any way Edgar's subordinate.[52]

Local Institutions: Shire, Hundred and Vill

The West Saxon kings had not only to conquer but also govern their
enlarged realm. As they overran the other kingdoms south of the Thames
they replaced the former *regiones* and *provinciae* with shires on the West
Saxon pattern, based on the burhs established by Edward and Æthelflæd.
It was a long and gradual process. Most midland shires are named for the
first time in the eleventh century, though some may go back to Edward the
Elder's time.[53] Older Mercian provinces, especially in the north-west,
persisted at least until the middle of the tenth century and perhaps beyond.[54]

The shire-community was made up of the local landowners, who were
also the suitors of the shire court, where they met as neighbours to settle
judicial disputes and criminal accusations, witness sales of land, publish
wills, distribute liability to tax and raise military levies for defence.[55] The
shire courts may have been, in origin, 'public' as opposed to 'royal' assemblies, but by the tenth century their activities were regulated by royal
legislation; Edgar ordered the *scirgemot* to meet twice a year and claimed
the royal rights (*cynescypes gerihta*) held by his father in each shire.[56] From
the viewpoint of the West Saxon kings, the shires and their courts were
predominantly units of royal control.

By the middle of the tenth century, shires were subdivided into hundreds, themselves further divided into tithings.[57] The structure is described
in the *Hundred Ordinance* (known as I Edgar, Edgar's first code). It is
largely concerned with the judicial aspect of the hundred, whose court

met every four weeks, and dates either from the reign of Eadred, or the early years of Edgar.[58] The duties of the hundredmen and tithingmen included the pursuit and capture of thieves, but the hundred also had military functions. Æthelweard the Chronicler, who, as ealdorman of the Western Shires, was in a position to know, describes the shire levies as 'hundreds' (*centurias*), and in the eleventh century the men of Swineshead, Hunts, 'paid geld in the hundred and went with [the men of the hundred] against the enemy'.[59]

The tithing's main purpose was to provide surety; its members jointly ensured each others' performance of their legal duties, and if one failed to answer to any charge, the rest could be fined in the hundred court.[60] The unit of ten implied in the word 'tithing' has been interpreted as a group of ten men, but it could equally well relate to a district of ten hides, equivalent perhaps to the vill.[61] The 'reeves of the vill' who appear in the legislation of Edgar's son, Æthelred, might be the 'tithingmen' in another guise.[62] By the time of the Domesday survey, each vill was represented by the priest, the reeve and six *villani*, and the *Leges Henrici Primi*, a twelfth-century legal tract, allows the priest, the reeve and 'four of the more substantial men of the vill' (*quattuor de melioribus uille*) to deputize for their lord or his steward in the hundred court.[63]

The court of the vill may be mentioned in the third code of Æthelred II, which, after establishing the fines for breach of the peace in the court of the Five Boroughs and the individual shires, adds the fine for breach of the peace in an ale-house.[64] Edgar's Fourth Code provides a rare glimpse of it in action, in its provisions for the buying of cattle. Not only must the transaction be concluded before the proper witnesses, but anyone who sets out to make such a purchase must publicly state his intention beforehand. If, however, someone journeying abroad buys cattle 'unexpectedly', without such prior warning, he shall make a public declaration when he returns home, and the cattle concerned shall be brought to the common pasture of the vill (*tunscipe*). If the purchaser neglects to make such a declaration, the men of the vill (*tunesmen*) are themselves to notify the head of the hundred of this lapse, and the cattle are to be confiscated.[65]

Ealdormen and Ealdordoms

In the ninth century each shire of Wessex had its own ealdorman, but by the time of Athelstan this was no longer practical and the districts

assigned to individual ealdorman grew larger. The names of 29 ealdormen appear in Athelstan's surviving charters, more or less evenly divided
between English and Scandinavian forms. No more than 15 attest any
single charter, and it is probable that, as in the later tenth century, there
were no more than a dozen in office at any given time.

The best-known of Athelstan's ealdormen is his namesake, Athelstan
Half-king, whose ealdordom comprised not only East Anglia, but also the
territories which had been eastern Mercia.[66] Naturally the Half-king
needed subordinates to govern this vast swathe of land and some can be
identified: Thurferth, who was perhaps ealdorman of Northampton;
Scule, whose territory was probably in Suffolk; and Halfdan, possibly in
Hertfordshire.[67]

This pattern, of lesser ealdormen within the districts of greater ones,
was to become general over the next half-century. After 954, the ealdordom of Northumbria covered not only the old Danish kingdom of York
and the north midlands, but also the remnant of English Bernicia; the
lands of St Cuthbert (the *Haliwerfolc*) between the Tees and the Tyne,
and the lands between the Tyne and Tweed ruled by the lords of Bamburgh. Eadulf, who died in 912, was succeeded by his son Ealdred (912–
33), an adherent both of Edward the Elder and of Athelstan.[68] Osulf, who
attests charters of Athelstan, Edmund and Eadred, often as 'high-reeve',
was probably Ealdred's son, and, from 954, the first ealdorman of all
Northumbria.[69] On his death in 963 he was replaced by Oslac (963–75),
whose Scandinavian name suggests that he came from York, or, since his
son Thored held land in Cambridgeshire, the east midlands; but though
Oslac may have had overall authority, the lands to the north of the Tyne
remained in the hands of the lords of Bamburgh.[70]

Such wide-reaching commands are not restricted to the former Danish
lands. By the 960s, western Mercia was a single ealdordom stretching
from Cheshire to Gloucestershire, in the hands of Ælfhere (956–83)
whose authority had originally encompassed only the central Mercian
shires based on Worcester. The men who held such commands became
the elite among the Old English aristocracy; Ælfhere himself came from
one of the collateral branches of the West Saxon family.[71] It is important
to remember, however, that there was no unit of administration higher
than the shire, which, by the late tenth century, was the special responsibility of the shire-reeve (sheriff), a royal official appointed not by the
ealdorman but by the king.[72] The greater ealdormen never became
provincial governors; they remained royal officers overseeing the king's
rights in the territories to which he had appointed them.

The King's Household

The will of King Eadred gives some idea of the establishment of his day.[73] His largest personal bequest was to his mother Eadgifu, whose attestations to the charters of both her sons show her prominence in their counsels.[74] Next comes a bequest to Archbishop Oda of 240 mancuses of gold (£30 of silver pennies); he also received £400 of silver to be disbursed on behalf of the people of Kent, Surrey, Sussex and Berkshire, 'that they may be able to purchase themselves relief from want, and from the heathen army, if they have need'. Similar bequests are made to Ælfsige, bishop of Winchester (951–8), on behalf of the people of Hampshire (£200), Wiltshire (£100) and Dorset (£100), and to Dunstan, on behalf of the people of Somerset and Devon (£200). Oscytel of Dorchester-on-Thames got £400 for the Mercians; the West Saxon bias in royal dispositions is still marked. Each bishop and each ealdorman received 120 gold mancuses (£15 of silver pennies). Next came the household officials, the *discþegn* (seneschal), *hræglþegn* (chamberlain) and *biriele* (butler), each of whom received 80 mancuses of gold (£10 of silver pennies).[75] The chaplains in charge of the king's relics (*haligdom*) each received 50 gold mancuses and £5 of silver pennies (equivalent to £11¼ of silver pennies). The remainder of the king's priests received £5 of pennies each, and each steward (*stigweard*) and lesser official, lay or ecclesiastic, received 30 gold mancuses (£3¾ of silver pennies).

Whether the priests of the king's household furnished scribes to write their lord's charters is a thorny question. On the one hand, opinion maintains that charters were invariably written by the beneficiary in the case of ecclesiastics, or, in the case of lay beneficiaries, by some religious community on their behalf.[76] On the other hand, the formulaic resemblances between charters of the same dates in favour of different beneficiaries has suggested the existence of 'a single agency ... entrusted with the responsibility for drawing up and writing several diplomas issued on the same occasion'; a chancery, in fact.[77] That the formulation of Edmund's surviving charters follows developments already in train under Athelstan also points to the existence of royal scribes trained to produce diplomas.[78] This is not to say that 'royal' scribes had a monopoly on charter-production. Other ecclesiastics wrote royal diplomas, either on their own behalf as beneficiaries, or for other beneficiaries on behalf of the king.[79] Indeed they were a natural source of talent for the production of written documents. Dunstan seems to have had a hand in the production of charters for Eadred and his successors. Eadred's charter of 949 granting

Reculver to Christ Church, Canterbury may have been written by Dunstan himself, and the group of charters known as the 'Dunstan B' diplomas written for various beneficiaries between 951 and 975 were probably produced by a scribe trained by Dunstan at Glastonbury.[80] Another group of diplomas, characterized by the use of alliterative prose, were perhaps produced under the direction of Coenwald, bishop of Worcester (929–57/8).[81]

To draw too fine a distinction between 'royal' scribes attached to the king's household and 'non-royal' scribes in ecclesiastical scriptoria would be anachronistic. Most of the Benedictine houses were founded (or re-founded) and endowed by successive kings, and it is entirely in the spirit of the proprietary church in this period that founders should continue to draw upon the resources, in wealth and manpower, of the ecclesiastical centres which they patronized. The king's valuables, for instance, not only treasure but also title-deeds and charters, were stored for safekeeping in various churches, including Glastonbury.[82]

The Royal Council

The basic problem for all medieval governments was to maintain contact between the itinerant household of the king and the local communities. One solution was to convene regular meetings attended both by court-iers and by local magnates. The great councils of Athelstan, whose impressive size and comprehensive coverage are demonstrated in the witness-lists to his surviving charters, helped to draw the leading men of the more distant provinces into the circle of royal power and patronage.[83] How far these councils were an innovation is unclear, since comparable evidence is lacking for the reign of Edward the Elder, but Athelstan's itinerary was more widely extended than that of his father (or indeed of his immediate successors).[84]

The king's council included the ecclesiastical magnates. Church reform, enthusiastically promoted by most of the West Saxon kings, ensured that many were dedicated to the ideals of the Benedictine reform movement. Some of the hostility shown towards Eadwig was probably aroused by his promotion of his own friends and allies (notably Ælfhere of Mercia) at the expense of this 'old guard', represented by St Dunstan.[85] Edgar, in contrast, favoured the reformers; it was he who promoted Dunstan to the arcbishopric of Canterbury. The dominant influence at Edgar's court was Æthelwold, abbot of Abingdon, whom he promoted to the bishopric of Winchester in 963.[86] Edgar had been educated by Æthelwold at Abingdon, and the bishop was also a friend of Edgar's queen, Ælfthryth, whom he married in 964 or 965.

Law and Legislation

The legislative tradition revived by Alfred was continued by his successors. Edward the Elder's Exeter code refers back to legislation which had not been properly enforced, and Athelstan issued at least three codes.[87] There are three from the short reign of Edmund and, though no code in Eadred's name is known, he may have been responsible for the *Hundred Ordinance*. There are three codes from Edgar's time, four if the *Hundred Ordinance* (I Edgar) is rightly attributed to him.[88]

None of Athelstan's codes are dated, but II Athelstan (the second code of Athelstan) issued at Grately (Hants) is earlier than V Athelstan promulgated at Exeter, for the Exeter code was issued because the decrees of Grately had not been properly enforced; the fragmentary Thunderfield code is later than either.[89] There are also two injunctions issued by the king to his reeves, one (I Athelstan) concerning the payment of tithe and other ecclesiastical dues, and the other (the *Ordinance on Charities*) arranging for the dispensing of alms.[90] A third injunction is appended to VI Athelstan (for which see below) in which the king commands each of 'his bishops and his ealdormen and all his reeves' to observe his legal enactments, and extract pledges to the same effect from 'those under his jurisdiction'.[91]

Enforcement of the king's laws also required the goodwill of the local community. The Grately Code was proclaimed at an assembly of Kentish magnates at Faversham, whose proceedings are recorded in III Athelstan, a report to the king from the leading men of Kent, described as 'the bishops . . . and all the thegns, nobles (*comites*) and free men (*villani*)'.[92] It acknowledges receipt of a written copy (*scriptum*) of the Grately enactments, and the guidance of the king's councillors (*sapientes*) whom he had sent to expound them, and sets out the decrees agreed by the Kentish assembly to implement the king's commands.

Such texts provide some insight into the way in which local communities actually worked. The code known as IV Athelstan is similar to the Kentish report, but is not addressed to the king; it has been described as 'a "private" record of royal decrees, drawn up by another party for special reasons and purposes' which are now unclear.[93] It mentions the Grately Code, but is mainly concerned with the ordinances of V Athelstan, which were 'established at Exeter . . . and again at Faversham [Kent], and on a third occasion at Thunderfield [Surrey]'. The legislation of Thunderfield is mentioned again, along with the Grately and Exeter codes, in VI Athelstan, a record of the arrangements made to implement the king's decrees by 'the bishops and reeves of London . . . both nobles and commoners (*ge eorlisce ge ceorlisce*)'.[94] Another example of local action is the *Ordinance concerning the Dunsæte*, which regulates the relations between communities living on the borders between England and Wales, describing itself as an agreement between the 'English witan (*Angelcynnes witan*) and the counsellors of the Welsh people'.[95]

Much of Edmund's legislation concerns the preservation of order. His first code, in which the hand of Oda, archbishop of Canterbury, has been detected, was promulgated at London, and relates to the Church. II Edmund was issued to promote 'peace and concord'; the king and his counsellors are said to be 'greatly distressed by the manifold illegal deeds of violence which are in our midst'.[96] What follows is an attempt to regulate and control the blood feud. It prohibits vengeance except against the slayer himself, and any assault, even upon him, which violates the sanctuary of a church or a royal manor-house (*burh*). The process of mediation between the kindreds of the slayer and the slain is to be overseen by the local authorities (*witan*), to ensure the payment of wergeld (the blood-price) and the avoidance of the feud. II Edmund also contains the earliest recorded reference to *hamsocn*, the crime of attacking a man in his own house.[97] It is equated with *mundbryce*, breach of the king's protection, and its judgement is reserved to the king. The penalty is loss of all the offender's property 'and it shall be for the king to decide whether his life shall be preserved'.

III Edmund, issued at Colyton, Devon perhaps in 945, is also concerned with public disturbance, notably theft and cattle-rustling. Its first clause orders the administration of a general oath of fidelity to the king. The terms of the oath, to be sworn on appropriate relics, are recited; 'to be faithful to King Edmund, even as it behooves a man to be faithful to his lord, favouring what he favours and discountenancing what he discountenances'.[98] The wording is very close to the exemplar of the hold-oath sworn by men to their lords, and all lords are required to take responsibility for their commended followers, whether retained in their household, or holding lands attached to their estates.[99] Specifically they are not to take into their service any fugitives from the law. The local community is also called into service; all, both nobles and commoners, are commanded to unite and seize thieves, whether dead or alive, and to cooperate in the tracking of stolen cattle, and any who refuse aid or who hinder the process of law are to be fined. In Edmund's legislation the functions of the four pillars of medieval society, kingship, lordship, community and family, are clearly evident; but in view of its tenor it is ironic that the king himself was killed in the course of a brawl between one of his household and a convicted outlaw.[100]

The next surviving piece of royal legislation is the *Hundred Ordinance*, which belongs either to the time of Eadred or to that of Edgar; it is at all events earlier than III Edgar, which refers to it. II and III Edgar probably represent a single act of legislation, promulgated at Andover (Hants). II Edgar covers ecclesiastical matters, notably the payment of various church dues. It is particularly noteworthy for its regulation of the relationship between the ancient minsters and the new 'estate-churches', built by secular magnates, which eventually formed the basis for the later medieval parish-structure.[101] III Edgar represents the secular aspect of the code, being mainly concerned with access to justice, the prevention of unjust judgements (a perennial theme) and the establishment of surety (*borh*); every man is to have a surety to take responsibility for his performance of his legal obligations.

IV Edgar, issued at *Wihtbordestan* (unidentified), probably dates from the 970s, the closing years (as it happened) of Edgar's reign. It is of particular interest for its recognition of the legal customs of the king's Danish subjects. The subject of the density of Scandinavian settlement in England is a thorny one and not likely soon to be resolved, but most would agree that the north and east saw a considerable influx of Danish and other Scandinavian peoples in the late ninth and early tenth centuries. With the West Saxon conquest, some departed.[102] But many remained; in 918, for instance, Edward the Elder had the burh at Nottingham manned 'both with Englishmen and Danes'.[103] Danish landholders who submitted to English lordship were allowed to retain their estates, but those who did not, or did so too late, were dispossessed. The account of a lawsuit prosecuted in the 970s describes how, after the death of King Edgar in 975, the sons of one Boga of Hemmingford claimed land at Bluntisham in Huntingdonshire on the grounds that it had belonged to their uncle Tope whose grandmother had submitted to King Edward at Cambridge. The jurors, however, said that Edward had taken Huntingdon before Cambridge, and a submission at Cambridge would therefore have come too late to save the lands of Tope's grandmother.[104]

The assimilation of the Danish population, especially in York and the north, must have been one of the major priorities in the 950s and 960s. It was probably in this period that the confederacy of the Five Boroughs (Lincoln, Stamford, Nottingham, Derby and Leicester) was established, as a regional system of defence for the southern provinces of York.[105] Edgar's Fourth Code belongs to the same process. It allows to the Danes 'such good laws as they best decide on', a concession granted 'because of your loyalty, which you have always shown me'.[106] The identity of the Danes in question is shown later in the code, when the king commands that 'Earl Oslac and all the host (here) dwelling in his aldormanry are to give their support that this may be enforced'.[107] The 'Danes' whose customs were to be recognized were the inhabitants of the former kingdom of York, now incorporated in the ealdordom of Northumbria, over which Oslac presided; the area which came to be called the Danelaw.[108] But the recognition was limited; IV Edgar asserts the king's rights to legislate 'for all the nation, whether Englishmen, Danes or Britons, in every province of my dominion'.[109] Edgar's arrangements were continued by his son and successor, Æthelred II, whose third code (III Æthelred, issued at Wantage in the 990s), legislates specifically for the Five Boroughs; but by the end of Æthelred's reign, the area, including York, was shired on the West Saxon pattern.[110]

The last clause of III Edgar points in the same direction. It commands that 'one coinage shall be current throughout all the king's realm and no-one shall refuse it'. By Edgar's time, the intrinsic value of the English penny was nearly half what it had been in the time of Alfred, one hundred years earlier.[111] Though the intervening kings had made attempts at reorganization, there had been no general re-coinage, and pennies of Alfred's time would still have been legal currency, had any remained. In the last years of his reign, Edgar instituted a reform which not only restored standards of fineness and weight, but also imposed a uniform design. Henceforth the coinage regularly bore not only the name of the king and his title (rex Anglorum) but also the name of the mint where it was struck and the moneyer who struck it. Edgar's 'Reform' issue continued in circulation until the beginning of Æthelred II's reign, when a re-coinage was ordered. Thereafter five successive re-coinages were undertaken during Æthelred's reign, and another 45 between 1016 and 1135. The purpose may have been fiscal, for a charge was probably levied for re-coining old money, and the moneyers had to pay for the new dies. The ability of the English kings to control the quality of their coinage is one of the most striking illustrations of the efficiency of their government.

8

RULE AND CONFLICT, 978–1066

He is reported to have declared to his nobles at length that each of his
successors would be able to boast that he was king of the English.
(John of Worcester)[1]

King Edgar's death in 975 at the age of 32 was perhaps unexpected. He
left two sons, Edward aged about sixteen by Æthelflæd *eneda* ('the white'),
and Æthelred son of Queen Ælfthryth who was eight or nine. Support for
Æthelred's succession was orchestrated by his mother, Æthelwold of
Winchester and Ælfhere of Mercia, while the archbishops, Dunstan and
Oswald, and Æthelwine of East Anglia declared for Edward. The participation of the two most powerful laymen south of the Trent produced a
dangerous confrontation, but before the end of the year Edward had
gained general acceptance. On 18 March 978, however, he was murdered at Corfe (Dorset) by adherents of his half-brother. The corpse was
hastily buried at Wareham, and only after its discovery and proper inter-
ment at Shaftesbury Abbey was Æthelred consecrated king.[2]

It was in Æthelred's time that the viking raiders returned to England
and the reign ended in the conquest of the country by the Danes. The
raids of the 980s were perhaps largely launched from elsewhere in the
British Isles. In 1000, Æthelred led a joint land and sea expedition
against Cumbria and the Isle of Man, perhaps as a punitive measure;
Man's ruler, Gothfrith Haraldson (d. 989) was raiding North Wales in
the 970s and 980s, and perhaps England as well.[3] Other raiders may have
come from further afield using the duchy of Normandy as a safe haven.
In 990 the papal envoy Leo, bishop of Trevi, negotiated a truce between
Æthelred and Duke Richard I, solemnized at Rouen on 1 March 991.[4]

97

The same desire to neutralize Norman support for their Scandinavian cousins may have prompted the marriage of Æthelred with Duke Richard's daughter, Emma, in 1002. She was his second wife; the first, Ælfgifu, is a shadowy figure, daughter of Thored, earl of Northumbria.[5]

The character of the viking attacks changed in the 990s. The raid of 991, which concentrated on Essex and East Anglia, has received much attention since it culminated in the battle of Maldon, Essex, in which Byrhtnoth, ealdorman of Essex, was killed. The defeat was commemorated in a celebrated poem, possibly composed at Ely, where Byrhtnoth was buried.[6] One of the viking leaders was perhaps Olaf Tryggvasson, later king of Norway, and another Swein Forkbeard, already king of Denmark; fleets led by both these men and others from the Scandinavian countries were operating in England between 991 and 1006.[7] Their objective was to acquire not land but plunder. The late tenth and early eleventh centuries saw the forging of the kingdoms of Denmark, Norway and Sweden, and the aspiring rulers required cash and treasure for the furtherance of their ambitions. Indeed it was after his agreement with Æthelred II in 994, whereby he received £22000 in gold and silver, that Olaf Tryggvasson made his successful bid for the kingdom of Norway.[8] Between 1003 and 1006 Swein Forkbeard led annual expeditions to England, apparently with the aim of gathering booty and exacting tribute. In 1006, for instance, his armies were harbouring on the Isle of Wight:

> and then towards Christmas they betook themselves to the entertainment waiting them, out through Hampshire into Berkshire, to Reading; and always they observed their ancient custom, lighting their beacons as they went. They then turned to Wallingford and burnt it all, and were one night at Cholsey, and then turned along Ashdown to Cuckhamsley Barrow, and waited there for what had been proudly threatened, for it had often been said that if they went to Cuckhamsley, they would never get to the sea. They then went home another way... There the people of Winchester could see that army, proud and undaunted, when they went past their gate to the sea, and fetched themselves food and treasures from more than 50 miles from the sea.[9]

Another beneficiary of English tributes was the prosperous Swede, Ulv of Borresta (Uppland), who 'took three gelds in England: first Toste paid; then Thorkell paid; then Cnut paid'.[10] Toste cannot be identified, but Thorkell is Thorkell *inn Havi* (the Tall), leader of 'the immense raiding-army which we called Thorkell's army', which devastated much of southern England between 1009 and 1012.[11] With the appearance of this host, the fabric of the English state began to crack.[12] Thorkell's force established its base in north Kent, whence, over the next three years, it raided Wessex, East Anglia and eastern Mercia. In September 1011, Canterbury was besieged and betrayed and a number of high-ranking captives including Archbishop Ælfheah held to ransom. A great tribute was raised, and £48 000 was paid to the army just after Easter (13 April) 1012. The archbishop, however, refused to allow a personal ransom to be paid for him, and on 19 April he was murdered by the viking army. Thorkell himself (who was probably a nominal Christian) was not involved in the killing; indeed it was perhaps as a result of it that he entered Æthelred's service, with 45 ships, while the remainder of his force 'dispersed as widely as it had been collected'.[13]

The *Chronicle* records that Thorkell's men were paid and provisioned in 1013, but gives no details of the money involved. It was in August of the same year that Swein Forkbeard reappeared to establish a base for himself at Gainsborough, Lincs, and before its end the English magnates accepted him as 'full king'. It was probably at this time that Swein's son Cnut married the English heiress Ælfgifu of Northampton, daughter of Ealdorman Ælfhelm of Northumbria. Æthelred fled (on Thorkell's ships) to Normandy, returning only after Swein's death, on 3 February 1014.[14] Later in the same year the royal fleet at Greenwich was paid £21 000; they may have been Thorkell's ships, but during his sojourn in Normandy Æthelred seems also to have engaged the services of the Norwegian Viking, Olaf Haraldsson the Stout (St Olaf).[15] The payments made to these stipendiary fleets in 1012 and 1014 were the origin of the heregeld, levied until (at least) 1051.[16]

On Swein's death, the Danish army at Gainsborough chose Cnut his son as king, presumably of England, since his elder brother Harald succeeded in Denmark.[17] Æthelred appears for the last time in personal command of his forces when, 'with his full force' (*ful fyrd*), he drove Cnut from Gainsborough.[18] But the cracks in the fabric had not been repaired. It was the thegns of the north who had first submitted to Swein in 1013, without a blow struck; it was only after crossing Watling Street that Swein's armies began to ravage the countryside.[19] In 1015 it seems that Æthelred decided to punish the recalcitrant northerners. At an assembly in Oxford, Sigeferth and Morcar, 'the chief thegns belonging to the Seven Boroughs', were killed by Æthelred's chief advisor Eadric Streona, ealdorman of Mercia; all their property was seized and Sigeferth's widow was imprisoned at Malmesbury. But Edmund ætheling, the king's eldest surviving son, 'went and took the woman against the king's will and married her'; he then went north to appropriate the estates of Sigeferth and Morcar, and 'the people all submitted to him'.[20]

Edmund's defiance of his father is perhaps connected with the fact that it was his half-brother Edward, Emma's son, who acted as his father's envoy to the English magnates in 1014; Edward, as the eldest son of a crowned queen, might be considered more 'throne-worthy' than an elder half-brother whose mother had enjoyed no such eminence.[21] Edmund was clearly staking out his claims. Uhtred of Bamburgh was already his brother-in-law, and his bride brought him the allegiance of the Danelaw.[22] Moreover her sister-in-law Ealdgyth, widow of the murdered Morcar, was the cousin of Ælfgifu of Northampton who had married Cnut, probably in 1013. Like Edmund's wife, Ælfgifu had reasons for enmity towards Æthelred II and Eadric of Mercia, for it was Eadric, with the king's connivance, who had killed her father Ælfhelm in 1006.[23]

The hostility between Edmund and Eadric contributed to the collapse of the English when Cnut returned to the attack in 1015. Æthelred was seriously ill, and it was left to Edmund to defend the kingdom. But cooperation between him and Eadric Streona proved impossible. In 1015, for instance, as Æthelred lay sick at Cosham, Eadric collected an army in the south and Edmund in the north, but 'when they united, the ealdorman wished to betray the ætheling, and on that account they separated without fighting, and retreated from their enemies'.[24] Having made enemies of both Edmund and Cnut's wife, Ælfgifu of Northampton, Eadric was in an invidious position. His best bet was to play the parties off against each other, which he did in 1015–6, supporting now one, now the other, in an attempt to balance out his foes. But this did not make for a united front against the Danes.

After Æthelred's death, on 23 April 1016, Edmund succeeded to the kingship, and in the course of the next six months called out the English fyrd five times, though on the first occasion, when he defeated Cnut at Penselwood, near Gillingham (Dorset), he had only 'the army which he had been able to collect in so short a time'.[25] The battle at Sherston (Wilts) fought in late June was inconclusive, but Edmund was victorious again at London and Brentford. At the battle of Otford (Kent) in the autumn of 1016 he put the Danes to flight and pursued them on horseback towards their encampment on the Isle of Sheppey. In the final battle, however, fought on 18 October at *Assandune* (Essex, but unidentified), Cnut was victorious. Only for this battle is the English casualty list provided, and it bears out the chronicler's description of a host drawn from 'all the

English nation' (*ealle Engla þeode*): Eadnoth, bishop of Dorchester-on Thames; Wulfsige, abbot of Ramsey; Ælfric, ealdorman of central Wessex; Godwine, ealdorman of Lindsey; Ulfcytel of East Anglia; and Æthelweard, son of Æthelwine, formerly ealdorman of East Anglia. It was Eadric Streona with the men of the Magonsæte who began the English rout.[26]

On the death of Edmund Ironside on 30 November 1016, the English magnates, lay and ecclesiastical, swore to accept Cnut as king and repudiated the remaining English æthelings.[27] Cnut was probably crowned early in 1017 by Lyfing, archbishop of Canterbury.[28] In the following summer he exiled Edmund's full brother, Eadwig, and married Æthelred's widow, Emma, presumably to neutralize any claims made by her sons by Æthelred, who were in exile with her brother in Normandy.[29] He did not, however, repudiate his English wife, Ælfgifu of Northampton, whose family connections were also valuable.[30]

By the end of the year Cnut felt secure enough to have Eadric Streona killed, with other English magnates whom he distrusted, at the Christmas court held at London.[31] The tribute of 1018 was the largest on record, £72000, plus £10500 from London; a rate of about £1 a hide throughout all England on the Domesday figures.[32] The sum involved has been regarded with scepticism, but as a one-off payment it is perhaps not incredible.[33] There are signs that it was regarded as particularly severe. Eadric, abbot of St Peter's, Gloucester (1022–58) had to loan two of the church's manors in return for a payment of £15 to redeem the rest of its lands from 'the great heregeld levied throughout England'; this may be a reference to arrears from the 1018 levy, perhaps also reflected in the reduced assessment obtained from Cnut by the community of St Milburg's at Much Wenlock, Shrops.[34] In 1018, Cnut paid off the bulk of his fleet, retaining 40 ships, and 'the Danes and the English came to an agreement at Oxford', in which it seems that Cnut agreed to uphold the laws of his English predecessors.[35]

In 1019, on the death of his brother Harald, Cnut became king of Denmark as well as England, and by the mid-1020s he had conquered Norway which was entrusted to Ælfgifu of Northampton as regent for their eldest son Swein. It was perhaps the need to delegate power in order to control so large a complex of kingdoms that led to the rise of the great earls in England, notably Godwine in Wessex and Leofric in Mercia.[36] But Cnut's 'northern Empire' did not outlast him. Towards the end of his reign the Norwegians drove out their Danish rulers and, flushed with success, invaded Denmark. This considerably complicated the already vexed question of who was to succeed to the kingship after Cnut. He died at Shaftesbury in November 1035, leaving sons by both his wives. Harthacnut, son of Queen Emma, was in Denmark dealing with the Norwegian invasion, but his rights in England were upheld by Emma supported by the royal housecarls and Godwine, earl of Wessex. Harthacnut's rival Harold, son of Ælfgifu of Northampton, had the backing of Leofric, earl of Mercia, the royal fleet based at London, and the thegns of the west and north.[37]

At a meeting held in Oxford, a compromise recognized Harold as regent for himself and his half-brother; according to John of Worcester, 'the kingdom of England was divided by lot', Harold holding Mercia and the north and Harthacnut the south.[38] This division is reflected in the coinage of the period. For a short time the coins of Cnut's last issue continued to circulate, before being replaced by the 'Jewel Cross' issue. This was struck in two forms; in the south the coins bore the name of Harthacnut and showed the bust of the king facing right, while the northern mints struck in the name of Harold and showed the king's bust facing left. The evidence suggests 'that there was unity in the issue from the start and that it was the result of an agreement between the two parties', presumably at the Oxford meeting in 1035. But Harthacnut's coinage did not last; the southern mints soon began to strike in the name of Harold, and thereafter the 'Jewel Cross' was replaced by the 'Fleur-de-lys' issue struck in Harold's name alone.[39]

The eclipse of Harthacnut and the rise of Harold brought about a change of allegiance on Earl Godwine's part. In 1036, Emma's exiled sons by her first husband, Æthelred II, advanced their own claims to the throne. Only the Norman writers mention Edward's unsuccessful expedition, launched from Normandy, but that of Alfred his brother is widely reported.[40] He landed in Kent and was intercepted by Godwine; he then fell into the hands of Harold I who had him taken to Ely and blinded, after which he either died of his injuries or was killed. The sources are divided between those which implicate Godwine in the murder of the ætheling (the 'C' version of the *Chronicle*, William of Jumièges and John of Worcester) and those which throw the whole responsibility on Harold I (the *Encomium* of Emma, the *Vita Edwardi*, and the 'D' *Chronicle*). Godwine's involvement in the death of 'the blameless ætheling' (as he is called in the 'C' *Chronicle*) was to cast a shadow over his future career.[41]

Godwine's rapprochement with Harold I had the result that, in 1037, Harthacnut 'was deserted because he was too long in Denmark', and Emma fled to Bruges. There was still some resistance to Harold. Archbishop

Æthelnoth is said to have refused to crown him, which may account for the king's seizure of Sandwich from Christ Church; it is significant that he gave the third penny (the earl's share) of the tolls to St Augustine's, a house connected with Earl Godwine.[42]

Only when Harold died, on 17 March 1040, was Harthacnut accepted as king; his first act was to have his half-brother's body dug up from its grave at Westminster and thrown into the Thames marshes. Harthacnut also 'burnt with great anger' against Earl Godwine and Lyfing, bishop of Worcester, whom Ælfric, archbishop of York, had accused of responsibility for Alfred's death. Lyfing was temporarily removed from the see of Worcester, given him by Harold I in 1038; Godwine had to buy the king's goodwill with a ship manned by 80 fully-armed warriors, and was required to swear publicly he had not advised nor desired the blinding of Alfred 'but that his lord King Harold had ordered him to do what he did'.[43] Yet, despite the king's disfavour Godwine was already too powerful and too well-entrenched to be removed.

The confrontation between the supporters of Harthacnut and Harold I in the years between 1035 and 1037 has much in common with that between the backers of Edward the Martyr and Æthelred II in the aftermath of Edgar's death. In neither case, however, did the stand-off end in violence, even though the *Chronicle*'s reference to the royal fleet and housecarls suggest that Leofric and Godwine, like Ælfhere and Æthelwine before them, had armed followings.[44] But in the uncertain politics of the decade between 1035 and 1042, the power of the great earls, particularly Godwine and Leofric, became more and more entrenched, and the potential rivalry between them more dangerous.

Harthacnut's attitude to taxation seems to have lost him the affection of his subjects, who by 1041 were regretting the welcome they had given him the previous year.[45] When his half-brother Edward arrived in the summer of the year 'he was sworn in as king'; and when Harthacnut died on 8 June 1042, 'all the people then received Edward as king, as was his natural right' (*swa him gecynde wæs*).[46] The early years of his reign saw the further aggrandizement of Earl Godwine and his family. In 1043, Edward gave an earldom based on Herefordshire to Godwine's eldest son, Swein.[47] On 23 January 1045 he married Godwine's eldest daughter, Edith, and soon afterwards promoted Harold, Godwine's second son, to the earldom of East Anglia, and Godwine's nephew, Beorn Estrithson, to the earldom of the east midlands.[48]

Godwine was unable, however, to gain the king's support for Beorn's brother Swein, Cnut's sister-son, in his struggle for the Danish kingdom with Magnus of Norway, son of Olaf Haraldsson. In 1042 Magnus arranged the murder of one of his chief Danish rivals, Harald, son (probably) of Thorkell the Tall, and launched a full-scale onslaught on Swein Estrithson.[49] Edward's attitude seems to have been to let the rivals fight it out. In 1044 he led a fleet of 35 ships to Sandwich, but the intention seems purely defensive, and in the same year Gunnhild, Cnut's niece and widow of the murdered Harald, was banished to Bruges, a clear attempt to placate Magnus.[50] In 1047 Godwine supported his nephew's plea for 50 English ships, but, as the 'D' *Chronicle* puts it, 'it seemed a foolish plan to everybody and it was hindered because Magnus had a great naval force'. Magnus drove Swein from Denmark, and only his death later in the year allowed Swein to return.

Another setback to Godwine's ambitions was the disgrace of his son Swein, though the young earl seems to have been the agent of his own ruin. In the spring of 1046 he abducted Eadgifu, abbess of Leominster; this may have been an act of unbridled passion, but marriage with her would have given Swein control of Leominster's vast estate in northern Herefordshire.[51] When the king refused his permission for the marriage, Swein fled to Flanders and thence, in 1048, to Denmark. Swein Estrithson and Magnus's successor in Norway, King Harald Hardrada, were fishing for an English alliance at this time, and Swein Godwineson apparently became embroiled in the political stew-pot; at all events, 'he ruined himself with the Danes', and in 1049 he was back in England.

In the interim, his lands and earldom had been apportioned between his brother Harold and his cousin, Beorn, who were none too pleased to see him.[52] Swein abducted and murdered Beorn, and was accordingly outlawed.[53] Beorn's death left the east-midland earldom vacant, but, though Godwine had another son of age to succeed, the king gave the appointment to his own nephew, Ralph.[54] He did, however, pardon and restore Swein in the summer of 1050, apparently through the intercession of Ealdred, bishop of Worcester.[55]

It is unlikely that Edward had supported Godwine willingly, and the years 1051 and 1052 saw the king trying, unsuccessfully, to rid himself of his greatest subject.[56] Thereafter it is hard to distinguish the actions and policies of Edward himself from those of Godwine's son Harold, who succeeded to the earldom of Wessex on his father's death in 1053. Indeed, in the 'D' version of the *Chronicle* the last decade of the old English monarchy appears mysterious and even sinister. Of Edward ætheling's return in 1054, it observes that 'we do not know for what reason it was brought about that he was not allowed to see the face of his kinsman King Edward';

and Earl Ælfgar's banishment and reinstatement in 1058 is dismissed with the exclamation that 'it is tedious to relate fully how things went'.[57] The 'C' text has nothing to record for the years 1057–64, and for the years 1062 and 1064, neither have 'D' and 'E'. The reticence of the sources makes the politics of Edward's later years particularly obscure.

It was a period which saw further advances in the fortunes of Godwine's sons. The death in 1054 of the elder son of Earl Siward of Northumbria, followed by his own in 1055, brought the earldom into the hands of Harold's next eldest brother, Tostig. When Earl Leofric died in 1057, Mercia went to his son Ælfgar, but Gyrth, Tostig's brother, received Ælfgar's previous earldom of East Anglia.[58] Earl Ralph also died in 1057, leaving a son who was a minor, and the east-midlands earldom was probably divided, the northern shires going to Tostig and the southern ones to his youngest brother Leofwine.[59]

Not everyone approved of the king's favour to the sons of Godwine. At the meeting in London where Tostig was appointed earl of Northumbria, Ælfgar, earl of East Anglia, was exiled. The various versions of the *Chronicle* provide a fruitful disagreement on the circumstances; 'C' says he was innocent of any fault, 'D' that he committed 'hardly any' crime, and 'E' that he admitted to 'being a traitor to the king and to all the people ... though the words escaped him against his will'.[60] Ælfgar's intemperance might stem from his own expectations in Northumbria, for his wife Ælfgifu was arguably the daughter of Ealdgyth, niece of a previous ealdorman of the region, and Morcar, thegn of the 'Seven Boroughs'.[61] Ælfgar fled to Ireland where he raised a fleet of 18 ships to add to his own. He then allied with Gruffudd ap Llewelyn, king of Gwynedd and (effectively) the rest of Wales into the bargain; either at this point or a little later, Gruffudd married Ælfgar's daughter Ealdgyth.[62] By the end of the year he had been reinstated, and in 1057 he succeeded his father Leofric as earl of Mercia. He was exiled again in 1058 and again reinstated with Gruffudd's help, but no further information is available.

It was Ralph, earl of Hereford since 1051, on whom the defence of the west fell in 1055. He met Gruffudd and Ælfgar near Hereford, but 'before any spear was thrown, the English army fled, because they were on horseback, and many were killed there – about four or five hundred men – and they killed none in return'.[63] It was Earl Harold and the levies of Wessex who saved the day, though Hereford was sacked and its minster-church burnt. Harold rebuilt the fortifications and arranged the peace-terms, which included the restitution of Ælfgar to his East Anglian earldom.

Ralph's incompetence probably cost him his command, though it was not until his death in 1057 that Harold received the earldom of Herefordshire.[64] It was in the wars against Gruffudd ap Llewelyn that Harold made his name as a military commander. Ælfgar's stormy career probably ended in 1062, though the date of his death is nowhere recorded.[65] In 1063 a joint land and sea expedition was launched against Gwynedd, Harold leading the fleet and Earl Tostig the land-army.[66] In the course of the fighting, King Gruffudd was killed by his own men and his half-brothers allied with Harold. It was perhaps at this time that Harold married Gruffudd's widow Ealdgyth, daughter of Earl Ælfgar, though without repudiating his handfast wife, Edith Swanneck; it was clearly a political alliance, designed to reconcile Harold with Edwin who had succeeded his father as earl of Mercia.[67]

Harold was clearly an able and ambitious man. The Bayeux Tapestry describes him as *dux Anglorum*, recalling the title *dux Francorum* born by Hugh the Great, count of Paris, whose son, Hugh Capet, supplanted the last of the Carolingian kings of France in 987.[68] Precisely when Harold began to think of himself as a possible successor to Edward we cannot know. The marriage of Edward and Edith was clearly intended to produce heirs; when Edward repudiated her in 1051, this may have been as much because of her childlessness as her relationship to Godwine. It was not impossible that Edward, now in his late forties, should have children by another wife, but in the interim it was natural for him to turn to his maternal kinsman, William of Normandy.[69] In 1054, however, Ealdred, bishop of Worcester, was sent to Germany to search for the king's nephew Edward, son of Edmund Ironside, who had been carried as a child to Hungary, to save him from Cnut's assassins.[70] The choice of Ealdred, an adherent of Harold, as envoy may be significant, though he was also one of the king's ablest negotiators. Harold himself, however, was at St Omer in November 1056, perhaps to meet the ætheling on his journey to England.[71] In the event Edward ætheling died in 1057 almost as soon as he set foot in the country, leaving a son, Edgar, who was probably no more than fourteen in 1066.[72] Meanwhile Edward had sent Harold to Normandy in 1064 to re-open negotiations with Duke William.[73] Having changed his mind at least once and probably twice, he changed it again on his deathbed and appointed Harold as his heir.[74] Harold was consecrated on 6 January 1066, the day of Edward's funeral, the first king to be crowned in Westminster Abbey; 'and he met little quiet in it as long as he ruled the realm'.[75]

9

THE ILL-COUNSELLED KING

When a child is king and a ceorl bishop and a slave ealdorman, it's bad news for the people.[1]

Æthelred II (978–1016) has been saddled with the worst reputation of all the Old English kings. His pejorative nickname, *unræd* ('ill-counselled') is recorded only from the thirteenth century, but his reign has been seen as a time of disaster, exacerbated by bad advice, vacillation, treachery and cowardice. His most recent biographer has done much to salvage his good name, but still with the proviso that he was 'a poor judge of men'.[2]

Æthelred's ill-fame springs, paradoxically, from the comparative richness of the evidence for his reign. All versions of the *Chronicle* are contemporary, and this, coupled with plentiful charters, laws and memoranda provides the basis for a reasonably full survey of Æthelred's time.[3] Unfortunately (from the king's standpoint), much of the surviving material is critical, if not of Æthelred personally at least of his advisors and ministers. Internal evidence shows that the writer of the base text of the *Chronicle*, from which the versions in 'C', 'D' and 'E' derive, came from the eastern shires, probably from London. He has little opinion of the Mercian and West Saxon councillors, displaying particular animus against Ælfric of Hampshire and Eadric of Mercia. He was, moreover, writing after the king's death and the Danish Conquest, and his knowledge of the outcome has adversely coloured his presentation of Æthelred's earlier years.[4]

The king's poor reputation obscures the fact that in his time the structure of Old English local administration begins to be clearly visible. The links between the localities and the itinerant court of the king also emerge, and, though it would be anachronistic in this period (and for some time to come) to speak of 'central' government, the sources throw some light on the machinery which enabled the king's officials to raise taxes and issue orders, including written orders. There is much more to the reign of Æthelred II than a catalogue of military defeats and disasters.

Local Organization: Ealdormen and Reeves

Æthelred was no more than 12 when he began to reign, and his early years were dominated by the magnates who had advised his father. This period of tutelage, coupled with memories of the disturbances on his father's death, may have made him uneasy about the power wielded by such people, for he seems to have taken advantage of the deaths of successive ealdormen to reduce the influence of their families.[5] Oslac of Northumbria had already been exiled, in 975, for unspecified reasons of which all versions of the *Chronicle* seem to disapprove.[6] His successor, Thored, may have been his son; he was also the young king's father-in-law, but this did not prevent him being removed in 992, and his successor Ælfhelm came from a north Mercian family unrelated to that of Thored.[7] Ælfhere of Mercia, who died in 983, was succeeded by his brother-in-law, Ælfric *cild*, but he was banished in 985 and not replaced. Nor did the king appoint a successor to Æthelwine, ealdorman of East Anglia, who died in 992. From 1004 to 1016, some of the ealdorman's functions in the region were carried out by Ulfcytel *snilling* (the bold), styled 'Ulfcytel of East Anglia' (*of East Englan*) in the annal recording his death in 1016 at the battle of *Assandune*. Yet he is never given the title of ealdorman (*dux*); he attests the king's charters simply as a thegn (*minister*).[8]

The ealdormen of the 990s seem to have more restricted spheres of authority than those of their predecessors. A charter of 997 is attested by Æthelweard the Chronicler, as 'ealdorman of the western shires' (western Wessex), Ælfric, 'ealdorman of the provinces of Winchester' (central Wessex), Leofsige 'of the East Saxons', Leofwine 'of the Hwiccian provinces' (central Mercia) and Ælfhelm 'of the Northumbrian provinces'.[9] Only in 1007 was the ealdordom of western Mercia revived, for the king's favourite, Eadric Streona. Eadric's rise coincided with the fall of Ælfhelm, who was murdered in 1006; indeed John of Worcester names Eadric as the instigator of this crime, committed with the king's connivance, and some colour is given to the allegation by the fact that Æthelred celebrated the Christmas feast of 1006 in Shropshire, a region with which Eadric was associated and which was well outside the normal royal itinerary.[10] Northumbria itself was entrusted to Uhtred of Bamburgh. Æthelred seems to have tried to bind these two powerful lords to himself by marrying them to his daughters, Eadric to Eadgyth and Uhtred to Ælfgifu.[11]

It is from Æthelred's reign that lesser royal officials begin to figure prominently in the surviving sources. The reeves in charge of the king's estates had always had wider fiscal and administrative duties over their localities. Edward the Elder's first code, a directive addressed to his reeves, concerns their judicial responsibilities, and his second code includes an injunction to each reeve to hold a meeting every four weeks to settle legal disputes.[12] The term reeve (*gerefa*) is in itself 'a pretty general sort of word, used for administrative agents at very different levels of importance'.[13] By the second half of the tenth century some discrimination between the various kinds of reeve becomes evident. The first references to the sheriff (*scir(es)man*, *scir-gerefa*) date from Æthelred II's reign; the earliest recorded by name is Wulfsige the priest, sheriff of Kent in the 980s.[14] Sheriffs and borough-reeves (*portgerefan*) are in turn distinguished from reeves in charge of individual vills or manors (*tungravii*, *tunesgerefan*).[15]

By the middle of the eleventh century lesser reeves were under the authority of the sheriff, who also accounted for the king's share of the judicial profits of the shire and hundred courts.[16] From the beginning the sheriff seems to be the king's man and his emergence might to a certain extent constrain the powers of the ealdorman. The same was probably true of the high-reeves (*heah-gerefan*) who appear at about the same time.[17] The third code of King Edmund prohibits trading except in the witness of the high-reeve (*summus praepositus*), priest, treasurer (*hordere*) or port-reeve.[18] The context suggests an urban official, but in the early eleventh century high-reeves are found leading the shire-levies, a function also fulfilled by ealdormen.[19] Some friction between ealdormen and high-reeves is suggested by the murder of Æfic the high-reeve by Ealdorman Leofsige of Essex in 1002, for which the ealdorman was banished.[20]

Local Organization: The Shire Court and Community

The sheriff is particularly associated with the shire and its court. It seems to have been in Æthelred's time that the shiring of England between the Thames and the Tees was completed.[21] This involved the assimilation of the Danish territories in the north. In his early years Æthelred legislated separately for 'English' England (I Æthelred, promulgated at Woodstock) and the Danes (III Æthelred, issued at Wantage). The Wantage Code specifically concerns the Five Boroughs (Lincoln, Stamford, Nottingham, Derby and Leicester), recognizing (like IV Edgar) the local customs of the area. The confederacy still existed in 1013, when its inhabitants submitted to King Swein Forkbeard along with the Northumbrians and the people of Lindsey.[22] It must also have been part of the 'Seven Boroughs', whose leading thegns were killed on Æthelred's orders in 1015.[23]

But the days of the confederacy were ending. In 1016 we hear for the first time of the shires of Lincoln and Nottingham; Derbyshire appears in 1048, and Leicestershire by 1066.[24] Yorkshire, recorded for the first time in 1065, included the northern part of what was to become Lancashire; the southern portion, known by the end of the tenth century as 'the land between Ribble and Mersey', was appended to Cheshire.[25] The shiring of the north did not reach 'English' Northumbria, which was left in the hands of the lords of Bamburgh, and the counties of Northumberland and Durham (the land of the *Haliwerfolc*) are post-Conquest creations.[26]

The procedures of the shire-court are illuminated by the vernacular notifications of the late tenth and early eleventh centuries. Less formal than diplomas, notifications were used for many purposes: leases, lawsuits, wills, contracts (including marriage-contracts), agreements, inventories, surveys, manumissions and fiscal records. Their English name, *[ge]swutelunga*, comes from the common opening formula, 'here it is declared in this document': *her swutelað on þissum gewrite*. The texts often employ rhythmic prose and alliteration and switch freely between the first and third persons, sometimes within the same sentence; both direct and indirect speech are used. Many are chirographs ('multiple writings'), a form used in England from the ninth century, in which several copies of the same text were written on a single parchment, the spaces between them being filled with the word C Y R O G R A P H U M (or variants thereof). The parchment was then cut through the letters, and the copies distributed among the interested parties. Usually only one such copy at most survives, but all chirographs contain a clause saying how many copies have been made, and who is to keep them.[27] They are not 'official' documents, for all were written for an interested party, but they demonstrate the general desire for written documentation, at least among the strata of society which might be expected to have some access to literacy.[28]

One such notification records a case heard before the court of Berkshire in the early 990s.[29] The parties, Wynflæd (the plaintiff) and Leofwine (the defendant) cannot be identified, though it might be suspected that Wynflæd was Leofwine's stepmother. Wynflæd laid claim to Hagbourne and Bradfield (Berks), on the grounds that she was given them by Ælfric (probably Leofwine's father) in exchange for Datchet (Bucks). Her statement of claim (*ontalu*), made before the king at the royal manor of Woolmer, Hants, was supported by a formidable array of witnesses, including Sigeric, archbishop of Canterbury, Ordbriht, bishop of Selsey, Ælfric, ealdorman of Hampshire, and the king's mother, Ælfthryth.[30]

Leofwine was informed of this and the case was referred to the shire-court of Berkshire at its traditional meeting-place of Cuckhamsley.[31] The king

> sent his seal (*insegel*) to the moot at Cuckhamsley by Abbot Ælfhere [of Bath] and greeted all the councillors (*witan*) who were assembled there, namely Bishop Æthelsige [of Sherborne] and Bishop Æscwig [of Dorchester-on-Thames] and Abbot Ælfric [of Malmesbury] and the whole shire, and prayed and commanded them to settle the case between Wynflæd and Leofwine as justly as they could.

Wynflæd, having made her formal claim, was allowed to produce proof of ownership (*ahnung*). Neither the archbishop nor the bishop of Selsey was present, but both sent 'declarations' (*geswutelunga*) to the shire-court, presumably in writing.[32] Queen Ælfthryth appeared in person, along with various other notables including the abbot of Abingdon, Æfic, seneschal (*discþegn*) to the æthelings, the abbesses of Nunnaminster and Reading 'and many a good thegn and good woman ... so that the full number was produced, including both men and women'. The shire-court, however,

> declared that it would be better for the oath to be dispensed with rather than sworn, because thereafter friendship would be at an end [between them] and [Leofwine] would be asked to return what he had seized and pay compensation and his wergeld to the king.

Leofwine therefore 'dispensed with the oath' and surrendered the disputed land to Bishop Æthelsige, declaring 'that henceforth he would make no further claim to it'. Wynflæd was required to return to Leofwine 'all his father's gold and silver that she had'. She produced the minimum amount 'to protect her oath' and, when Leofwine protested, declined to take an oath that all his father's property was there, saying (in effect) that he could not prove the contrary. The matter was then concluded in the witness of Ælfgar the king's reeve, presumably the sheriff of Berkshire, and other members of the shire court.

The 'methods of proof' in such cases are listed in a plea involving the bishop of Rochester in the late 970s: *talu*, 'statement of claim', *team* (vouching to warranty, that is tracing the claim back to its source) and *ahnung*, proof of ownership.[33] Wynflæd presumably could not vouch Ælfric to warranty since it seems from the context that he was dead, and her *talu* had been contested by Leofwine; therefore she produced her *ahnung*. This could involve the production of royal diplomas (*landbec*) or other documentation, though none are mentioned in this case.[34] Wynflæd relied upon her oath-helpers, people prepared to swear to the truth of her claim. Twenty-four persons are actually named, 11 men and 13 women and, given the Old English fondness for reckoning in twelves, the 'full number', to which the text refers, was perhaps 36.[35] Whether claiming property or answering a criminal charge, an individual had to find a set number of neighbours and friends prepared to take their oaths on his behalf. To do this successfully one had to be of good reputation. Untrustworthy (or unpopular) people would not be able to collect the required numbers of oath-helpers, and would therefore lose their cases.[36]

The importance of the oath and the role of the oath-helpers is underlined by the penalties for perjury, which could involve forfeiture and even mutilation.[37] This may explain why, in Wynflæd's case, the shire-court concluded that 'it would be better for the oath to be dispensed with rather than sworn'. It was presumably obvious that Wynflæd was going to carry the day; her supporters outweighed any counterclaim that Leofwine could produce. But if it went to the oath then, as the notification says, not only would 'friendship be at an end between them', but Leofwine would implicitly be convicted as a thief (in that he had been holding the disputed estates illegally) and perhaps as a perjurer. He might not only lose the property, but have to pay a fine equivalent to his wergeld to the king. By accepting the situation he avoided these dangers.[38]

The role of the sheriff in this affair is given little emphasis, except that it was concluded in the witness of 'the king's reeve', Ælfgar. Leofric the sheriff (*scyresman*) of Kent played a more prominent role in a dispute over Snodland, Kent, between 995 and 1005, involving Godwine bishop of Rochester, and Leofwine Ælfheah's son.[39] Leofric is the only laymen named among those who presided over the shire-court, and reappears as one of the negotiators of the eventual settlement. In an earlier dispute, involving land at Wouldham, Archbishop Dunstan secured possession by producing the relevant charter (*boc*) and by his own oath, accepted on the king's behalf by Wulfsige the sheriff (*scirigman*).[40]

The Written Word and Royal Administration

In the Berkshire notification, the case was opened by the production of the king's *insegl* ('seal, token'), brought by Ælfhere, abbot of Bath. Such royal envoys linked the local assemblies with the itinerant court of the king, and by 1066 the duty to assist and provision the king's messengers (*legati regis, missatici regis*) had been laid on some English towns.[41] Whether the accompanying command to hear the case was in writing or delivered orally by the abbot is unclear.[42] The account of Æthelred's negotiations with the English magnates in 1014 is equally ambiguous:

the king sent his son Edward hither with his messengers, and bade greet all his people, and said that he would be to them a gracious lord, and would remedy all the things which they all hated, and everything should be forgiven that had been done or said against him, on condition that they all unanimously without treachery submitted to him.[43]

The diplomatic style of vernacular documents seems to have been based on the formal language used in oral ceremonies.[44] When it is remembered that dispositive force was vested not in written documents but in the spoken words and accompanying gestures of the oral ceremony which they recorded, this is not surprising, but it does make it difficult to distinguish between references to written documents and written records of oral messages.

How often the pre-Conquest kings used written communications rather than oral messages it is impossible to say. King Alfred wrote of the man who received his lord's 'written message and seal' (*ærendgewrit and insegel*), asking (rhetorically) 'whether you could say that you could not recognize him by this means'.[45] In similar vein Ælfric the Homilist, at the end of the tenth century, remarks on the obstinacy of the king's thegn who, when his lord sends him a *gewrit*, will neither hear it nor look at it.[46] Edgar commanded that copies were to be made of his *Wihtbordesstan* code, and sent to the ealdormen of Mercia and East Anglia for distribution 'far and wide'.[47] The notification recording the Snodland dispute describes how the king sent

> a letter and his seal (*gewrit and his insegl*) to Archbishop Ælfric and gave orders that he and his thegns in East Kent and West Kent should settle the dispute between them justly, weighing both claim and counter-claim (*be ontale and be oftale*).[48]

The word *gewrit* could be applied to all manner of documents; the returns of the Domesday survey presented to the king at Lammas, 1086, are described as *ealle þa gewritan*.[49] Whether in the Snodland case the *insegl* was actually attached to the *gewrit*, or carried separately as a sign of the king's authority, has been much discussed; the earliest certain examples of writs with seals attached date from the time of Edward the Confessor.[50]

Few such documents are extant.[51] Public letters were addressed generally and intended to be read to the assembled shire-court; yet the Snodland *gewrit* does not survive, and is known only from the reference to it in the *geswutelung* which records the case. Once it had fulfilled its purpose the *gewrit* was of no further interest and was not preserved. Private letters intended for the eye of the recipient only are even less likely to be kept.[52] It is the transitory nature of such communications which makes their function and frequency so difficult to assess.

An eleventh-century glossary associates the office of custodian of the relics (*scrinarius*) with that of the chancellor (*cancellarius*), and both with the English office of burthegn (chamberlain).[53] Eadred's will speaks of the mass-priests 'whom I have put in charge of my relics' and it is from Æthelred's time that we have the first direct evidence of the keeping of a document with the royal relic-collection (*haligdom*).[54] If the royal priests sometimes kept documents of interest to the king, they may also on occasion have written them. The labour involved in the production of diplomas was not great; it has been calculated that in 956, the year which saw the issue of close on 60 surviving diplomas, no more than two scribes, each working for a month, would have been required.[55] There is direct evidence for at least one royal scribe in Æthelred's time, for in 984 the king gave land at Lew, Oxon to his *scriptor* and *minister* (thegn), Ælfwine.[56]

The unwillingness to countenance the idea of any kind of royal scriptorium before 1066 may stem from a mental picture of the developed Chancery of the thirteenth century, with its hierarchy of staff and voluminous records. In comparison, all early medieval 'chanceries', even where they are acknowledged to exist, were a different kind of animal.

Evidence for systematic record-keeping is virtually non-existent before the twelfth century.[57] As for personnel, it has been calculated that the Carolingian chancery of Charles the Bald, which was more active than that of any other Carolingian (let alone English) king, consisted of 'no more than a couple of notaries and a supervisor at any one time'.[58] It is worth remembering that up to 1095, the post-Conquest chancery of the Norman kings was composed of a chancellor (who kept the royal seal) and a single scribe; and that *Domesday Book*, the high-point of the post-Conquest administration was written not by a royal chancery scribe, but (most probably) by a member of the community of Durham Cathedral, working under his bishop's supervision.[59]

Military Organization

Æthelred's kingdom, and with it his posthumous reputation, was lost in the struggle against the viking raiders of the late tenth and early eleventh centuries. He has been compared unfavourably with his great-great-grandfather, but the dangers which he faced were very different from those confronting Alfred.[60] The viking wars of Æthelred's reign changed in character as time went on, and different strategies were required to confront them.[61] Æthelred has been widely criticized for the payment of danegeld, though no such strictures are levelled at the similar tributes paid by Alfred. The earliest recorded geld of Æthelred's reign is the £10000 paid in 991 to the army which defeated Byrhtnoth at Maldon; this was followed by the geld paid to Olaf Tryggvasson in 994.[62] Progressively greater sums are said to have been paid in later years: £24000 in 1002, £36000 in 1007, £48000 in 1012.

Doubts have been expressed about the credibility of such sums; it has been suggested that they merely represent (as large, round figures in medieval sources often do) 'a lot of money'.[63] One problem is that 'danegeld' is used in post-Conquest sources for the annual land-tax, usually assessed at 2s on the hide.[64] Historians apply the term both to the tribute (*gafol*) paid to successive viking armies, and to the army-tax (*heregeld*) levied between 1012 and 1051, though the two were very different.[65] Tribute, extorted by force or the threat of force, is likely to produce a higher yield than can be raised by normal taxation, and, seen in this light, the tributes of Æthelred's reign may not be so incredible.

Whatever the rate at which they were levied, the tributes were paid, although they caused much hardship even to the richest landowners.

Archbishop Sigeric sold the manor of Monks Risborough, Bucks, for £90 of silver and 200 mancuses (6000d) to save Canterbury in 994, and the monks of Worcester remembered that the various gelds and tributes levied by Æthelred and Cnut were heavy enough to require the melting-down and sale of church plate and treasure.[66] Even the king is found selling land to one Toti (himself a Dane), for 'a pound of silver in purest gold' to pay the tribute.[67]

Another criticism of Æthelred is that, unlike his father, he was unable to defend his kingdom from invasion. The encomium on Edgar incorporated into the *Chronicle* claims that during his reign 'there was no fleet so proud nor host so strong that it got itself prey in England'; a boast echoed by Ælfric the Homilist's statement that in his time 'no fleet was ever heard of except that of our own people who held this land'.[68] Great claims were made for Edgar's sea-power by post-Conquest historians. John of Worcester attributes to him a fleet of 3600 ships which were assembled every year after Easter, 1200 on the east coast, 1200 on the west and 1200 on the north, so that the king could circumnavigate the island each summer, 'for the defence of his kingdom against foreigners and to train himself and his men in military exercises'. William of Malmesbury has a similar account (though without giving the numbers of ships) and the thirteenth-century historian, Roger of Wendover, added a fourth fleet, bringing the total number of ships to 4800.[69]

Such exaggeration may be discounted, but Edgar had a substantial fleet at his disposal. The *Chronicle* records that immediately after his coronation in 973, Edgar

> took his whole naval force (*sciphere*) to Chester, and six kings came to meet him, and all gave him pledges that they would be his allies on sea and on land.[70]

The *Annales Cambriae* for the same year records 'a great gathering of ships at Chester by Edgar, king of the Saxons'.[71] The king's purpose seems to have been to impress the rulers of the north and west; according to John of Worcester, the kings who submitted to Edgar in 973 included Kenneth II of Scotland (971–95), Malcolm of Cumbria (975–97), Maccus Haraldsson, king of the Sudreys (Man and the Hebrides), Iago ap Idwal Foel of Gwynedd (950–79) and Hywel ap Ieuaf (979–85), his nephew and eventual supplanter. What the post-Conquest writers present as a 'submission' is perhaps more likely to represent a series of alliances, but the reality of English sea-power in the 970s may be taken as genuine.[72]

How was Edgar's fleet raised? The *Leges Henrici Primi*, a twelfth-century legal tract, says that the English shires were divided into 'hundreds and shipsokes' (*sipessocna*).[73] The term 'shipsoke' is not used in any pre-Conquest source, but traces of what may have been such units can be found. In the first decade of the eleventh century, Bishop Æthelric of Sherborne complained that he was no longer receiving the 'ship-scot' (*scypegesceote*) from 33 hides of 'the three hundred hides that other bishops had for their diocese'.[74] At about the same time, the canons of St Paul's, London, produced a list of estates belonging to their church which were liable to supply a total of 58 *scipmen*, presumably to the king. The original number may have been 60, which (assuming one man per five hides) implies a 300-hide unit; the see of London then held between 300 and 350 hides of land.[75]

Other religious houses had similar obligations. The best-documented is the triple hundred of Oswaldslow, Worcestershire, attached to the bishopric of Worcester. In the 1070s and 1080s, the bishop was involved in a dispute with the abbot of Evesham over the rights of the bishop in Oswaldslow, which included 'the king's geld and service and military expeditions by land and sea' (*expeditiones in terra et in mari*).[76] One of the bishop's witnesses was 'Eadric, who was in the time of King Edward the steersman of the bishop's ship, and the leader (*ductor*) of the same bishop's army in the king's service'.[77] As at St Paul's, the service due from the bishop of Worcester was assessed on his land, but, as at Sherborne, there is a hint that the service was (or could be) rendered in cash, for a writ of William I refers to the tax (*geld*) taken in King Edward's time for the building of ships.[78]

The original endowment of the abbey of Pershore in the same shire was 300 hides, and this too seems to have owed ship-service; its steersman, the commander of the ship and its complement of warriors held land at Pershore in 1066.[79] How old these triple-hundreds were is a question much debated. The charter which fathers Oswaldslow upon Edgar (S. 731) is a twelfth-century forgery, and Edgar's charter of 972 to Pershore (S. 786), detailing the 300-hide endowment, is also spurious. But Edgar was probably responsible for the creation of both. Pershore's triple hundred cannot logically pre-date its re-foundation as a Benedictine abbey around 972. The reformed community collapsed almost immediately, reviving only in the 1020s, and lost two-thirds of its endowment to Westminster Abbey in the reign of Edward the Confessor. The optimum occasion for the establishment of the triple hundred is the moment of foundation in the 970s.[80] Neither Pershore's triple hundred nor that of

Oswaldslow was territorially discrete, each consisting rather of a scatter of lands belonging to the religious house in question, and interpenetrating each other to an extent which suggests that they were created at the same time. If Pershore's triple hundred dates to Edgar's time, so also must that of Oswaldslow.[81] The fact that all the known shipsokes are ecclesiastical may be set down to the natural bias in the survival of written evidence.[82]

Shipsokes were probably not the only means of raising ships for the royal fleet. In his panegyric upon Edgar, Archbishop Wulfstan *lupus* tempers his praise with one complaint:

> Yet he did one ill-deed too greatly: he loved evil foreign customs and brought too firmly heathen manners within this land, and attracted foreigners and enticed harmful people to this country.[83]

Wulfstan can scarcely be speaking of the continental churchmen who visited England during Edgar's reign. William of Malmesbury, amplifying Wulfstan's words, specifies Saxons (Germans), Flemings and Danes, from whom the English learnt, respectively, ferocity, effeminacy and drunkenness, in none of which they had indulged heretofore.[84] William was probably thinking of his own times, but Wulfstan's reference to 'heathen manners' suggests men of Scandinavian origin. Perhaps, like Alfred before him, Edgar was hiring viking stipendiaries and their ships.[85] This expedient was certainly adopted by Æthelred. In 1001, Pallig (later said to have been Swein Forkbeard's brother-in-law) 'deserted King Æthelred in spite of all the pledges which he had given him' and joined a Danish force ravaging in Devon, 'with the ships which he could collect'. Pallig's treachery sheds some light on the king's order for the massacre of 'all the Danish men who were in England' on St Brice's Day (13 November), 1002.[86]

To judge from the *Chronicle*'s entry for 992, which records an order that 'all the ships that were of any use' should be assembled at London, the methods of raising vessels were in some disarray.[87] Another fleet was ordered out in 999, but delay and vacillation negated its efforts.[88] A more effective operation was launched in 1000 when the fleet ravaged the Isle of Man, while the land-army led by Æthelred in person devastated Cumbria.[89] In 1008, the king commanded that 'ships should be built unremittingly over all England, namely a warship (*scegð*) from 310 hides and a helmet and a corselet from 8 hides'.[90] The contemporary law-code promulgated at Enham (Alamein, Hants) ordered that ships be fitted out 'as diligently as possible, so that in every year they may all be equipped soon after Easter'.[91] Early in 1009 a fleet said to have been larger than any previously gathered was deployed at Sandwich, but a quarrel between two of the commanders led to the loss of 100 ships and the rest returned to their base at London.[92] This debacle was followed by the arrival in the same year of 'the immense raiding-army (*unfriðhere*) which we called Thorkell's army'.[93]

The description of the Danish wars in the *Chronicle* throws some light on the organization of the English defences at this time. There is little sign of the fortified burhs, many of which had presumably fallen into ruin, while others had developed their commercial interests and grown into towns. Some of the walled towns were still defensible, and older strongpoints like South Cadbury (Somerset), *Eanbyri* (Wiltshire) and Cissbury (Sussex) were refurbished.[94] In 1001 a Danish force was 'very stoutly resisted' at Exeter, and the storming of the city in 1003 is attributed to the treachery of the queen's reeve, the 'French *ceorl* Hugh'.[95] London also resisted several Danish assaults, all of them proudly recorded by the chronicler who was perhaps himself a Londoner.[96] Canterbury may have been less defensible; in 994 Archbishop Sigeric raised a geld to save the city from destruction, and the citizens (*burhwaru*) bought off Thorkell's army in 1009.[97] Yet its fall in 1011 is, like that of Exeter in 1003, attributed to treachery after a three-week siege. The citizens of Winchester may have watched with some outrage the Danish marchpast in 1006, but at least they were safe behind their walls.[98] But the general impression is that in Æthelred's day the walled towns and strongpoints were primarily places of refuge, though Wallingford (sacked in 1006) may have had some military function.[99]

As for the army in the field, it is clear that, as in the time of Alfred, the men of the shire fought together as a group led by local magnates and men appointed by the king. The English force at Maldon in 991 consisted of the men of Essex under their ealdorman, Byrhtnoth.[100] In 1001 the men of Hampshire, led by the king's high-reeves Æthelweard and Leofwine, were worsted at Dean, Sussex.[101] Later in the same year the army of Devon and Somerset fell victim to the same host at Pinhoe (Devon); the leaders, who were killed, were Kola the king's high-reeve and Eadsige the king's reeve, presumably reeve of Pinhoe.[102] In 1003 a 'great army' (*swið mycel fyrd*) was raised in Hampshire and Wiltshire, under the command of Ealdorman Ælfric whose cowardly behaviour (according to the *Chronicle*) allowed the Danes under King Swein Forkbeard to escape to their ships.[103] Ulfcytel of East Anglia, on the other hand, behaved impeccably. In 1004 he and the East Anglian witan made terms with King Swein, and when the truce was broken by the Danes, Ulfcytel 'secretly gathered his army' and engaged the enemy at Thetford. The English were defeated, but 'if their full strength had been there, the Danes would never have got back to their ships; as they themselves said that they never met worse fighting in England than Ulfcytel dealt to them'.[104] It was Ulf-cytel and his army who engaged the host of Thorkell the Tall at the battle of Ringmere, on 5 May 1010.[105] The East Angles fled, led by Thurcytel 'Mare's Head', but the men of Cambridgeshire stood firm; nevertheless they were overwhelmed and many were killed, including Athelstan, brother-in-law of the king, Oswig and his son, Wulfric Leofwine's son, and Eadwig brother of Æfic.[106]

A distinction was drawn between forces led by ealdormen, king's thegns and high-reeves, or local magnates, and large-scale armies commanded personally by the king. The Enham code of 1008 decrees that anyone who deserts an army led by the king in person 'shall be at the risk of his life or his wergeld', whereas absconding from a lesser army carried a fine of 120s.[107] The English army which assembled early in 1016, when Æthelred was ill, would not move without the presence of the king and disbanded. It was recalled only 'on pain of the full penalty' (presumably that specified in the Enham Code), but the king feared treachery and withdrew to the walls of London.[108] Another such army, drawn from 'the whole nation' (ealne þeodscipe) and led by Æthelred himself, was assembled in 1009 to meet the threat of 'the immense raiding-army' of Thorkell the Tall; the fact that it achieved nothing is attributed by the chronicler to the machinations of Eadric Streona, ealdorman of Mercia.[109] In 1006, the king ordered out 'the whole nation (eall þeodscip) from Wessex and Mercia' to oppose the fleet of King Swein Forkbeard, which arrived after mid-summer. This force was kept out all that autumn, though to no good effect; indeed the chronicler complains that the English army did as much harm as the Danes, before returning home at the approach of winter. It seems that about two months was the limit for the provisioning of such a force.[110]

How the armies, whether local or nationwide, were raised has long been debated. The question has been bedevilled by the long-running controversy over the origins of English feudalism. Those unwilling to allow any feudal element in pre-Conquest society have laid stress on the public and territorial aspects of military obligation, while their opponents have emphasised the importance of lordship, including tenurial dependence, on the composition of the English armies.[111] If the red herring of feudalism is removed and the contemporary evidence allowed to speak for itself, many of the difficulties vanish. The eleventh-century armies are clearly 'territorial' in the sense that the shire-levies form the tactical units. Even within the greater armies commanded by the king, the warriors seem still to have fought shire by shire under their own commanders; the rout at *Assandune* was allegedly begun by Eadric Streona, leading the men of the Magonsæte (Shropshire and Herefordshire). Ealdorman Æthelweard describes such levies as 'all the hundreds of the people' (*centurias populi*), and his contemporary, Ælfric the Homilist, regularly translates the biblical 'centurion' as *hundredes ealdor* (commander of the hundred).[112] Later in the century the men of Swineshead (Hunts) paid geld in Kimbolton Hundred, 'and went with them [the men of the hundred] against the enemy'.[113] Such hundred-contingents may have been raised on the basis of one man from every five hides; the evidence for such a quota is late and localized, but the principle is found in the *Burghal Hidage*.[114]

It is also clear that the shire-levies of the tenth and eleventh centuries included contingents made up of lords and their men. The East Saxon army at Maldon in 991 was spearheaded by the following of Ealdorman Byrhtnoth, men personally commended to him or serving in his household.[115] Ecclesiastics and their officers are also prominent. Ælfstan, bishop of London, with whose church one of the shipsokes is associated, was among the commanders in 992. So was Æscwig, bishop of Dorchester-on-Thames, another bishopric whose 300-hide endowment may have been a shipsoke.[116] It seems too that a substantial part of the force at Dean in 1001 was made up of a contingent provided by the bishop of Winchester. Apart from the two high-reeves, the named casualties can all be associated with the bishop: Wulfhere the bishop's thegn; Godwine of Worthy, son of a previous bishop, Ælfsige (d. 958); and Leofwine of Whitchurch, a manor which belonged to the bishopric.[117]

The West Saxon kings from Alfred onwards had exploited the ties of lordship to enforce royal control. The Third Code of King Edmund used the hold-oath to bind both nobles and commoners (*twelfhindi et twihindi*) to himself.[118] It is not surprising to find that by the end of the century lordship also articulated the structure of the *fyrd*. The ideology is expressed in the poem on the battle of Maldon. Much about it is controversial, but all agree that its theme is loyalty: the loyalty of Byrhtnoth's men to their lord, and Byrhtnoth's loyalty to Æthelred.[119] It has been argued that this is merely a poetic device, irrelevant to contemporary realities. It would indeed be foolish to believe that the tie between lord and man was marked in every case by the emotional charge celebrated in heroic verse;

but it would be equally foolish to deny that this was sometimes the case.[120]
The concept of loyalty, the loyalty of lord and man and of both to the
king, was one of the binding forces of Old English society. The king's
thegns, as his commended men, were attended in turn by the commended
men of their own followings. Professor Leyser wrote tellingly of 'the central role of leaders in holding together the little universes of their followers',
and their deaths in action could be catastrophic to morale; when they fell
their men might well seek to save themselves in flight.[121] Indeed most
battles (including the battle of Maldon) ended with the death or flight of
the chief commander; as the *Chronicle* says, 'when the leader (*heretoga*)
gives way, the whole army will be very much hindered'.[122]

An army which relied on the mutual loyalty of its members was particularly vulnerable to treachery and deceit. As the Danish onslaught intensified, more and more pressure was put on local resources, until 'finally
there was no leader (*heafod man*) who would collect an army, but each fled
as best he could, and in the end no shire would even help the next'.[123]
The damage to morale during the years between 1009 and 1012 becomes
evident when Swein Forkbeard reappeared in 1013. One by one the
magnates of England submitted to him, first in the north, then the midlands, then in Wessex itself, so that eventually 'all the nation regarded
him as full king'. The Londoners were the last to hold out, but at length
even they capitulated and at Christmas 1013 Æthelred fled across the sea
to the protection of his brother-in-law, Duke Richard II of Normandy.[124]

Only after Swein's death on 3 February 1014 did Æthelred return. In a
sermon preached after the king's reinstatement, Archbishop Wulfstan
lupus fulminated against the treachery of the English magnates:

> a full great treachery it is also in the world that a man should betray his
> lord to death, or drive him in his lifetime from the land; and both have
> happened in this country: Edward [the Martyr] was betrayed and then
> killed . . . and Æthelred was driven out of his country.[125]

Medieval kingship was a fragile creation, dependent upon the common
interest of rulers and their magnates. A king who lost the loyalty of his followers could lose everything, including his kingdom and even his life;
and if his men lost their mutual allegiance to him and to each other, they
forfeited much of their ability to resist invasion and conquest.

10

THE DANISH CONQUEST

Before him there had never been in England a king of such great authority . . . lord of all Denmark, of all England, of all Norway and also of Scotland.[1]

In the eleventh century the English royal house could trace its origins, without employing too much fiction, back to the seventh century. Cnut's dynasty had no such antiquity, though his propagandists soon began to manufacture one.[2] But despite their attempts to make him a descendant of Ivar *inn beinlusi*, his historical ancestry goes back only to his great-grandfather, Gorm the Old (d. 958), known chiefly from the runestone he erected to his wife Thyre ('Denmark's pride') at Jelling (Jutland). Jelling, the centre of the family's power, was developed by Gorm's son Harald Bluetooth (958–87), whose own runestone boasts that 'he won for himself all Denmark and Norway and made the Danes Christian'. Towards the end of his reign, however, he was deposed by his son, Swein Forkbeard, and died on 1 November 987.[3] In Swein's time, the centre of royal power in Denmark began to shift from Jelling in Jutland towards the eastern lands, notably to Roskilde in Sjælland, soon to become the richest of the Danish bishoprics.[4] Impressive though the achievements of Harald and Swein were, neither the Danish kingdom nor its nascent church were as developed as their counterparts in England.

The sources for Cnut's reign are comparatively poor. The *Chronicle* dwindles to a few 'uninformative and . . . increasingly sparse' annals, the earliest of which were written at least a decade after the events described.[5] There is a fuller account of the reigns of Cnut's sons, Harold I 'Harefoot' (1035–40) and Harthacnut (1040–2). The period from 1016 to 1041 is covered by the *Encomium Emmae Reginae*, a propagandist work commissioned by Cnut's queen and widow from a monk of Saint-Bertin's, Flanders.[6] The earliest sections of *The Life of King Edward who lies at Westminster* (Vita Edwardi Regis) are also useful.[7] Scandinavian sources include inscriptions, fragments of skaldic poetry incorporated into later sagas, and the works of the twelfth- and thirteenth-century Scandinavian historians.[8] There are references to English affairs in the works of other continental writers, notably Adam of Bremen, William of Jumieges and Thietmar of Merseberg.[9]

Few of Cnut's charters survive, and even fewer from the reigns of Harold I and Harthacnut.[10] Of the 35 or so charters extant in Cnut's name, about half are not authentic as they stand, though some of the dubious examples may contain genuine material. They are also unevenly distributed, being concentrated at the beginning and end of the reign, with a hiatus in the late 1020s and early 1030s.[11] Cnut was the last pre-Conquest king to promulgate laws, most of which are the work of Wulfstan *lupus*, archbishop of York (d. 1023).[12]

Danes and English

English society after the Danish conquest is sometimes described as 'Anglo-Scandinavian' rather than 'Anglo-Saxon'.[13] Many of Æthelred's leading thegns perished in the battles and purges of 1015 and 1016, and the succession of a Danish king inevitably brought men from Scandinavia into the English establishment.[14] The assessment of their significance depends on the view taken of the numbers involved in comparison to the surviving English.[15] The case for 'a major upheaval among the landowning class' has been forcefully put, but, persuasively argued though it is, the lack of a Danish equivalent of *Domesday Book* means that the ratio of Danes to English, even in the upper reaches of society, remains a matter of conjecture.[16] It is particularly difficult to distinguish between new immigrants and descendants of the families who settled in the east and north in the wake of the ninth-century incursions, many of whom (particularly in East Anglia and the east midlands) must by now have been as much 'English' as 'Danish'.[17]

Though the English sources refer to Cnut's followers as 'Danes', they were not all from Denmark; Eric of Lade, who married Swein Forkbeard's daughter Gytha, was a Norwegian. Some may have been from even further afield, for Cnut had kinsmen among the ruling houses of central Europe through his mother, daughter of Miesko, duke of the Poles.[18] A charter of 1026 is attested by *Wrytsleof dux*, who may have been related to Cnut's maternal kindred.[19] He could also have been Wendish, for Harald Bluetooth married a Wendish princess, Tove, daughter of Mistivoi, king of the Obodrites (965/7–*c*. 995); and her nephew Gottschalk was harboured in Cnut's court.[20] Tovi 'the Wend', who held land at Great Barrington, Gloucs, may have arrived with Gunnhild, Cnut's niece, who married Hakon, earl of Worcestershire, and who is said to have been the daughter of 'Wyrtgeorn, king of the Wends'.[21]

All the Scandinavian newcomers to England in Cnut's time were laymen; there were as yet no Danish bishops or clerks to be promoted to English sees and abbeys. Indeed the movement of personnel was in the opposite direction, for English ecclesiastics were among the missionaries active at this time within Scandinavia itself.[22] For foreign churchmen in Cnut's entourage we have to look elsewhere.[23] Henry, supposed to have been Cnut's treasurer, was a German, who subsequently became bishop of the Orkneys and eventually of Lund.[24] Wythman, *teutonicus natione*, became abbot of Ramsey in 1016.[25] The royal priest Duduc, variously described as a 'Saxon' and a 'Lotharingian', was promoted to the bishopric of Wells, probably in 1033. Two of Harthacnut's priests eventually became bishops; Herman, a Lotharingian, of Ramsbury and Sherborne, and Leofric, an Englishman trained in Lotharingia, of Exeter.[26]

It has been suggested that Cnut's baptismal name, Lambert, reflects a devotion to Saint Lambert of Liege.[27] In fact Lambert was a name currently in use in the family of his Polish mother, but Cnut's interest in Lotharingia is shown by his visit to Cologne, perhaps during his return journey from Rome in 1027.[28] The links between Scandinavia and Germany were more long-standing; German missionaries were as, if not more, influential in the Christianization of the north as Englishmen, and had indeed achieved the conversion of Denmark in Harald Bluetooth's time.[29] As king of Denmark, Cnut needed to establish good relations both with the German church, especially the archbishopric of Hamburg-Bremen which claimed metropolitan rights over all the northern churches, and with the German Emperor, the southern neighbour of the Danes. When he attended the coronation of Conrad II at Rome in 1027 he negotiated with pope and emperor 'concerning the needs of all the peoples of my kingdom, whether English or Danes'.[30] In his letter recording the event, addressed to 'the whole race of the English', he chooses to emphasise the concessions on tolls levied on English merchants and pilgrims to Rome, but it is probable that he also acknowledged the rights of Hamburg-Bremen, long a matter of dispute.[31]

Churchmen from Lotharingia, a centre of reform, were to play an important role in the reorganization of the English Church throughout the eleventh century.[32] The ecclesiastical establishment, however, remained predominantly English. In the opening years of Cnut's reign the major figure was that of Archbishop Wulfstan II of York, Wulfstan *lupus*, who continued to advise Cnut as he had advised Æthelred II.[33] His hand has been detected in Cnut's law-codes, beginning with the text of the agreement reached at Oxford in 1018, 'according to Edgar's law'. Like much early legislation, the 1018 code is of political rather than legal significance, but it lays down a programme of matters for future consideration. More influential were the later codes, I Cnut (covering ecclesiastical matters) and II Cnut (the secular code), promulgated between 1020 and Wulfstan's death in 1023.[34] They represent the summation of previous enactments, and soon came to be regarded as the epitome of English law.[35]

The King's Household

Sir Frank Stenton's picture of Cnut 'surrounded by a large company of specialized fighting men [who] formed a highly organized military guild' is no longer tenable.[36] Nor is the idea of a Scandinavianized court. Scandinavian terms (*stallari, huskarl, liðesman*) do not necessarily imply the Scandinavian nature of the office described, any more than a Scandinavian personal name implies that the bearer was Scandinavian, or even of Scandinavian descent.[37]

In the case of the stallers, it has been denied that their office had anything to do with the Danish king; the Old English word *stallere, steallere* is seen not as a derivation from Old Norse *stallari*, but 'simply an Anglicization of the Franco-Norman constable or *comes stabuli*'.[38] The argument rests on the assertion that no contemporary source mentions the title, whereas there are several references from the reign of Edward the Confessor.[39] However, Osgod Clapa, called *stallere* in 1046, attests charters of Cnut and Harthacnut from 1026 to 1042 as *miles* and *minister*, both of which might represent the vernacular 'staller'. Herman of Bury writing at the end of the eleventh century calls him *maior domus*, which suggests some official position in the king's household.[40] Osgod may have had authority over London and the royal fleet stationed there.[41]

Osgod is often found in association with Tovi the Proud, patron of Waltham Holy Cross.[42] The *Waltham Chronicle* compiled in the late twelfth century calls Tovi a staller, and describes him in fulsome terms as 'the first man in England after the king'.[43] This can be discounted as exaggeration but he was clearly high in Cnut's counsel, for between 1016 and 1035 he is found at a shire-court at Aylton, Herefords, 'on the king's business'.[44] It was at the wedding-feast of Tovi and Osgod's daughter Gytha in 1042 that King Harthacnut collapsed and died 'as he stood at his drink'.[45] Tovi's grandson, Esgar, who held at least some of his lands, was also a staller, in the service of King Edward.[46]

There remains the question whether the office of staller represents an innovation of Cnut's time, or is merely an old position given a new style when bestowed upon the king's Scandinavian followers, in the same way that the English title 'ealdorman' is replaced by Old Norse 'earl' (*jarl*).[47] The original meaning of *stallari* seems to be someone with a high place in the king's hall and it is perhaps relevant to cite in this context Archbishop Wulfstan *lupus*' words on the higher grade of royal thegn, who had 'a seat and special office in the king's hall' and 'rode in his household band on his missions'.[48] There is little in the known careers of Osgod and Tovi (or the later stallers of King Edward) to suggest that their functions were, in general, greatly different from those carried out in the tenth century by the men described as *pedisequi*, a title 'which describes a man in close personal relations to the king'.[49] The best known is Wulfstan of Dalham, called *sequipedus* (a variant of *pedisequus*) in a charter of Eadred of 956; he was among the king's thegns who attended a council at London in Edgar's reign, acted as the same king's representative in Cambridgeshire, and, as the king's officer, assisted Bishop Æthelwold to eject the clerks from the Old Minster, Winchester, in 963.[50]

What has been said of the stallers applies equally to the housecarls ('men of the household, retainers'). All great lords, ecclesiastical and lay, kept households which included fighting-men, or at least men who could perform military or quasi-military functions. In the vernacular they were known as thegns or *cnihtas* ('knights'), and in Latin are styled *milites*, *ministri* or *bellatores*. Cnut presumably had such a contingent of household warriors, whom he retained in his service after he became king. Such men may have been used to garrison important strongpoints; 15 acres at Wallingford, Bucks, is described as 'the land where the housecarls used to live', and the four Dorset boroughs (Dorchester, Bridport, Wareham and Shaftesbury) paid annual sums 'for the use of the king's housecarls'.[51]

The only reference to Cnut's housecarls in action comes from Osbern of Canterbury's account of the translation of St Ælfheah's body from London to Canterbury in 1023. Its historicity has been defended, but Osbern was writing in the third quarter of the eleventh century, and the passage in which the king's housecarls defend the party carrying the archbishop's relics from the angry Londoners has the appearance of a *topos* (a formal and traditional story).[52] On the death of Cnut in 1035, Harthacnut remained in Denmark, while his mother, Queen Emma, took up residence in Winchester 'with the housecarls of her son the king'.[53] In 1040, Harthacnut imposed a severe geld and (according to John of Worcester) 'sent his housecarls (*huscarlas*) throughout the provinces of his kingdom to extort the tribute'. Two of them, Feader and Thurstan, were killed by the men of Worcester on 4 May 'in an upper room in one of the towers of Worcester monastery to which they had fled to hide'. On 12 November the king sent a force commanded by his five leading earls 'and almost all his housecarls', which ravaged Worcester and the surrounding area for four days; but the townspeople defended themselves on an island in the Severn and were subsequently allowed to return to their homes.[54] Such expeditions, however, were hardly new; for a comparable use of punitive force we need look no further than King Æthelred II's harrying of the diocese of Rochester in 986.[55]

Like the king's thegns, housecarls also figure in non-military roles. The incident at Worcester in 1041 has suggested that housecarls might be used as geld-collectors; one might compare, on a lesser scale, the sending by one Toki of his *cnihtas*, Sexi and Leofwine, to Archbishop Eadsige of Canterbury, to negotiate a renewal of his lease on Halton, Bucks.[56] Housecarls also attest charters in the company of their lords. Earl Leofric's agreement on the endowment of Stow St Mary, Lincs, is witnessed (*inter alia*) by King Edward and 'all the king's housecarls and chaplains' (*on eallra þæs kynges huscarlan and on his mæssepreostan*).[57] Around the same time (about 1050) another agreement, involving the abbey of St Albans, was attested (*inter alia*) by Earl Leofric, and by 'Vagn and all the earl's housecarls'.[58] The Scandinavian names in the *Liber Vitae* of Thorney Abbey, which are associated with those of Earls Thorkell, Hakon, Eric, Eilaf and Ulf, probably represent the household retainers of one or more of the earls, entering the fraternity of the abbey along with their lord or lords.[59] In an administrative context we have two writs of King Edward, both relating to the appointment of St Wulfstan as bishop of Worcester in 1062; they are addressed (*inter alia*) to the Norman immigrant Richard [fitzScrob], and in one of them he too is called 'Richard my housecarl'.[60]

Individual members of royal retinues usually become visible only when their lords reward them with land. The Scandinavian names recorded in the 'English' areas of England (the south and west) have been taken to imply the settlement of Cnut's Danish followers in the 1020s and 1030s.[61] Karli the king's *cniht*, who witnessed a Kentish marriage-agreement between 1016 and 1020, was presumably a Scandinavian in Cnut's following; his sons, Godric and Godwine were holding land in Kent on the eve of the Norman Conquest.[62] A more celebrated group of housecarls are the Dorset landowners, Aghmund, Bovi and Urk (or Orc).[63] All are described in the Latin texts as *ministri* (thegns), but the endorsement to Bovi's charter, dated 1033, calls him a housecarl, and Urk is addressed as a housecarl in a vernacular writ of Edward the Confessor; it seems likely that if we had similar evidence for Aghmund he too would have been styled housecarl.[64] Names of Scandinavian origin which appear among the pre-Conquest landowners in Dorset (Askell, Azur, Beorn, Bruni, Her, Toli, Thormund and Toki (*Toxus*) the priest) may indicate other housecarls settled in the shire.[65]

In 1066 the four Dorset boroughs (Dorchester, Bridport, Wareham and Shaftesbury) discharged their assessment to geld by payments 'for the use of the king's housecarls', which might suggest that the first housecarls in Dorset had performed some military role, perhaps as garrisons.[66] If so, this situation is unlikely to have lasted very long. The best-known of the three named housecarls is Urk, who with his wife Tole founded Abbotsbury Abbey and established the Abbotsbury Gild, activities which suggest that like other men of Scandinavian origin he 'melted into the Anglo-Saxon landscape, assuming the role appropriate to one of his standing and taking an interest in the welfare of the local population'.[67] Bovi, likewise, may have been the founder of the abbey at Horton, which was in existence by 1062.[68] Neither as a group nor as individuals do housecarls seem markedly different from thegns, and by the time of Domesday, 'housecarl' and 'thegn' could be used interchangeably of the same man. It seems that the housecarls were, in origin, the household followers of Cnut and his earls, mostly of Scandinavian origin and therefore described (like the stallers) by a Scandinavian word.

The lithesmen of London make their first appearance in 1035, when, with Earl Leofric and the northern thegns, they 'chose Harold [I] to the regency (*to healdes*) of all England'.[69] They are perhaps identical with the Danes who recovered Harold's body after Harthacnut, his half-brother and successor, had it dug up and thrown into the Thames marshes, reburying it in 'the cemetery they had in London'.[70] In 1049 the London lithesmen recovered the body of Cnut's murdered nephew, Beorn Estrithson, bearing it to Winchester for burial next to his uncle.[71]

The lithesmen (men of the *lið*, 'fleet') manned the ships maintained by the English kings from Æthelred II to Edward the Confessor. They were undoubtedly Scandinavians, but their use as stipendiary troops, the tax instituted to pay them and their association with London are not innovations of Cnut's time, but go back to the closing years of Æthelred II's reign. The word *lið* is a Scandinavian loan, 'the domestic name for those bands making havoc in western Europe or combining trade and plunder in Russia', of which Cnut's *þingmannalið* was merely the most celebrated.[72] Another was the force led by Thorkell the Tall, hired by Æthelred in 1012.[73] The payments made to it in 1013 and 1014 have already been discussed, and it seems that Cnut used the precedent to maintain a fleet of his own, retaining 40 ships (Thorkell's fleet numbered 45) when he paid off the rest of his force in 1018. The wages of their crews were paid by the annual heregeld.

At the end of the eleventh century the monks of Worcester still remembered the burden of this tax, particularly since those who could not pay it risked losing their lands to those who could.[74] Cnut's Secular Code proclaims that

> he who has performed the obligations on an estate with the witness of the shire [and he who owned it before would not or could not] is to have it uncontested for his lifetime and to give it to whom he pleases after his lifetime

and the endorsement to Bovi the housecarl's charter records that he 'defended the land successfully at law with his own money in payment of the tax due upon it, the whole shire being witness'.[75]

By the end of the reign, the fleet had been reduced to 16 ships, paid for 'at eight marks to the *hamele*'.[76] This number was maintained during the reign of Harold I (1035–40), but Harthacnut made himself unpopular by demanding the same rate for a fleet of 60 or 62 ships, £21 099 in all.[77] In 1041 the heregeld was levied again, raising £11 048 for 32 ships.[78] The fleet was maintained by Harthacnut's half-brother Edward the Confessor, but again the number of ships was reduced; by 1050 there were 14 ships, nine of which were dismissed in that year, and the remainder were paid off in 1051 taking their ships with them.[79] With the stipendiary fleet went the heregeld, abolished (as the *Chronicle* says) 'in the thirty-ninth year after it had been instituted'.[80]

Earls and Earldoms

In 1017, Cnut divided the English kingdom, 'Wessex for himself, East Anglia for Thorkell, Mercia for Eadric and Northumbria for Eric'.[81] This has been seen as a revolutionary step and an ominous precedent for the future, but the division is foreshadowed in Edgar's Fourth Code.[82] Nor did it last long.[83] Eadric Streona was murdered before the year's end, and it is not clear that anyone was appointed to replace him as earl of all Mercia. Thorkell, the dominant figure in Cnut's early years, fell out with the king and returned to Denmark in 1021; the next earl to have authority over all East Anglia was Harold Godwineson (in 1045). Eric of Lade briefly succeeded Thorkell as senior earl, but himself drops out of sight after 1023. He probably never controlled northern Northumbria, which passed from Earl Uhtred's brother Eadulf to his son Ealdred, and the next earl to have authority over southern Northumbria is Siward, who attests for the first time in 1033.

From Cnut's time, the title of ealdorman was replaced by that of earl. The change, foreshadowed in the tenth century, is probably due to the presence of Scandinavians among the ranks of the ealdormen, but it would have to be shown that the change in nomenclature was accompanied by a change in function for it to be of real significance.[84] This seems not to be the case. Thorkell's power in East Anglia resembles that wielded by his predecessor Æthelwine *amicus dei*, Æthelred's premier ealdorman from 983 to 992. In Wessex, which Cnut kept in his own hands, there seem at first to have been two (or possibly three) ealdormen, as in the time of the tenth-century kings.[85]

Many of Cnut's earls are little more than names, and in some cases it is not even certain where their spheres of authority lay. The position is clearest in Mercia, where the archives of the church of Worcester provide a fuller picture than is available elsewhere.[86] The appointment of Eadric Streona as ealdorman of Mercia in 1007 did not, it seems, affect the position of Leofwine, described as ealdorman 'of the Hwiccian provinces' (the Worcester area) in 997.[87] Both survived the Danish conquest, attesting a lease of Wulfstan *lupus* dated 1017.[88] Leofwine maintained and perhaps even advanced his position after the murder of Eadric, though his eldest son, Northman (who was killed with Eadric in 1017) may have been an adherent of the disgraced ealdorman.[89]

Cnut appointed three Danish earls to the shires of the Mercian ealdordom. Earl Ranig may have been given Herefordshire as early as October or November 1016, though there are no charters from the years 1016–17 to confirm this.[90] Ranig attests the earliest surviving charters from 1018, as does Earl Eilaf who probably held Gloucestershire, and in 1019 they are joined by Earl Hakon whose authority lay in Worcestershire. Since this had been Leofwine's ealdordom, and since he remained in office until 1023, it has been assumed that he was promoted to the earldom of all Mercia on Eadric's murder in 1017, but he may have been merely an English colleague of the Scandinavian Earl Hakon. Two of Leofwine's sons, Leofric and Edwin, held positions of authority in the west, perhaps as sheriffs, Leofric in Worcestershire and Edwin in Herefordshire.[91] Cnut's treatment of Mercia suggests a continuation of the policies of Æthelred's reign when, as we have seen, ealdormen were appointed to spheres more restricted than those of Edgar's time. Mercia after Eadric's murder looks very different from the other earldoms, but if we had the same kind of evidence for Northumbria and East Anglia we might find that Eric and Thorkell also had 'subordinate' earls within their respective spheres.[92]

Four of Cnut's eight surviving writs include the sheriff as well as the earl and/or the ecclesiastical authorities in their address.[93] This, and the presence of men like Osgod Clapa and Tovi the Proud, suggests a continuing reliance on royal officials of lesser rank operating under closer royal control as a check on the authority of the earls. If, however, Cnut wished to reduce that authority, then, like Æthelred, he abandoned the attempt, for by the 1030s two great earls stand out above all the rest: Leofric of Mercia and Godwine of Wessex.

It has been suggested that Cnut's reign saw the final destruction (begun in Æthelred's reign) of the close-knit aristocracy which supported the tenth-century kings, and its replacement by 'new men', unrelated to each other or the king.[94] In fact most of the more powerful earls were the king's kinsman, though by marriage rather than blood. Eric of Lade was his brother-in-law, the husband of his half-sister Gytha, Swein Forkbeard's daughter: their son Hakon, earl of Worcestershire, married Cnut's niece Gunnhild.[95] Eilaf was brother to the Danish Jarl Ulf, husband of Cnut's full sister Estrith; Eilaf's own sister Gytha was the wife of Godwine of Wessex.[96] Only the disappearance of the Scandinavian earls from English affairs after about 1030 (and of the Scandinavian kings after 1042) prevented the development of a new 'Anglo-Scandinavian' establishment.[97]

Godwine is the archetypal 'new man', the most famous, perhaps one should say the most notorious of Cnut's earls.[98] His father, Wulfnoth *cild*, was accused of some unspecified crime at the meeting of the great

ship-levy in 1009.[99] Wulfnoth's ability to detach 20 ships from the royal
fleet suggests a man of rank, as does his appellation *cild* ('child', 'young
man', 'warrior'). The *Chronicle*'s description of him as 'Wulfnoth *cild* the
South Saxon' implies that he was at least of local importance; one thinks
of Æthelnoth *cild* 'the Kentishman', the most prominent of the south-
eastern thegns in King Edward's reign.[100] Some of the very extensive
lands in Sussex later in the possession of Godwine and his family may have
belonged to Wulfnoth.[101]

It has been too readily assumed that Wulfnoth was guilty as charged,
though John of Worcester believed that the allegation brought against
him was unjust.[102] His accuser was Brihtric, brother of Eadric Streona,
ealdorman of Mercia, author of the downfall of other thegns and ealdormen, including Sigeferth and Morcar murdered in 1015.[103] Sigeferth's
widow then married the ætheling Edmund, but the connection may go
back further, for both Sigeferth and Morcar were beneficiaries under the
will of Edmund's brother Athelstan ætheling (d. 1014). Another of Athelstan's bequests was to one Godwine son of Wulfnoth, who was to have the
estate at Compton which had been his father's; the names are common,
but Earl Godwine later held an estate at Compton, Sussex.[104] If Godwine
and Wulfnoth were members of an 'æthelings' party', opposed to that of
Eadric Streona, then Brihtric's accusation against Wulfnoth in 1009
takes on a more sinister aspect.

Whatever the family's position under Æthelred, it is in Cnut's time that
Godwine emerges into the limelight. He attests as earl from 1018, but can
only have held central and eastern Wessex, for Æthelweard, ealdorman
of the Western Shires, was banished only in 1020.[105] The *Vita Edwardi*
records Godwine's gradual rise to power.[106] Of all his English adherents,
Cnut found Godwine 'the most cautious in counsel and the most active in
war'. He took him to Denmark, where he 'tested more closely his wisdom', and 'admitted [him] to his council and gave him his sister [*sic*] as
wife'; on his return to England, he made Godwine 'earl and *baiulus* of
almost all the kingdom'. This probably refers to Cnut's visit to Denmark
in 1022–3, when he was reconciled with Thorkell the Tall; Thorkell vanishes from sight after 1023, and it is from this point that Godwine displaces
Eric of Lade at the head of the earls signing Cnut's charters.[107] It was
probably now that he became earl of all Wessex, though he did not hold
Kent until after the death of Archbishop Æthelnoth in 1038.[108] It is easy
to see why Godwine was valuable to the new king. Sandwich, Kent, was
the usual assembly-place for the English fleet at the beginning of the cam-
paigning season, as London was its permanent base and arsenal; a man

whose land and influence lay in the south-east would be of particular use to a king whose ambitions included Scandinavia as well as England.

By the middle of the eleventh century the landed wealth of Godwine's heirs exceeded that of the king, but the stages whereby this fortune was acquired cannot be reconstructed. It was perhaps from Cnut that Godwine received the many large, formerly royal manors which he held in Kent, Sussex and Hampshire, but the only surviving charter of Cnut in Godwine's favour is a grant of land at Polhampton, Hants, which included property in Winchester.[109] It seems to have been in Cnut's time that Godwine acquired some of the lands of the defunct community at Minster-in-Thanet; the purchaser from whom Ælfstan, abbot of St Augustine's, Canterbury, bought half of the minster lands at some time before 1030 is unnamed, but Ælfstan is said to have given him Folkestone in exchange, and Folkestone is later found in the possession of Earl Godwine.[110] Godwine seems to have had a 'special relationship' with St Augustine's; the 'E' version of the *Chronicle*, which was being compiled there in the mid-eleventh century, is noticeably partial towards him and his sons.

Godwine may also have been patron of the refounded minster at Dover, removed into the safety of the hilltop burh, and now represented by the early eleventh-century church (perhaps built by Godwine) of St Mary in Castro.[111] He was certainly a close associate of the royal clerk, Eadsige, who succeeded Æthelnoth as archbishop of Canterbury in 1038.[112] It was in Eadsige's time (1038–50) that control of Kent passed to Earl Godwine, as well as several of the manors belonging to Christ Church which were recovered only after the Norman Conquest.[113]

Godwine's closest rival, Leofric son of Ealdorman Leofwine, first attests as earl in 1032, though he may have been promoted in the late 1020s. John of Worcester indeed has Leofric succeed to the earldom of his brother Northman killed in 1017, but there is no evidence that Northman ever held the rank of earl.[114] Whatever the extent of his father's power, Leofric himself was certainly earl of Mercia. His family, which (unlike that of Godwine) can be traced back into the tenth century, may have come from the east, rather than the west midlands.[115] In the Confessor's reign, Sexi of Woodwalton, Hunts, a benefactor of Ramsey Abbey, claimed kinship with Earl Leofric; descendants of the family may have survived in the east midlands even after 1066, and the religious establishments there remembered them kindly.[116] In the west, however, Leofwine's family (with some exceptions) had a reputation as spoliators of the episcopal church of Worcester, though they were benefactors of Evesham Abbey, a house often at odds with its diocesan bishop.[117] Godwine, on the other hand, was a friend of Lyfing, bishop of Worcester (1038–46), and Lyfing's successor, Ealdred.[118]

The abbot of Evesham at this time was Ælfweard (1014–44), who was also from 1035 bishop of London. He was allegedly a kinsman of Cnut, but is more likely to have been related to Cnut's English wife, Ælfgifu of Northampton.[119] It was perhaps in the late 1020s that Leofric's son Ælfgar married Ælfgifu, who has been plausibly identified with the daughter of Ælfgifu of Northampton's cousin Ealdgyth and her husband Morcar.[120] If this hypothesis is correct, then both the leading earls of the 1030s were related to Cnut, Godwine through his marriage to the king's sister-in-law, Gytha, and Leofric through his son's marriage to a kinswoman of Ælfgifu of Northampton and her sons by Cnut. An alliance between the Mercian earls and the family of Ælfgifu of Northampton might also explain why, in 1035, Leofric backed her son Harold I against his half-brother Harthacnut.[121]

The reign of Harthacnut also saw the rise of Siward, earl of Northumbria. It is usually assumed that Siward was Danish, but nothing certain is known of his origins. He attests as earl for the first time in 1033, but was probably at that time in effective control of only the southern part of Northumbria, the old kingdom of York. In Bamburgh, Eadulf *cudel* had been succeeded by his nephew Ealdred, probably about 1019, but he was murdered in 1038. His half-brother Eadulf succeeded him, but in 1041 'Harthacnut betrayed Earl Eadulf under his safe-conduct and he was then a pledge-breaker'. The tone of this notice, common to the 'C' and 'D' versions of the *Chronicle*, suggests disapproval, at least in some quarters, of the king's action, but nothing is known for certain of the background. The removal of Eadulf opened up the north for Siward. He married the murdered earl's niece, Ælfflæd, and it was this alliance that allowed him to extend his authority over Northumbria north of the Tees.[122]

It was probably in the same period, the 1040s, that Siward regained control of southern Cumbria from the Scots, for an undated writ in the name of Gospatric, a later ruler of 'the lands which were Cumbrian', refers to the *grith* ('peace') established there by Earl Siward.[123] The context is perhaps Siward's patronage of the future king of Scots, Malcolm Canmore, in exile after the death of his father Duncan in 1040; it was Siward who, in 1054, killed Duncan's successor Macbeth and restored Malcolm to his father's throne.[124] How long the region remained in English hands is uncertain. To judge from Gospatric's writ it was never shired, but retained its native British customs with an anglicized overlay.[125] At some time, perhaps in 1069 or 1070, Malcolm Canmore regained control, for only the southernmost portions of what later became Cumberland and Westmorland were surveyed in 1086. It was not until William II's capture of Carlisle in 1092 that southern Cumbria was finally incorporated into England.[126]

11

AUTHORITY AND
AMBITION, 1042–66

Then some of them thought it would be a great piece of folly if they joined battle, for in the two hosts there was most of what was noblest in England, and they considered that they would be opening a way for our enemies to enter the country and to cause great ruin among ourselves.

(*Anglo-Saxon Chronicle* 'D', 1051)

The shadow of 14 October 1066 hangs over Edward the Confessor, last of the West Saxon dynasty, and his successor Harold II Godwineson, last of the Old English kings.[1] Modern historians have tended to concentrate on the weaknesses in the kings and their kingdom which permitted the extinction of the West Saxon line, and the conquest of the country.[2] Yet in these years the English regained southern Cumbria, established a client-kingdom in north Wales, and won one of their most decisive victories over a viking host at the battle of Stamford Bridge.[3] These are scarcely the achievements of a kingdom in terminal decline.

The *Chronicle* is contemporary for this period and each version has its own standpoint, 'C' being hostile to Earl Godwine and his family, while 'E' (kept, until the middle of the eleventh century, at St Augustine's, Canterbury) is noticeably favourable to them.[4] The twelfth-century chronicler John of Worcester particularly favours Harold II. Another partisan work is the *Vita Edwardi*, originally commissioned by Queen Edith, probably in 1065, as a biography of her family.[5] Adam of Bremen is a valuable source for the period, provided it is remembered that one of his informants was

Swein Estrithson, king of Denmark (1047–76); and the later years are covered by the Norman historians, William of Jumieges and William of Poitiers, and the Bayeux Tapestry.[6] Sixty-four charters and a hundred writs of Edward survive, and a single writ of Harold. The reigns of Edward and Harold are also illuminated retrospectively by the great candle of Domesday Book, fruit of the survey conducted in 1085–6 at the command of William the Conqueror.[7]

The French Connection

Harthacnut and Edward were sons of Emma of Normandy. Harthacnut, however, was reared in England and Denmark, whereas Edward's early adulthood was spent with his mother's kindred. He seems never to have forgotten his rights as Æthelred II's eldest surviving son, but by the time he returned to England in 1041, in his late thirties, his tastes and inclinations were as much French as English.[8]

Just as Cnut brought Scandinavian followers to England, so Edward was accompanied by Frenchmen.[9] It is natural that they should have received more attention than Cnut's Danes, for the Norman Conquest proved permanent, whereas that of the Danes was transitory. Men like the king's nephew, Ralph, who was made an earl, his friend Robert of Jumieges, briefly archbishop of Canterbury, and his kinsman Robert fitzWimarc, who became a staller, have been seen as outriders of that great post-Conquest host, who swept away the pre-Conquest nobility of England. It is important, however, to avoid hindsight in assessing their role in Edward's reign.[10] Of course they were ethnically French, but the fact that Earl Ralph and Robert fitzWimarc gave their sons insular names argues a degree of assimilation to their adopted country.[11] Robert also displayed a noticeably cautious response to Duke William's invasion, perhaps because a considerable part of his land came from Harold II.[12] After the Conquest, indeed, all Edward's 'Frenchmen' were regarded as *anglici*.[13]

Edward cannot have given the see of London to Robert of Jumieges before 1044, and since his attestations as bishop begin only in 1046 the king may have had difficulty enforcing his appointment.[14] This was certainly the case with the king's promotion of his Norman priest Ulf to the bishopric of Dorchester-on-Thames in 1049.[15] Ralph had to wait until 1050 for his earldom, though his mother Godgifu, who was dead by 1049, held lands in England, presumably given by her brother.[16] It is in 1050 also that the Norman priests William, later bishop of London, and

Peter, whom William I elevated to the bishopric of Lichfield, begin to attest Edward's charters.[17] Robert fitzWimarc does not attest genuine charters until 1059, but his castle at Clavering, Essex, was standing in 1052.[18] One Norman who did not do well out of Edward's accession was his mother Emma, who had identified herself rather too closely with her second husband and her son Harthacnut, to Edward's detriment.[19] To judge from the surviving charters, more Englishmen and Danes than Frenchmen received advancement from the new king in the 1040s.[20]

1051–2: A Crisis of Authority?

In the years 1051–2 there was a stand-off between the king and Earl Godwine. The *Vita Edwardi* traces its roots to the archiepiscopal election of 1050. Archbishop Eadsige, a close associate of Godwine, died on 29 October 1050 whereupon his monks and clergy elected Ælric, a monk of Christ Church and a kinsman of the earl.[21] In mid-Lent, 1051, at a council held in London, the king quashed the election in favour of Robert of Jumieges, 'while all the clergy protested with all their might against the wrong'.[22] Their complaints were ignored and Robert set out for Rome to receive his pallium.

Robert's bishopric of London was given to Spearhafoc, abbot of Abingdon, and Abingdon itself to Rothulf. It is true that two of the three new appointees were Norman (though Rothulf had spent most of his life in Scandinavia) but they were also 'king's men': Spearhafoc had been the king's goldsmith, and Rothulf was his kinsman through his mother Emma.[23] There seems to have been little solidarity between them and indeed Robert refused to consecrate Spearhafoc. Edward was eventually compelled to give London to William, a Norman but also (perhaps more importantly) a royal clerk, as was the Englishman Cynesige appointed to the archbishopric of York left vacant by the death of Ælfric on 29 January 1051.[24] This was promotion which might have been expected by Ealdred, bishop of Worcester, whose predecessors Oswald and Wulfstan *lupus* had held both sees; but perhaps Ealdred, like the monk Ælric, was too close to Earl Godwine. In short, Edward's ecclesiastical appointments certainly look 'anti-Godwinist', but the men selected were chosen for their closeness to the king as much as for their nationality.

Frenchmen and foreigners (*welisce men*) are prominent in the *Chronicle*'s accounts of the crisis, of which 'E' is the fuller.[25] It concentrates on the activities of Eustace, count of Boulogne, the king's one-time brother-in-law.[26]

He arrived 'soon after the bishop' (Archbishop Robert, who returned from Rome on 28 June) and

> went to the king and told him what he wished, and then went home-
> wards. When he came east to Canterbury, he and his men took refresh-
> ment there, and went to Dover. When he was some miles or more on
> this side of Dover, he put on his mail-shirt, and all his companions did
> likewise. So they went to Dover. When they got there, they wished to
> lodge where it suited their own convenience. Then one of Eustace's
> men came and wished to stay at the home of a householder (husbunda)
> against his will, and he wounded the householder, and the householder
> killed him. Then Eustace got upon his horse and his companions upon
> theirs, and went to the householder (husbunda) and killed him upon his
> own hearth.[27] And afterwards they went up towards the town and
> killed, within and without, more than twenty men. And the townsmen
> (burhmenn) killed nineteen on the other side and wounded they did not
> know how many.

There is no hint of what the king and Eustace discussed, but Eustace was clearly expecting trouble at Dover (men do not ride in full mail unless they must). The main fight between his followers and the burhmenn took place in the old Iron Age hillfort on the cliff, where in the early eleventh century a new minster-church had been built, possibly under the patronage of Godwine.[28] It may have been the king's intention that Eustace should take over this defensible site, perhaps to establish a castle there.[29] One of the complaints in the 'E' Chronicle is that 'the foreigners (welisce menn) then had built a castle in Herefordshire in Earl Swein's province, and had inflicted every possible injury and insult upon the king's men in those parts'. This castle, probably at Hereford itself, is almost certainly 'Pentecost's castle', one of the two to which the 'Frenchmen' (Frencisce menn) fled after Godwine's return in 1052.[30] The other is 'Robert's castle', presumably Clavering, Essex, in Harold's earldom of East Anglia.[31] If Eustace's attack on Dover was an unsuccessful attempt at a third strong-point, in Godwine's own earldom, it may be that the king was deliberately intruding his own men into the provinces of all three earls.

Edward's attempt to use French men and French fortifications against Godwine and his sons is striking, but it would be a mistake to see the con-frontation as a simple matter of 'French' versus 'English'. Both parties had foreign support. The earl was negotiating the marriage of his third son Tostig with Judith, half-sister of Baldwin V of Flanders, which adds an extra dimension to Edward's discussions with Eustace of Boulogne, an opponent of Baldwin.[32] Conversely, Edward was supported not only by Archbishop Robert, Earl Ralph and his other Frenchmen, but also by Leofric of Mercia and his son Ælfgar, and Siward of Northumbria. Ralph may have received Swein's earldom in Hereford when the family was expelled, but East Anglia went to Ælfgar, and the western shires of Godwine's earldom to the king's English kinsman Odda of Deerhurst.[33]

In the event, Godwine forced the king to reinstate him and his sons (though Swein did not return to England with his brothers in 1052).[34] This was both personally damaging to Edward and another stage in the aggrandizement of Earl Godwine, or rather, since he died on 15 April 1053, of his son Earl Harold. Whether it also tarnished the office of kingship is debateable. One of the striking elements in the earl's defiance is the unwillingness of his own men to follow him in any direct confrontation with the king. They were, to quote the 'E' text of the *Chronicle*, 'reluctant to have to stand against their royal lord (*cynehlaford*)', and when, at a council held at London in late September, 'the king asked for all those thegns that the earls had had . . . they were all handed over to him'. The 'E' text is noticeably partisan to Godwine, and 'D' presents the earls as 'ready to do battle against the king', but in fact they did not, and even 'D' records the dwindling of Godwine's support during the month of September and the transfer of Harold's thegns, at least, to the king's allegiance. After the exile of the family in late September, all that Ealdred of Worcester (a supporter of Godwine) dared do was allow the escape of Earl Harold via Bristol to Ireland, and even that seems to have earned him the king's disfavour.[35]

The events of 1052 show the limitations of Godwine's influence. *Domesday Book* reveals the extent of the family's landholdings both in Wessex proper and in the Western Shires.[36] Yet when Harold landed at Porlock, Som, in the summer of 1052, 'there was a great force gathered there to oppose him', and his father met with similar opposition both in the Isle of Wight and at Portland, Dorset.[37] Once the combined fleets began to move east into the ancestral lands of the family, the picture changed; 'all the men of Kent, and all the *butsecarles* from the district of Hastings, and from the region round about there by the sea-coast and all Essex and Surrey and much else beside' declared for the earls.[38] Yet the king still had a force of 50 ships waiting for them at London, and a land-army augmented by the men of Earls Leofric and Siward.[39] Once again, as in 1051, the decisive factor was the unwillingness on either side to push the confrontation to the limit: 'it was hateful to almost all of them to fight against men of their own race, for there was little else that was worth anything apart from Englishmen on either side'.[40]

In 1052, the councillors prevailed upon the king to back down. Godwine was allowed to clear himself of all charges, he and his sons were reinstated, the king took back his wife (whom he had repudiated the previous year) and 'they outlawed all the Frenchmen who had promoted injustices and passed unjust judgements and given bad counsel in this country'. The *Chronicle* specifically names Archbishop Robert, Ulf of Dorchester-on-Thames, and William, who had received Spearhafoc's bishopric of London.[41] Yet even now the opponents cannot be split into 'French' versus 'English', nor did the king's supporters lose out entirely. The reinstatement of Godwine and Harold meant the demotion of Earls Odda and Ælfgar, but Odda kept his title and was probably compensated with an earldom in Worcestershire; as for Ælfgar, he received East Anglia once again when Harold succeeded to Wessex on Godwine's death in 1053. The archbishopric went to Stigand, to be held in plurality with Winchester.[42] He is often presented as an adherent of Godwine but his connections seem rather to have been with the recently-deceased Emma, and he is perhaps best regarded as a royal clerk, as was Wulfwig who received Ulf's bishopric of Dorchester-on-Thames; William, who had also been a royal clerk, was recalled to the see of London. Another Norman clerk who remained in the king's entourage was his kinsman Osbern, to whom William I gave the bishopric of Exeter.[43] As for the laymen, Earl Ralph not only retained his own earldom but added that of Swein Godwineson in Herefordshire. Osbern Pentecost was expelled, but got safe passage from Leofric of Mercia to Scotland.[44] Robert fitzWimarc remained undisturbed at Clavering, Essex, as did his son-in-law Richard fitzScrob, of Richard's Castle, Herefords.[45]

The King's Government

Edward has been criticized for abolishing the heregeld and disbanding the lithesmen, but the 14 ships and their crews dismissed in 1050 and 1051 were only a small part of the royal fleet, and one perhaps too closely linked to Godwine.[46] The English ship-levy was perhaps more reliable and certainly larger. In 1049 the West Saxon contingent contained 42 ships, and there were ships from Mercia too, as well as those which remained with the king.[47] In 1052 Edward was able to deploy 40 warships (*snacca*) at Sandwich, commanded by Earls Ralph and Odda.[48] Like the ships of the lithesmen, these vessels seem to have been based at London for they returned there after their unsuccessful attempt to intercept Earl Godwine, 'so that other earls and other oarsmen (*hasæton*) should be appointed to them'.[49] Presumably they were among the 50 ships with which Edward confronted Godwine at London later in the year.

The home-base of the Mercian contingent is never mentioned, but probably lay in the Severn region, perhaps at Bristol, where Earl Swein maintained a vessel, used by his brother Harold in his escape to Ireland in 1051. It was from Bristol too that Harold led the *sciphere* around the coasts of Wales from south to north to harry Gruffudd ap Llewelyn in 1063.[50] Perhaps it was for a ship-base there that the city of Gloucester, in 1066, had to supply '36 measures (*dicras*) of iron, and 100 iron rods, drawn out, as nails for the king's ships'.[51]

Other English towns and sea-ports provided vessels for the royal fleet; Maldon, in Essex, had to build a ship as part of its customary payments to the king.[52] They could also contribute to the manning of vessels; the burgesses of Warwick had to provide the king with either four boatmen (*batsueins*) or £4 in pennies, the inhabitants of Malmesbury contributed 20s 'to provision the boatmen (*buzecarles*)' and each house in Colchester paid 6d a year 'to provision the king's stipendiaries (*soldariorum regis*) on expeditions by land and sea' (a total sum of £15.5s.3d per annum).[53] The burgesses of Lewes also rendered 20s, for 'those who had charge of the arms in the ships', and the burgesses of Leicester owed four horses to carry arms 'or whatever else is required' to London.[54]

Edward seems to have made special arrangements with the sea-ports along the south-eastern coast, which prefigure the later organization of the Cinque Ports.[55] By 1066, Dover owed 20 ships, each with 21 men, for 15 days service each year; Sandwich owed the same service as Dover, and Romney owed unspecified 'service at sea'.[56] Such ships were manned by *butsecarles* ('boatmen'); those of Hastings are mentioned in 1052, as are the ships of Pevensey, Dungeness, Romney, Hythe, Folkestone, Dover and Sandwich.[57] In 1052 the *butsecarles* of the south-east supported Earl Godwine against the king, but were less enthusiastic about assisting Tostig against his brother, King Harold in 1066; Tostig did indeed take some of the *butsecarles* of Sandwich with him when he sailed north to raid in Lindsey ('some willingly and some unwillingly') but they deserted him after his encounter with Earl Edwin, and he had only 12 *snacca* on his arrival in Scotland. Their temporary defection does not seem to have hampered Harold, who assembled at Sandwich 'a shipfyrd and a landfyrd larger than any king had assembled before in this country'.[58] He maintained this force in arms for nearly four months (it was stood down on 8 September), a formidable feat for a medieval commander.[59]

As for the abolition of the heregeld, what Edward lost in cash he probably gained in popularity, for it was clearly a heavy burden; 'it always came before other gelds which were variously paid, and it oppressed people in many ways'.[60] The 'other gelds' presumably continued to be levied. One of them was perhaps ship-scot, for one of William I's writs refers back to 'the time in King Edward's reign when the geld was taken to build ships' (*ad navigium faciendum*), and in 1066 the borough of Stamford, Lincs, paid geld for 12½ hundreds *in exercitum et navigio* as well as for 'Danegeld'.[61] References to other gelds are rare, but before 1066 Archbishop Stigand had full rights ('sake and soke') over his urban property at Guildford, Surrey, 'except when the common geld is laid on the town, which no-one can escape' (*nisi commune geldum in villa venerit unde nullum evadat*).[62] The 12 lawmen of Stamford likewise had full rights over their properties 'except for geld' and some other royal dues.[63] In Hertford too, there was property which rendered no customary dues except the king's geld 'when it was collected'.[64] In Berkshire the 'common geld' was assessed at 7d on the hide, half due 'before Christmas' and the remainder at Pentecost.[65] Whether geld was already the annual imposition it became after 1066 is impossible to say, but the entries for Guildford and Hertford cited above suggest not.

Geld was assessed on the hide and the fact that the hidage of an estate could vary as between the king's service and that of the lord suggests a certain sophistication in that assessment.[66] No documentation survives from the pre-Conquest period, though the recording of pre- as well as post-Conquest hidages in *Domesday Book* (regularly in the south-east) suggests that at least some pre-Conquest lists of collection or assessment (or both) existed in 1086.[67] What they might have been like is suggested by the two geld-related documents which survive from the reign of William I, the Northamptonshire Geld Roll and the Geld Rolls for the south-western shires preserved in Exon Domesday.[68]

The fact that the Northamptonshire Geld Roll is written in English might suggest that its form goes back to pre-Conquest models.[69] It relates to a geld taken between 1075 and 1083.[70] It seems to be concerned with assessment rather than collection, giving for each hundred the total hidage, the hidage in demesne, the hidage assessed to geld (*gewered*), the hidage which is exempt (*unwered*) or from which no geld has been received (*ne com nam peni*) and the hidage which is 'waste' (unaccounted for).[71]

The Geld Rolls for the south-western shires (Wiltshire, Dorset, Somerset, Devon and Cornwall) relate to the actual collection of a 6s geld, probably in 1086.[72] Like the 'common geld' of the Berkshire custumal, it was due in two instalments, the later described as 'after Easter' or 'after the feast of St Mary'; the earlier term was probably some time in September.[73] The collectors worked in groups of four, whether four to each hundred or four to each shire is unclear.[74] In Devon they received the geld from one hide (6s) for their trouble. Some are named; *Celwi* (Ceolwig), a collector for Chippenham Hundred, Wilts, might be the Ceolwine (*Celeinus*) who held 3½ virgates of demesne at the royal manor of Chippenham, by the grant of Eadric the pre-Conquest sheriff of Wiltshire.[75] If so, he was perhaps a sheriff's officer. Florence Harmer suggested that geld was collected by the officials of the shire and hundred and the hundredmen appear as collectors in Devon and perhaps Cornwall.[76] In Wiltshire they are simply *collectores* or *congregatores* (the latter occur also in Dorset) but in Somerset they appear as *fegadri* or *fegundri*, which may be a Latinization of their vernacular name.[77]

Another group of officers, the *portatores*, appear in Somerset and Devon. In Somerset they received expenses for providing waggons, strongboxes, wax (for seals) and a scribe.[78] The Devon *portatores*, William the usher (*hostiarius*) a royal sergeant, and Ralph de la Pommeraye a substantial local landowner, carried the geld to 'the king's treasury at Winchester' (*ad thesaurum regis Wintonie*).[79] Here the written accounts of the geld collectors were checked by a body of officials described as 'the king's barons' *barones regis*.[80]

This is (to the best of my knowledge) the earliest reference to a treasury at Winchester, usually assumed to date back at least to the time of Cnut.[81] Winchester was one of the chief residences of the pre-Conquest kings. Its walls had deterred even Swein Forkbeard's Vikings and it was the site of three royal monasteries and a royal palace.[82] Its significance as an administrative centre is highlighted by the number of royal officials who, in 1086 and afterwards, held property in the city and the surrounding shires. They are described in Domesday as 'king's thegns' (*taini regis*) or (if they have continental names) 'king's sergeants' (*servientes regis*).[83] They are not the king's thegns of Cnut's Secular Code, great lords who owed half an earl's wergeld, but men of middling rank, dignified by being in the king's service.[84] Some held before 1066: Henry the treasurer and Theodoric the king's cook (Winchester), Wulfgeat the huntsman and his son Cola the huntsman (Hampshire, Berkshire and Wiltshire), Edwin the huntsman and Godwine the falconer (Hampshire), Oda the treasurer and Godwine the reeve (Dorset).[85]

One of the earliest references to the palace at Winchester occurs in the *Chronicle*'s account of Earl Godwine's death; he collapsed as he was dining with the king, and was carried by his sons into the king's private chamber (*into þæs kinges bure, in regis cameram*).[86] The chamber or 'bower' (*bur*) was the private part of a residence, where the lord's treasure and personal property was kept in the charge of chamberlains (*burþegnas, camerarii, cubicularii*).[87] An apocryphal story tells of thefts from a strong-box, carelessly left unlocked, which were observed by the apparently-sleeping Edward; he allowed the thief two bites at the cherry, but when he returned for the third time warned him of the imminent approach of Hugolin the chamberlain.[88] Hugolin or Hugo was a real person who attests Edward's charters as *camerarius* or *cubicularius* in the period 1060–2, and held land in Berkshire, Oxfordshire and Warwickshire.[89] The post-Conquest Ramsey Chronicle associates him with the keeping of documents in the king's *gazophilacium* ('treasury'), perhaps identical with the royal *haligdom*, the repository of both relics and charters.[90]

A strong-box in the care of a royal chamberlain might meet the daily needs of the itinerant king, but for the assessment, collection and storage of geld (and especially of heregeld) something more elaborate was required. V. H. Galbraith observed that 'the Anglo-Saxon financial system, which collected the Danegeld, was not run from a box under the bed', and D. M. Metcalf, having calculated the size of the box required, remarked 'Some box, some bed'.[91] The south-western Geld Rolls suggest a body of officials who received cash and checked accounts, functions performed in the twelfth century by the Lower Exchequer with its chamberlains and clerks.[92] Similar duties could have been performed by the Confessor's chamberlains, and in fact two pre-Conquest 'treasurers' are known: Henry, who held land in Winchester before 1066 and received lands in Hampshire from William I, and Oda who held half a hide at Wimborne Minster, Dorset.[93]

Other royal officials appear among the witnesses to Edward's charters. It is from the 1050s that Robert fitzWimarc rises to prominence as staller, and with him Ralph the staller, born in Norfolk of an English mother and a Breton father.[94] The most interesting figure, however, is the royal priest Regenbald, who was perhaps a Lotharingian. He attests charters between 1050 and 1065, once as *regis sigillarius* (keeper of the seal) and once as *regis cancellarius* (chancellor), and the king granted him the rights of a diocesan bishop. His presence (and that of other priests of continental origin) in the king's household might help to explain the continental influences seen in the drafting of some of Edward's charters.[95]

The duty of the *sigillarius* was to keep the king's seal. Three of the surviving original writs of Edward bear (or bore) wax impressions of the double-sided royal seal.[96] On each face was an image of the king in majesty, with the inscription '+SIGILLUM EADVVARDI ANGLORUM BASILEI'. The design probably dates from the 1050s, and the same 'majesty' portrait is found on some contemporary coins; it may be related to the development of ceremonial 'crown-wearings' at the major feasts, themselves based on German imperial models.[97] The seal's design is certainly based on that of the German Emperors, though (like the seals of the French kings) this was single-sided and impressed on the face of the document. Edward's seal was suspended on a strip cut from the bottom of the parchment (the sealing-tag); the writ could be folded and tied with a wrapping-tie (also cut from the bottom of the parchment) in such a way that the pendant seal was still displayed. It has been suggested that the double-sided seal was first used to authenticate the writs of Cnut, and represented his dual role as king both of the English and the Danes, but in the absence of direct evidence this must remain conjectural.[98]

A United Kingdom?

In 1065, Edward was faced with a revolt in Northumbria. Though widely regarded as a sign of local 'separatism' within an imperfectly united realm, this was clearly directed neither against Edward nor the rule of Wessex.[99] The target was Earl Tostig. His unpopularity probably stemmed from the levels of tax demanded, but the fact that the northerners demanded the renewal of 'the laws of Cnut' suggests that he also tried to iron out the local differences between the Danelaw and the rest of England, recognized in the legislation of Edgar and Æthelred II.[100]

It was Harold who negotiated the agreement in which the king effectively gave way to the northerners' demands. Their primary stipulation was the outlawry of Tostig, and the promotion of Morcar, Earl Ælfgar's younger son, to his place. It is clear from the *Vita Edwardi* that Edward was most unwilling to grant this, and the implication is that Harold was the prime mover against his brother; indeed Tostig is said to have accused him of inciting the northerners against him.[101] There may have been some substance to this charge, for Morcar was Harold's brother-in-law. It has been assumed that Morcar was an outsider in the north, chosen as a compromise candidate acceptable both to the Anglo-Scandinavians of York and the English of Bamburgh.[102] The *Vita Edwardi*, however, presents him and his brother Earl Edwin as old enemies of Tostig, and they may have kinsmen and friends in the north. Edwin as well as Morcar was one of the major landholders in Yorkshire and Lincolnshire in 1066, and their mother Ælfgifu was arguably the grand-niece of an earlier Northumbrian ealdorman and daughter of Morcar, one of the leading northern magnates murdered in 1015.[103] By supporting Morcar, then, Harold aligned himself with both Mercians and Northumbrians, a political gain which overode any familial feelings for a brother whose rule had led to disaster in the north. Tostig withdrew in dudgeon to Flanders, returning in 1066 to harry both his brother and the Mercian earls; he was killed, with Harald Hardrada, at the battle of Stamford Bridge.

Perhaps because of the adulation lavished upon them by the *Vita Edwardi* and latterly by E. A. Freeman (in his great *History of the Norman Conquest of England*), Godwine and Harold have come to be regarded as the evil genii of the house of Wessex and the English kingship. T. J. Oleson wrote scathingly that 'the ambitions of this house, which stopped at nothing, explain the turbulence of much of the Confessor's reign and the failure of the Anglo-Saxon monarchy to maintain itself against foreign powers'.[104] Robin Fleming too speaks of 'disturbing hints of the overweening power of Cnut's most famous creation, Earl Godwine, and of the weakness of the Dane's eventual successor' and sees Edward in his latter years as 'a weak king, pushed and bullied by a family of highly-competent and slightly unscrupulous earls'.[105] Frank Barlow, who takes a more positive view of the king's abilities ('a realist, Edward probably accepted . . . a situation which he could not greatly change') nevertheless observes that 'the rule of Edith, Harold and Tostig brought the country to ruin'.[106]

These are the kind of judgements passed upon Æthelred II, though in this case with little contemporary support. Even the 'C' text of the *Chronicle*, which is hostile to Godwine's kin, includes a eulogy of Harold in its commemorative verse on Edward: 'a noble earl who all the time had loyally followed his lord's commands with words and deeds, neglecting nothing that met the needs of the people's king'.[107] Harold was a popular choice for the kingship. There is no sign in 1066 of the general loss of nerve so apparent at the end of Æthelred II's reign. Apart from Tostig, whose grievances we have already observed, there was no opposition to Harold in England, and no disputed election such as occurred in 975 and 1035.[108] His maintenance of the fyrd, both on sea and land, during the summer and autumn of 1066 indicates his ability to command the loyalty of the English, as well as his military skill.[109] The earls of Mercia and Northumbria were his brothers-in-law, and he took special care after his coronation to allay any reservations among the northerners.[110] His spectacular victory at Stamford Bridge won him unquestioning support; the 'D' *Chronicle*, not noticeably favourable to his house, describes him as 'Harold our king' in its account of the engagement.

It is worth remembering what earls could not do. They could not mint their own coinage, neither could they issue charters.[111] Nor could they hold their own courts, though they were entitled to a third share of the revenues from borough, shire and hundred courts in their respective earldoms.[112] But there was no tier of local administration higher than the shire, whose importance is shown by the coincidence of the shired area of the kingdom with the effective limits of royal power. Neither Northumberland nor Durham were shired by the West Saxon kings, which is why William I's commissioners were unable to survey the region north of the Tees in 1085–6; not only were the natives hostile, but the local institutions through which the commissioners operated (created by the West Saxon rulers) did not exist there.

The suitors of the shire-court (the *meliores*, 'better men') were the landholders prominent in the locality, who are addressed in the king's writs along with the earl, the bishop and the sheriff. A full study of such communities is lacking, but preliminary investigation suggests that their members were primarily king's men. A rare glimpse of Godwine as earl of Wessex is provided by a vernacular notification recording an agreement concluded at Exeter before the shire-court of Devon, some of whose members are named as witnesses. These included two royal kinsmen, Odda of Deerhurst (later earl of the western Shires during Godwine's exile), and Ordgar, patron of Tavistock Abbey, both of them wealthy landholders, with a group of men of more modest standing several of whom are nevertheless found (like Odda and Ordgar) among the witnesses to royal charters.[113] A similar mix existed in the shire-community of Kent as it appears in *Domesday Book*, when its members included men like Æthelnoth *cild* of Canterbury and Wulfweard white, royal officials with lands spread over several shires, and lesser landholders whose interests were confined to Kent, but who were nevertheless king's men.[114]

Godwine and his sons may have been collectively richer than the king, but their earldoms were not provincial governorships. Royal control of the local institutions meant that earldoms did not develop into principalities on the lines of the French duchies. Nor is there any indication of any desire that they should; the English, as William of Poitiers remarked, 'were accustomed to serve a king and wished only for a king to be their lord'.[115] It was not an independent Wessex but the kingship of the English at which Harold aimed. As king, he had all the powers and privileges of Edward plus his own personal wealth in land and men, which effectively doubled the size of the royal estates. The imbalance of wealth between king and earls was now in the former's favour. In the event this prize fell into the hands of his Norman successors, whose fortune it was to wield 'the formidable authority of the royal majesty which we stress as worthy of attention for its continual and beneficial pre-eminence over the laws'.[116]

NOTES

1 Through a Glass Darkly: The Origins of English Kingship

1. Diana Greenway (ed.), *Henry, Archdeacon of Huntingdon, 'Historia Anglorum': The History of the English People* (Oxford, 1996), pp. 16–17 and see pp. lx–lxi.
2. For the archaeology see Martin Welch, *Anglo-Saxon England* (London, 1992), and the review by John Hines, *Medieval Archaeology*, 37 (1993), 314–5. For the historical sources, see D. N. Dumville, 'Sub-Roman Britain: History and Legend', *History*, 62 (1977), 173–92; Barbara Yorke, 'Fact or fiction? the written evidence for the fifth and sixth centuries AD', *ASSAH*, 6 (1993), 45–50.
3. Unless otherwise stated, all references to the *Anglo-Saxon Chronicle* (cited, by year, as *ASC*) are to Dorothy Whitelock, D. C. Douglas and Susie I. Tucker (eds), *The Anglo-Saxon Chronicle: a Revised Translation*, 2nd edn (London, 1965). Bede is cited (as *HE*) in the edition of Bertram Colgrave and R. A. B. Mynors (eds), *Bede's Ecclesiastical History of the English People* (Oxford, 1969).
4. Latin text and translation in John Morris (ed.), *Nennius: British History and the Welsh Annals* (Chichester, 1980) and see D. N. Dumville, 'The Historical Value of the *Historia Brittonum*', *Arthurian Literature*, 6 (1986), 1–59. The *Historia Brittonum* is cited as *HB*.
5. Michael Winterbottom (ed.), *Gildas: The Ruin of Britain and Other Works* (Chichester, 1978); see M. Lapidge and D. N. Dumville (eds), *Gildas: New Approaches* (Woodbridge, 1984); Patrick Sims-Williams, 'Gildas and the Anglo-Saxons', *Cambridge Medieval Celtic Studies*, 6 (1983), 1–30. It has recently been argued that Gildas wrote in the last quarter of the fifth century (Nicholas Higham, *The English Conquest: Gildas and Britain in the Fifth Century* (Manchester, 1994) pp. 118–45).
6. J. M. Kemble, *The Saxons in England* (London, 1849) i, p. 22.
7. Patrick Sims-Williams, 'The Settlement of England in Bede and the *Chronicle*', *ASE*, 12 (1983), 1–41.
8. The West Saxon *adventus* has most recently been recalibrated by D. N. Dumville ('The West Saxon Genealogical Regnal List and the Chronology of early Wessex', *Peritia*, 4 (1985), 21–66), who calculates that the arrival of Cerdic and Cynric was originally placed in 532, and the beginning of Cerdic's reign in 538. See also Kenneth Harrison, *The Framework of Anglo-Saxon History to AD 900* (Cambridge, 1976), pp. 120–41; Barbara Yorke, *Kings and Kingdoms of Early Anglo-Saxon England* (London, 1990), pp. 130–2; Martin Welch, 'The Kingdom of the South Saxons: The Origins', in *Origins*, pp. 81–2.

9. Sims-Williams, 'The Settlement of England in Bede and the *Chronicle*', 27.
10. The *Anglo-Saxon Chronicle* was put together in Wessex, in Alfred's reign (871–99) when the West Saxon kings ruled both Kent and Sussex. The assertion that Stuf and Wihtgar were 'kinsmen' of Cerdic and Cynric may be related to the advertised ancestry of Alfred. Although (like all the West Saxon kings) he claimed descent from Cerdic, his mother was allegedly a descendant of Stuf and Wihtgar, described as Jutes by the king's biographer Asser (Simon Keynes and Michael Lapidge, *Alfred the Great* (Harmondsworth, 1983), p. 68 and note 8).
11. Sims-Williams, 'The Settlement of England in Bede and the *Chronicle*', 5–26.
12. *HE* i, 15; ii, 5.
13. Bede makes Oeric's son Ohta the father of Iurminric and grandfather of Æthelberht. In the eighth-century Kentish royal genealogy, Oisc and Ohta change places: Oisc is the son of Ohta and father of Iurminric (D. P. Kirby, *The Earliest English Kings* (London, 1991), p. 15). The same order is found in the *Historia Brittonum* (*HB* chapters 56, 58; Nicholas Brooks, 'The Creation and Early Structure of the Kingdom of Kent', in *Origins*, pp. 61–4).
14. *HE* i, 15; ii, 5; Brooks, 'The Creation and early Structure of the Kingdom of Kent', pp. 68–9. The fact that the Kentish pedigree appears in two parts in the *Historia Ecclesiastica* may in itself suggest the linking together of two originally separate traditions.
15. The Anglian collection was put together in Mercia in 796, but probably derives from a Northumbrian collection made between 765 and 774; it contains the royal genealogies of Bernicia, Deira, Mercia, Lindsey, Kent, East Anglia and Wessex, with regnal lists for Northumbria and Mercia (D. N. Dumville, 'The Anglian Collection of Royal Genealogies and Regnal Lists', *ASE*, 5 (1976), 23–50). For the West Saxon collection, see Kenneth Sisam, 'Anglo-Saxon Royal Genealogies', *Proceedings of the British Academy*, 39 (1953), 287–348; D. N. Dumville, 'The West Saxon Genealogical Regnal List: Manuscripts and Texts', *Anglia*, 104 (1986), 1–32; *idem*, 'The West Saxon Genealogical Regnal List and the Chronology of early Wessex', 21–66. Pedigrees for individual West Saxon rulers, often at variance both with those in the Anglian collection and with the West Saxon genealogical regnal list, appear in the *Chronicle* (Yorke, *Kings and Kingdoms*, pp. 128–9). For a discussion of the East Saxon material, see Barbara Yorke, 'The Kingdom of the East Saxons', *ASE*, 14 (1985), 1–36.
16. D. N. Dumville, 'Kingship, Genealogies and Regnal Lists', in P. H. Sawyer and I. N. Wood (eds), *Early Medieval Kingship* (Leeds, 1977), pp. 72–104.
17. Stenton, *ASE*, 39 and see note 87 below.
18. *HE* i, 15; Sims-Williams, 'The Settlement of England in Bede and the *Chronicle*', 21.
19. Bede (*HE* iii, 1) describes how 'all those who compute the dates of kings' agreed to delete the reigns of Edwin's apostate successors in Bernicia and Deira and assign the year in question to the reign of the next king, Oswald. Thus the only contemporary reference to the compilation of king-lists shows them being manipulated for ideological purposes (Dumville, 'Kingship, Genealogies and Regnal Lists', 81, 97).

20. Lewis Thorpe (trans.), *Gregory of Tours, History of the Franks* (Harmondsworth, 1974), pp. 219, 513; *HE* i, 25. The marriage took place before the death of Bertha's mother Ingoberg in 588–9, but, since Bertha must have been born between 561 and 568, probably not before the late 570s (Brooks, 'The Creation and Early Structure of the Kingdom of Kent', p. 66 and footnotes 60, 62, p. 253).

21. Brooks, 'The Creation and Early Structure of the Kingdom of Kent', p. 64. All the recorded seventh-century names containing the first element *Irmin-*, *Iurmin-* belong to members of the Kentish royal line, except for that of Iurminburg, second wife of King Ecgfrith of Northumbria, whose origins are unknown. Æthelberht's son Eadbald married Ymme (Emma), daughter of Erchinoald, mayor of the palace of Neustria (I. N. Wood, 'Frankish Hegemony in England', in M. O. Carver (ed.), *The Age of Sutton Hoo* (Woodbridge, 1992), pp. 239–40). The name of her son, Eorcenberht, preserves the first element (*Erchin-*, *Eorcen-*) of that of her father.

22. Sonia Chadwick Hawkes, 'Anglo-Saxon Kent, *c.* 425–725', in P. E. Leach (ed.), *Archaeology in Kent to AD 1500*, CBA Research Report, 48 (1982), pp. 65–78.

23. I. N. Wood, 'The Franks and Sutton Hoo', in Ian Wood and Niels Lund (eds), *People and Places in Northern Europe, 500–1600* (Woodbridge, 1991), pp. 1–14; *idem*, 'Frankish Hegemony in England', pp. 235–41 (but cf Brooks, 'The Creation and Early Structure of the Kingdom of Kent', p. 66 and footnote 62, p. 253).

24. *HE* ii, 15; Dumville, 'The Anglian Collection', pp. 31, 33–4, 37.

25. M. O. Carver, 'The Anglo-Saxon Cemetery at Sutton Hoo: An Interim Report', in Carver (ed.), *The Age of Sutton Hoo*, pp. 343–71; but see also Kirby, *Earliest English Kings*, p. 66. It has been proposed that the Sutton Hoo burials commemorate the East Saxon, rather than the East Anglian kings (Michael Parker Pearson, Robert van de Noort and Alex Woolf, 'Three Men and a Boat: Sutton Hoo and the East Saxon Kingdom', *ASE*, 22 (1993), 27–50).

26. Yorke, *Kings and Kingdoms*, p. 9.

27. Martin Carver, 'Kingship and Material Culture in Early Anglo-Saxon East Anglia', in *Origins*, pp. 141–58, esp. pp. 149–52. The implications of a burgeoning elite for the origins of kingship are not unambiguous, for the emergence of a rich and powerful aristocracy may hamper rather than enhance royal power (Guy Halsall, 'Social Change around AD 600: An Austrasian Perspective', in Carver (ed.), *The Age of Sutton Hoo*, pp. 265–78).

28. C. J. Arnold, *The Archaeology of Early Anglo-Saxon England* (London and New York, 1988), pp. 163–93; Steven Bassett, 'In Search of the Origins of Anglo-Saxon Kingdoms', in *Origins*, pp. 23–4.

29. Apart from Sutton Hoo and the Wuffingas, Benty Grange (Derbys) has been linked with the unknown rulers of the *Pecsætan*, a people still distinct in the seventh century though soon to be absorbed by the Mercians (Welch, *Anglo-Saxon England*, pp. 88–96). Caenby, Lincs, may be the grave of one of the kings of Lindsey (Bruce Eagles, 'Lindsey', in *Origins*, p. 210).

30. Dumville, 'Kingship, Genealogies and Regnal Lists', p. 91; Christopher Scull, 'Before Sutton Hoo: Structures of Power and Society in Early East Anglia', in Carver (ed.), *The Age of Sutton Hoo*, p. 5.

31. For the problems of assessing 'wealth' and its relation to 'status', see Edward James, 'Burial and Status in the Early Medieval West', *TRHS* fifth series, 39 (1989), 23–40; Arnold, *An Archaeology of the Early Anglo-Saxon Kingdoms*, pp. 142–93. The consensus seems to accept a relationship, albeit rarely straightforward, between grave-goods, wealth and status, but what this might imply for the origins of kingship is still in dispute.

32. Scull, 'Before Sutton Hoo', pp. 8–10, 15–20. For early Welsh society, see Wendy Davies, *Wales in the Early Middle Ages* (Leicester, 1982), pp. 59–71.

33. *HE* i, 15.

34. Susan Reynolds, *Fiefs and Vassals* (Oxford, 1994), pp. 25–6.

35. James Campbell, 'Bede's *Reges* and *Principes*', in *Essays in Anglo-Saxon History* (London, 1986), pp. 86–7.

36. *HE*, v, 23, and see Kirby, *Earliest English Kings*, pp. 5–7. There were two kingdoms in Northumbria, Bernicia in the north and Deira in the south.

37. See note 1 above. It was in the sixteenth century that the term Heptarchy was first coined for the Seven Kingdoms.

38. The 'people who dwell west of the River Severn' are probably the Magonsæte (Kirby, *Earliest English Kings*, pp. 5–7; Patrick Sims-Williams, *Religion and Literature in Western England, 600–800* (Oxford, 1990), pp. 40–3; but see also Kate Pretty, 'Defining the Magonsæte', in *Origins*, pp. 171–83). The Hwicce dwelt in the area now divided between Worcestershire, Gloucestershire and south Warwickshire, and the *Lindisfare* are the people of Lindsey.

39. They might include the *Hæstingas* (*gens hestingorum*) recorded in 771 (*HR*, 771, *EHD* i, 243 and see Peter Drewett, David Rudling and Mark Gardiner, *The South-east to AD 1000* (London, 1988), p. 276; Martin Welch, 'The Kingdom of the South Saxons: The Origins', in *Origins*, pp. 75–83). The land of the *Hæstingas* was still distinct in the eleventh century (*ASC* 'D', 1011, 1049).

40. For the text and its transmission, see D. N. Dumville 'The Tribal Hidage: an Introduction to its Texts and their Transmission', in *Origins*, pp. 225–30 and for the date, *idem*, 'Essex, Middle Anglia and the Expansion of Mercia', in *Origins*, pp. 129–33. See also Chapter 4 below.

41. The *Tribal Hidage* does not include the Northumbrian kingdoms of Deira and Bernicia. This is usually explained by assuming that it is a Mercian document, and that Deira and Bernicia were not under Mercian control. However their non-appearance might imply a Northumbrian provenance for the *Tribal Hidage*, since 'an early medieval king did not impose tribute on his own people' (Nicholas Brooks, 'The Formation of the Mercian Kingdom', in *Origins*, pp. 159, pp. 167–8). For the hide, see Chapter 4 below.

42. Margaret Gelling, 'The Early History of Western Mercia', *Origins*, pp. 183–201; see also note 38 above.

43. Dumville, 'Essex, Middle Anglia and the Expansion of Mercia', p. 129; Wendy Davies and Hayo Vierck, 'The Contexts of the Tribal Hidage: Social Aggregates and Settlement Patterns', *Frümittelalterliche Studien*, 8 (1974), 223–93.

44. *HE* iii, 20; iv, 6, 19; Pauline Stafford, *The East Midlands in the Early Middle Ages* (Leicester, 1985), pp. 31–3.

45. *HE* iv, 19 (Ely); v, 19 (Oundle); ii, 14, iii, 24 (*Loidis*). *Loidis* was part of the British kingdom of Elmet (the *Elmed sætna* of the *Tribal Hidage*, assessed at 600 hides).

46. *HE* iii, 21.

47. Dumville, 'Essex, Middle Anglia and the Expansion of Mercia', pp. 130–34.

48. Dumville, 'Essex, Middle Anglia and the Expansion of Mercia', pp. 122–40 (the quotation is on page 130); see also Wendy Davies, 'Middle Anglia and the Middle Angles', *Midland History*, 2 (1973–4), 18–20.

49. Yorke, *Kings and Kingdoms*, p. 157.

50. James Campbell, 'The End of Roman Britain' in James Campbell (ed.), *The Anglo-Saxons* (Oxford, 1982), pp. 16–7; A. S. Esmonde Cleary, *The Ending of Roman Britain* (London, 1989), pp. 172–87.

51. Gildas, ed. Winterbottom, pp. 29–33, 99–102; Davies, *Wales in the Early Middle Ages*, pp. 92–102; 110. For Vortipor's memorial stone, see Davies, *loc. cit.*, p. 96; James Campbell, 'The Lost Centuries: 400–600', in Campbell (ed.), *The Anglo-Saxons*, pp. 21–2.

52. Kent, Deira, Bernicia and Lindsey.

53. For Wroxeter, see Pretty, 'Defining the *Magonsæte*', pp. 171–83, Gelling, 'The Early History of Western Mercia', pp. 186–7; for Chichester, see M. G. Welch, *Early Anglo-Saxon Sussex*, BAR British series, 112 (1983), 247–50. This is not, of course, to argue that urban institutions survived at either of these centres, nor at any other.

54. Barry Cunliffe, *Wessex to AD 1000* (London, 1993), pp. 281–2.

55. For St Albans, see Keith Bailey, 'The Middle Saxons', in *Origins*, pp. 109–10; of particular significance is Bede's statement that the church and cult of the British martyr had continued *usque ad hanc diem* (*HE* i, 7), for the medieval settlement grew round the *martyrium*, leaving the Romano-British town abandoned (Guy de la Bedoyere, *Roman Towns in Britain* (London, 1992), p. 126). For Wighton and Burgh Castle, see Scull, 'Before Sutton Hoo', pp. 14–15; and for Great Chesterford, see Bassett, 'In Search of the Origins of Anglo-Saxon Kingdoms', pp. 25–6.

56. Edward James, 'Cemeteries and the Problem of Frankish Settlement in Gaul', in P. H. Sawyer (ed.), *Names, Words and Graves: Early Medieval Settlement* (Leeds, 1979), pp. 55–89.

57. Yorke, *Kings and Kingdoms*, pp. 6–7; Drewett, Rudling and Gardiner, *The South-east to AD 1000*, pp. 251–2, 265.

58. Heinrich Härke, 'Changing Symbols in a Changing Society: The Anglo-Saxon Weapon Burial Rite in the Seventh Century', in Carver (ed.), *The Age of Sutton Hoo*, pp. 149–65, esp. pp. 154–5, 163–4; for the Gallo-Romans, see Patrick J. Geary, *Before France and Germany: The Creation and Transformation of the Merovingian World* (Oxford and New York, 1988), pp. 82–96.

59. The West Saxon dynasty goes back to Cerdic (British Ceretic) and the British name Cædwalla (Cadwallon) was born by one of the attested seventh-century kings (Kirby, *Earliest English Kings*, p. 16). The British name Caedbaed/Cædbæd occurs in the genealogy of the kings of Lindsey (Dumville, 'The Anglian Collection of Royal Genealogies', pp. 31, 33, 37). English kings might, of course, find wives from the surviving British kingdoms; Oswiu of Northumbria married Rhiainfellt, of the royal line of Rheged (*HB*, chap. 57;

D. N. Dumville, 'The Origins of Northumbria: Some Aspects of the British Background', in *Origins*, p. 220).

60. The problem of 'continuity' from Romano-Britons to English is discussed by Esmonde Cleary, *The Ending of Roman Britain*, pp. 162–205.

61. Sims-Williams, *Religion and Literature in Western England*, pp. 54–86. One such community might have dwelt at Uley, Gloucs, where a Romano-British temple to Mercury appears to have been adapted to Christian use (Ann Woodward, *Shrines and Sacrifice* (London, 1992), pp. 101–3, 112–3, 117–9).

62. James Campbell, 'Observations on the Conversion of England', in *Essays in Anglo-Saxon History*, pp. 71–3; Jane Stevenson, 'Christianity in Sixth- and Seventh-century Southumbria', in Carver (ed.), *The Age of Sutton Hoo*, pp. 185–7. See also Yorke, *Kings and Kingdoms*, pp. 6–7.

63. The minimalist approach has recently been stated by Nicholas Higham, *Rome, Britain and the Anglo-Saxons* (London, 1992), but see the review by John Hines in *Medieval Archaeology*, 37 (1993), 314–18.

64. See the discussion in Scull, 'Before Sutton Hoo', pp. 8–9.

65. *HE* i, 15, Wallace-Hadrill, *Commentary*, p. 22. The presence among the invaders of other Germanic peoples (Franks, Frisians and Scandinavians have all been detected) does not invalidate Bede's general point. He himself lists other Germanic peoples from whom the *Angli vel Saxones* 'derive their origin': Frisians, Rugians, Danes, Huns, Old Saxons and *Boruhtware* (*HE* v, 9; Wallace-Hadrill, *Commentary*, p. 181).

66. The chief centre of the Kentish kings was Canterbury (*Cantwaraburh*) 'the fortified place of the people of Kent' which must relate to its Romano-British name, *Durovernum Cantiacorum*, 'the alder-fort (or, walled town by the alder-swamp) of the *Cantiaci*' (Brooks, 'The Creation and Early Structure of the Kingdom of Kent', pp. 57–8; A. L. F. Rivet and Colin Smith, *The Place-names of Roman Britain* (London, 1979), pp. 299, 353–4).

67. *HE* i, 15; Rivet and Smith, *The Place-names of Roman Britain*, pp. 487–9.

68. *HE* iv, 13; see Barbara Yorke, 'The Jutes of Hampshire and Wight and the Origins of Wessex', in *Origins*, pp. 90–1. As late as the twelfth century, John of Worcester described the New Forest as lying *in provincia Jutarum*, and as being called *Ytene*, 'of the Jutes', in English (Benjamin Thorpe (ed.), *Florence of Worcester, Chronicon ex Chronicis* (London, 1848–9) i, p. 276; ii, pp. 44–5).

69. *HE* i, 25; Eagles, 'Lindsey', p. 210; Dumville, 'Essex, Middle Anglia and the Expansion of Mercia', p. 127.

70. Wallace-Hadrill, *Commentary*, pp. 226–8; Kirby, *Earliest English Kings*, pp. 22–3, 64–5.

71. Dumville, 'The Origins of Northumbria', pp. 213–22; for a more optimistic view of the evidence, see Nicholas Higham, *The Northern Counties to AD 1000* (London and New York, 1986), pp. 250–60.

72. Eagles, 'Lindsey', pp. 206–12; Barbara Yorke, 'Lindsey: The Lost Kingdom Found?', in A. Vince (ed.), *Pre-Viking Lindsey* (Lincoln, 1993), pp. 141, 142–3; Margaret Gelling, 'The Name Lindsey', *ASE*, 18 (1989), 31–2.

73. R. Coates, 'On some Controversy Surrounding *Gewissæ/Gewissei, Cerdic* and *Ceawlin*', *Nomina* 13 (1989–90), 1–11; see also John Blair, *Anglo-Saxon Oxfordshire* (Stroud, 1994), p. 37.

74. See Chapter 2 below.

75. Yorke, 'The Jutes of Hampshire', pp. 93–4; Heather Edwards, *The Charters of the Early West Saxon Kingdom*, BAR British series, 198 (1988), 309. For the charters of the early West Saxon kings, see S.233, 235, 237, 243–4. Aldhelm refers to Centwine simply as *rex Saxonum* (M. Lapidge and J. L. Rosier, *Aldhelm, the Poetic Works* (Woodbridge, 1985), p. 48) and Cædwalla is *rex Saxonum* in the epitaph on his tomb at Rome, cited by Bede (*HE* v, 7). Ine is *Wesseaxna kyning* in the preamble to his law-code, but this survives only as an appendix to the laws of Alfred, by whose time the royal style 'king of the West Saxons' was well-established.

76. S. 233, a charter which is not genuine as it stands but whose subscriptions have been taken from a series of contemporary records.

77. The Middle Saxons, who never had an independent existence, are probably an artificial grouping of lesser peoples comparable to the Middle Angles (Dumville, 'Essex, Middle Anglia and the Expansion of Mercia', pp. 134–4; Bailey, 'The Middle Saxons', pp. 108–22).

78. *HE* iv, 5.

79. *HE* iv, 17.

80. Kirby, *Earliest English Kings*, pp. 20–3.

81. *HE* ii, 5; *ASC*, 829 (the oldest manuscript, 'A', has *Bretwalda*, 'ruler of Britain', and the rest *Brytenwalda*, possibly 'wide-ruler').

82. S. 89, translated in *EHD* i, no. 67, pp. 458–9. The charter is attested by (among others), Æthelric 'sub-king and companion of the most glorious prince Æthelbald', who can be identified as king of the Hwicce.

83. S. 155, a charter of Offa's successor Coenwulf, dated 799, calls Offa *rex et decus Britanniae*, 'king and glory of Britain' (see also *EHD* i, no. 195, p. 779 and Chapter 3, note 4 below).

84. Patrick Wormald, 'Bede, the *Bretwaldas* and the Origin of the *gens Anglorum*', in Patrick Wormald, Donald Bullough and Roger Collins (eds), *Ideal and Reality in Frankish and Anglo-Saxon Society* (Oxford, 1983), pp. 106–11.

85. F. M. Stenton, 'The Supremacy of the Mercian Kings', *EHR*, 33 (1918), 433–52, reprinted in D. M. Stenton (ed.), *Preparatory to Anglo-Saxon England* (Oxford, 1970), pp. 48–66; Stenton, *ASE*, pp. 206–24. See also Eric John, *Reassessing Anglo-Saxon England* (Manchester, 1996), p. 54: '[Offa] preferred to make southern and eastern England part of Mercia and to rename Mercia England whether their inhabitants liked it or not'. For the date of Offa's succession, see Kirby, *Earliest English Kings*, p. 163.

86. Dumville, 'The Anglian Collection of Royal Genealogies', pp. 45–50 and see note 15 above. See also the genealogy of Offa in *ASC*, 757.

87. Sam Newton, *The Origins of Beowulf and the Pre-Viking Kingdom of East Anglia* (Woodbridge, 1993), pp. 64–71. Stories of Offa, king of Angeln, were still circulating in twelfth-century Denmark and were known to the thirteenth-century English historian, Matthew Paris. For the removal of the Angles from Angeln (now in Denmark), see *HE* i, 15; *ASC* 'E', 449 adds that Angeln 'ever after remained waste'.

88. For the notion of a 'greater Anglia', see Kirby, *Earliest English Kings*, pp. 174–5, 179; but see also Dumville, 'Kingship, Genealogies and Regnal Lists', p. 93.

89. Ian Stewart, 'The London Mint and the Coinage of Offa', in Mark Blackburn (ed.), *Anglo-Saxon Monetary History* (Leicester, 1986), pp. 39, 42.

90. *VG* chapter 1; Hugh Pagan, 'The Coinage of the East Anglian Kingdom from 825 to 870', *BNJ*, 52 (1982), 41–83; Bede refers to Rædwald of East Anglia as *rex Anglorum* (*HE* ii, 12). Compare the title *rex Saxonum* used by the early West Saxon kings (note 75 above). Popes Boniface and Honorius address Edwin of Northumbria as *rex Anglorum*, and Pope Gregory the Great uses the same title when addressing the Jutish King Æthelberht of Kent (*HE* i, 32 ii, 10, 17); both (according to Bede) exercised *imperium*. Pope Vitalian addresses the Anglian king, Oswiu of Northumbria, another *Bretwalda*, as *rex Saxonum*, but he was probably using the normal terminology on the continent, where the English were known as the Saxons of England (or Britain) as opposed to the Saxons of Saxony (Susan Reynolds, 'What do we Mean by "Anglo-Saxon" and "Anglo-Saxons"?', *Journal of British Studies*, 24 (1985), 395–414).

91. Yorke, *Kings and Kingdoms*, p. 114.

92. *WG*, chapters 5, 6, pp. 80–3.

93. Wormald, 'Bede, the *Bretwaldas* and the Origins of the *Gens Anglorum*', pp. 99–129.

94. P. H. Sawyer, *From Roman Britain to Norman England* (London, 1978), pp. 86–9; see also Esmonde Cleary: 'Continuity into Anglo-Saxon England must be sought not from Roman Britain but from post-Roman Britain' (*The ending of Roman Britain*, p. 200).

95. Scull, 'Before Sutton Hoo', p. 8.

2   The Time of the Warlords

1. James Campbell, 'Bede II', in *Essays in Anglo-Saxon History*, p. 35; D. P. Kirby, in 'Northumbria in the time of Wilfrid', *Saint Wilfrid at Hexham* (Newcastle upon Tyne, 1974), pp. 2–4.

2. Bertram Colgrave (ed.), *The Life of Bishop Wilfrid by Eddius Stephanus* (Cambridge, 1927) (cited as *VW*); for the identity of the author, see D. P. Kirby, 'Bede, Eddius and the *Life of Wilfrid*', *EHR*, 98 (1983), 101–4.

3. Yorke, *Kings and Kingdoms*, p. 138; idem, 'The Jutes of Hampshire', pp. 92–4; Blair, *Anglo-Saxon Oxfordshire*, pp. 35–41.

4. *HE* iv, 12, 15; for the translation of *strenuissimus*, see Wallace-Hadrill, *Commentary*, p. 84.

5. *VW*, chapters 40, 42. Cædwalla was helped by Bishop Wilfrid, himself at that time himself an exile in Sussex.

6. *VW*, chapter 40. Centwine's abdication may have been voluntary not forced, but his withdrawal probably enabled Cædwalla to make a bid for the kingship (Clare Stancliffe, 'Kings who Opted Out', in Wormald *et al.* (eds), *Ideal and Reality in Frankish and Anglo-Saxon Society*, pp. 154–5).

7. *HE* iv, 15. Berhthun and Andhun, who ruled in West and East Kent respectively after the death of Æthelwealh, are described as *duces regii*, 'royal military commanders'.

8. Yorke, 'The Jutes of Hampshire', pp. 93–4; Kirby, *Earliest English Kings*, p. 22. See also Chapter 1 above.

9. Yorke, 'The Jutes of Hampshire', pp. 91–3; *Kings and Kingdoms*, pp. 137–8; *ASC*, 686.

10. Kirby, *Earliest English Kings*, pp. 58–9; Yorke, *Kings and Kingdoms*, pp. 136–7; 139–40; *idem*, 'The Jutes of Hampshire', p. 93. Bede's story of how King Cenwealh quarrelled with his Frankish bishop, Agilbert and 'divided' Agilbert's see by appointing another bishop to Winchester (*HE* iii, 7) probably marks 'not the division of the see of Dorchester but its abandonment': the date seems to be the late 650s or early 660s and Dorchester-on-Thames was a Mercian see in the 670s (Blair, *Anglo-Saxon Oxfordshire*, p. 44). For Hamwic, see Chapter 4 below.

11. See below.

12. *HE* iii, 24; Brooks, 'The Formation of the Mercian Kingdom', p. 162.

13. Greenway (ed.), *Henry of Huntingdon, Historia Anglorum*, pp. 98–9. Henry may have used a lost set of early annals (Wendy Davies, 'Annals and the Origins of Mercia', in Ann Dornier (ed.), *Mercian Studies* (Leicester, 1977), pp. 1–29), but Professor Greenway argues that 'the material extra to the *Anglo-Saxon Chronicle* represents no more than Henry's amplification of the Chronicle's laconic entries' (Diana Greenway, 'Authority, Convention and Observation in Henry of Huntingdon's *Historia Anglorum*', *ANS*, 18 (1996), 109; *idem, Henry of Huntingdon, Historia Anglorum*, pp. cii–civ. See also Sims-Williams, *Religion and Literature in Western England*, p. 95). The East Anglian origins of the Mercians are accepted by Kirby, *Earliest English Kings*, p. 65, and (with reservations about the 'early annals') by Brooks, 'The Formation of the Mercian Kingdom', pp. 162–4.

14. Yorke, *Kings and Kingdoms*, p. 102 (but see also pp. 124–5). For the *Tomsæte*, first mentioned in the ninth century, see Chapter 5 below.

15. *HE* ii, 14; Sims-Williams, *Religion and Literature in Western England*, p. 25 and notes 41, 42. For the regnal lists, see Dumville, 'The Anglian Collection', pp. 29 and note 3, 33, 36, 40. Bede's interest in Cearl stemmed from his protection of the exiled Edwin, who married his daughter (see note 38 below).

16. *HE* ii, 20: *vir strenuissimus de regio genere Merciorum* (see note 4 above).

17. *HE* iii, 21; v, 24; see Chapter 1, note 46 above. Bede approved of Peada because it was in his time that the Middle Angles were converted.

18. A. Ozanne, 'The Peak-dwellers', *Medieval Archaeology*, 6 (1962), 15–52.

19. Brooks, 'The Formation of the Mercian Kingdom', pp. 168–9; Gelling, 'The Early History of Western Mercia', pp. 188–91.

20. D. W. Rollason, *The Mildryth Legend* (Leicester, 1982). The family has been studied by H. P. R. Finberg, 'The Princes of the Magonsæte', in *ECWM*, pp. 217–24, but see now Sims-Williams, *Religion and Literature in Western England*, pp. 47–53.

21. H. P. R. Finberg, 'The Princes of the Hwicce', *ECWM*, pp. 167–80; Bassett, 'In Search of the Origins of Anglo-Saxon Kingdoms', pp. 6–18; Sims-Williams, *Religion and Literature in Western England*, pp. 29–39.

22. The South Saxon king, Æthelwealh, who was baptised at Wulfhere's court, had married the Hwiccian princess Eafe (*HE* iv, 13). See below, note 71.

23. Kirby, *Earliest English Kings*, pp. 58–9, 115–16; Blair, *Anglo-Saxon Oxfordshire*, pp. 42–52.

24. *HE* ii, 20; iii, 9.

25. Oswald was, however, Edwin's nephew; his mother was Acha, daughter of Ælle of Deira, and second wife of Oswald's father Æthelfrith, king of Bernicia (*HB* chap. 63; *HE* i, 34).

26. Dumville, 'The Origins of Northumbria', pp. 213–22. Ælle is the king of Deira who appears in the story of St Gregory and the English slaves (*WG* chapters 9,12; *HE* ii, 1); for the problems of dating his reign, see Molly Miller, 'The Dates of Deira', *ASE*, 8 (1979), 41–2; 45–51.

27. *ASC*, 547; *HB* chapter 61; Kenneth Jackson, 'On the Northern British Section in Nennius', in N. K. Chadwick (ed.), *Celt and Saxon: Studies in the Early British Border* (Cambridge, 1964), pp. 27–9; Higham, *The Northern Counties to AD 1000*, pp. 257–8. See, however, the criticisms of Dumville, 'The Historical Value of the *Historia Brittonum*', pp. 14–19.

28. His first wife was Bebbe, who gave her name to Bamburgh (*HE* iii, 6; *HB* chapter 63).

29. *HE* ii, 14, 15; Wallace-Hadrill, *Commentary*, p. 254. Edwin may already have met Paulinus in East Anglia (*VG* chapter 16). For the role of Rhun, former king of Rheged, in Edwin's conversion, see Charles Phythian-Adams, *Land of the Cumbrians: a Study in British Provincial Origins* (Aldershot, 1996), pp. 56–7.

30. Bede (*HE* ii, 14) records his mass baptisms in the River Glen, near the royal vill of Yeavering in Bernicia, and in the River Swale, near Catterick in Deira; also (*HE* ii, 16) his baptism of Blæcca, *praefectus* of Lincoln and the building at Lincoln of a stone church, in which Paulinus later consecrated Honorius as archbishop of Canterbury.

31. *HE* ii, 5. Bede's insistence on the 'equality' between the Kentish and Northumbrian kings is probably based upon the equality of their respective bishops, for in 634 Pope Honorius sent *pallia* both to Paulinus, as bishop of York, and to Honorius, archbishop of Canterbury, and referred to both as 'metropolitans' (*HE* ii, 17; 18). Had this arrangement not been cancelled by the collapse of the York mission after Edwin's death, Pope Gregory the Great's plan for two archbishoprics (*HE* i, 29) would have been fulfilled; as it was York had to wait until 735 to be raised to archiepiscopal rank.

32. *HE* ii, 9; the *Chronicle* says that Edwin killed five kings in Wessex in 626. Bede's Cwichelm is presumably the Cwichelm said (in the *Chronicle*) to have died in 636, after his baptism, and also Cwichelm son of Cynegils, recorded in the *Chronicle* in 648; he may have been ruling with (or under) his father Cynegils, for the two are associated in the *Chronicle* in 614 and again in 628 (Yorke, *Kings and Kingdoms*, p. 143; but see also Kirby, *Earliest English Kings*, p. 51).

33. The speed of Eanfrith's coup suggests that he was in Cadwallon's entourage (Kirby, *Earliest English Kings*, p. 87). He was probably a son of Æthelfrith's first wife, Bebbe, whereas Oswald and Oswiu were the children of Edwin's sister Acha.

34. *HE* iii, 1, 2. The year between Edwin's death and Oswald's accession was assigned to Oswald by 'those who compute the dates of kings', in order to abolish the memories of the tyrant Cadwallon, and the apostate kings of Deira and Bernicia (*HE* iii, 1 and see Chapter 1 above).

35. For Oswald's career and subsequent cult, see Clare Stancliffe and Eric Cambridge (eds), *Oswald: Northumbrian King to European Saint* (Stamford, 1995).

36. Oswald's sanctity was first demonstrated when a horse was cured of colic by rolling upon the earth where his blood was spilt (*HE* iii, 9); a most suitable miracle for the first Englishman to become a saint.
37. *HE* iii, 11.
38. *HE* ii, 20. They were Uscfrea, Edwin's son by Æthelburh, and Yffi son of Osfrith, Edwin's elder son by his first wife Cwenburh, daughter of the Mercian king Cearl (see note 15 above). The æthelings were members of the royal dynasty; in the later period the sons and grandsons of ruling kings.
39. The site is unidentified, but was probably not Oswestry (Gelling, 'The Early History of Western Mercia', pp. 188–9).
40. *HE* iii, 16.
41. Penda had Oswald's head and arms cut off and hung on stakes. Oswiu buried the head at Lindisfarne (it was later placed in the coffin of St Cuthbert), while the arms were enshrined in a silver reliquary at Bamburgh (*HE* iii, 6, 12). The rest of Oswald's bones seem to have lain on the battlefield until they were retrieved by Oswiu's daughter Osthryth, wife of Æthelred of Mercia, who translated them to Bardney (*HE* iii, 11).
42. He was a son of Osric, who briefly succeeded Edwin as king of Deira in 633–4.
43. *HE* iii, 15. Oswiu already had two children, Alhfrith and Alhflæd who must have been born no later than 635, since both were adult in 653; their mother was probably Rieimmelth (Rhiainfellt) of Rheged (*HB* chapter 57; Phythian-Adams, *Land of the Cumbrians*, p. 58). Aldfrith, son of an Irish princess of the Ui Neill, was probably born after Oswiu's marriage to Eanflæd (Kirby, *Earliest English Kings*, pp. 143–4 and see below).
44. Eanflæd was born on Easter Eve 626, on the same day that her father was delivered from Cwichelm's assassin (*HE* iii, 9), and her son Ecgfrith was in his fortieth year when he perished at the battle of *Nechtanesmere* in 685 (*HE* iv, 26).
45. *HE* iii, 14.
46. *HE* iii, 24.
47. *HE* iii, 14. Bede has little to say about Oethelwald beyond the fact that he gave land for a monastery at Lastingham to Cedd, bishop of the East Saxons (*HE* iii, 23). This must have been after the baptism of King Sigeberht of Essex (*c*. 653) and before *c*. 658, when Alhfrith was ruling in Deira (*VW* chapter 7). It is likely that Oethelwald was expelled from Deira after the battle of the *Winwæd* in 655 (see note 60 below).
48. Talorcan died in 657 after a four-year reign (Kirby, *Earliest English Kings*, p. 94; A. P. Smyth, *Warlords and Holy Men: Scotland AD 80–1000* (London, 1984), pp. 61–2).
49. Kirby, *Earliest English Kings*, p. 143.
50. *HE* iii, 22. Bede gives no date, but Cedd, who led the East Anglian mission, was detached from his work in Middle Anglia, whither he had been sent in 653.
51. *HE* iii, 21.
52. Cedd and his companions may not have been first in the field, for Thomas, second bishop of the East Angles (*c*. 647–*c*. 653), was a man of the *Gyrwe* (see Chapter 1 above), which implies some prior knowledge of the Christian faith among at least some middle Anglian people.

53. *HE* iii, 21. Rædwald had been 'initiated into the mysteries of the Christian faith' at the court of King Æthelberht in Kent, but, 'seduced by his wife and by certain evil teachers', he compromised by adding a Christian altar to a temple of the old gods. Bede's contemporary Aldwulf, king of the East Angles (d. 713), claimed to have seen this temple as a boy (*HE* ii, 15).

54. *HE* iii, 16, 17. The first raid is dated no closer than the episcopate of Aidan (634–51) and could have taken place in Oswald's reign, or perhaps in the aftermath of the battle of *Maserfeld*. Bede's sole interest in recording these events is to demonstrate Aidan's sanctity. On the first occasion he was on the Inner Farne when he saw the flames rising above Bamburgh and his prayers caused the wind to change, driving the conflagration back onto the Mercian besiegers. On the second occasion, the royal vill where he died was burnt by the Mercians, but the wooden buttress of the church against which he had leant to take his last breath was miraculously unscathed.

55. *Iudeu* may be the *urbs Giudi* recorded by Bede, which lay 'halfway along' the Firth of Forth (*HE* i, 12; Kirby, *Earliest English Kings*, p. 90).

56. *HB* chapters 64–5, and see Chapter 4 below. *Catguommed* is 'a not very good pun' on Cadafael's name, 'battle-seizer' (Jackson, 'On the Northern British Section in Nennius', pp. 36–8). The *Annales Cambriae* record that in 658 'Oswiu came and took plunder', perhaps in revenge for Cadafael's part in the campaign.

57. *HE* iii, 24; the reconstruction of the campaign which follows is based on Kirby, *Earliest English Kings*, pp. 94–5, and Jackson, 'On the Northern British Sections in Nennius', pp. 35–9, but see Dumville, 'The Historical Value of the *Historia Brittonum*', p. 16.

58. For the *duces regii*, see Chapter 4 below.

59. Judith McClure, 'Bede's Old Testament Kings', in Wormald *et al.* (eds), *Ideal and Reality in Frankish and Anglo-Saxon Society*, pp. 88–90.

60. It did not do him much good; he is not heard of after the battle and was probably driven out by Oswiu, whose son Alhfrith was king of Deira by *c.* 658 (*VW* chapter 7).

61. In Bede's version, Penda refused the tribute, because he desired 'to destroy and exterminate' the whole Northumbrian people.

62. See the map in Brooks, 'The Formation of the Mercian Kingdom', p. 161. The site lies within the old British kingdom of Elmet.

63. Diuma and Ceollach, the first two bishops, were appointed in Oswiu's time, and Trumhere, the third, was abbot of Gilling, founded by Oswiu in expiation for the murder of Oswine (*HE* iii, 24 and see note 46 above). Oswiu's lay *principes* were driven out when the Mercians rebelled against his rule (see note 65 below).

64. *HE* iii, 24. Peada's murder recalls that of Oswine of Deira, and both should be laid at Oswiu's door.

65. *HE* iii, 24.

66. *HE* iii, 7. It was probably only at this point that the Middle Saxons (first recorded by that name in 704) gained a separate identity (Dumville, 'Essex, Middle Anglia and the Expansion of Mercia', p. 134; Keith Bailey, 'The Middle Saxons', in *Origins*, p. 111).

67. *HE* iii, 22, 30; Yorke, 'The Kingdom of the East Saxons', p. 32. Æthelwald succeeded Æthelhere, killed at the *Winwæd*, as king of the East Angles.

68. S.1165 (*EHD* i, no. 54, pp. 440–1). For the authenticity of Frithuwold's charter (probably drafted by Chertsey's founder Eorcenwald), see Patrick Wormald, *Bede and the Conversion of England: the Charter Evidence*, The Jarrow lecture (Jarrow, 1984), pp. 9–11. Eorcenwald, later bishop of London, was probably related to the Kentish kings.

69. Ann Dornier, 'The Anglo-Saxon Monastery of Breedon-on-the-Hill, Leicestershire'; Alex Rumble, '*Hrepingas* Re-considered', both in Dornier (ed.), *Mercian Studies*, pp. 157–8, 169–71.

70. John Blair, 'Frithuwold's Kingdom and the Origins of Surrey', in *Origins*, pp. 97–110, esp. pp. 105–7.

71. *HE* iv, 13. The *Chronicle* dates Æthelwealh's baptism to 661 but it may be later (Kirby, *Earliest English Kings*, pp. 115–6). Æthelwealh was killed, and the Jutish lands seized by Cædwalla of Wessex in 685.

72. His father may be the king of Wessex who attempted to have Edwin assassinated in 626 (see above, note 32).

73. Blair, *Anglo-Saxon Oxfordshire*, p. 44.

74. The genealogy of the kings of Lindsey is included in the Anglian collection (see Dumville, 'The Anglian Collection of Royal Genealogies', pp. 31, 33, 37); it is notable for containing the names 'Biscop' and 'Bede', which has suggested to some that Benedict Biscop, founder of Monkwearmouth-Jarrow, and Bede himself were kin to the kings of Lindsey. For the history of the kingdom, see Eagles, 'Lindsey', pp. 202–12; Yorke, 'Lindsey: the Lost Kingdom Found?', pp. 141–50.

75. *HE* iii, 21, 24; iv, 3.

76. Bede records Alhfrith's quarrel with his father but typically gives no details. He was still king of Deira in 664, but is not heard of thereafter (*HE* iii, 14, 25, 28; *VW* chapters 8–10). His Mercian wife Cyneburh seems to have returned home after his demise, for she and her sister Cyneswith were buried and venerated at the monastery which she is said to have founded at Castor, Northants (David Rollason, *Saints and Relics in Anglo-Saxon England* (Oxford, 1989), pp. 119, 202–3).

77. *HE* iv, 21; *VW* chapter 24.

78. *HE* iv, 26.

79. For Northumbria in the eighth century, see Kirby, *Earliest English Kings*, pp. 142–62.

3   The Shadow of Mercia

1. The *Continuations* are printed and translated in *HE*, pp. 572–7. The northern annals from the *Historia Regum*, cited as *HR*, are translated in *EHD* i, pp. 262–70. They end in 802 but another version, extending to 806, which 'often differs materially from the Latin tradition', underlies the 'northern recension' (the 'D' and 'E' texts) of the *Anglo-Saxon Chronicle* (D. N. Dumville, 'Textual Archaeology and Northumbrian History Subsequent to Bede', in

D. M. Metcalf (ed.), *Coinage in Ninth-Century Northumbria*, BAR British series, 180 (1987), 48–9). See also C. R. Hart, 'Byrhtferth's Northumbrian Chronicle', *EHR*, 95 (1982), 558–82; M. Lapidge, 'Byrhtferth of Ramsey and the Early Sections of the *Historia Regum* Attributed to Symeon of Durham', *ASE*, 10 (1982), 97–122.

2.　Peter Godman (ed.), *Alcuin: The Bishops, Kings and Saints of York* (Oxford, 1982).

3.　Bertram Colgrave (ed.), *Felix's Life of St Guthlac* (Cambridge, 1956), cited as *VG*.

4.　M. Tangl (ed.), *Die briefe des heligen Bonifatius und Lullus, Monumenta Germaniae Historica, Epistolae Selectae* i (Berlin, 1916); E. Dümmler (ed.), *Alcuini siue Albini Epistolae, Epistolae Karolini Ævi* ii (Berlin, 1895). Some of Boniface's letters are translated in C. H. Talbot (ed.), *The Anglo-Saxon Missionaries in Germany* (London, 1954), and some of Alcuin's in Stephen Allott, *Alcuin of York* (York, 1974); see also *EHD*, i, nos. 167–9, 171–81, 192–5, 198–203. The letter of Alcuin cited in the chapter heading is *EHD* i, no. 195, pp. 779–80; for Offa as *decus Britanniae*, see also Chapter 1, note 83 above.

5.　Pre-Conquest royal and private charters and memoranda are calendared in P. H. Sawyer, *Anglo-Saxon Charters: an Annotated List and Bibliography*, Royal Historical Society (London, 1968), cited as S.; this is currently being revised and updated by Susan Kelly and Simon Keynes. For their interpretation, see F. M. Stenton, *The Latin Charters of the Anglo-Saxon Period* (Oxford, 1955); Wormald, *Bede and the Conversion of England: the Charter Evidence*, Jarrow Lecture 1984.

6.　*VW* chapter 20. For the *Tribal Hidage*, see Chapter 4 below.

7.　*VW* chapter 20. Eddius, full of praise for Wulfhere when he supports Wilfrid, describes him as 'proud of heart and insatiable in spirit' when he descends on Northumbria in force. Bede, typically, is interested in the event only because it brought Lindsey back into Northumbrian hands and enabled Archbishop Theodore to give the province a bishop of its own (*HE* iv, 12).

8.　The *Chronicle* gives Æscwine a reign of three years, from 674–76.

9.　*HE* iii, 11; *ASC*, 704, 716. It was Osthryth who translated the remains of her uncle King Oswald to Bardney, much against the will of the community (see Chapter 2 above).

10.　*VW* chapter 40 and see Chapter 5, note 36 below. William of Malmesbury's assertion that Beorhtwald was Wulfhere's son is no more than an inference (*GP*, p. 251).

11.　*HE* v, 24, pp. 564–5.

12.　Ceolwald is recorded only in the Mercian king-list preserved at Worcester (*HC* ii, p. 369).

13.　*VG*, chapters 40, 49. The church of St Guthlac at Hereford may have been founded in Æthelbald's time (Sims-Williams, *Religion and Literature in Western England*, pp. 60, 146).

14.　*VG* chapter 45. For the title *patricius* and its significance, see Chapter 5 below. Heardberht's last attestation is to a Hwiccian charter of 757, after the murder of his brother (S.55), also subscribed by Æthelbald's kinsman and ultimate successor, Offa, and the family may have originated in this region.

15.　The Mercian genealogies have only one generation, that of Æthelbald's father Alwih, between Æthelbald and Eowa (killed in 642); the father of Eanulf is also said to have been a son of Eowa (Dumville, 'The Anglian Collection of Royal Genealogies', pp. 31, 33). Eanulf founded St Peter's, Bredon, in Hwiccian territory (Worcestershire), during the time of Bishop Ecgwine of Worcester (d. 717); he was probably considerably older than Æthelbald (S.116; *ECWM* no. 208, p. 90; Sims-Williams, *Religion and Literature in Western England*, p. 153). For Æthelbald's other grants to him, see S. 146–7.

16. See Chapter 1 above.

17. See Chapter 4 below, and S. 100, an undated charter of Æthelbald, disposing of land in Middlesex.

18. Yorke, *Kings and Kingdoms*, p. 50; *idem*, 'The kingdom of the East Saxons', pp. 1–36, especially pp. 31–6.

19. For Wihtred, see Kirby, *Earliest English Kings*, p. 12.

20. Susan Kelly, *Charters of St Augustine's Abbey, Canterbury, and Minster-in-Thanet* (Oxford, 1995), pp. 198–200. Eadberht I may have been the father of King Eardwulf, who issued two charters in favour of Rochester (in West Kent) in or before 762 (S. 30, 31).

21. Tatwine, priest of Breedon-on-the-Hill, Leics, in 731; Nothelm, a priest of London, in 734/5; and Cuthberht, formerly bishop of Hereford, in 740; see Kirby, *Earliest English Kings*, pp. 30–1.

22. *HE* iv, 15; *ASC*, 710. For the charters of Nothelm/Nunna, see S. 42–5, 22.

23. For Ine's laws, see *EHD* i, no. 32, pp. 364–72. Wealdhere's letter is translated in *EHD* i, no. 64, p. 729; see also Chapter 5 below.

24. Yorke, *Kings and Kingdoms*, pp. 140–2; *idem*, *Wessex in the Early Middle Ages* (Leicester, 1995), pp. 79–83.

25. *ASC* 'A', 733. For the significance of Somerton, see Chapter 5 below.

26. Kirby, *Earliest English Kings*, pp. 133–4. S. 93, a spurious grant of Æthelbald to Abingdon, is attested by Æthelheard *in expeditione ultra fluvium Sabrina adversus Britonem gentem*, which may come from a genuine document; for Cuthred's presence in Æthelbald's host, see *ASC* 'A', 743. For Æthelbald's grants of 'West Saxon' land, see S. 96, 1410, 1679; especially significant is S. 1258, relating to the minster at Cookham, Berks (see below, at note 49).

27. *ASC*, 752; *HR* 750, *EHD* i, p. 241; *HE*, pp. 574–5.

28. *ASC*, 757; *HR* 757, *EHD* i, p. 241. The *Continuations* add that he was killed 'at night . . . in shocking fashion' (*HE*, pp. 574–5).

29. For the suggestion that Offa's reign began in 758 rather than 757, see Kirby, *Earliest English Kings*, p. 163. Beornred may have come from another branch of the Mercian ruling dynasty, perhaps the same which produced the ninth-century Mercian kings, Beornwulf (823–6), Beorhtwulf (840–52) and Burgred (852–74), and Beorhtsige son of Beornoth ætheling, who was killed in 903 (*ASC*); see Yorke, *Kings and Kingdoms*, p. 119; C. R. Hart, 'The Kingdom of Mercia', in Dornier (ed.), *Mercian Studies*, pp. 54–7).

30. Martin Biddle and Birthe Kjølbye Biddle, 'The Repton Stone', *ASE*, 14 (1985), 233–92; Leslie Webster and Michelle Brown (eds), *The Transformation of the Roman World*, British Museum (London, 1997), p. 225.

31. C. E. Blunt, 'The Coinage of Offa', in R. H. M. Dolley (ed.), *Anglo-Saxon Coins: Studies Presented to F. M. Stenton* (London, 1961), pp. 39–62.

32. Kelly, *Charters of St Augustine's Abbey, Canterbury*, pp. 200–203.

33. S. 33, 105; A. Campbell (ed.), *Charters of Rochester* (London, 1973), nos 6–7, pp. 7–8, 9–11.

34. S. 32; Campbell, *Charters of Rochester*, no. 5, p. 6.

35. S. 34; Campbell, *Charters of Rochester*, no. 7, pp. 8–9.

36. S. 107; Nicholas Brooks, *The Early History of the Church of Canterbury* (Leicester, 1984), p. 114.

37. Stenton, *ASE*, p. 207. Kirby casts doubt on this assumption (*Earliest English Kings*, pp. 165–6) but see Kelly, *Charters of St Augustine's, Canterbury*, pp. 200–203.

38. S. 38.

39. Kirby, *Earliest English Kings*, pp. 166–9. Ecgberht's father Ealhmund was (according to the West Saxon genealogies) the son of Eafa, and a descendant of Ine's brother Ingild (see also note 82 below).

40. A letter from Charlemagne to Offa (*EHD* i, no. 197, pp. 781–2) refers to the plight of the priest Odberht, the Frankish form of the OE name Eadberht. Eadberht *Præn's* name suggests a connection with the dynasty of the Oiscingas (Kelly, *Charters of St Augustine's, Canterbury*, p. 202).

41. Brooks, *The Early History of the Church of Canterbury* pp. 114–120; for Jænberht's kinsman, Ealdhun *praefectus*, see Chapter 5 below. Kirby, *Earliest English Kings*, pp. 169–72, takes a different view of the significance of these events.

42. *EHD* i, no. 204, pp. 791–3 (a letter of Offa's eventual successor Coenwulf to Pope Leo III).

43. *HR* 771, *EHD* i, p. 243. A charter of Osmund, king of the South Saxons, dated 770, is confirmed by Offa (S. 49); see also S. 46, 50. For the *Hæstingas*, see Chapter 1, note 39 above.

44. Stewart, 'The London mint and the Coinage of Offa', pp. 27–43.

45. Stewart, 'The London mint and the Coinage of Offa', pp. 30–1. Æthelberht's murder presumably took place at or near Hereford, where he was buried, and whose cathedral is dedicated to him; a cult soon arose around his remains (D. W. Rollason, 'The cults of murdered royal saints in Anglo-Saxon England', *ASE*, 11 (1983) 9). The later *lives* of Æthelberht make him succeed his father Æthelred in 779.

46. Kirby, *Earliest English Kings*, pp. 178–9.

47. Cuthred died in 756, to be succeeded by Sigeberht, who was then deposed in favour of Cynewulf; it was Sigeberht's brother, the ætheling Cyneheard, who killed Cynewulf in 786 (*ASC*, 757).

48. S. 96; F. M. Stenton, *The Early History of the Abbey of Abingdon* (Reading, 1913, reprinted Stamford, 1989), p. 23, note 1; Sims-Williams, *Religion and Literature in Western England*, pp. 225–8.

49. The fortunes of Cookham down to 798 are related in S. 1258, translated in *EHD* i, no. 79, pp. 468–70. For the Mercian/West Saxon border in the eighth and ninth centuries, see Yorke, *Wessex in the Early Middle Ages*, pp. 61–4, and for its eastern reaches (the Vale of the White Horse) Blair, *Anglo-Saxon Oxfordshire*, pp. 54–6.

50. *ASC*, 779.

51. S. 265.

52. Sims-Williams, *Religion and Literature in Western England*, pp. 159–60.

53. S. 1257, translated in *EHD* i, no. 77, pp. 466–7.

54. For the papal legation, see Chapter 5 below.

55. Barbara Yorke, *Wessex in the Early Middle Ages* (Leicester, 1995), p. 63. Asser (*Life of Alfred*, chapters 14–15) claims that she 'began to behave like a tyrant after the manner of her father', denouncing and, if necessary, killing all who opposed her; after Beorhtric's death she was forced to flee abroad and 'died a miserable death in Pavia'.

56. He fled to Frankia (see note 39 above), but returned to claim the kingship on Beorhtric's death in 802 (see note 82 below).

57. See Chapter 5 below.

58. *ASC*, 787; for Ecgfrith's royal style, see S.148–151.

59. *EHD* i, no. 202, pp. 786–8.

60. *EHD* i, no. 196, p. 780. Hringstan is otherwise unknown.

61. Offa died on 26 July 796, and Ecgfrith 141 days later, on 14 December (*ASC*, 796, 797).

62. *HE* iii, 7; presumably the repudiated sister returned home, for her enraged brother Penda expelled Cenwealh from Wessex in revenge. It has also been suggested that Coenwulf was a kinsman of the Hwiccian kings (Bassett, 'In search of the origins of Anglo-Saxon kingdoms', pp. 8–17).

63. Kirby, *Earliest English Kings*, pp. 177–9.

64. For Pope Leo's letter condemning Eadberht, see *EHD* i, no. 205, pp. 793–4. Eadberht was imprisoned at the minster of Winchcombe until 811, when he was released; his subsequent fate is unknown.

65. For Cuthred's charters, issued in his own name or jointly with his brother, see S. 39–41, 157, 159–61.

66. S.157; the charter, which runs in the names of both kings, is preserved because Swithhun subsequently gave the land to Rochester (Campbell, *Charters of Rochester*, no. 16, pp. 19–20). Swithhun is probably the *comes* who attests a Kentish charter of 804 (S. 159), but nothing more is known of him beyond the suspicion that he might be related to the Swithnoth who received land in Chart Sutton from Coenwulf in 814 (S. 173).

67. Simon Keynes, 'The control of Kent in the ninth century', *Early Medieval Europe*, 2 (1993), 115.

68. *ASC*, 825, and see above, note 39.

69. S. 165, 168, 170, 187; Yorke, 'The Kingdom of the East Saxons', pp. 24, 36.

70. He probably fled to Mercia, as did at least one other member of the East Saxon dynasty; Sigeric, who received land in Hertfordshire from the bishop of London between 827 and 839, is described in the document recording this grant as a *minister* (thegn) of Wiglaf, king of the Mercians, but appears in the witness-list as *rex Orientalium Saxonum* (S.1791).

71. S. 153.

72. Brooks, *The Early History of the Church of Canterbury*, pp. 125–7. For Ceolwulf's letter to Pope Leo and the pope's reply, see *EHD* i, nos 204–5, pp. 791–4.

73. Brooks, *The Early History of the Church of Canterbury*, pp. 132–42. The crux of the dispute was control of the Kentish minster churches, see Chapter 5 below.

74. S. 186; C. E. Blunt, C. S. S. Lyon and B. H. I. H. Stewart, 'The Coinage of Southern England, 796–840', *BNJ*, 32 (1963), 14–5, 21, 66–7, 70–1.

75. *ASC* 'D', 'E', 792; *HR* 792, *EHD* i, p. 247.

76. *HR* 790, 796, *EHD* i, pp. 246, 248; for a reference to Eardwulf's miraculous escape from death, see *EHD* i, no. 199, pp. 784–5.

77. In 800, another of Eardwulf's rivals, Alhmund (St Alkmund), son of King Alhred (765–74), was murdered 'with his fellow-exiles *(cum suis profugis)*' by Eardwulf's men; the place of their exile is not named, but Alhmund was buried at 'Northworthy' (Derby), where he was venerated as a saint (Rollason, 'The Cults of Murdered Royal Saints in Anglo-Saxon England', p. 2).

78. *The Royal Frankish Annals,* translated in P. D. King (ed.), *Charlemagne: Translated Sources* (Kendal, 1987), pp. 100–1.

79. Kirby, *Earliest English Kings*, pp. 156–7, 196.

80. See note 39 above.

81. S. 154 (reading 'Beorhtric' for 'Ecgberht') see *ECWM* no. 233, p. 97; Kirby, *Earliest English Kings*, p. 179 and note 122 (p. 184). Sims-Williams accepts the date of the charter (799), but regards the reference to the peace-treaty as 'an antiquarian addition' *(Religion and Literature in Western England*, p. 171, note 127).

82. Kirby, *Earliest English Kings*, pp. 192–4.

83. *ASC*, 802.

84. S. 1435.

85. S. 187; Brooks, *The Early History of the Church of Canterbury*, p. 136; *ASC*, 823.

86. Baldred and Beornwulf may have belonged to a collateral branch of the Mercian royal kindred (Yorke, *Kings and Kingdoms*, pp. 119, 122). Baldred's coinage appears a little earlier at Rochester than at Canterbury, suggesting that his authority was recognized first in West Kent (Hugh Pagan, 'Coinage of Southern England, 798–874', in Blackburn (ed.), *Anglo-Saxon Monetary History*, p. 47).

87. Kirby, *Earliest English Kings*, pp. 188–9; *ASC*, 822, 825, 826, 827. The Chronicle implies that Baldred was expelled immediately after the battle of *Ellendun* but Beornwulf's authority was recognized in Kent as late as March 826 (S. 1267) and the conquest of Kent may not have been completed until after the death of Ludeca in 827 (Brooks, *The Early History of the Church of Canterbury*, p. 136 and note 22, pp. 352–3). For the expulsion of Sigered of Essex, see above, note 70.

88. Kirby, *Earliest English Kings*, p. 191. For Beornwulf's putative kinsmen, see note 29 above, and for Ceolwulf II, who was probably a son of Ælfflæd and Wigmund, see Chapter 6 below.

4   Strategies of Power

1. E. Talbot Donaldson, *Beowulf: a New Prose Translation* (New York, 1966), p. 1.

2. *Maxims Ib*, in T. A. Shippey (ed.), *Poems of Wisdom and Learning in Old English* (Cambridge, 1976), pp. 68–9.

3. *HE* iii, 6, 14.

4. James Campbell, 'The Sale of Land and the Economics of Power in Early England: Problems and Possibilities', *Haskins Society J.*, 1 (1989), 34.

5. A. W. Haddan and W. Stubbs (eds), *Councils and Ecclesiastical Documents* (Oxford, 1871), p. 182; *VG* chapter 17.

6. *HE* ii, 5; iv, 26.

7. *VW* chapter 20.

8. *HE* iii, 11. See also Bede's account of the expulsion of Oswiu's men in 658 by the defeated Mercians, who thus recovered 'their lands and their liberty at the same time' (*HE* iii, 14).

9. T. M. Charles-Edwards, 'Early Medieval Kingships in the British Isles', in *Origins*, pp. 29–31 and (on the possibility that Ecgfrith of Northumbria might have received tribute in cash) pp. 32–3.

10. *HE* ii, 9; iii, 24; iv, 13, 16.

11. *HE* i, 25 (*iuxta consuetudinem aestimationis Anglorum*); ii, 9; iv, 16 (*iuxta aestimationem Anglorum*).

12. T. M. Charles-Edwards, 'Kinship, Status and the Origins of the Hide', *P&P*, 56 (1962), 3–33; the quotation is on p. 19.

13. Charles-Edwards, 'Kinship, Status and the Origins of the Hide', pp. 17–9; the source is the *Senchus fer nAlban* (see below, note 24).

14. The early codes are printed and translated in F. L. Attenborough, *The Laws of the Earliest English Kings* (Cambridge, 1922, reprinted New York, 1963), pp. 4–17 (Æthelberht), 18–23 (Hlothhere and Eadric), 24–31 (Wihtred) and 36–61 (Ine); see also *EHD* i, nos. 29–32, pp. 357–72. The main edition is that of Felix Liebermann, *Die Gesetze der Angelsachsen*, 3 vols (Halle, 1903–16). They are cited here by the name of the king and the chapter number.

15. Ine, 64–6; Æthelberht, 25. *Hlafæta* means (literally) 'loaf-eater', one who receives bread; the 'giver of bread' is the *hlaford*, 'lord'.

16. Margaret Gelling, *Signposts to the Past* (London, 1978), pp. 106–29. They are topographical names, which describe an area, not habitative, relating to the settlements in which people lived.

17. J. M. Dodgson, 'The significance of the distribution of English place-names in -*ingas*, -*inga* in south-east England', *Medieval Archaeology*, 10 (1966), 1–29; reprinted in Kenneth Cameron (ed.), *Place-name Evidence for the Anglo-Saxon Invasion and the Scandinavian Settlements*, English Place-name Society (Nottingham, 1975), pp. 27–54.

18. See, in general, Bassett, 'In search of the Origins of Anglo-Saxon Kingdoms', pp. 1–27; and for particular cases, John Blair, *Early Medieval Surrey* (Stroud, 1991), pp. 12–24, *idem, Anglo-Saxon Oxfordshire*, pp. 1–41.

19. Speculation has included Surrey and Hampshire (Davies and Vierck, 'The Contexts of the Tribal Hidage', pp. 236, 279; Yorke, 'The Jutes of Hampshire', p. 92); Middlesex (C. R. Hart, 'The Tribal Hidage', *TRHS* 5th series, 21 (1971), 151; Bailey, 'The Middle Saxons', p. 112); and Berkshire (C. R. Hart, 'The kingdom of Mercia', in Dornier (ed.), *Mercian Studies*, pp. 47, 48).

20. For the extensive archaeological work at Repton, see the summary in Stafford, *The East Midlands in the Early Middle Ages*, pp. 106–8.

21. *HE* iii, 30; iv, 12; *VW*, chapter 20. Wulfhere is favoured by Wendy Davies (Davies and Vierck, 'The Contexts of the Tribal Hidage', pp. 226–7) and Pauline Stafford (*The East Midlands in the Early Middle Ages*, pp. 94–6), but the early years of his brother Æthelred, who defeated Ecgfrith at the battle of the Trent in 679, are another possibility (*HE* iv, 21; Dumville, 'Essex, Middle Anglia and the Expansion of Mercia', pp. 129–33). The reign of Offa (758–96) has also been suggested (Hart, 'The kingdom of Mercia', p. 44; *idem*, 'The Tribal Hidage', p. 157). See also notes 22 and 23 below.

22. Brooks, 'The Formation of the Mercian kingdom', pp. 159–68; *HE* iii, 11.
23. Simon Keynes, 'England, 700–900', Rosamund McKitterick (ed.), *The New Cambridge Medieval History, ii: c. 700–900* (Cambridge, 1995), pp. 21–5. P. H. Sawyer has suggested that, in its present form, the *Tribal Hidage* 'was compiled in the ninth or tenth century by a West Saxon' (*From Roman Britain to Norman England* (London, 1978), p. 111 and see Kirby, *Earliest English Kings*, pp. 9–12).
24. The *Senchus* is edited, translated and discussed by John Bannermann, in *Celtica*, 7 (1966), 142–62; 8 (1968), 90–108; 9 (1971), 217–65, and in *Studies in the History of Dalriada* (Edinburgh, 1974), pp. 27–68; see also Marjorie O. Anderson, *Kings and Kingship in Early Scotland* (Edinburgh, 1973), pp. 158–65; Alan Orr Anderson, *Early Sources of Scottish History, AD 500–1286* (Edinburgh, 1922; republished Stamford, 1990) i, pp. cl–cliii. The first survey may date from the time of Domangart (660–73), under whose leadership the Dal Riata were temporarily united, and the second is perhaps a generation later.
25. *HE* ii, 5, accepting the translation and interpretation of Thomas Charles-Edwards and Patrick Wormald, in Wallace-Hadrill, *Commentary*, pp. 220–2.
26. Campbell, 'Bede's *Reges* and *Principes*', p. 91. Berhthun and Andhun, who took on Cædwalla of Wessex after he killed King Æthelwealh of Sussex in 685, are also described as *duces regii* (*HE* iv, 15).
27. *HE* ii, 9; iv, 26.
28. At the battle of the *Winwæd* (655), Cadafael of Gwynedd withdrew from the host of Penda of Mercia, and Oethelwald of Deira from that of his uncle Oswiu of Northumbria, to await the outcome of the engagement (*HB* chapters 64–5; *HE* iii, 24).
29. Ine, 51. The noun *fyrd* comes from the verb *faran*, 'to go' (compare the modern words thorough*fare* and *fare*well).
30. Richard P. Abels, *Lordship and Military Obligation in Anglo-Saxon England* (Berkeley, Los Angeles and London, 1988), pp. 10–42.
31. Translation in Michael Lapidge and Michael Herren, *Aldhelm: the Prose Works* (Ipswich, 1979), pp. 170–1. In the time of Offa of Mercia (758–96), the men of Hringstan followed him to exile in Frankia (*EHD* i, no. 196, p. 780 and see Chapter 3 above).
32. *HE* iv, 22.
33. This is made clear by the words of the *comes* when Imma finally admits his identity: 'Now you ought to die, because all my brothers and kinsmen were killed in the battle; but I will not kill you, for I do not intend to break my promise'.
34. *VW* chapter 2.
35. Benedict Biscop, the founder of Monkwearmouth-Jarrow, served in King Oswiu's warband until he reached the age of 25, when 'the king gave him possession of the amount of land due to his rank' (*HA* chapter 1).
36. Abels, *Lordship and Military Obligation in Anglo-Saxon England*, p. 32.
37. *HE* iii, 14.
38. T. M. Charles-Edwards, 'The Distinction Between Land and Moveable Wealth in Anglo-Saxon England', in P. H. Sawyer (ed.), *Medieval Settlement* (London, 1976), pp. 182–3.

39. Stephen S. Evans, *The Lords of Battle: Image and Reality in the Comitatus in Dark-Age Britain* (Woodbridge, 1997).

40. Stenton, *ASE*, pp. 277, 290. Stenton may have been mistaken in seeing the majority of peasants as free men bearing arms, but what he says about the military abilities of those upper-ranking free peasants who did fight is perfectly reasonable.

41. Abels, *Lordship and Military Obligation in Anglo-Saxon England*, p. 28.

42. Reynolds, *Fiefs and Vassals*, pp. 38–9. For the Celtic structure, see note 13 above.

43. *HAA* chapter 34, translated in *EHD* i, no. 155, p. 706. The king in question might be Oswine of Deira, for Ceolfrith's family were connected with the monastery at Gilling, Yorks, founded by Oswiu in expiation of Oswine's murder; Ceolfrith's brother Cynefrith and his kinsman Tunberht (later bishop of Hexham) were successive abbots, and Ceolfrith himself began his monastic career there (*HAA* chapter 2, *EHD* i, no. 155, p. 697).

44. *VW* chapter 2. It was one of the *regales socii* upon whom Wilfrid had waited in his father's house who introduced the young man into the household of Queen Eanflæd, Oswiu's Kentish wife.

45. S. 186, translated in *EHD* i, no. 83, pp. 474–5. Abbess Eangyth's letter to St Boniface (see note 49 below) complains of the services due to the queen, bishop, *praefectus*, and other magnates (*potestates et comites*) as well as the king. For *fæstingmen*, ealdormen and *praefecti*, see Chapter 5 below.

46. Æthelberht, 2; *VW* chapter 39.

47. For the scandal at Coldingham, see *HE* iv, 25.

48. *HE* iii, 26.

49. Tangl (ed.), *Die briefe des heligen Bonifatius und Lullus*, no. 14 (Barbara Yorke, '"Sisters under the Skin"? Anglo-Saxon Nuns and Nunneries in Southern England', *Reading Medieval Studies*, 15 (1989), 99).

50. S. 1257 (dated 781); Donald A. Bullough, 'What has Ingeld to do with Lindisfarne?', *ASE*, 22 (1993), 106–7, note 46.

51. James Campbell, 'Bede's Words for Places', in *Essays in Anglo-Saxon History*, pp. 108–17; the quotation is on p. 109.

52. Ine 70, i. The amber was a measure used for both liquids and dry goods; it varied from time to time and place to place, and it is not possible to give a modern equivalent.

53. S. 146, translated in *EHD* i, no. 78, pp. 467–8.

54. Peter Sawyer, 'The Royal *Tun* in Pre-Conquest England', in Wormald *et al* (eds), *Ideal and Reality in Frankish and Anglo-Saxon Society*, pp. 273–99.

55. S. 207. Offa had freed the Kentish churches from service at royal vills two years earlier (S. 134). See also Henry Chadwick, *Studies on Anglo-Saxon Institutions* (Cambridge, 1905), pp. 249–52.

56. See Chapter 5 below.

57. *HE* iv, 13, 14; for the translation of *possessiunculi*, see Campbell, 'Bede's words for places', p. 112. The date must be between 680 and 685.

58. S. 235, translated *EHD* i, no. 58. For the authenticity of the charter, see Wormald, *Bede and the Conversion of the English: the Charter Evidence*, pp. 9–10, 25, and for the estate, Blair, *Early Medieval Surrey*, pp. 25–7 and map, figure 9.

59. Later evidence suggests that when only a part of the whole was granted, the structure was often preserved by dividing each settlement between grantor and grantee (David Roffe, 'The *Descriptio Terrarum* of Peterborough Abbey', *Historical Research*, 65 (1992), 1–16. It was, of course, also possible to detach and grant away the individual settlements (Gelling, *Signposts to the Past*, pp. 196–206).

60. *HE* ii, 14. The *viculi* and *loci* were presumably the smaller settlements of the *regio* dependent upon Yeavering.

61. Brian Hope-Taylor, *Yeavering: an Anglo-British Centre of Early Northumbria* (London, 1977). There is a series of plans of successive stages, based on those of Hope-Taylor, in Higham, *The Northern Counties to AD 1100*, p. 265; see also Welch, *Anglo-Saxon England*, pp. 43–7 and colour plate 1.

62. Campbell, *The Anglo-Saxons*, p. 57 (see *HE* iii, 13). For a similar suggestion relating to the Roman theatre at Canterbury, see below, note 96.

63. Yorke, *Wessex in the Early Middle Ages*, pp. 76–9.

64. Nicholas Brooks, 'The Development of Military Obligations in Eighth- and Ninth-century England', Kathleen Hughes and Peter Clemoes (eds), *England Before the Conquest* (Cambridge, 1971), p. 77.

65. Higham, *The Northern Counties to AD 1000*, pp. 266–7.

66. Abels, *Lordship and Military Obligation in Anglo-Saxon England*, pp. 54–5; R. A. Hall (ed.), *Viking-Age York and the North*, CBA Research Report no. 27 (1978), 32; and, for a more cautious assessment, R. A. Hall, 'Sources for Pre-Conquest York', Wood and Lund (eds), *People and Places in Northern Europe*, p. 90. The 'fortified town' (*oppidum municipium*) where Osric of Deira besieged Cadwallon in 634 is probably not York, but some Welsh stronghold, perhaps the *Caer Mincip* mentioned by Nennius (*HE* iii, 1; Campbell, 'Bede's words for places', p. 103, note 8).

67. *Anon Life*, chapter 8; Bede, *Prose Life*, chapter 27.

68. *VW* chapter 36: the king instructed his reeve (*praefectus*) Osfrith to cast Wilfrid into the 'hidden dungeons, where the sun rarely shone by day', but Eddius may not have been speaking literally. For the identification of *Inbroninis* with Fenwick (or some place nearby), see Campbell, 'Bede's Words for Places', p. 119.

69. Campbell, 'Bede's words for places', pp. 100, 104. Eddius uses the same word (*urbs*) for both *Inbroninis* and Dunbar, where Wilfrid was also imprisoned (*VW* chapter 38). For the place-name element *-burh*, see Gelling, *Signposts to the Past*, pp. 143–8.

70. *HE* iii, 16, 17; see also Chapter 2 above.

71. Ine, 45. There is a similar provision in the laws of Æthelberht of Kent, but here the word used is *tun*, 'enclosure, settlement, farmstead' (Æthelberht, 5, 13, 17; for *tun* as a place-name element, see Campbell, 'Bede's Words for Places', pp. 113–5). The offence is, however, distinct from *edorbryce*, breaking into the fenced homestead of a free man (Æthelberht, 27, 29).

72. *ASC*, 757.

73. See Chapter 6 below.

74. S.102, *EHD* i, no. 64, pp. 449–50.

75. The Romano-British name for both centres was *Salinae*, *Salinis* ('at the salt-pans'), a name preserved (in the case of Droitwich) into the ninth century as

Saltwic (Gelling, *Signposts to the Past*, p. 34; S. 223, F. E. Harmer, *Select English Historical Documents of the Ninth and Tenth Centuries* (Cambridge, 1914), p. 23).

76. Ine, 25, 25, i. Compare the *mangere* ('monger', tradesman) at Canterbury, whom King Æthelwulf of Wessex granted to his thegn Dudda in 839 (S. 287, and see Brooks, *The Early History of the Church of Canterbury*, p. 29).

77. *Anon Life* ii, 5; Bede (*Prose Life*, chapter 12) softens their friendless state and of course God provided for them; this is the famous story of the osprey who dropped a fish for Cuthbert's meal, and received half of it back as a reward for its trouble.

78. Wihtred, 28; Ine, 20. Wihtred's Code was issued in 695.

79. Hlothhere and Eadric, 15.

80. See Chapter 2 above.

81. *HE* iii, 9.

82. Bede, *Prose Life*, chapter 7.

83. Ine, 23. The king's share in both cases was two-thirds of the wergeld; compare the king's 'two pennies', Chapter 11, note 112 below.

84. P. H. Sawyer, 'Kings and Merchants', in Sawyer and Wood (eds), *Early Medieval Kingship*, pp. 144–6.

85. Hlothhere and Eadric, 7–10.

86. Richard Hodges, *Dark-Age Economics: the Origins of Towns and Trade, AD 600–1000* (London, 1982), pp. 47–86.

87. Pope Boniface sent King Edwin 'a robe embroidered with gold and a garment from Ancyra' (the latter probably silk), and gave to his wife, Queen Æthelburh 'a silver mirror and an ivory comb adorned with gold' (*HE* ii, 10, 11).

88. Wood, 'The Franks and Sutton Hoo', pp. 1–14; Drewett, Rudling and Gardner, *The South-East to AD 1000*, pp. 278–82.

89. Arnold, *The Archaeology of Early Anglo-Saxon England*, pp. 51–73; Sawyer, 'Kings and Merchants', pp. 149–52.

90. Hlothhere and Eadric, 16. The same code provides elsewhere for cases regarding stolen property in general to be dealt with 'at the king's hall' (Hlothhere and Eadric, 7), presumably at the nearest royal vill.

91. S. 1165, translated in *EHD* i, no. 55, pp. 440–1. Old English sources use 'port' to mean any trading-settlement, whether inland, or (the present-day usage) on the coast. For Frithuwold's kingdom, see Blair, 'Frithuwold's Kingdom and the Origins of Surrey', pp. 97–107.

92. *HE* ii, 3; iv, 21.

93. Alan Vince, *Saxon London: an Archaeological Investigation* (London, 1990), pp. 54–6. Dr Vince suggests that Hlothhere was not the only king to maintain a hall at London; the Mercians and their subordinates also had interests in the trading-centre (see Frithuwold's charter cited in note 91 above), as did Ine of Wessex, who in the preamble to his Law-Code describes Eorcenwald, bishop of London (675–93) as 'my bishop' (Ine, Prologue).

94. Vince, *Saxon London*, pp. 13–25, 54–6, 61–3, 81–2, 103–5.

95. Hall, 'Sources for Pre-Conquest York', pp. 84–90.

96. Brooks, *The Early History of the Church of Canterbury*, p. 25; see also Welch, *Anglo-Saxon England*, colour plate 6.

97. Tim Tatton-Brown, 'The towns of Kent', in Jeremy Haslam (ed.), *Anglo-Saxon Towns in Southern England* (Chichester, 1984), pp. 4–5, 21–2; Brooks, *The Early History of the Church of Canterbury*, pp. 22–5.

98. Margaret Sparks and Tim Tatton-Brown, 'The History of the *Villa* of St Martin's, Canterbury', *Archaeologia Cantiana*, 104 (1987), 200–13.

99. Hodges, *Dark-Age Economics*, pp. 70–3. For Ipswich, see Helen Clarke and Bjorn Ambrosiani, *Towns in the Viking Age* (Leicester, 1991), pp. 19–22, 34–5.

100. For a summary of the latest research on *Hamwic*, see Yorke, *Wessex in the Early Middle Ages*, pp. 302–9. *Hamm* means 'land which is hemmed in', whether by water or some other feature (Gelling, *Place-names in the Landscape*, pp. 41–50).

101. Yorke, *Wessex in the Early Middle Ages*, p. 68.

102. Sawyer, 'Kings and merchants', p. 153; Hodges, *Dark-Age Economics*, p. 70.

103. *The Royal Frankish Annals*, in King (ed.), *Charlemagne: Translated Sources*, pp. 99–100; P. H. Sawyer, *Kings and Vikings* (London, 1982), pp. 72–3. For Reric, see Clarke and Ambrosiani, *Towns in the Viking Age*, p. 109.

104. Susan Kelly, 'Trading Privileges from Eighth-century England', *Early Medieval Europe*, 1 (1992), 3–28; the quotation is on pp. 25. By the end of the ninth century the Mercian rulers were levying dues on the salt carried between Droitwich and Worcester, assessed on the pack-load and on the waggon-load (S. 223).

105. *EHD* i, no. 197, pp. 781–2.

106. Clarke and Ambrosiani, *Towns in the Viking Age*, pp. 28, 39.

107. David Peacock, 'Offa's Black Stones', *Antiquity*, 71 (1997), 709–15.

108. 'He paid such attention to the upbringing of his sons and daughters that he never sat down to table without them when he was at home, and never set out on a journey without taking them with him ... These girls were extraordinarily beautiful and greatly loved by their father. It is a remarkable fact that, as a result of this, he kept them with him in his household until the very day of his death, instead of giving them in marriage to his own men or to foreigners, maintaining that he could not live without them. The consequence was that he had a number of unfortunate experiences ... However, he shut his eyes to all that happened, as if no suspicion of any immoral conduct had ever reached him, or as if the rumour was without foundation' (Einhard, *Life of Charlemagne*, in Lewis Thorpe, *Two Lives of Charlemagne* (Harmondsworth, 1969), p. 75). The illegitimate children of Charlemagne's daughters included the Frankish historian Nithard, son of Agilbert, lay-abbot of Saint-Riquier.

109. Kirby, *Earliest English Kings*, pp. 175–6.

110. D. M. Metcalf, in Campbell (ed.), *The Anglo-Saxons*, pp. 62–3.

111. Ian Stewart, 'The Earliest English Denarial Coinage, *c.* 680–750', in David Hill and D. M. Metcalf (eds), *Sceattas in England and on the Continent*, BAR British series, 128 (1984), 5–26. Though the *thrymsa* was used in the earliest Kentish Law-code, that of Æthelberht, to calculate payments and fines, these were not necessarily paid in coin (Vince, *Saxon London*, pp. 110–1). In the reign of Æthelred of Mercia (675–91), Abbot Hædde of *Medeshamstede* bought from the king 15 hides of land for 500 *solidi*, specified as twelve

beds, consisting of feather mattresses and pillows with muslin and linen sheets, a slave and a slave-girl, a gold brooch, and two horses with two wagons (S. 1804; Campbell, 'The Sale of Land and the Economics of Power', p. 27).

112. D. M. Metcalf, 'Monetary Affairs in Mercia in the Time of Æthelbald (716–757)', in Dornier (ed.), *Mercian Studies*, pp. 87–106 (but see also Blair, *Anglo-Saxon Oxfordshire*, pp. 82–4); C. E. Blunt, 'The Coinage of Offa', in Dolley (ed.), *Anglo-Saxon Coins: Studies Presented to Sir Frank Stenton*, pp. 39–62; Stewart, 'The London Mint and the Coinage of Offa', pp. 27–44.

113. Stewart, 'The London Mint and the Coinage of Offa', p. 28; Pagan, 'Coinage in Southern England, 796–874', p. 50.

5 All the King's Men

1. *HE* iii, 14. Both *minister* and *miles* translate 'thegn'; Old English nobles were both servants and warriors of their lord the king. For the Ælfric quotation, see S. Keynes, *The Diplomas of King Æthelred 'the Unready', 978–1016* (Cambridge, 1980), pp, 206–7.

2. *HE* ii, 16 (see Chapter 2 above).

3. *HE* ii, 9. For a non-royal household, see *HE* v, 6, pp. 465–9.

4. Attenborough, *Laws of the Earliest English Kings*, pp. 36–7; *EHD* i, no. 32, p. 364.

5. Attenborough, *Laws of the Earliest English Kings*, pp. 24–5; *EHD* i, no. 31, p. 362.

6. *HE* iii, 9. It is not always easy to distinguish between a witenagemot and a synod, since both the business transacted and those present may overlap; but a synod was called and presided over by churchmen, whereas the witan assembled at the command and under the presidency of a king.

7. *HE* iii, 6; L. M. Larson, *The King's Household in England Before the Norman Conquest* (Madison, Wisconsin, 1904), p. 181.

8. *Beowulf*, lines 331–6; Larson, *The King's Household*, p. 181. Compare Cuthbert's office of guestmaster (*praepositus hospitium*) at Melrose (*Prose Life*, chapter 7).

9. *HE* ii, 9; see also the *nuntii* despatched by Æthelfrith of Northumbria to King Rædwald of the East Angles (*HE* ii, 12).

10. S. 186, 190, translated in *EHD* i, nos. 83, 85, pp. 474–5, 477–9.

11. S. 168–70, 188, 1434, 1436.

12. Larson, *The King's Household*, pp. 123–4. Larson compares the position of Unferth the *thyle* ('counsellor'), who, in *Beowulf*, sat at the feet of King Hrothgar, but adds that 'the association is no doubt a fancied one'. For the tenth-century *pedisequi*, see S. 520, 569, 768 and E. O. Blake (ed.), *Liber Eliensis*, Camden Society third series, 92 (1962), xiii; also Chapter 10, notes 49–50 below.

13. For the household of Eanflæd, Oswiu's queen, see *HE* iii, 25; *VW* chapter 2, and for that of Bertha, wife of Æthelberht of Kent, *HE* i, 25. Penda's queen,

Cynewise, had charge of the young Ecgfrith when he was a hostage in Mercia at the time of the battle of the *Winwæd* (*HE* iii, 24).

14. *HE* iv, 3. Imma (see Chapter 4 above) had been a member of Æthelthryth's household before moving to that of her brother-in-law Ælfwine.

15. The abrupt and deliberate change of status is a *topos* (a conventional anecdote); at Monkwearmouth, Eosterwine, a kinsman of Benedict Biscop and hence out of the top drawer of the Northumbrian aristocracy, undertook the most menial work – winnowing, threshing, milking ewes and cows, baking bread, cooking and gardening – and continued to do so even after he became abbot (*HA* chapter 8).

16. Pepin I, who deposed the last Merovingian king, Childeric III, in 751, had been mayor of the palace of Austrasia (eastern Frankia).

17. Osbald, *patricius* of Æthelwald Moll's son, King Æthelred, was briefly king after Æthelred's murder in 796, though he seems not to have had any hand in it; he later entered a monastery and died, as abbot, in 799, whereas Æthelred's slayer was himself killed by Torhtmund, one of the king's thegns, whom Alcuin commended to Charlemagne (*HR*, 796, 799, *EHD* i, pp. 248, 250; *EHD* i, no. 206, pp. 794–5).

18. For Æthelwald, Brorda and the other *patricii*, and for the origins and significance of the title, see Alan Thacker, 'Some Terms for Noblemen in Anglo-Saxon England, *c.* 650–900', *ASSAH*, 2 (1981), 213–21.

19. The Old English Bede is in an Anglian dialect, and its author was probably a Mercian adherent of King Alfred (Dorothy Whitelock, 'The Old English Bede', *Proceedings of the British Academy*, 48 (1962), 57–90).

20. *VW* chapter 18. For the title, and those who bore it in the eighth and ninth centuries, see Thacker, 'Some Terms for Noblemen in Anglo-Saxon England', pp. 210–13.

21. *HE* ii, 16.

22. *VW* chapters 36–38.

23. *Anon Life* chapter 8. Four of the witnesses to Kentish charters in the early ninth century are described as *praepositi*: Beornhard (S. 159, 161); Wulfheard and Eadred (S. 159); and Heahfrith (S. 1265). Chadwick added a second Beornhard and Eadred, who attest a memorandum of Archbishop Æthelheard (S. 1259), but they are more likely to be provosts of Christ Church than royal reeves (Chadwick, *Studies in Anglo-Saxon Institutions*, pp. 251–2; Brooks, *The Early History of the Church of Canterbury*, p. 155).

24. Hlothhere and Eadric, 16.

25. *HE* iv, 1.

26. S. 155, 1259, 1264; Brooks, *The Early History of the Church of Canterbury*, pp. 33, 114–5, 158.

27. Æthelnoth's will is written on the dorse of a charter of King Cuthred, giving him land at Eythorne, Kent, in 805; it is in the same hand as the main text, but in English (S. 41, 1500). For Eastry and its *regio*, see S. 1264, 1268.

28. It was once thought that Abba was a free man rather than a noble, for his wergeld is specified as 'two thousand', omitting the unit of cash, and 2000d would be the wergeld of a Kentish ceorl. The missing unit, however, may be the *thrymsa* (3d), 2000 of which would be the wergeld of a thegn (S. 1482; Harmer, *Select English Historical Documents of the Ninth and Tenth Centuries*, p. 78).

29. Apart from various food-rents, Abba left 1500d to the abbot and community at Folkestone, a *mancus* of gold (30d) to every priest in Kent, and 1d to 'every servant of God'; Heregyth his wife made her own gift to Christ Church of an extensive food-rent from Challock.

30. *EHD* i, no. 177, p. 755; Brooks, 'The Development of Military Obligation in Eighth- and Ninth-century England', p. 77. For reevish oppression in the late Old English state, see James Campbell, 'Some Agents and Agencies of the Late Anglo-Saxon State', in J. C. Holt (ed.), *Domesday Studies* (Woodbridge, 1987), pp. 216–7.

31. S. 186 (dated 822), translated in *EHD* i, no. 83, pp. 474–5, includes among its exemptions the 'entertainment... of reeves (*prefecti*) and tax-gatherers (*ex-actores*)'.

32. *HE* v, 24, pp. 566–7; *VW* chapter 60.

33. *HE* iv, 26 (*ASC*, 684); *HE* v, 24, pp. 564–5; for the title, see Chapter 4, note 26 above.

34. *VW* chapter 19; *Two Chronicles* ii, p. 34.

35. Thacker, 'Some Terms for Noblemen in Anglo-Saxon England', pp. 215–6.

36. *VW* chapter 40; S. 1169.

37. *ASC*, 648; S. 1164, translated in *EHD* i, no. 55, pp. 442–3 (see also the preamble to Ine's laws); S. 236, 1165, 1170; Lapidge and Herren, *Aldhelm: the Prose Works*, p. 170; Yorke, *Wessex in the Early Middle Ages*, pp. 79–93.

38. Similar strategies were used in Mercia, as when Penda made his son Peada king of the Middle Angles.

39. *HE* iii, 24; the Mercians were led by three *duces*, Immin, Eafa and Eadberht, who had presumably been supplanted by Oswiu's men after the *Winwæd* in 655.

40. Yorke, *Kings and Kingdoms*, p. 162. In the rather similar (tenth-century) context of the emergent duchy of Normandy, Dr Potts has remarked 'how swiftly assumptions of regional unity can break down under local pressure' (Cassandra Potts, '*Atque unum ex diversis gentibus populum effecit*: Historical Tradition and the Norman Identity', *ANS*, 18 (1996), 140).

41. Yorke, *Wessex in the Early Middle Ages*, p. 79.

42. The ealdormen and the 'important councillors' (*geðungenes witan*) are also linked in Ine 6, ii.

43. Ine, 50. For the ninth-century references, see note 46 below.

44. Ine, 8, 36, i. Compare the 'assembly or meeting' (*meðel oððe þing*), where the 'judges of the people of Kent' (*Cantwara deman*) preside (Hlothhere and Eadric, 8).

45. Ine, 39; for the lord's right of jurisdiction, see Ine 50.

46. All references are from the *Anglo-Saxon Chronicle*, and the ealdormen lead the shire-levies in battle.

47. Yorke, *Wessex in the Early Middle Ages*, pp. 84–92.

48. *ASC*, 827; for Ealdorman Mucel, see note 56 below.

49. *ASC*, 802.

50. See Chapter 7, note 54 below.

51. S. 197.

52. Blair, 'Frithuwold's Kingdom'; Dornier, 'The Anglo-Saxon Monastery of Breedon-on-the-Hill, Leicestershire', pp. 155–68; Blair, *Anglo-Saxon Oxfordshire*, pp. 52–4. See also Chapter 2 above.

53. *ASC*, 853; Blair, *Anglo-Saxon Oxfordshire*, pp. 93–4. He received land at Pang-bourne, Berks, from Bishop Ceolred of Leicester and King Beorhtwulf of Mercia in 844 (S. 1271; *EHD* i, no. 87, pp. 480–1), and was killed in 871, at the battle of Reading, Berks, when his body was taken to *Northworthig* (Derby) for burial (*ASC*, 871; Æthelweard, *Chron*, p. 37).

54. Asser, chapter 29. Asser adds that Æthelred Mucil's wife Eadburh, whom he knew personally, came 'from the royal stock of the king of the Mercians', which is probably correct, for Ealdorman Æthelwulf, brother of Ealhswith, was indeed a kinsman of the Mercian kings (S. 1442).

55. Keynes and Lapidge, *Alfred the Great*, pp. 240–1.

56. S. 190, translated in *EHD* i, no. 85, pp. 477–9; Campbell, 'Bede's *Reges* and *Principes*', p. 89; Thacker, 'Some Terms for Noblemen in Anglo-Saxon Eng-land', p. 204. Mucel Esne's son is presumably the ealdorman Mucel who attests between 814 and the 849s (see note 48 above); his father may be the ealdor-man Esne who attests Mercian charters of the late eighth and early ninth centuries (Keynes and Lapidge, *Alfred the Great*, pp. 240–1).

57. Keynes, 'The Control of Kent in the Ninth Century', pp. 112–18.

58. A memorandum of 844 (S. 1188) describes him as 'ealdorman and *princeps* of the province of East Kent' but this may reflect the practice of the mid-ninth century, when two Kentish ealdormen (for East Kent and West Kent respect-ively) were the norm; there is no sign of a second ealdorman in Oswulf's time.

59. Julia Crick, 'Church, Land and Lay Nobility in Early Ninth-Century Kent: the Case of Ealdorman Oswulf' *Historical Research*, 61 (1988), 251–9.

60. Alfred, 38,ii; S. 198; see Chadwick, *Studies in Anglo-Saxon Institutions*, p. 239.

61. S. 296, 1510. For Ealhhere, see Brooks, *The Early History of the Church of Canter-bury*, pp. 148–9.

62. Presumably in pre-Christian times, the priests of the old gods had also attend-ed; Bede mentions one such priest, Coifi, at the Northumbrian witenagemot which decided to accept Christianity, but of course the circumstances may have been exceptional (*HE* ii, 13).

63. See for instance the conversion of Peada, king of the Middle Angles, who was baptised not only with his gesiths and thegns (*cum comitis ac militibus*) but also with their respective *familiae* (*HE* iii, 21).

64. *VW* chapter 17.

65. Ine, 4, 61.

66. John Blair, 'Minster Churches in the Landscape', in Della Hooke (ed.), *Anglo-Saxon settlements* (Oxford, 1988), pp. 35–58.

67. Brooks, *The Early History of the Church of Canterbury*, pp. 132–42.

68. This theme is explored by J. M. Wallace-Hadrill, *Early Germanic Kingship in England and on the Continent* (Oxford, 1971).

69. For the Merovingians, see Wood, 'Frankish hegemony in England', pp. 235–41; for the Carolingians, see Wallace-Hadrill, *Early Medieval Kingship in England and on the Continent*, pp. 98–151.

70. *ASC*, 786; *HR* 796, *EHD* i, p. 248. *ASC* 'D', 796 (the 'northern' version of the *Chronicle*) adds that Eardwulf was consecrated and enthroned by Archbishop Eanbald, supported by Æthelberht, Higbald and Badwulf, bishops of Hex-ham, Lindisfarne and Whithorn respectively.

71. Brooks, *The Early History of the Church of Canterbury*, pp. 117–8. For the connections between Offa and Charlemagne, see Chapter 4 above.

72. Stewart, 'The London Mint and the Coinage of Offa', pp. 30, 34–5, 41.

73. S. 186 (translated in *EHD* i, no. 83, pp. 474–5); Brooks, *The Early History of the Church of Canterbury*, pp. 135–6.

74. Janet L. Nelson, *Politics and Ritual in Early Medieval Europe* (London, 1986), pp. 285, 324.

75. See Chapter 7, note 29 below.

76. Metcalf, 'Monetary Affairs in Mercia in the Time of Æthelbald', pp. 88–90 and figure 12.

77. *HE* ii, 5.

78. Patrick Wormald, '*Lex Scripta* and *Verbum Regis*: Legislation and Germanic Kingship, from Euric to Cnut', in Sawyer and Wood (eds), *Early Germanic Kingship*, pp. 105–38.

79. Bede's account of Æthelberht's Code links it with the Kentish royal genealogy (*HE* iii, 3) just as the slightly later code of Rothari, king of the Lombards (643) is prefaced by a regnal list and royal genealogy (Wallace-Hadrill, *Commentary*, pp. 60–1).

80. They say nothing, for instance, about property and inheritance, the matters which perhaps were of greatest concern to most people.

81. *EHD* i, no. 202, pp. 786–7. See also Alcuin's letter of the same year to Coenwulf of Mercia (Allott, *Alcuin of York*, pp. 59–60).

82. Patrick Wormald, 'In Search of King Offa's Law-code', in Wood and Lund (eds), *People and Places in Northern Europe*, pp. 25–45. There is a partial translation of George's report in *EHD* i, no. 191, pp. 836–40.

83. Ælfwald himself was assassinated in 788 and his nephew and successor Osred was murdered in 792.

84. The English word for interpreter is *wealhstod*, which literally implies one who understood the language of the British (Old English *wealhas*, 'foreigners'). By the end of the seventh century the word was common enough to be used as a personal name; Bishop Wealhstod of the people beyond the Severn (the *Magonsæte*) was a contemporary of Bede (J. R. R. Tolkien, 'English and Welsh', in *Angles and Britons* (Cardiff, 1963), pp. 23–4; *HE* v, 24). *Wealh* is the ancestor of 'Welsh'; the Britons of Wales call themselves the Cymry (Gelling, *Signposts to the Past*, pp. 93–6).

85. Bede says that King Cenwealh, 'who knew only the Saxon language (*Saxonum... linguam*) grew tired of [Agilbert's] barbarous speech' and expelled him from Wessex; this may be disingenuous (there were other considerations), but at the Synod of Whitby, Agilbert told King Oswiu that Wilfrid could better expound their common views 'in the English tongue (*lingua Anglorum*)', whereas he himself would have to use an interpreter (*HE* iii, 7, 25 and see Wallace-Hadrill, *Commentary*, pp. 99–100). For Augustine's interpreters, see *HE* i, 25; Wallace-Hadrill, *Commentary*, pp. 33–4.

86. *HE* iii, 3.

87. The *futhorc*, like the alphabet, is named from its opening letters, in this case the signs *feoh*, *ur*, *thorn*, *os*, *rad* and *cen*. See R. I. Page, *An Introduction to English Runes* (London, 1973).

88. A cache of runic letters on birch-bark from Bergen, in Norway, which
     dates from the fourteenth century, deals for the most part with day-to-day
     business transactions and personal messages (A. Liestol, 'Correspondence
     in Runes', *Medieval Scandinavia*, 1 (1968), 17–27).

89. R. I. Page, *Runes and Runic Inscriptions* (Woodbridge, 1995), p. 287.

90. King Chilperic (561–84) adopted extra symbols into the Roman alphabet to
     express characteristically Frankish sounds (including *th* and *w*), but he used
     letters from the Greek alphabet, which did not catch on (Thorpe (trans.),
     Gregory of Tours, The History of the Franks, p. 312).

91. Susan Kelly, 'Anglo-Saxon Society and the Written Word', in Rosamund Mc-
     Kitterick (ed.), *The uses of Literacy in Early Medieval Europe* (Cambridge, 1990),
     pp. 36–62.

92. Bede, *Letter to Ecgberht*, p. 115, translated in *EHD* i, no. 170, pp. 737–8. At
     the time of his death, Bede himself was engaged in an English translation of
     the Gospel of St John 'to the great profit of the Church' (*HE*, pp. 582–3).

93. See the lists in Wormald, *Bede and the Conversion of England: the Charter Evid-
     ence*, pp. 24–6.

94. *VW* chapter 17.

95. Bede, *Letter to Ecgbert*, p. 415; translated in *EHD* i, no. 170, p. 741. Note the
     importance of the subscriptions; the validity of the grant depended on the
     oral ceremony before witnesses, whose names were appended to the written
     record (see also below, note 102).

96. Stenton, *Latin Charters of the Anglo-Saxon Period*, p. 31; see also Stenton, *ASE*,
     pp. 141–2.

97. Pierre Chaplais, 'Who Introduced Charters into England? The case for St
     Augustine', in F. Ranger (ed.), *Prisca Munimenta* (London, 1973), pp. 88–107.

98. Wormald, *Bede and the Conversion of England: the Charter Evidence*, pp. 11–19.

99. A. G. Kennedy, 'Disputes about *Bocland*: the Forum for their Adjudication',
     ASE, 14 (1985), 175–95.

100. S. 1165, 1171, 235; see Wormald, *Bede and the Conversion of England: the Char-
     ter Evidence*, p. 10. Mr Wormald detects the influence of Eorcenwald not
     only on the diplomatic forms of later charters in favour of his own see at
     London, but also on subsequent West Saxon and even Mercian diplomatic
     practice.

101. S. 1256; Susan Kelly, *Charters of Shaftesbury Abbey* (Oxford, 1996), no. 1, pp.
     3–20. The memorandum, and the charter to which it relates (S. 1164), is
     translated in *EHD* i, no. 55, pp. 442–3.

102. For the importance of the subscriptions, see above, note 95.

103. The surviving charter of Cenred (S. 1164) is not the 'original', but Cyneheard's
     emended text. The 'original' has vanished with the anonymous monastery
     to which it was granted, but both the land at Fontmell and the defunct min-
     ster at Tisbury passed into the hands of the royal nunnery at Shaftesbury,
     in whose cartulary both Cyneheard's *libellus* and his memorandum survive.

104. Kelly, 'Anglo-Saxon Society and the Written Word', p. 45.

105. See Chapter 3 above.

106. For the significance of secular literature in this period, see Patrick Worm-
     ald, 'Bede, *Beowulf* and the Conversion of the Anglo-Saxon Aristocracy', in

Robert T. Farrell (ed.), *Bede and Anglo-Saxon England*, BAR British series, 46 (1978), 32–95.

107. Godman (ed.), *Alcuin: The Bishops, Kings and Saints of York*, pp. 70–1. For Aldfrith's education and his books, see *HE* iv, 26, v, 15, *HA* chapter 15. He is the king to whom Aldhelm addressed a Latin work on poetic metre (Lapidge and Herren, *Aldhelm: The Prose Works*, pp. 31–3).

108. *VW* chapter 60. There is more than a hint that the archbishop could not understand the papal Latin.

109. *EHD* i, no. 178, pp. 756–7 (my italics). Herefrith died in 747 (*HE*, pp. 574–5); one hopes this had no connection with his delivery of Boniface's cross letter to King Æthelbald.

110. For Ælfric's words and their significance, see Keynes, *The Diplomas of Æthelred*, pp. 136–7.

111. *EHD* i, no. 179, pp. 757–8. The letter to Æthelbald itself is translated in *EHD* i, no. 177, pp. 751–56.

112. Pierre Chaplais, 'The Letter from Bishop Wealdhere to Archbishop Brihtwold of Canterbury: the Earliest Original Letter Close Extant in the West', in M. B. Parkes and Andrew G. Watson (eds), *Medieval Scribes, Manuscripts and Libraries: Essays Presented to N. R. Ker* (London, 1978), pp. 3–23. The letter is translated in *EHD* i, no. 64, p. 29 (my italics).

6 Out of the North: The Impact of the Vikings

1. Michael Swanton (ed.), *The Anglo-Saxon Chronicle* (London, 1996), p. 55.

2. Northumbrian history in the early ninth century is almost irrecoverable and even the sequence of its kings is uncertain; see Kirby, *Earliest English Kings*, pp. 196–7 and the articles in Metcalf (ed.), *Coinage in Ninth-Century Northumbria*.

3. For East Anglia in this period, see C. R. Hart, 'The Eastern Danelaw', *The Danelaw* (London, 1992), pp. 37–41.

4. See Chapter 3, note 87 above.

5. Yorke, 'The kingdom of the East Saxons', pp. 24, 36. The last East Saxon kings probably fled to Mercia, see Chapter 3, note 70 above.

6. Keynes, 'The Control of Kent in the Ninth Century', p. 112.

7. Pagan, 'Coinage in Southern England', pp. 46–7, 55–7.

8. See Chapter 3 above.

9. Rollason, 'The Cults of Murdered Royal Saints in Anglo-Saxon England', pp. 5–9; for Ceolwulf II, see below.

10. S. 197; Keynes, 'The Control of Kent in the Ninth Century', p. 127.

11. *ASC*, 853; Asser, chapter 69.

12. Yorke, *Wessex in the Early Middle Ages*, pp. 95–6, and see Chapter 5 above.

13. Abels, *Lordship and Military Obligation in Anglo-Saxon England*, pp. 43–66.

14. Bede, *Letter to Ecgberht*, pp. 414–15, translated in *EHD* i, no. 170, pp. 740–1.

15. S. 1182, translated *EHD* i, no. 72, p. 460. Dunwald's will is extant only in a late medieval transcript, and the original charter of Æthelheard does not survive at all. For the earliest Mercian charters (S. 114, dated 779, and S. 128,

dated 788), see Stenton, *Latin Charters of the Anglo-Saxon Period*, pp. 38–9, 59–60.

16. The case for the remission of all dues was argued by Eric John (*Land Tenure in Early England* (Leicester, 1960), pp. 64–79; see also *Reassessing Anglo-Saxon England*, pp. 13–14). The counter-arguments are rehearsed by Brooks, 'The Development of Military Obligation in Eighth- and Ninth-century England', pp. 72–7.

17. S. 255, translated in *EHD* i, no. 69, pp. 455–7; Mary-Anne O'Donovan, *Charters of Sherborne* (Oxford, 1988), pp. liv, 2.

18. S. 92; for Boniface's complaints, see Chapter 5 above.

19. S. 134.

20. S. 168 (dated 811), 186 (dated 822). For Aldwulf, see Chapter 3 above.

21. Brooks, 'The Development of Military Obligation in Eighth- and Ninth-Century England'.

22. Philip Rahtz, 'The Archaeology of West Mercian Towns', in Dornier (ed.), *Mercian Studies*, pp. 111–14, 123–7; cf. Clarke and Ambrosiani, *Towns in the Viking Age*, p. 39.

23. Rahtz, 'The Archaeology of West Mercian Towns', p. 117; Clarke and Ambrosiani, *Towns in the Viking Age*, pp. 44–5.

24. Jeremy Haslam, 'Market and Fortress in England in the Reign of Offa', *World Archaeology*, 19i, (1987), 76–93. For Oxford, see Blair, *Anglo-Saxon Oxfordshire*, pp. 89–92, and for London, Vince, *Anglo-Saxon London*, pp. 85–6.

25. B. Durham et al, 'The Thames Crossing at Oxford: Archaeological Studies, 1979–82', *Oxoniensia*, 49 (1984), 82–7; P. Crummy, J. Hillam and C. Crossan, 'Mersea Island: the Anglo-Saxon Causeway', *Essex Archaeology and History*, 14 (1982), 77–86; Nicholas Brooks, 'Church, Crown and Community: Public Work and Seigneurial Responsibilities at Rochester Bridge', in T. Reuter (ed.), *Warriors and Churchmen: Studies Presented to Karl Leyser* London (1992), pp. 1–20; *idem*, 'Medieval bridges', *Haskins Society J.*, 7 (1995), 18, 23.

26. Stenton, *ASE*, pp. 212–15.

27. Patrick Wormald in Campbell (ed.), *The Anglo-Saxons*, pp. 120–1.

28. David Hill, *An Atlas of Anglo-Saxon England* (Oxford, 1981), p. 75. The most recent survey of the Dyke is Frank Noble, in Margaret Gelling (ed.), *Offa's Dyke Reviewed*, BAR British series, 114 (1983).

29. Margaret Gelling, 'The Place-name Burton and Variants', in Sonia Chadwick Hawkes (ed.), *Weapons and Warfare in Anglo-Saxon England* (Oxford, 1989), pp. 145–53.

30. Ann Williams, 'A Bell-house and a Burh-geat: Lordly Residences in England before the Norman Conquest', *Medieval Knighthood*, 4 (1992), 231–2.

31. The movements of viking armies in the ninth century are mapped in Hill, *An Atlas of Anglo-Saxon England*, pp. 36–42.

32. *ASC*, 851. At this time the chronicler begins the year on 24 September, so Ceorl's victory of '851' was actually achieved in the autumn of 850 and the Vikings spent the winter of 850–851 in Thanet.

33. For Ivar's involvement in Ireland, see Alfred P. Smyth, *Scandinavian York and Dublin* i (Dublin, 1975), pp. 16–20.

34. *ASC*, 871. For the distinction between royal armies and those commanded by lesser men, see also below, Chapter 9, note 107.

35. *ASC*, 872; for 'the immense tribute of the barbarians, in that same year when the pagans stayed in London', see S. 1278, translated in *EHD* i, no. 94, pp. 490–1.

36. S. 354; Simon Keynes, 'The West Saxon Charters of King Æthelwulf and his Sons', *EHR*, 109 (1994), 1137–8.

37. The 'Great Summer Army' arrived after the battle of *Meretun* (possibly Martin, Dorset) in which Bishop Heahmund of Sherborne was killed, on 22 March 871, but before the death of King Æthelred, after Easter (15 April) in the same year (A. P. Smyth, 'Guthrum and the Second Summer Army', *Scandinavian Kings in the British Isles, 850–880* (Oxford, 1977), pp. 240–54, at note 4; Æthelweard, *Chron*, p. 39).

38. Excavation at Repton has revealed the Danish defences of 873–4 (M. Biddle and B. Kjølbye-Biddle, 'Repton, 1984', *Bulletin of the CBA Churches Committee*, 21 (1984), 6–8; M. Biddle *et al*, 'Coins of the Anglo-Saxon Period from Repton, Derbyshire', in Blackburn (ed.), *Anglo-Saxon Monetary History*, pp. 111–22).

39. In S. 215 (translated in *EHD* i, no. 95, pp. 491–2), a charter of 875, he is described as 'by the grant of the gratuitous grace of God, king of the Mercians'. On Ceolwulf II, see Kirby, *Earliest English Kings*, pp. 215–7; Yorke, *Kings and Kingdoms*, p. 119, 123; Alfred P. Smyth, *Alfred the Great* (Oxford, 1995), pp. 51–5.

40. See above, note 8. Ceolwulf II may have been a brother or half-brother of St Wigstan (Ann Williams, Alfred P. Smyth and David Kirby, *A Biographical Dictionary of Dark-Age Britain* (London, 1991), p. 78). Ceolwulf I had been deposed in favour of Beornwulf, to whom Burgred, whom Ceolwulf II displaced in his turn, was perhaps related.

41. *ASC*, 876.

42. Smyth, *Scandinavian York and Dublin*, i, pp. 19–20. Ivar had died in 873.

43. Æthelweard (*Chron*, p. 41) says that 'the barbarians divided up the kingdom for themselves into two shares' (*barbari in sortes sibi duas dividunt regnum*).

44. *ASC*, 877; Keynes and Lapidge, *Alfred the Great*, pp. 246–7.

45. Æthelweard, *Chron*, p. 42.

46. Pagan, 'Coinage in Southern England', pp. 62–3 and note 33.

47. *ASC*, 878.

48. Fans of historical fiction will find a splendid account in C. Walter Hodges, *The Marsh King*.

49. Guthrum's departure from western Mercia may be connected with the death in 878–9 of his ally Ceolwulf II (D. N. Dumville, 'The Treaty of Alfred and Guthrum', *Wessex and England from Alfred to Edgar* (Woodbridge, 1992), p. 7 and note 37).

50. Text translated in Keynes and Lapidge, *Alfred the Great*, pp. 171–2, notes on pp. 311–13; for the date, see Dumville, 'The Treaty of Alfred and Guthrum', pp. 1–27.

51. *ASC*, 880, 890. The *Annals of St Neot's* record his burial at the royal estate of Hadleigh, Suffolk (Keynes and Lapidge, *Alfred the Great*, p. 282, note 7).

52. Ann Williams, 'The Vikings in Essex', *Essex Archaeology and History*, 27 (1996), 92–101.

53. *ASC*, 838.

54. Keynes, 'The Control of Kent in the Ninth Century', pp. 111–31.

55. Keynes and Lapidge, *Alfred the Great*, p. 68. If Osburh was the mother of Æthelwulf's eldest son Athelstan, who became king of Kent in 839, the marriage pre-dates *Ellendun* (825) but she need not have been Æthelwulf's only wife (Janet Nelson, 'Reconstructing a Royal Family: Reflections on Alfred', in Wood and Lund (eds), *People and Places in Northern Europe*, pp. 54–8). The couple were certainly married by 839.

56. S. 1438; Brooks, *The Early History of the Church of Canterbury*, pp. 323–5. For the dispute, see Chapter 5, note 67 above.

57. The ratio of lay to ecclesiastical beneficiaries is the more significant when it is remembered that charters to laymen are usually preserved only if the land subsequently passed to the church.

58. Keynes, 'The Control of Kent in the Ninth Century', pp. 125–6, 128.

59. In a Rochester charter, Ecgberht refers to his son Æthelwulf 'whom we have made king in Kent' (S. 271, Campbell, *Charters of Rochester*, no. 18, p. 21). The text has been tampered with but is probably based on 'a genuine document of the late 820s' (Keynes, 'The Control of Kent in the Ninth Century', p. 121 and note 50). In 830 Æthelwulf attested one of his father's charters as *rex Cantraorium* (*sic*) and further Kentish charters of 836 and 838 in Ecgberht's name acknowledge the consent of Æthelwulf as king. By 838 Æthelwulf was issuing charters in his own name, with his father's assent (S. 282, 279–80; 286, 323).

60. *ASC*, 839; S. 289, 291, 293, 296, 300, 324. Of the remaining charters of Æthelwulf, S. 297 is a cartulary-text, lacking witnesses, and S. 299 is issued in the joint names of Æthelwulf and Athelstan. Athelstan *rex* also attests S. 319, which has the impossible date of 874, possibly an error for 844. He does not attest S. 321, dated 880 (*sic*) which is almost certainly spurious (Campbell, *Charters of Rochester*, p. xxvi).

61. Pagan, 'Coinage of Southern England', pp. 46–7, 50.

62. Æthelberht attests S. 315–6, both dated 855, as *rex*; if, as has been suggested, S. 316 should be re-dated to 853, Æthelberht may have been given Kent immediately on the death of his brother Athelstan, between 851 and 853.

63. Keynes and Lapidge, *Alfred the Great*, pp. 314–15, notes 3 and 4.

64. Keynes, 'The Control of Kent in the Ninth Century', pp, 128–30. Alfred's heir, Edward, seems to have been king of Kent in the 890s; he attests a charter of 898 as *rex* (S.350), and it was he who defended the south-east (Surrey and Essex as well as Kent) against a viking assault in 893 (Æthelweard, *Chron*, pp. 49–50; Williams, 'The Vikings in Essex', pp. 94–5). In his will (S. 1507), Alfred bequeathed to Edward his booklands in Kent, presumably the same which Eadred, Edward's son by his third wife Eadgifu, daughter of the Kentish ealdorman Sigehelm, left to his mother (S. 1515).

65. See, for instance, Ann Williams, 'Some Notes and Considerations on Problems Connected with the English Royal Succession, 860–1066', *ANS*, 1 (1979), 144–67.

66. Keynes, 'The West Saxon Charters of King Æthelwulf and his Sons', pp. 1128–31.

67. Asser was bishop by 900, and may have been appointed as early as 892; he died in 907 or 908. It has been claimed, most recently by Professor Smyth, that the *life* of Alfred is not the work of Asser but a later compilation, of little

relevance to ninth-century conditions (Smyth, *Alfred the Great*, pp. 147–367). This view has not, however, won general acceptance; see the review-article by Simon Keynes, 'On the Authenticity of Asser's *Life of King Alfred*', *Journal of Ecclesiastical History*, 47 (1996), 529–51.

68. Keynes and Lapidge, *Alfred the Great*, *passim*.
69. For a perceptive overview of Alfred's achievement, see Janet L. Nelson, '"A King Across the Sea": Alfred in Continental Perspective', *TRHS* 5th series, 36 (1986), 45–68.
70. S. 218.
71. This entry has been seen as a misplaced doublet of that recording the capture of London in 886, but this need not be the case (Dumville, 'The treaty of Alfred and Guthrum', pp. 6–7). Asser says that Alfred took London only 'after the burning of cities and the massacre of peoples', which suggests an extended and fierce campaign (Asser, chapter 83).
72. Alfred's recognition as king in Mercia may have been what encouraged the kings of south Wales to seek his protection; Asser presents them as 'driven by the might and the tyrannical behaviour of Ealdorman Æthelred and the Mercians' (Asser, chapter 80, see Keynes and Lapidge, *Alfred the Great*, pp. 96, 262–3).
73. For Alfred's royal titles, see Keynes, 'The West Saxon Charters of King Æthelwulf and his Sons', pp. 1147–9; Keynes and Lapidge, *Alfred the Great*, pp. 38–9.
74. *ASC*, 893.
75. In its account of the battle of Farnham and the siege of Thorney in 893, the *Chronicle* merely records the triumph of the 'English army', whereas Æthelweard names the commander as the ætheling Edward, assisted by King (*sic*) Æthelred of the Mercians (*Chron*, pp. 50–1).
76. Æthelweard, *Chron*, pp. 49–50. Irish sources also call Æthelred a king and his wife Æthelflæd a queen (Joan Newlyn Radnor (ed.), *Fragmentary Annals of Ireland*, (Dublin, 1978), pp. 169, 181).
77. Not all of Æthelred's charters acknowledge Alfred's permission; see, for instance, S. 219, dated 884. For the meeting-places of the Mercian witan in Æthelred's time, see Hill, *An Atlas of Anglo-Saxon England*, p. 47.
78. S. 346.
79. Keynes, 'The West Saxon Diplomas of King Æthelwulf and his Sons', pp. 1134–41.
80. The translation of Bede's *Historia Ecclesiastica* is in an Anglian dialect.
81. See Alfred's letter prefaced to the *Pastoral Care*, translated in Keynes and Lapidge, *Alfred the Great*, pp. 124–6.
82. Keynes and Lapidge, *Alfred the Great*, pp. 141, 300.
83. Asser (chapter 106) describes how 'ealdorman and reeves and thegns (who were illiterate from childhood) applied themselves in an amazing way to learning how to read, preferring rather to learn this unfamiliar discipline (no matter how laboriously) than to relinquish their offices of power' (Keynes and Lapidge, *Alfred the Great*, p. 110).
84. Attenborough, *Laws of the Earliest English Kings*, pp. 36–93.
85. Attenborough, *Laws of the Earliest English Kings*, pp. 114–5. For an optimistic view of the evidence, taking due account of contrary opinion, see Simon

Keynes, 'Royal Government and the Written Word in Late Anglo-Saxon England', in McKitterick (ed.), *The Uses of Literacy in Early Medieval Europe*, pp. 226–57.

86. *ASC*, 896. For the battle, see note 99 below. *Geneat* means 'companion, retainer', though perhaps not of thegnly rank.

87. S. 186 (822), translated in *EHD* i, no. 83, pp. 474–5, grants exemption from the entertainment of 'keepers of dogs, horses and hawks'; S. 215 (875), translated in *EHD* i, no. 95, pp. 491–2, frees the diocese of the Hwicce (Worcester) from 'feeding the king's horses and those who lead them'; S. 197 (844 for 848) and S. 278 (835) grant freedom from the feeding of the king's horses and 'those in charge of them' (*ministrorum eorum*).

88. Ine, 33; Larson, *The King's Household*, pp. 176–8; Keynes and Lapidge, *Alfred the Great*, p. 291, note 42.

89. S. 348, translated in Keynes and Lapidge, *Alfred the Great*, pp. 179–81.

90. The king's valuables were kept in his private room (his chamber or *bur*, 'bower') and 'custody of the one implies some office in respect of the other' (Keynes and Lapidge, *Alfred the Great*, p. 330, note 15). Ælfric *thesaurius* re-appears, as Ælfric *hræglþegn* (*hrægl*, 'clothing'), in S.1445, translated in *EHD* i, no. 102, pp. 501–3.

91. Asser, chapter 2; Keynes and Lapidge, *Alfred the Great*, p. 68 and note.

92. Asser, chapters 100–1; Keynes and Lapidge, *Alfred the Great*, p. 106 and notes. A similar arrangement was made for the 'fighting-men' (*bellatores*); half served in the host, half remained at home, 'except for those men who were to garrison the burhs'.

93. It was from Alfred's time that the word 'thegn' ('servant') finally ousted the earlier 'gesith' ('companion') as the term for an Old English nobleman (H. R. Loyn, 'Gesiths and Thegns in Anglo-Saxon England from the Seventh to the Tenth century', *EHR*, 64 (1955), 529–49).

94. Lordship even outweighed the ties of kinship; it was forbidden for the feud to be pursued against one's lord (Alfred, 42,6).

95. Asser, chapter 91.

96. Asser, chapter 76.

97. Alfred was not, of course, the first English, or even the first West Saxon king to appreciate the importance of sea-power; see Matthew Strickland, 'Military Technology and Conquest: the Anomaly of Anglo-Saxon England', *ANS*, 19 (1997), 374–5.

98. *ASC*, 893; the ships captured on the Lea in 895 were also fetched to London. Mention of Rochester is a reminder that the fleet sent by Alfred against the East Angles in 885 had come from Kent (*ASC*, 885); it may be that the history of the Medway shipyards is older than we thought. A charter of Æthelred I (S.339; Campbell, *Charters of Rochester*, no. 26, pp. 30–32), dated 868, refers to two channels off the Medway, called *Pirifliat* and *Scipfliot* : 'presumably tidal inlets used by the ships coming up to a beach on the north-east side of the city' (Tatton-Brown, 'The Towns of Kent', p. 14).

99. *ASC*, 896.

100. Smyth, *Alfred the Great*, pp. 111–13.

101. Niels Lund (ed.), *Two Voyagers at the Court of King Alfred* (York, 1984).

102. See, e.g., *ASC* 'E', 1048.

103. S. 339; Campbell, *Charters of Rochester*, p. 31 and note 2.

104. Asser, chapter 54; Keynes and Lapidge, *Alfred the Great*, pp. 83–4, 248. Æthelweard says that the English were commanded by Odda, ealdorman of Devon (*Chron*, p. 43).

105. *ASC*, 893 and see Keynes and Lapidge, *Alfred the Great*, p. 287, note 9; Asser, chapters 49, 92, 98 (see also Keynes and Lapidge, *Alfred the Great*, p. 271, note 229).

106. *ASC*, 895; the fortification has not been identified but was not Hertford (Dumville, 'The Treaty of Alfred and Guthrum', pp. 8–9, note 47). Unable to use their ships, the Vikings decamped into Mercia.

107. Smyth, *Alfred the Great*, pp. 135–43, especially 139–40. The question of Carolingian influence on Alfred's policies is discussed by Nelson, '"A King Across the Sea"', pp. 47–52.

108. *ASC*, 892. Possibly Castle Toll, Newenden, Kent (B. K. Davison, 'The Burghal Hidage Fort of *Eorpeburnan*: a Suggested Identification', *Medieval Archaeology*, 16 (1972), 123–7). But see David Hill and Alexander R. Rumble (eds), *The Defence of Wessex: the Burghal Hidage and Anglo-Saxon Fortifications* (Manchester, 1996), pp. 98–9, 201–2.

109. Text and translation in Hill and Rumble (eds), *The Defence of Wessex*, pp. 24–35; translation only, Keynes and Lapidge, *Alfred the Great*, pp. 193–4.

110. Patrick Wormald, 'BL Cotton Ms Otho Bxi: a Supplementary Note', in Hill and Rumble (eds), *The Defence of Wessex*, p. 64.

111. Nicholas Brooks, 'The Administrative Background of the Burghal Hidage', in Hill and Rumble (eds), *The Defence of Wessex*, p. 128.

112. A pole or *gyrd* equals 5½ modern yards (16 feet 6 inches) and an 'acre's breadth' was 4 poles (22 yards or 66 feet). Forty poles equals a furlong (220 yards or 660 feet).

113. Estates are commonly said to 'defend' themselves against fiscal obligations; see Hill and Rumble (eds), *The Defence of Wessex*, appendices I and II, pp. 176–81.

114. For Alfred's division of the fyrd into two parts, each to serve six months in turn, see above, note 92, and for the operation of the division in his son's time, *ASC*, 917. In 893, according to the *Chronicle*, an English army besieging a force of Danes at Thorney Island, in the River Colne, broke off their engagement, even as the relieving force approached, because their provisions were exhausted and they had 'completed their period of service' (*ASC*, 893). Æthelweard, however, says (*Chron*, p, 49) that the besiegers successfully completed the siege. See also Abels, *Lordship and Military Obligation in Anglo-Saxon England*, pp. 62–6.

115. Brooks, 'The Administrative Background of the Burghal Hidage', pp. 128–150.

116. S. 223; Harmer, *Select English Historical Documents*, no. 13, pp. 22–3 (text), 54–5 (translation), 106–7 (notes). There is a translation in *EHD* i, no. 99, p. 498. The agreement cannot be dated more closely than 889–899.

117. Like military service, the more serious judicial cases were always reserved to the king, even in grants of bookland.

118. Brooks, 'The Administrative Background of the Burghal Hidage', p. 143.

119. S. 1648; Vince, *Saxon London*, pp. 20–22. A charter apparently relating to the same transaction and running in the names of Alfred and Æthelred as *subregulus et patricius Merciorum*, is preserved at Worcester (S. 346; T. Dyson, 'Two Saxon Land-Grants for Queenhythe', in J. Bird, H. Chapman and J. Clark (eds), *Collectanea Lundoniensa: Studies Presented to R. Merrifield*, London and Middlesex Archaeological Society Special Paper II (1978), 200–15). The bishop of Worcester's land in London was known as *Hwætmundestan*.

120. *Eorpeburnan*, Portchester, Chisbury, Bredy, Halwell, Pilton, Watchet, Lyng, Sashes, Eashing (Brooks, 'The Administrative Background of the Burghal Hidage', p. 144).

121. Asser, chapter 91.

122. Watchet, for instance, seems not to have been fortified when it was attacked in 988 (*ASC*).

123. Asser, chapter 91; cf chapter 106.

124. Alfred, 4.

125. S. 362, translated in *EHD* i, no. 100, pp. 499–500. Note that the Mercian witan is still separate from that of the West Saxons. Wulfhere was probably ealdorman of Wiltshire, and perhaps a kinsman of Wulfthryth, queen of Æthelred I (S. 340, dated 868, is attested by Wulfthryth *regina* and Wulfhere *princeps*; Nelson, '"A King Across the Sea"', pp. 54–5; Smyth, *Alfred the Great*, pp. 446–7).

126. *EHD* i, no. 222, pp. 811–13.

127. *Chron Abingdon* i, 50; for the history of Wouldham, see S. 1458.

128. S. 1507; Keynes and Lapidge, *Alfred the Great*, p. 177 and note 97, p. 324.

129. The Worcester agreement cited above (note 116) shows that he had appropriated for himself the tolls on salt entering the city from Droitwich.

7   The Making of England

1. IV Edgar 1, translated in *EHD* i, no. 41, p. 399.

2. Stafford, *The East Midlands in the early middle ages*, pp. 46–50.

3. *Historia de Sancto Cuthberto*, in Thomas Arnold (ed.), *Symeonis Monachi Opera Omnia*, Rolls Series (London, 1882–5) i, pp. 196–214; extracts in *EHD* i, no. 6, pp. 261–3); *HR*, translated extracts in *EHD* i, pp. 251–4 and see C. R. Hart, 'Byrhtferth's Northumbrian Chronicle', *EHR*, 95 (1982), 558–82; M. Lapidge, 'Byrhtferth of Ramsey and the Early Sections of the *Historia Regum* Attributed to Symeon of Durham', *ASE*, 10 (1982), 97–122.

4. H. O. Coxe (ed.), *Roger of Wendover, Flores Historiarum* (London, 1841–4), extracts translated in *EHD* i, no. 4, pp. 255–8.

5. John Williams ab Ithel (ed.), *Annales Cambriae* (London, 1860); Thomas Jones (ed. and trans.), *Brut y Twysogyon or The Chronicle of the Princes, Peniarth Ms 20 Version* (Cardiff, 1952); 'Chronicle of the Kings of Scots', in Anderson, *Kings and Kingship in Early Scotland*, pp. 249–53, and see Anderson, *Early sources of Scottish history* i, pp. 425–77 *passim*; S. Mac Airt and G. Mac Niocaill (eds), *The Annals of Ulster (to AD 1131), Part I: Text and Translation* (Dublin, 1983).

6. The *Life* of St Dunstan by 'B', in William Stubbs (ed.), *Memorials of St Dunstan*, Rolls Series (London, 1874), pp. 3–52, extracts in *EHD* i, no. 234, pp. 826–31; Michael Lapidge and Michael Winterbottom (eds), *Wulfstan of Winchester: the Life of St Æthelwold* (Oxford, 1991); Ælfric's *Life* of Æthelwold, in Michael Winterbottom (ed.), *Three Lives of English Saints* (1972); *Life* of St Oswald by Byrhtferth of Ramsey in J. Raine (ed.), *Historians of the Church of York and its Archbishops*, Rolls Series (London, 1879) i, pp. 399–475, extracts in *EHD* i, no. 236, pp. 839–43. Extracts from the works of Æthelwold himself and those of Ælfric the homilist are translated in *EHD* i, pp. 831–9, 846–54.

7. Æthelweard, *Chron*, ed. Campbell.

8. F. T. Wainwright, 'Aethelflaed, Lady of the Mercians', *Scandinavian England* (Chichester, 1975), pp. 305–24.

9. Ealdorman Æthelred's participation in the Tettenhall campaign is recorded by Æthelweard (*Chron*, p. 52), but, according to the *Mercian Register*, it was Æthelflæd who fortified *Bremesbyrig* in the same year (note 15 below).

10. *Wigingamere* may be Linslade near Wing, Bucks (B. Nurse, J. Pugh and I. Mollet, *A Village in Time. The History of Newport, Essex* (Newport, 1995), p. 10).

11. *ASC*, 914.

12. *ASC*, 915, 916.

13. *ASC*, 917.

14. The *Mercian Register* is preserved in *ASC* 'B', compiled between 977 and *c.* 1000, and 'C', written up at Abingdon *c.* 1044 (S. Taylor, *The Anglo-Saxon Chronicle: a Collaborative Edition, 4, Ms B* (Cambridge, 1983), pp. xxiii, xxxiv, xliv–xlvii, 49–51). The text is translated in *ASC*, pp. 62–8.

15. The personal name *Breme* is the first element in both *Bremesbyrig* ('Breme's burh') and the early form of Bromsgrove (*Bremesgraf*, 'Breme's grove'); T. Slater, 'Urban Genesis and Medieval Town Plans in Warwickshire and Worcestershire', in T. Slater and P. J. Jarvis (eds), *Field and Forest: an Historical Geography of Warwickshire and Worcestershire* (Norwich, 1982), p. 80.

16. *ASC*, 914, for 'the men from Hereford and Gloucester and the nearest burhs'; for Worcester, see Chapter 6 above.

17. The 'Derby' captured by Æthelflæd was probably the refurbished Roman fort at Little Chester (R. A. Hall, 'The Five Boroughs of the Danelaw: a Review of Present Knowledge', *ASE*, 18 (1989), 159–61).

18. Smyth, *Scandinavian York and Dublin* i, pp. 60–74, 93–116.

19. *Mercian Register*, 918. Mercians, Scots and Northumbrians fought against Ragnall at the second battle of Corbridge in 918 (F. T. Wainwright, 'The Battles at Corbridge', *Scandinavian England*, pp. 163–79; Smyth, *Scandinavian York and Dublin* i, p. 93).

20. Christine Mahany and David Roffe, 'Stamford: the Development of an Anglo-Scandinavian Borough', *ANS*, 5 (1983), 197–291.

21. *ASC*, 918.

22. Edward had already taken London and Oxford, with their dependent territories, into his hands (*ASC*, 911).

23. *ASC*, 920; Smyth, *Scandinavian York and Dublin* i, pp. 110–2; *idem, Warlords and Holy Men*, pp. 198–201. Ealdred and Uhtred received lands from Edward and Æthelred (and therefore before the latter's death in 911), subsequently

confirmed by Athelstan (S. 396–7; P. H. Sawyer, *Charters of Burton Abbey* (Oxford, 1979), pp. 5–7).

24. William of Malmesbury explains his presence there as a response to a revolt by the men of Chester, with Welsh support; Edward subdued the town and replaced the garrison (*GR* i, pp. 144–5; Stenton, *ASE*, p. 339).

25. For Athelstan, see D. N. Dumville, 'Between Alfred the Great and Edgar the Peaceable: Æthelstan, first king of England', *Wessex and England from Alfred to Edgar*, pp. 141–72; Michael Wood, 'The Making of King Æthelstan's Empire: an English Charlemagne?', Wormald *et al* (eds), *Ideal and Reality in Frankish and Anglo-Saxon History*, pp. 250–72.

26. She was Athelstan's full sister, daughter of Edward the Elder's first wife, Ecgwynn (*GR* i, p. 136); Athelstan had a daughter of the same name (Blake (ed.), *Liber Eliensis*, p. 292). Roger of Wendover identifies her with St Edith (Eadgyth) of Polesworth, Warks (*Flores Historiarum* i, p. 385).

27. The coronation liturgy known as the Second English *Ordo*, composed (probably) for the consecration of Edward the Elder, refers to the kingship of 'both peoples', the West Saxons and the Mercians, but was later altered to include the Northumbrians as well (Janet L. Nelson, 'The Second English *Ordo*', *Politics and Ritual in Early Medieval Europe*, pp. 361–74).

28. The meeting-place was perhaps the Roman fort of *Brocavum* (Brougham Castle) at the confluence of the Eamont and the Lowther (Michael Lapidge, 'Some Latin Poems as Evidence for the Reign of Athelstan', *ASE*, 9 (1981), 91–2, note 140). For Owen of Cumbria, see Phythian-Adams, *Land of the Cumbrians*, p. 112.

29. Lapidge, 'Some Latin Poems as Evidence for the Reign of Athelstan', pp. 83–93, 98; C. E. Blunt, 'The coinage of Athelstan, 924–39: a survey', *BNJ*, 42 (1974), 56. Athelstan is the first king to be represented with a crown and the Second English *Ordo* (note 27 above) is the first to specify the use of a crown (Janet L. Nelson, 'The Earliest Royal Ordo: some Liturgical and Historical Aspects', *Politics and Ritual in Early Medieval Europe*, pp. 356–8). See Chapter 5, note 76, above.

30. *ASC*, 927, conflates the meetings at *Eamot* and Hereford; for the Cornish, see *GR* i, pp. 147–8, translated in *EHD* i, no. 8, pp. 280–1, and S. 399, 400, both issued 'in the royal fortress' (*arce regis*) of Exeter in 928. Several Welsh kings attest the later charters of Athelstan (Simon Keynes, *An Atlas of Attestations in Anglo-Saxon Charters, c. 670–1066* (Cambridge, 1995), table XXXVI).

31. I. Williams (ed.), *Armes Prydein: The Prophecy of Britain from the Book of Taliesin*, trans. Rachel Bromwich, Medieval and Modern Welsh series, vi (Dublin, 1972), and see Alfred P. Smyth, *Scandinavian York and Dublin* ii (Dublin 1979), pp. 65–72.

32. *ASC*, 934; *HR*, 934, *EHD* i, p. 252.

33. The name means 'the fortified place of *Brun*'. Professor Smyth (*Scandinavian York and Dublin* ii, pp. 41–55) argues for a location in the forest of *Bruneswald* on the Northants/Hunts borders, commemorated in Leighton Bromswold (Hunts) and Newton Bromswold (Northants); Michael Wood ('Brunanburh revisited', *Saga-book of the Viking Society*, 20 part 3 (1980), 200–17) prefers Brinsworth (Yorks, WR), in which case Olaf and Constantine were on their way home when Athelstan's force attacked.

34. *ASC*, 937; Dumville, 'Æthelstan, First King of England', p. 142.

35. Æthelweard, *Chron*, p. 54.

36. Smyth, *Scandinavian York and Dublin* ii, pp. 39–40.

37. D. N. Dumville, 'Learning and the Church in the Reign of King Edmund I', *Wessex and England from Alfred to Edgar*, pp. 173–84.

38. *ASC*, 878.

39. These events are recorded only in the northern annals, see *EHD* i, no. 3c, p. 253 (cf. no. 4, p. 257). The truce was brokered by Archbishop Oda of Canterbury and Archbishop Wulfstan of York.

40. He was the son of Sigtrygg *Caech* (see above), though not by King Athelstan's sister. A Sigtrygg was minting coins at York in the early 940s but nothing more is known of him (C. E. Blunt, B. H. I. H. Stewart and C. S. S. Lyon, *Coinage in Tenth-Century England* (London, 1989), p. 211).

41. *ASC*, 942.

42. *ASC*, 945; Roger of Wendover, *EHD* i, p. 257; Smyth, *Warlords and Holy Men*, pp. 222–3; Phythian-Adams, *Land of the Cumbrians*, pp. 112–13, 119.

43. Dorothy Whitelock, 'The Dealings of the Kings of England with Northumbria in the Tenth and Eleventh Centuries', in Peter Clemoes (ed.), *The Anglo-Saxons: Studies Presented to Bruce Dickins* (London, 1959), p. 77; reprinted in *History, Law and Literature in Tenth- and Eleventh-century England*.

44. Peter Sawyer, 'The Last Scandinavian Rulers of York', *Northern History* 31 (1995), 39–44. I am very grateful to Marios Costambeys for help with the chronology of this period.

45. Roger of Wendover (*EHD* i, p. 257).

46. *EHD* i, nos. 234, 238, pp. 900–1, 920; Æthelweard, *Chron*, p. 55.

47. Keynes, *The Diplomas of Æthelred II*, pp. 48–69.

48. *ASC* 'B' and 'C' have Edgar succeeding to the Mercian kingdom in 957, whereas 'D' records that when Eadred died, Eadwig received Wessex and Edgar Mercia.

49. For Edgar's charters as king of the Mercians, see S. 667, 673, 674, 675, 676, 676a, 677, 678, 679.

50. *ASC*, 'D', 'E', 973 have six kings, but Ælfric the homilist has eight (*EHD* i, p. 853) as does John of Worcester, who names the participants (*JnW* ii, pp. 422–3). See Chapter 9 below.

51. Eric John, *Orbis Britanniae* (Leicester, 1966), pp. 1–63, 276–89; Janet L. Nelson, 'Inauguration rituals', in Sawyer and Wood (eds), *Early Medieval Kingship*, pp. 63–71.

52. Smyth, *Warlords and Holy Men*, pp. 215–238, especially 232–3. Edgar's 'Cession of Lothian' is recorded by Roger of Wendover, (*EHD* i, 258 and note 2).

53. Stenton, *ASE*, pp. 336–7. Worcestershire may be the territory which supported the burh established by Æthelred and Æthelflæd in the 890s (Ann Williams, 'An Introduction to the Worcestershire Domesday', in Ann Williams and R. W. H. Erskine (eds), *The Worcestershire Domesday* (London, 1988), pp. 9–11; *idem*, 'An Introduction to the Gloucestershire Domesday', in Ann Williams and R. W. H. Erskine (eds), *The Gloucestershire Domesday* (London, 1989), pp. 12–4).

54. S. 677, dated 958, *ASC* 1016 (the Magonsæte); S. 723, dated 963 (the *Wrocensæte*); S. 712a, also 963 (the *Pecsæte*; see Nicholas Brooks *et al*, 'A New Charter of King Edgar', *ASE*, 13 (1989), 137–55).

55. See Chapter 9 below.

56. III Edgar, 5,1; IV Edgar, 2a; Patrick Wormald, 'Charters, Law and the Settlement of Disputes in Anglo-Saxon England', Wendy Davies and Paul Fouracre (eds), *The Settlement of Disputes in Early Medieval Europe* (Cambridge, 1986), pp. 162–3.

57. In the Danelaw (York and the north-east midlands), the wapentake replaces the hundred, and the term 'hundred' is applied to a smaller territorial unit comparable to the tithing.

58. H. R. Loyn, 'The Hundred in England in the Tenth and Eleventh Centuries', H. Hearder and H. R. Loyn (eds), *British Government and Administration* (Cardiff, 1974), pp. 1–15; reprinted in H. R. Loyn, *Society and Peoples: Studies in the History of England and Wales, c. 600–1200* (London, 1992), pp. 111–34. Old English law-codes are cited by the name of the issuing king preceded by the number (in Roman Figures) traditionally assigned to the code, should the king have issued more than one.

59. Æthelweard, *Chron*, p. 28; *GDB*, fo. 208 and see Chapter 9 below.

60. H. R. Loyn, *The Governance of Anglo-Saxon England, 500–1087* (London, 1984), pp. 146–7.

61. Vills were not settlements but units of administration, which might contain a number of settlements. The vill must also be distinguished from the manor, the unit of estate management, which might also contain several settlements or parts of settlements. Vill and manor might coincide, but a manor could include settlements in more than one vill.

62. Tithingmen (*decimales homines*) are associated with the priest and *tungravius* (vill-reeve) in VII Æthelred, 2,5; see also IV Æthelred, 3 (A. J. Robertson, *Laws of the Kings of England from Edmund to Henry I* (Cambridge, 1925, reprinted 1974), pp. 72–3, 114–5).

63. *Inquisitio Eliensis*, in N. E. S. A. Hamilton (ed.), *Inquisitio Comitatensis Cantabrigiensis* (London, 1876), p. 97; L. J. Downer (ed.), *Leges Henrici Primi* (Oxford, 1972), pp. 100–1. The testimony of the vill is mentioned twice in Little Domesday and once in Domesday Book itself (*LDB*, ff. 285v, 393, *GDB*, fo. 44v: Julian Munby (ed.), *Domesday Book: Hampshire* (Chichester, 1982), no. 23, 3). See Robin Fleming, 'Oral testimony and the Domesday Inquest', *ANS*, 17 (1995), 101–2.

64. III Æthelred II, 1,2; compare VI Athelstan, 8,1, where the hundredmen and tithingmen of London meet monthly 'when the butts are being filled'.

65. IV Edgar, 7–8.

66. C. R. Hart, 'Athelstan "Half-king" and his Family', *ASE*, 2 (1973), 115–44.

67. Hart, 'Athelstan "Half-king"', p. 122; Blake (ed.), *Liber Eliensis*, pp. xiv, 111. Thurferth might be the Danish jarl who submitted to Edward the Elder in 917.

68. See above, note 23.

69. Above, note 43; for the title 'high-reeve', see Chapter 9, note 17 below.

70. Whitelock, 'The Dealings of the Kings of England with Northumbria in the Tenth and Eleventh Centuries', pp. 76–82. Only York and the midlands were shired on the West Saxon pattern; north of the Tees, the local administration was left virtually unchanged by the pre-Conquest kings.

71. Ann Williams, '*Princeps Merciorum Gentis*: the Family, Career and Connections of Ælfhere, Ealdorman of Mercia, 956–83', *ASE*, 10 (1982), 143–72.

72. See Chapter 9 below.

73. S. 1515.

74. Keynes, *An Atlas of Attestations to Anglo-Saxon Charters*, table XXXIa.

75. S. 706 (962) is a grant of Edgar to Titstan *fidelis cubicularius*, glossed *burþegn* in the endorsement.

76. Pierre Chaplais, 'The Origin and Authenticity of the Royal Anglo-Saxon Diploma' and 'The Anglo-Saxon Chancery: from the Diploma to the Writ', reprinted in Ranger (ed.), *Prisca Munimenta*, pp. 28–42, 43–62; *idem*, 'The Royal Anglo-Saxon "Chancery" of the Tenth Century Re-visited', in H. Mayr-Harting and R. I. Moore (eds), *Studies in Medieval History Presented to R. H. C. Davis* (London, 1985), pp. 41–51.

77. Keynes, *The Diplomas of Æthelred*, pp. 14–83; the quotation appears on p. 79.

78. Dumville, 'Æthelstan, First King of England', pp. 151–3.

79. Edward the Confessor commanded the bishop of Dorchester-on-Thames to write the charter recording his grant of Taynton, Oxon, to the abbey of Saint-Denis at Paris (S. 1105).

80. S. 546; Simon Keynes, 'The "Dunstan B" Charters', *ASE*, 23 (1994), 165–93.

81. Keynes, *The Diplomas of Æthelred*, p. 82, note 165.

82. Stubbs (ed.), *Memorials of St Dunstan*, p. 29.

83. Dumville, 'Æthelstan, First king of England', p. 148; Keynes, *An Atlas of Attestations in Anglo-Saxon Charters*, tables XXXVI, XXXVII and XXXIX.

84. Hill, *An Atlas of Anglo-Saxon England*, pp. 87–9.

85. 'B's *life* of Dunstan says Eadwig 'ruined with vain hatred the shrewd and wise and admitted with loving zeal the ignorant and those like himself' (*EHD* i, no. 234, p. 830).

86. Barbara Yorke, 'Æthelwold and the Politics of the Tenth Century', in Barbara Yorke (ed.), *Bishop Æthelwold: His Career and Influence* (Woodbridge, 1988), pp. 65–88.

87. Keynes, 'Royal Government and the Written Word in Late Anglo-Saxon England', pp. 235–41.

88. Attenborough, *The Laws of the Earliest English Kings*; Robertson, *The Laws of the Kings of England from Edmund to Henry I*.

89. Attenborough, *Laws of the earliest English Kings*, pp. 150–1; Keynes, 'Royal Government and the Written Word', p. 239.

90. Keynes, 'Royal government and the Written Word', pp. 235–6.

91. VI Athelstan, 11 (Attenborough, *Laws of the Earliest English Kings*, pp. 168–9; *EHD* i, no. 38, p. 391).

92. The same association of nobles and free men is found in VI Athelstan and III Edmund.

93. Keynes, 'Royal Government and the Written Word in Late Anglo-Saxon England', p. 239.

94. *EHD* i, no. 37, pp. 387–91.

95. Benjamin Thorpe, *Ancient Laws and Institutes of England* (London, 1840) i, pp. 352–7; facsimile and translation in Noble, *Offa's Dyke Reviewed*, pp. 103–9. The two communities were separated by a river, usually taken to be the Wye, but see Sims-Williams, *Religion and Literature in Western England*, pp. 9, note 30, 45–6.

96. Robertson, *Laws of the Kings of England from Edmund to Henry I*, pp. 8–9; *EHD* i, no. 38, pp. 391–2.

97. Rebecca V. Colman, 'Domestic Peace and Public Order in Anglo-Saxon Law', in J. Douglas Woods and David A. E. Pelteret (eds), *The Anglo-Saxons: Synthesis and Achievement* (Waterloo, Ontario, 1985), pp. 49–61.

98. Robertson, *Laws of the Kings of England from Edmund to Henry I*, pp. 12–13. For the 'tendency to associate kingship with personal lordship' see Abels, *Lordship and Military Obligation in Anglo-Saxon England*, p. 84.

99. III Edmund 7 (*homines suos et omnes qui in pace et in terra sua sunt*). For the hold-oath, see William Stubbs, *Select Charters and Other Illustrations of English Constitutional History*, 9th edn (Oxford, 1921), pp. 73–4.

100. *ASC* 'D', 946 says he was stabbed by Leofa, and John of Worcester (*JnW* ii, pp. 398–9) adds that the man was a convicted outlaw and that Edmund intervened to save his seneschal, whom Leofa had attacked. For the bonds of medieval society, see Susan Reynolds, *Kingdoms and Communities in Western Europe, 900–1300* (Oxford, 1984).

101. John Blair, 'Introduction: from Minster to Parish Church', in John Blair (ed.) *Minsters and Parish Churches: the Local Church in Transition, 950–1200* (Oxford, 1988), pp. 1–19.

102. Like Jarl Thurcetel of Bedford and his men (note 12 above).

103. *ASC*, 918. See also Jarl Thurferth of Northampton, note 67 above.

104. Blake (ed.), *Liber Eliensis*, pp. xi, 98–9.

105. David Roffe, 'The Origins of Derbyshire', *Derbyshire Archaeological J.*, 106 (1986), 111–16; 'Hundreds and Wapentakes', in Ann Williams and G. H. Martin (eds), *The Lincolnshire Domesday* (London, 1992), pp. 40–42.

106. IV Edgar 12; Robertson, *Laws of the Kings of England from Edmund to Henry I*, pp. 36–7.

107. IV Edgar, 15; Robertson, *Laws of the Kings of England from Edmund to Henry I*, pp. 38–9; *EHD* i, no. 41, p. 400. The Southumbrian ealdormen, Ælfhere of Mercia and Æthelwine of East Anglia are merely told to distribute the copies of the law-code which will be sent to them, 'that this measure may be known to both the poor and the rich'.

108. The 'Danelaw' did not, of course, include the far north-east, which had never been settled by Scandinavians.

109. See note 1 above.

110. See Chapter 9 below.

111. Mark Blackburn, 'Æthelred's Coinage and the Payment of Tribute', Donald Scragg (ed.), *The Battle of Maldon, AD 991* (Oxford, 1991), pp. 156–69; John Brand, *Periodic Change of Type in the Anglo-Saxon and Norman Periods* (Rochester, 1984).

8   Rule and Conflict, 978–1066

1. *JnW* ii, pp. 424–5; the words are attributed to Edgar, in 973. The sources for this chapter are discussed in the detailed surveys of Æthelred II, Cnut and Edward, Chapters 9–11 below.

2. For Edward the Martyr's reign, see D. J. V. Fisher, 'The Anti-monastic Re-action in the Reign of Edward the Martyr', *Cambridge Hist. J.*, 10 (1950–2), 254–70; Keynes, *The Diplomas of Æthelred*, pp. 163–74.

3. *Annales Cambriae*, pp. 19–21; *Brut y Tywysogyon*, pp. 8–10; *Annals of Ulster*, pp. 420–1.

4. Stubbs (ed.), *Memorials of St Dunstan*, pp. 397–8; *EHD* i, no. 230, pp. 823–4. A viking fleet which had been operating in England since 997 went to Nor-mandy in 1000 (*ASC*, 1000).

5. Keynes, *The Diplomas of Æthelred*, p. 187 and note 118.

6. D. G. Scragg, *The Battle of Maldon*, (Manchester, 1981). There is an exten-sive bibliography on this poem; for a survey of current opinions, see the articles in Scragg (ed.), *The Battle of Maldon, AD 991*, and Janet Cooper (ed.), *The Battle of Maldon: Fiction and Fact*, (London, 1993).

7. Simon Keynes, 'The Historical Context of the Battle of Maldon', in Scragg (ed.), *The Battle of Maldon, AD 991*, pp. 88–90; Niels Lund, 'The Armies of Swein Forkbeard and Cnut: *leding* or *lið*?', *ASE*, 15 (1986), 105–18.

8. *ASC*, 994, gives £16000; the higher figure, which appears in the treaty between Æthelred and the viking leaders (II Æthelred), may include the local tributes said to have been arranged by Archbishop Sigeric for Kent, Ealdorman Ælfric for central Wessex, and Ealdorman Æthelweard for the south-western shires (Keynes, 'The Historical Context of the Battle of Mal-don', pp. 103–7). Similar payments were extorted in 1004 from Ulfcytel of the East Angles, and in 1009 from the people of East Kent.

9. *ASC*, 1006.

10. Ulv's memorial runestone, cited in Lund, 'The Armies of Swein Forkbeard and Cnut', pp. 117–8; *idem*, 'The Danish Perspective', Scragg (ed.), *The Bat-tle of Maldon, AD 991*, pp. 117–18.

11. *ASC*, 1009. Cnut is the son of Swein Forkbeard, and the future king of England, Denmark and Norway.

12. For Thorkell's career, see A. Campbell (ed.), *Encomium Emmae Reginae*, Camden Society third series, 72 (1949), 73–82.

13. *ASC*, 1012. Thietmar of Merseberg, translated in *EHD* i, no. 28, pp. 320–1.

14. *ASC*, 1014. For the negotiations between Æthelred and the English mag-nates, see Chapter 9 below.

15. *EHD* i, no. 13, p. 306. Like Olaf Tryggvasson before him, Olaf Haraldsson used his windfall to make himself king of Norway, until he was ousted by Cnut in 1028 (Peter Sawyer, 'Cnut's Scandinavian Empire', in Alexander Rumble (ed.), *The Reign of Cnut, King of England, Denmark and Norway* (Leices-ter, 1994), pp. 17–21).

16. See Chapter 10 below.

17. *ASC*, 1014 and see Chapter 10 below.

18. *ASC*, 1014. For the meaning of *ful fyrd*, see Chapter 9, note 109 below.

19. *ASC*, 1013.

20. *ASC*, 1015.

21. Some such argument may have been used in 975 to advance the claims of Æthelred, son of Queen Ælfthryth, against his half-brother Edward, whose mother had probably not been crowned (Nelson, 'Inauguration rituals', p. 67). Ælfthryth's elder son Edmund (who predeceased his father) attests

S. 745 as *legitimus*, ahead of his elder half-brother. For Edward as his father's envoy, see *ASC*, 1014 and Chapter 9 below.

22. See Chapter 9, note 11 below.

23. The family can be reconstructed from the will of Ælfhelm's brother, Wulfric Spot (d. 1002) who disposed of a huge estate in northern Mercia and southern Northumbria (S. 1536; Sawyer, *Charters of Burton*, pp. xli–xliii, 53–6). For Ælfhelm's murder, see Chapter 9, note 10 below.

24. *ASC*, 1015.

25. *JnW* ii, pp. 486–7.

26. *ASC*, 1016; C. R. Hart, 'The site of *Assandune*', *The Danelaw*, pp. 553–65.

27. *JnW* ii, pp. 494–7.

28. All versions of the *Chronicle*, including 'A', make Cnut succeed to 'all the kingdom of the English' in 1017; the coronation at London, by Lyfing, is recorded by the twelfth-century chronicler, Ralph of Diceto (William Stubbs (ed.), *The Historical Works of Master Ralph of Diceto* Rolls Series (London, 1876) i, p. 169).

29. Simon Keynes, 'The Æthelings in Normandy', *ANS*, 13 (1991), 173–205, esp. pp. 181–5. The infant sons of Edmund, Edward and Edmund, were smuggled abroad to save them from the fate which eventually befell their uncle, Eadwig, murdered on Cnut's orders (*ASC* 'C', 1017).

30. See above, note 23. Earl Harold Godwineson also kept two wives concurrently (see note 67 below).

31. *JnW* ii, pp. 504–5; the *Chronicle* places the murder of Eadric before Cnut's marriage with Emma.

32. M. K. Lawson, *Cnut: the Danes in England in the Early Eleventh Century* (London, 1993), pp. 189–90.

33. D. M. Metcalf argued that it should be seen against the 'unusual and intense minting-activity' which produced Cnut's first 'Quatrefoil' issue, itself much lighter in weight than the last issue of Æthelred's 'Small Cross' pennies ('Large Danegelds in Relation to War and Kingship: their Implications for Monetary History and some Numismatic Evidence', in Hawkes (ed.), *Weapons and Warfare in Anglo-Saxon England*, pp. 179–89). See, however, Blackburn, 'Æthelred's coinage and the payment of tribute', pp. 164–6 and especially note 12.

34. S. 1424; *GDB* fo. 252v; Lawson, *Cnut*, pp. 191–4.

35. *ASC* 1018; A. G. Kennedy, 'Cnut's law-code of 1018', *ASE*, 16 (1983), 53–81.

36. See Chapter 10 below.

37. *ASC*, 1035; all versions deny that Harold I was the son, either of Cnut or of Ælfgifu of Northampton. John of Worcester (*JnW* ii, pp. 520–1) relates the slander that he was the son of a shoemaker, and his brother Swein the son of priest's concubine, and that Ælfgifu in each case only pretended to be pregnant, and had the children smuggled into her chamber; a similar story is told of Harold's birth in the *Encomium Emmae Reginae* (Campbell (ed.), pp. 38–41).

38. *JnW* ii, pp. 520–3.

39. Tuuka Talvio, 'Harold I and Harthacnut's *Jewel Cross* Type Reconsidered', in Blackburn (ed.), *Anglo-Saxon Monetary History*, pp. 273–90; the quotation is on p. 287.

40. Keynes, 'The Æthelings in Normandy', pp. 195–6.

41. Elisabeth van Houts (ed.), *The Gesta Normannorum Ducum of William of Jumieges, Orderic Vitalis and Robert of Torigni*, 2v (Oxford, 1992–5) i, pp. 130–1, ii, pp. 106–7; *JnW* ii, pp. 523–5 (John is not here following his normal source, the 'D' *Chronicle*); Campbell (ed.), *Encomium Emmae Reginae*, pp. 41–7; Frank Barlow (ed.), *The Life of King Edward the Confessor* (London, 1962), p. 20 (hereafter cited as *Vita Edwardi*).

42. Campbell, *Encomium Emmae Reginae*, pp. 40–1; S. 1467 and see Chapter 9 below.

43. *JnW* ii, pp. 530–3.

44. For the unwillingness of the great earls to come to blows, see also Chapter 11 below.

45. *ASC*, 1041 and see Chapter 10 below.

46. *ASC* 'C', 'D', 1042. 'E' has Edward chosen king even before his half-brother's funeral, though he was not crowned until 3 April (Easter Day) 1043 (*ASC*).

47. Earl Ranig, the previous earl of Herefordshire, is last heard of in 1041 (*JnW* ii, pp. 532–3).

48. The date of Edward's marriage to Edith, 'ten nights before Candlemas' (2 February) is given by *ASC* 'C', 1044, which, since 'C' begins the year at Lady Day (25 March), represents 23 January 1045. For Harold's appointment, see T. J. Oleson, *The Witenagemot in the Reign of Edward the Confessor* (Oxford, 1955), p. 126. Thuri, the previous incumbent of Beorn's earldom, survived into Edward's reign, but the date of his death is unknown (S.1228; Simon Keynes, 'A Lost Cartulary of St Alban's Abbey', *ASE*, 22 (1993), 267–8). Beorn and Swein were the sons of Estrith, Cnut's full sister, and Jarl Ulf, Godwine's brother-in-law.

49. F. J. Tschan (tr.), *Adam of Bremen, History of the Archbishops of Hamburg-Bremen* (New York, 1959), pp. 108–9; Campbell (ed.), *Encomium Emmae Reginae*, pp. 84–5; Ann Williams, '"Cockles amongst the wheat": Danes and English in the West Midlands in the First Half of the Eleventh Century', *Midland History*, 11 (1986), 9–10.

50. *ASC* 'D', 1044 and see Chapter 10, note 95 below. John of Worcester (ii, pp. 540–1) says her sons (Hemming and Thorkell) were also exiled.

51. C. P. Lewis, 'An Introduction to the Herefordshire Domesday', in Ann Williams and R. W. H. Erskine (eds), *The Herefordshire Domesday* (London, 1988), pp. 20–1. Leominster was subsequently disbanded, to the ultimate benefit of Swein's sister, Queen Edith (*GDB* ff. 180–180v).

52. *ASC* 'C', 'E', 1049; 'D', however, says Beorn promised to help him, as does John of Worcester.

53. Beorn's murder had serious repercussions in Denmark, where Swein Estrithson seems to have regarded Godwine's whole family as responsible for his brother's death (Tschan (tr.), Adam of Bremen, pp. 92, 125).

54. Godwine's third son Tostig attests from 1044 as *minister* and *nobilis*; Ralph attests, as earl, from 1050 (Keynes, *An Atlas of Attestations in Anglo-Saxon Charters*, table LXXIV); Ann Williams, 'The King's Nephew: the Family and Career of Ralph, Earl of Hereford', in Christopher Harper-Bill, Christopher Holdsworth and Janet L. Nelson (eds), *Studies in Medieval History presented to R. Allen Brown* (Woodbridge, 1989), pp. 327–43).

55. Ealdred had just negotiated, at Rome, the removal of the see of Devon and Cornwall from Crediton to Exeter; the royal charter recording this is attested

(*inter alia*) by Earl Swein (S. 1021; Frank Barlow, *The English Church, 1000–1066* (London, 1963), pp. 116–7, 154–5; Vanessa J. King, 'Ealdred, Archbishop of York: the Worcester Years', *ANS*, 18 (1996), 127).

56. See Chapter 11 below.

57. For these events, see below.

58. There are no charters for the years 1055–8, and Gyrth first attests as earl in 1059, but he had held Norfolk during the temporary exile of Ælfgar in 1055 (Barlow (ed.), *Vita Edwardi*, p. 33). Ælfgar held East Anglia during the exile of Harold in 1051–2 and after Harold's succession to Wessex in 1053.

59. Williams, 'The King's Nephew: the Family and Career of Ralph, Earl of Hereford', pp. 338–40. Leofwine attests as earl from 1059 (see previous note). He held Herts, Middx and probably Bucks, but the evidence linking him with Kent, Surrey and Staffs is unreliable.

60. *ASC*, 1055; for the various versions of the *Chronicle*, see Chapter 10, note 5 below.

61. See Chapter 10, note 120 below.

62. Kari Maund, 'The Welsh Alliances of Earl Ælfgar of Mercia and his Family in the Mid Eleventh Century', *ANS*, 11 (1989), 186–8.

63. *ASC* 'C', 1055. Ralph received Hereford when Swein was exiled in 1051; unlike his brothers, he never returned to England (see Chapter 11 below).

64. Bishop Athelstan of Hereford died on 10 February 1056, and was succeeded by Harold's priest Leofgar, who 'wore his moustaches during his priesthood until he became a bishop' and then actively campaigned against Gruffudd, until he was killed on 16 June 1056. The subsequent truce with Gruffudd was brokered by Leofric of Mercia, Harold, and Ealdred, bishop of Worcester; there is no reference to Earl Ralph's participation (*ASC* 'C', 1056).

65. Maund, 'The Welsh Alliances of Earl Ælfgar of Mercia and His Family', p. 188.

66. *ASC* 'D', 'E', 1063; Frank Barlow, *Edward the Confessor* (London, 1970), pp. 210–11. In the twelfth century, Gerald of Wales and John of Salisbury recommended Harold's 1063 campaign to Henry II as an epitome of how an attack against the Welsh should be launched (Frederick C. Suppe, *Military Institutions on the Welsh Marches: Shropshire, 1066–1300* (Woodbridge, 1994), p. 17).

67. Edith (Eadgyth) was the mother of Harold's older children. The union was presumably a 'handfast match' (*more Danico*), like the first marriage of Cnut to Ælfgifu of Northampton; since such unions were not recognised by the Church, re-marriage, even in the lifetime of the first spouse, was perfectly possible. Harold's lands in north Mercia may have been Ealdgyth's dowry (Barlow, *Edward the Confessor*, p. 243 and note 6; Ann Williams, 'Land and Power in the Eleventh Century: the estates of Harold Godwineson', *ANS* 3 (1981), 176).

68. Rosamund McKitterick, *The Frankish Kingdoms Under the Carolingians, 751–987* (London, 1983), pp. 314–5.

69. The offer of the English succession was made either via Robert of Jumieges (as the Norman historians allege) or directly, when (as the 'D' *Chronicle* asserts) William visited England in the autumn of 1051.

70. *ASC* 'C' and 'D' record the embassy, but not the purpose, which is supplied by John of Worcester (*JnW* ii, pp. 574–7).

71. Philip Grierson, 'A Visit of Earl Harold to Flanders in 1056', *EHR*, 51 (1936), 90–7.
72. Edgar was the same age as William of Normandy's eldest son, Robert Curthose, born about 1052 (Nicholas Hooper, 'Edgar the Ætheling: Anglo-Saxon Prince, Rebel and Crusader', *ASE*, 14 (1985), 29). He may not have been brought to England until 1058 (King, 'Ealdred, Archbishop of York: the Worcester Years', pp. 127–8, 130).
73. Barlow, *Edward the Confessor*, pp. 220–9.
74. *ASC* 'C', 'D', 1065, 'E' 1066, *JnW* ii, pp. 600–1; Barlow (ed.), *Vita Edwardi*, p. 79; Raymonde Foreville (ed.), *Guillaume de Poitiers, Histoire de Guillaume le Conquerant* (Paris, 1962), pp. 172–4.
75. *ASC* 'C', 'D', 1065.

9   The Ill-Counselled King

1. Verse on King Æthelred II, thirteenth century, original cited in Simon Keynes, 'The Declining Reputation of King Æthelred the Unready', in David Hill (ed.), *Ethelred the Unready: Papers from the Millenary Conference*, BAR British series, 59 (1978), 227.
2. Simon Keynes, 'A Tale of Two Kings: Alfred the Great and Æthelred the Unready', *TRHS* 5th series, 36 (1986), 213.
3. For the laws, see Patrick Wormald, 'Æthelred the Lawmaker', in Hill (ed.), *Ethelred the Unready*, pp. 47–80. For the charters, see Keynes, *The Diplomas of Æthelred*; idem, 'Crime and Punishment in the Reign of Æthelred the Unready', Wood and Lund (eds), *People and Places in Northern Europe*, pp. 67–81.
4. Keynes, 'The Declining Reputation of King Æthelred the Unready', pp. 227–53. The 'A' text is independent, but has only one substantial entry for Æthelred's reign, the annal for 1001.
5. Pauline Stafford, 'The reign of Æthelred II, a Study in the Limitations on Royal Policy and Action', in Hill (ed.), *Ethelred the Unready*, pp. 15–46.
6. The 'A', 'B' and C' texts describe (in verse) how 'the valiant man Oslac was driven from the country, over the tossing waves, the gannet's bath, the tumult of waters, the homeland of the whale; a grey-haired man, wise and skilled in speech, he was bereft of his lands'. The 'D' and 'E' texts merely say that 'the famous (*se mæra*, 'glorious, splendid') earl' was exiled.
7. Earl Thored appears for the last time in 992 and Ælfhelm begins to attest as ealdorman (*dux*) in 993 (*ASC*, 992; Keynes, *An Atlas of Attestations in Anglo-Saxon Charters*, table LXII). He might be Thored Gunnar's son (for whom see *ASC*, 966), but the fact that Earl Thored's son Athelstan, the king's brother-in-law, was killed with the men of Cambridgeshire at the battle of Ringmere (*ASC*, 1010) suggests that he was Thored son of Oslac, who held land in Cambridgeshire (Blake (ed.), *Liber Eliensis*, p. 106).
8. Keynes, *An Atlas of Attestations in Anglo-Saxon Charters*, table LXIII; *idem*, *The Diplomas of Æthelred*, pp. 208–9 and note 199; *ASC*, 1004, 1010, 1016.

9. S. 891. Such geographical designations are almost unique, but Ælfhelm is called 'Ealdorman of the Northumbrian Provinces' in S. 1380 (996 for 994), whose witness-list may reflect a genuine document of the 990s (Keynes, *The Diplomas of Æthelred*, p. 104, note 62).

10. *JnW* ii, pp. 456–9; for Æthelred's itinerary, see Hill, *Atlas of Anglo-Saxon England*, p. 91. Eadric led the Magonsæte, the people of Shropshire and Herefordshire, at the battle of *Assandune* in 1016 (*ASC*, 1016).

11. They were children of the king's first wife, Ælfgifu, daughter of Earl Thored; for Uhtred and Ælfgifu, see Christopher Morris, *Marriage and Murder in Eleventh-century Northumbria: A Study of De Obsessione Dunelmi*, Borthwick Paper no. 82 (York, 1992). The marriage may have taken place as early as 1008, though a later date is perhaps more likely. In the later middle ages it was believed that Ulfcytel of East Anglia also married a daughter of Æthelred, but the tradition is unreliable (Campbell (ed.), *Encomium Emmae Reginae*, p. 89).

12. I Edward (Keynes, 'Royal government and the written word', pp. 234–5); II Edward, 8.

13. Campbell, 'Some Agents and Agencies of the late Anglo-Saxon State', p. 205.

14. S. 1458, A. J. Robertson, *Anglo-Saxon Charters*, 2nd edn (Cambridge, 1956), no. 41, pp. 84–7. Later reformers forbade priests to act as reeves (Roger Fowler (ed.), *The Canons of Edgar* (Oxford 1972), p. 25, note 14).

15. IV Æthelred, 3; VII Æthelred, 2,5; Robertson, *Laws of the Kings of England from Edmund to Henry I*, pp. 72–3, 114–5; Campbell, 'Some Agents and Agencies of the Late Anglo-Saxon State', pp. 205–8.

16. *GDB*, fo. 69; Frank and Caroline Thorn (eds), *Domesday Book: Wiltshire*, (Chichester, 1979), no. 24p. The king took two-thirds of the revenue from the shires and hundreds and the earl one-third (see Chapter 11, note 112, below).

17. The title 'high-reeve' was also used of the lords of Bamburgh, but in their case it is perhaps a translation of the Scottish *mormaer* (both words could be translated as 'great steward'); see Smyth, *Warlords and Holy Men*, pp. 235–6.

18. II Edmund 5; Robertson, *Laws of the Kings of England from Edmund to Henry I*, pp. 14–5. Cf the 'king's reeve' who can deputise for the ealdorman in the court of the Five Boroughs (III Æthelred, 1,1; Robertson, *Laws of the Kings of England from Edmund to Cnut*, pp. 64–5; *EHD* i, no. 43, p. 403).

19. In 1001, two high-reeves, Æthelweard and Leofwine, were among the casualties suffered by the levies of Hampshire at Dean, Sussex; in the same year the high-reeve Kola was killed at Pinhoe, leading the forces of Devon and Somerset (*ASC* 'A', 1001).

20. *ASC*, 1002; S. 926 (Campbell, (ed.) *Charters of Rochester*, no. 33, pp. 45–7); Stenton, *Latin Charters of the Anglo-Saxon Period*, pp. 76–81.

21. Eadric Streona amalgated the shire of Winchcombe with that of Gloucester to form Gloucestershire (*HC* i, pp. 280–1). Oxfordshire, Cambridgeshire, Hertfordshire, Buckinghamshire, Bedfordshire, Huntingdonshire and Northamptonshire all appear for the first time in Æthelred's reign (*ASC*, 1010, 1011, 1016).

22. *ASC*, 1013.

23. *ASC*, 1015. The remaining boroughs were presumably York itself and Bamburgh, the other regions which had submitted to Swein in 1013.

24. *ASC*, 1016; Stamford was still separate at this point, for the Danish army went 'along the Fen to Stamford, *and then* into Lincolnshire' (my italics). For Derbyshire, see *ASC* 'D', 1048; Leicestershire is first recorded in Domesday Book.

25. *ASC* 'C', 1065; C. P. Lewis, 'An Introduction to the Lancashire Domesday', in Ann Williams and G. H. Martin (eds), *The Lancashire Domesday* (London, 1991), pp. 5–6.

26. For the *Haliwerfolc*, see Chapter 7 above. The community of St Cuthbert removed from Chester-le-Street to its final home at Durham in 998.

27. S. 939 is the central part of a tripartite chirograph, recording a lawsuit concerning the will of Æthelric of Bocking in the late tenth century; one copy (the survivor) went to the archives of Canterbury, one to the king's *haligdom* (see note 54 below), and Æthelric's widow kept the third.

28. A rather pessimistic view of lay literacy appears in Patrick Wormald, 'The Uses of Literacy in Anglo-Saxon England', *TRHS* 5th series, 27 (1977), 95–114; but see *idem*, 'Charters, Law and the Settlement of Disputes in Anglo-Saxon England', pp. 161–2 and note 65.

29. S. 1454, Robertson, *Anglo-Saxon Charters*, no. 66, pp. 136–9.

30. For the *ontalu* and *oftalu* (claim and counter-claim), see S. 1456 (note 48 below).

31. The shire-court was the appropriate place for such disputes, because any sales or exchanges of land were made in the witness of the shire (S. 1473, Robertson, *Anglo-Saxon Charters*, no. 103, pp. 192–3; Kennedy, 'Disputes about *Bocland*: the Forum for their Adjudication', pp. 175–95).

32. Queen Ælfthryth sent such a written declaration to the shire-court of Somerset in the later 990s (S. 1242, F. E. Harmer, *Anglo-Saxon Writs* (Manchester, 1952), no. 108, pp. 396–7).

33. S. 1457, Robertson, *Anglo-Saxon Charters*, no. 59, pp. 122–3.

34. Godric, bishop of Rochester, produced the documents (*swutelunga*) relating to the estate of Snodland before the shire-court of Kent (S. 1456, Kennedy, 'Disputes about *Bocland*: the Forum for their Adjudication', pp. 181–5).

35. Cf the thirty-six people to be chosen as witnesses in IV Edgar, 3.4.

36. Persons of particular ill-repute were not even allowed to try: Edward the Elder's first code ordains that men found guilty of perjury shall never again be allowed to clear themselves by oath, but must go to the ordeal (I Edward, 3).

37. II Cnut, 36–7: whoever swears a false oath on the relics and is convicted shall lose a hand or half his wergeld; false testimony which falls short of this (i.e. which does not involve an oath) incurs a fine, and the offender's 'testimony henceforth shall be valueless'.

38. One might also suspect that there was something to be said on Leofwine's side, though his case is never presented; the curious appendix, in which Wynflæd is unwilling to state on oath that she has produced all his father's treasure suggests that she could be in some trouble herself. See Wormald, 'Charters, Law and the Settlement of Disputes in Anglo-Saxon England', pp. 160, 165–6.

39. S. 1456; Robertson, *Anglo-Saxon Charters*, no. 69, pp. 140–3.

40. S. 1458; Robertson, *Anglo-Saxon Charters*, no. 41, pp. 84–7.

41. Dover, Wallingford and Torksey (*GDB* ff. 1, 56, 337); compare the hospitality owed to royal *fæstingmen* in the early charters (Chapter 5 above).

42. By 1066, *sigillum* (*insegel*) could be used to describe both the royal seal and the writ to which it was attached (*GDB*, ff. 50, 51, 60v, 169, 208 bis, 374; Harmer, *Anglo-Saxon Writs*, pp. 543–5).

43. *ASC*, 1014.

44. O'Donovan, *Charters of Sherborne*, p. 48.

45. Keynes and Lapidge, *Alfred the Great*, p. 141.

46. Keynes, 'Royal Government and the Written Word', p. 247. The thegn might have to have this *gewrit* read to him, but he could at least examine it, though Ælfric's words do not necessarily imply that his notional thegn could not read.

47. IV Edgar, 15,1.

48. S. 1456.

49. *ASC*, 1086; *gewritan* presumably translates the term *breves* used in the text of Domesday Book itself. Compare the later usage of the term 'writ', e.g. 'Holy Writ' (the Bible).

50. See Chapter 11 below.

51. Two alleged writs of Æthelred are preserved, but neither is regarded as genuine (S. 945–6).

52. For a non-royal example, see the letter of Bishop Wealdhere (Chapter 5 above).

53. The glossary, produced at Abingdon, is discussed by Keynes, *The Diplomas of Æthelred*, pp. 145–7.

54. S. 1515 (see Chapter 7, note 73 above); S. 939 (see note 27 above). For this and later references to documents stored in the king's *haligdom*, see Simon Keynes, 'Regenbald the Chancellor (*sic*)', *ANS*, 10 (1987) 190 and note 36.

55. Chaplais, 'The Royal Anglo-Saxon "Chancery" of the Tenth Century Re-visited', p. 43.

56. S. 853; see also Felix, who wrote letters for King Æthelwulf of Wessex in the ninth century (Keynes, *The Diplomas of Æthelred*, pp. 135–6). The description of Ælfwine as *minister* may imply that he was a layman, and furthermore that his expertise in writing would thus be confined to the vernacular, but some laymen were competent in Latin; Ealdorman Æthelweard the Chronicler, for example.

57. M. T. Clanchy, *From Memory to Written Record: England, 1066–1307*, 2nd edn (Oxford, 1993).

58. Nelson, '"A King Across the Sea": Alfred in Continental Perspective', p. 50.

59. Pierre Chaplais, 'William of Saint-Calais and the Domesday Survey', in Holt (ed.), *Domesday Studies*, pp. 71–5; Michael Gullick, 'The manuscripts', in Ann Williams and R. W. H. Erskine (eds), *Domesday Book: Studies* (London, 1987), pp. 98–105.

60. Keynes, 'A Tale of Two Kings', pp. 205–6; P. H. Sawyer, 'The Two Viking Ages of Britain', *Medieval Scandinavia*, 2 (1969), 163–76, 203–7.

61. Keynes, 'The Historical Context of the Battle of Maldon', pp. 81–113, especially 85–98.

62. £16000 (*ASC*), £22 000 according to the treaty with the Vikings (see Chapter 8, note 8 above).

63. John Gillingham, '"The Most Precious Jewel in the English Crown": Levels of Danegeld and Heregeld in the Early Eleventh Century', *EHR*, 104 (1989), 373–84; *idem*, 'Chronicles and Coins as Evidence for Levels of Tribute and Taxation in late Tenth- and Early Eleventh-Century England', *EHR*, 105 (1990), 939–50. The *Chronicle*'s figures have been defended by M. K. Lawson, 'The Collection of Danegeld and Heregeld in the Reigns of Æthelred II and Cnut', *EHR*, 99 (1984), 721–38; *idem*, '"Those Stories look true": Levels of Taxation in the Reigns of Æthelred II and Cnut', *EHR*, 104 (1989), 385–406; *idem*, 'Danegeld and Heregeld Once More', *EHR*, 105 (1990), 951–61.

64. For post-Conquest 'danegeld', see Judith Green, 'The Last Century of Danegeld', *EHR*, 96 (1981), 241–58.

65. Keynes, 'The Historical Context of the Battle of Maldon', p. 101.

66. S. 882, dated 994, translated in *EHD* i, no. 118, pp. 527–9; *HC* i, pp. 248–9.

67. S. 943 (dated between 1006 and 1011), printed in *ECEE*, pp. 190–1.

68. *ASC* 'D', 'E', 975; Ælfric, *Life of St Swithun*, translated in *EHD* i, p. 853.

69. *JnW* ii, pp. 424–7; *GR* i, pp. 177–8; *Flores Historiarum* i, pp. 415–6.

70. *ASC* 'D', 'E', 973.

71. *Annales Cambriae*, pp. 19–20. Ælfric the homilist refers to what seems to be the same event, though he specifies eight kings, and gives neither place nor date (*Life of St Swithun*, translated in *EHD* i, p. 853).

72. Stenton concluded that 'no Anglo-Norman writer, inventing a list of names with which to garnish an ancient annal, could have come as close as this to fact or probability' (*ASE*, pp. 369–70). For the Scottish viewpoint, see Smyth, *Warlords and Holy Men*, pp. 215–238, especially 232–3.

73. Downer (ed.), *Leges Henrici Primi*, 6,1b, p. 97.

74. S.1383, printed and translated in Harmer, *Anglo-Saxon Writs*, no. 63, pp. 269–7.

75. Robertson, *Anglo-Saxon Charters*, no.72, pp. 144–5; Pamela Taylor, 'The Endowment and Military Obligations of the See of London: a Re-assessment of Three Sources', *ANS*, 14 (1992), 292–99.

76. *HC* i, pp. 80–3; Frank and Caroline Thorn (eds), *Domesday Book: Worcestershire* (Chichester, 1982), Appendix V, Worcester H.

77. For Eadric's office of *ductor*, compare that of the bishop's *archiductor*, described in the *indiculum* attributed to Archbishop Oswald (*HC* i, pp. 292–6, translated in R. Allen Brown, *The Origins of English Feudalism* (London, 1973), pp. 133–4).

78. *HC* i, pp. 77–8; Thorn and Thorn (eds), *Domesday Book: Worcestershire*, Appendix H. Crowle, in Oswaldslow, owed 'military expeditions by land and sea' (*HC* i, pp. 264–5); Bishampton was held before 1066 by four free men (*liberi homines*) owing *expeditiones et navigia*, the same service being due from the 1086 tenants (*GDB*, fol. 173).

79. *GDB*, fo. 174v. By this time, two-thirds of the Worcestershire endowment of Pershore Abbey had been transferred to Edward the Confessor's abbey at Westminster.

80. Ann Williams, *Land, Power and Politics: the Family and Career of Odda of Deerhurst* (Deerhurst, 1997), pp. 5, 10–11.

81. Williams, 'An Introduction to the Worcestershire Domesday', pp. 17–8.

82. Nicholas Hooper, 'Some Observations on the Navy in Late Anglo-Saxon England', in Harper-Bill *et al* (eds), *Studies in Medieval History Presented to R. Allen Brown*, pp. 208–13.

83. *ASC* 'D', 'E', 959.

84. *GR* i, pp. 164–5.

85. Sawyer, *From Roman Britain to Norman England*, p. 127; see also Hooper, 'Some Observations on the Navy in Late Anglo-Saxon England', pp. 204–5. For Alfred's foreign troops, see *ASC*, 896 and W. H. Stevenson (ed.), *Asser's Life of Alfred* (Oxford, 1904), pp. 38–9.

86. *ASC* 'A', 1001, 'C', 'D', 'E', 1002; for Pallig, see Keynes, *The Diplomas of Æthelred*, pp, 204–5. The massacre of the Danes at Oxford, who may have been merchants rather than stipendiary troops, is recorded in S. 909, translated in *EHD* i, no, 127, pp. 545–7. For later viking stipendiaries, see Chapter 8 above.

87. *ASC*, 992; the ensuing battle was inconclusive, though the chronicler attributes this to the incompetence of the English commanders, notably Ealdorman Ælfric of Hampshire.

88. *ASC*, 999.

89. *ASC*, 1000. The chronicler says that the fleet failed to rendezvous with the land-force, but it is equally possible that the attack was aimed from the first against both the Norse of Man and the satellites of the Scots king in Cumbria.

90. *ASC*, 1008; the figure of 310 may be an error for 300.

91. V Æthelred, 27.

92. *ASC*, 1009. For the quarrel between Brihtric and Wulfnoth, see Chapter 10 below.

93. See Chapter 8 above.

94. Richard Abels, 'Tactics, Strategy and Military Organization', in Scragg (ed.), *The Battle of Maldon, AD 991*, p. 145.

95. *ASC*, 1001, 1003. The appelation *ceorl*, 'non-noble', may be pejorative. The queen was Emma, daughter of Duke Richard I of Normandy.

96. *ASC*, 994, 1009, 1013. In 1016, the force gathered by Edmund ætheling refused to move unless they had the personal attendance of the king and the citizens (*burhwaru*) of London.

97. Note 66 above; *ASC*, 1009. Had the latter payment not been agreed, the Danes 'would quickly have captured the burh'.

98. *ASC*, 1006, and see Chapter 8 above.

99. It was the last place downstream where the Thames could still be forded; the pre-Conquest fortifications are usually taken to be those of Alfred. See Chapter 10, note 51 below.

100. *Eastseaxena ord*, where *ord* means 'point, hence spear, vanguard'; Scragg, *The Battle of Maldon*, pp. 59 (line 69), 72.

101. *ASC* 'A', 1001.

102. The two versions of the *Chronicle* do not agree over the details of the English force; 'A', which is less pejorative than the main chronicle, says that Kola and Eadsige fought 'with what army they could gather', whereas the main text (in 'C', 'D' and 'E') speaks of an 'immense army' (*ormæt fyrd*), which fled from the enemy.

103. *ASC*, 1003.

104. *ASC*, 1004. The chronicler's praise of Ulfcytel is in strong contrast to the disfavour shown to the Mercian and West Saxon commanders, but he may be right about Ulfcytel's reputation, for Sigvatr Thordarsson, an Icelandic skald in the employ of Olaf Haraldsson 'the Stout' (St Olaf), calls East Anglia 'Ulfcytel's land' (*Olafsdrapa*, verse 8, *EHD* i, no. 12, p. 305).

105. *ASC*, 1010. One of the leaders on the viking side was the Olaf Haraldsson, later an ally of Æthelred (*EHD* i, nos. 12–3, pp. 305–6 and see previous note).

106. For Athelstan, see above, note 7. Æfic may have been the high-reeve murdered by Ealdorman Leofsige (above, note 20).

107. V Æthelred, 28; see also VI Æthelred, 35 and Chapter 6, note 34, above.

108. *ASC*, 1015, 1016.

109. *ASC*, 1009. Compare the *ful fyrd* with which Æthelred expelled Cnut in 1014 (Chapter 8, note 18 above).

110. *ASC*, 1006; two months service was required from the levies of Berkshire in King Edward's reign (*GDB* fo. 56v). In 1066, however, King Harold II Godwineson kept the sea-fyrd and the land-fyrd out 'all summer and autumn', a total of about four months from early May until 8 September (*ASC*, 'C', 1066 and see Chapter 11 below).

111. The arguments are summarized in Abels, *Lordship and Military Obligation in Anglo-Saxon England*, pp. 2–4.

112. Æthelweard, *Chron*, p. 28; Abels, *Lordship and Military Obligation in Anglo-Saxon England*, p. 182.

113. *GDB*, fo. 208.

114. The Berkshire custumal, recorded in Domesday, states that 'if the king sent an army anywhere, one *miles* went from every five hides' (*GDB* fo. 56v). For the *Burghal Hidage*, see above, Chapter 6.

115. Abels, 'Tactics, Strategy and Military Organization', p. 146; *idem*, *Lordship and Military Obligation in Anglo-Saxon England*, pp. 137–40, 159–61.

116. Hooper, 'Some Observations on the Navy in late Anglo-Saxon England', p. 21; *VCH Oxfordshire* vii, p. 2. One of Æscwig's successors, Eadnoth, fell at *Assandune* in 1016.

117. According to Domesday, Whitchurch 'had always belonged to the monastery'(*GDB* fo. 41); it was (allegedly) given by Edward the Elder (S. 378). In 1066, there were two subsidiary holdings, at Freefolk and Whitnal, both apparently held as temporary loans from the church; perhaps one was the land of Leofwine of Whitchurch. Godwine's land, which came to him from his father (S. 1491), was probably at Martyr Worthy, Hants, held in 1066 by the monks of the Old Minster, Winchester (*GDB* fo. 41).

118. III Edmund, 1 (see Chapter 7 above). 'Twelfhind' and 'twihind' refer to the wergelds (1200s and 200s) of thegns and ceorls respectively. See Abels, *Lordship and Military Obligation in Anglo-Saxon England*, p. 84.

119. Ælfwine Ælfric's son declares that the thegns of Mercia will have no cause to reproach him for deserting his lord, and Leofsunu of Sturmer, a minor local thegn, expresses the same concern, though on a smaller scale: 'the steadfast warriors around Sturmer will not need to taunt

me . . . that I came home lordless'. Byrhtnoth in turn speaks of his duty to defend 'the land of Æthelred, my lord' (Scragg, *The Battle of Maldon*, pp. 58, 64, 65).

120. *ASC*, 1010 draws the same distinction between the faithful men, who fight and die, and the cowards, who save themselves by flight, as does *The Battle of Maldon*. See also Ann Williams, 'The Battle of Maldon and "The Battle of Maldon": History, Poetry and Propaganda', *Medieval History*, 2 (1992), 38–9.

121. Karl Leyser, 'Early medieval warfare', in Cooper (ed), *The Battle of Maldon: Fiction and Fact*, p. 97.

122. *ASC*, 1003.

123. *ASC*, 1010.

124. *ASC*, 1013.

125. *The Sermon of the Wolf to the English*, trans. *EHD* i, no. 240, pp. 856–7. Wulfstan's self-given appellation *lupus*, 'wolf' is a pun on the first element of his name.

10   The Danish Conquest

1. Greenway (ed.), *Henry of Huntingdon, Historia Anglorum*, pp. 366–7. Cnut's claim to the lordship of Scotland is based on an agreement with Malcolm II (1005–34) and the other northern kings in 1031 (*JnW*, ii, pp. 512–3; *ASC* 'D', 'E' and see B. T. Hudson, 'Cnut and the Scottish kings', *EHR*, 107 (1992), 350–60).

2. Roberta Frank, 'King Cnut in the Verse of his Skalds', in Rumble (ed.), *The Reign of Cnut*, pp. 110–13.

3. Niels Lund, '"Denemearc", "Tanmarker but" and "Tanmaurk ala"', in Wood and Lund (eds), *People and Places in Northern Europe*, pp. 161–9.

4. Niels Lund, 'Cnut's Danish Kingdom', in Rumble (ed.), *The Reign of Cnut*, pp. 32–3.

5. Lawson, *Cnut*, p. 49. The 'C' *Chronicle* was compiled at Abingdon *c.* 1044, and continued to be written there until the Conquest (Patrick W. Connor, *The Anglo- Saxon Chronicle: a Collaborative Edition, 10; the Abingdon Chronicle, 956–1066* (Cambridge, 1996), p. xxxiv). 'D' was put together at some northern house in the late eleventh or early twelfth centuries, and 'E' as it stands dates from 1121, when it was copied and continued at Peterborough, although entries were being written at St Augustine's, Canterbury, in the mid-eleventh century (D. M. Dumville, 'Some Aspects of Annalistic Writing at Canterbury in the Eleventh and Early Twelfth Centuries', *Peritia* 2 (1983), 23–57; for 'D', see also Patrick Wormald, *How do we Know so Much About Anglo-Saxon Deerhurst?* (Deerhurst, 1993), pp. 9–17, 26–7).

6. Campbell (ed.), *Encomium Emmae Reginae*.

7. Barlow (ed.), *Vita Edwardi*.

8. Birgit Sawyer, 'The Evidence of Scandinavian Runic Inscriptions', in Rumble (ed.), *The reign of Cnut*, pp. 23–6; Frank, 'King Cnut in the verse of his skalds', pp. 106–24; Eric Christiansen (ed.), *Saxo Grammaticus, Danorum Regum Heroumque Historia, Books X–XVI*, BAR International series, 84 (1980).

9. Tschan (tr.), *Adam of Bremen*; van Houts (ed.), *Gesta Normannorum Ducum*. For Thietmar, see the extracts translated in *EHD* i, no. 27, pp. 318–21.

10. Harthacnut's name appears on three charters, two of dubious authenticity, and two writs, which may be genuine (S. 993–7). Harold I is represented only by a memorandum (S. 1467) recording a dispute between Christ Church, Canterbury and the rival house of St Augustine's.

11. Keynes, 'Cnut's earls', in Rumble (ed.), *The Reign of Cnut*, pp. 48–52.

12. M. K. Lawson, 'Archbishop Wulfstan and the Homiletic Element in the Laws of Æthelred and Cnut', *EHR*, 107 (1992), reprinted in Rumble (ed.), *The Reign of Cnut*, pp. 140–64; Pauline Stafford, 'The laws of Cnut and the history of Anglo-Saxon Royal Promises', *ASE*, 10 (1982), 173–90; Kennedy, 'Cnut's Law-Code of 1018', pp. 57–81.

13. R. Allen Brown, *The Normans and the Norman Conquest*, 2nd edn (Woodbridge, 1985), p. 65.

14. The most prominent were the earls of Northumbria, East Anglia and the west midlands (see below).

15. Simon Keynes concludes that 'there was more "continuity" than none, and rather less than a lot' ('Cnut's earls', p. 79, note 206), while for Lawson, the Danish landowners formed 'a sizeable minority' in the predominantly English shires (Lawson, *Cnut*, p. 168). For some English survivors, see H. P. R. Finberg, 'The House of Ordgar and the Foundation of Tavistock Abbey', *EHR*, 58 (1943); Ann Williams, 'A West-Country Magnate of the Eleventh Century: the Family, Estates and Patronage of Beorhtric Son of Ælfgar', in K. S. B. Keats-Rohan (ed.), *Family Trees and the Roots of Politics* (Woodbridge, 1997), pp. 41–68; *idem*, *Land, Power and Politics: the Family and Career of Odda of Deerhurst*.

16. Katharin Mack, 'Changing Thegns: Cnut's Conquest and the English Aristocracy', *Albion*, 16 (1984), 375–87. For a more restricted and less cataclysmic analysis, see Williams, '"Cockles amongst the Wheat"', pp. 1–22.

17. Gillian Fellows-Jensen, 'Danish Place-Names and Personal Names in England. The Influence of Cnut?', in Rumble (ed.), *The Reign of Cnut*, pp. 123–140.

18. Cnut's mother, not named in any contemporary source, was the widow of Eric of Sweden when she married Swein; she bore him three children (Harald, Cnut and Estrith), but he seems to have repudiated her, and she returned to Poland, whence her sons fetched her after their father's death (Tschan (tr.), Adam of Bremen, p. 78; Campbell (ed.), *Encomium Emmae Reginae*, p. 19).

19. S. 962; Keynes, 'Cnut's earls', pp. 64–5. His name 'presumably represents an Anglicized form of the Slavic name Vratislav'.

20. For Tove, see Tinna Damgaard-Sorensen, 'Danes and Wends: a Study of Danish Attitudes to the Wends', Wood and Lund (ed.), *People and Places in Northern Europe*, pp. 176–7. She may have been Harald's second wife, for Adam of Bremen names Gunnhild as Swein Forkbeard's mother (Tschan (tr.), p. 56). A re-marriage would help to explain the rift between Harald and Swein, and it was to the Wends that Harald fled when Swein rebelled against him in 987. For Gottschalk, see Tschan (tr.), Adam of Bremen, pp. 100–1.

21. *GDB*, fo. 164. For Tovi's byname *Widenesci* (*recte Winedesci*), see Gösta Tengvik, *Old English Bynames* (Uppsala, 1938), p. 136. For Gunnhild, see note 95 below.

22. Lesley Abrams, 'Eleventh-Century Missions and the early Stages of Ecclesiast-
    ical Organization in Scandinavia', *ANS*, 17 (1995), 21–40; *idem*, 'The Anglo-
    Saxons and the Christianization of Scandinavia', *ASE*, 24 (1995), 213–49.
23. Lawson, *Cnut*, p. 129; Simon Keynes, 'Giso, Bishop of Wells (1061–88)',
    ANS, 19 (1997), 205–7.
24. Tschan (tr.), Adam of Bremen, p. 192.
25. Keynes, 'Giso, Bishop of Wells', pp. 207–9; *Chron Ramsey*, pp. 135–44.
26. Herman attests two charters of Harthacnut as a royal priest (S. 982, 993),
    the second of which is also attested by Leofric (Keynes, 'Giso, Bishop of
    Wells', pp. 208–9).
27. Lawson, *Cnut*, p. 129 and note 57; for the name, see Tschan (tr.), Adam of
    Bremen, p. 91; J. Gerchow, 'Prayers for King Cnut: the Liturgical Commem-
    moration of a Conqueror', in C. Hicks (ed.), *England in the Eleventh Century*
    (Stamford, 1992), pp. 235–6.
28. Michael Hare, 'Cnut and Lotharingia: Two Notes', *ASE*, forthcoming. I am
    very grateful to Mr Hare for the opportunity to read this paper before pub-
    lication.
29. Adam of Bremen (Tschan (tr.), p. 56) claims that Swein Forkbeard's baptis-
    mal name was Otto, from his godfather, the German Emperor; the name
    may be correct, if not the alleged circumstances (Hare, 'Cnut and Lotharing-
    ia: Two Notes').
30. *EHD* i, no. 49, pp. 416–8.
31. Lund, 'Cnut's Danish Kingdom', pp. 39–42. For earlier agreements on
    tolls, see Simon Keynes, 'The Anglo-Saxon Entries in the Liber Vitae of
    Brescia', in Jane Roberts and Janet L. Nelson (eds), *Alfred the Wise: Studies in
    Honour of Janet Bately* (Cambridge, 1997), p. 99.
32. Keynes, 'Giso, bishop of Wells', pp. 203–71.
33. Dorothy Whitelock, 'Archbishop Wulfstan, Homilist and Statesman', *TRHS*
    4th series, 24 (1942), 42–60.
34. Robertson, *Laws of the Kings of England from Edmund to Henry I*, pp. 154–219;
    translated extracts in *EHD* i, no. 50, pp. 419–30.
35. The *Chronicle* reports that after the northern rising of 1065, Earl Harold
    renewed 'the Law of King Cnut' (*ASC* 'D','E', 1065 and see Chapter 11
    below).
36. Stenton, *ASE*, p. 412. For the terminology, see Hooper, 'Military Develop-
    ments in the Reign of Cnut', p. 89; Lund, 'The Armies of Swein Forkbeard
    and Cnut', pp. 110–2.
37. The Warwickshire landowner Thorkell of Arden had a Scandinavian name,
    as did his brothers Ketilbjorn and Guthmund, but they were almost certain-
    ly of English descent (Ann Williams, 'A Vicecomital Family in Pre-Conquest
    Warwickshire', *ANS*, 11 (1989), 279–95).
38. R. H. C. Davis, 'Did the Anglo-Saxons have Warhorses?', in Hawkes (ed.),
    Weapons and Warfare in Anglo-Saxon England, p. 143.
39. Thored *steallare* attests S. 981, an alleged grant of Cnut to Christ Church,
    Canterbury, but the charter is spurious.
40. Herman of Bury, *Miraculi Sancti Eadmundi*, in Thomas Arnold (ed.), *Memori-
    als of St Edmund's Abbey, Bury*, Rolls Series (London, 1890–96) i, pp. 54–6.
    Harthacnut's *maior domus* Styr is recorded by John of Worcester, with his

steward (*dispensator*) Eadric and his executioner (*carnifex*) Thrond (*JnW* ii, pp. 530–1).

41. Pamela Nightingale, 'The Origin of the Court of Husting and Danish influence on London's Development into a Capital City', *EHR*, 102 (1987), 559–78.

42. Keynes, *An Atlas of Attestations in Anglo-Saxon Charters*, tables LXX, LXXV.

43. Leslie Watkiss and Marjorie Chibnall (eds), *The Waltham Chronicle* (Oxford, 1994), pp. xvi–xix, xxxvi, 1–27, 62–3. Later writers use similar words of Osgod Clapa (*ut secundus a rege non minus quam rex ipse cunctis formidandus haberetur*, Arnold (ed.), *Memorials of St Edmund's Abbey, Bury* i, pp. 135–6, cf p. 364).

44. S. 1462.

45. *ASC*, 1042.

46. Tovi attests the will of Ælfric *modercope* (S. 1490, dating from 1042–3); he might be the Tovi *comes* to whom Edward granted land at *Bergh* (unidentified) in 1048 (S. 1017, *ECNENM*, pp. 251–2). Esgar attests the Confessor's charters from 1059 to 1066, as the king's steward (*dapifer*) and as *procurator* of the royal household; a number of royal writs also include him in their address-clauses (Keynes, *An Atlas of Attestations in Anglo-Saxon Charters*, table LXXV(1); *idem*, 'Regenbald the chancellor (*sic*)', pp. 205–6).

47. It is usually assumed that both Osgod and Tovi were Danes in Cnut's following, though Osgod may have been an Englishman (Williams, 'The King's Nephew: the Family and Career of Ralph of Hereford', pp. 333–4).

48. Larson, *The King's Household*, pp. 146–52, esp. p. 148; *Geþynco*, in Liebermann, *Die Gesetze der Angelsachsen*, i, p. 456, translated *EHD* i, no. 52A, p. 432.

49. Dorothy Whitelock, 'Introduction', Blake (ed), *Liber Eliensis*, p. xiii. A different view of the stallers and their significance is taken by Katharin Mack, 'The Stallers: Administrative Innovation in the Reign of Edward the Confessor', *J. Med. Hist*, 12 (1986), 123–34.

50. S. 157 (Robertson, *Anglo-Saxon Charters*, no. 59, pp. 122–5, 367); S. 572; Blake (ed.), *Liber Eliensis*, pp. xiii–xiv, 73, 80, 86n, 93, 97, 109–110; *Chron Abingdon* ii, p. 260); Larson, *The King's Household*, pp. 123–4. The *Liber Eliensis* describes him as 'one who was in the king's confidence' (*quidam qui erat regis a secretis*) and the meaning of *pedisequus, sequipedus* seems to be 'one who sits at the feet' (see also Chapter 5 above).

51. *GDB*, ff. 56, 75 and compare the half-mark paid from Exeter *ad opus militium* (fo. 100); Hooper, 'Military Developments in the Reign of Cnut', pp. 92–3.

52. Alexander R. Rumble and Rosemary Morris, '*Translatio Sancti Ælfegi Cantuariensis archiepiscopi et martiris*', Rumble (ed.), *The Reign of Cnut*, pp. 281–315, esp. 286–8. Nicholas Hooper is more inclined to accept Osbern's description as a genuine reminiscence of Cnut's time ('The Housecarls in England in the Eleventh Century', *ANS*, 7 (1984), 172, note 62).

53. *ASC* 'E', 1035; 'C' and 'D' record Emma's residence at Winchester, but do not mention the king's housecarls.

54. *JnW* ii, pp. 532–3. The *Chronicle* ('C' and 'D' only) says merely that two unnamed housecarls were killed in the monastery while attempting to collect the geld. The five earls were Thuri of the east midlands ('the middle people'), Leofric of Mercia, Godwine of Wessex, Siward of Northumbria and

Ranig of Herefordshire. For later references to the use of housecarls, whether of the king or of his earls, in a military capacity, see *ASC*, 1054, 1065.

55. *ASC*, 986; Keynes, *The Diplomas of Æthelred*, pp. 178–80.
56. Campbell, 'Some Agents and Agencies of the Late Anglo-Saxon State', pp.
     201–5; Hooper, 'Military Developments in the Reign of Cnut', pp. 95–6;
     S. 1466, printed in Robertson, *Anglo-Saxon Charters*, no. 90, pp. 174–5.
57. Robertson, *Anglo-Saxon Charters*, no. 115, pp. 214–5.
58. Keynes, ' A Lost Cartulary of St Albans Abbey', pp. 266–7. The Latin sum-
     mary (S.1425) translates *huscarlan* as *barones*. Vagn (*Waga, Wagen*) was a pros-
     perous landholder in Warwickshire and Staffordshire, giving his name to
     Wootton Wawen (*GDB* ff. 242v, 250).
59. Dorothy Whitelock, 'Scandinavian Personal Names in the Liber Vitae of
     Thorney Abbey', *Saga-Book of the Viking Society*, 12 (1940), 132–40; reprinted in
     History, Law and Literature in Tenth- and Eleventh Century England (London, 1981).
60. Harmer, *Anglo-Saxon Writs*, nos 116–7, pp. 411–2.
61. John Insley, 'Some Scandinavian Personal Names from South-west England',
     Nam och Bygd, 70 (1982), 77–93; *idem*, 'Some Scandinavian Personal Names
     from South-west England from Post-Conquest Records', *Studia Anthroponymica
     Scandinavia*, 3 (1985), 25–58.
62. S. 1461, Robertson, *Anglo-Saxon Charters*, pp. 150–1; *GDB*, ff. 5v, 8, 8v, 9:
     Ann Williams, 'Lost Worlds: Kentish Society in the Eleventh Century', *Medieval
     Prosopography*, forthcoming. See also S. 1221, a Christ Church forgery,
     recording the gift of Saltwood, Kent, by Haldan *scearpa*, a *princeps* of Cnut,
     for the souls of his wife Leofdæg and Leofflæd, the original donor (Keynes,
     'Cnut's earls', p. 62).
63. S. 955, dated 1019 (Kelly, *Charters of Shaftesbury Abbey*, no. 30); S. 969, dated
     1033 (O'Donovan, *Charters of Sherborne*, no. 20); S. 961, dated 1024 and
     S.1602d, probably 1033 (Simon Keynes, 'The Lost Cartulary of Abbotsbury',
     ASE, 18 (1989), 229–30).
64. S. 1063, Harmer, *Anglo-Saxon Writs*, no. 1.
65. Ann Williams, 'Introduction to the Dorset Domesday', *VCH Dorset* iii
     (1969), 33–4.
66. *GDB* fo. 75; the rate was 1 mark of silver per 10 hides. See also note 51 above.
67. Keynes, 'The Lost Cartulary of Abbotsbury', pp. 208–9. The Abbotsbury
     Gild Statutes are translated in *EHD* i, no. 139.
68. S.1032; Robertson, *Anglo-Saxon Charters*, no. 120, pp. 220–3. Horton, which
     became a cell of Sherborne in 1122, was also endowed by the Devonshire
     magnate Ordwulf (O'Donovan, *Charters of Sherborne*, pp. lx–lxi).
69. *ASC* 'E', 1035.
70. *JnW* ii, pp. 530–1.
71. *ASC* 'E', 1049 and see Chapter 11, note 46 below.
72. Lund, 'The Armies of Swein Forkbeard and Cnut', pp. 105–18, esp. pp. 110–12.
73. See Chapter 8 above.
74. *HC*, pp. 277–8; Ann Williams, 'The Spoliation of Worcester', *ANS*, 19
     (1997), 384–5.
75. II Cnut, 79, translated in *EHD* i, no. 50, p. 430 (the passage in brackets
     occurs in only one of the surviving versions of the text); S. 989; O'Donovan,
     Charters of Sherborne, p. 72.

76. *ASC* 'E', 1040. The *hamele*, which 'refers to the rope or withy grommet securing an oar to its single thole', is used for a unit of the ship's company (probably representing a single man); see N. A. M. Rodger, 'Cnut's Geld and the Size of Danish Ships', *EHR*, 110 (1995), 392–403.

77. *ASC*, 1040: 'C' and 'D' give 60 ships and 'E' 62 ships, but all versions agree that the sums involved were very burdensome. Compare the £21 000 paid to the fleet in 1014 and the £22 000 agreed in Æthelred's treaty of 994 with Olaf Tryggvasson (see Chapter 8 above).

78. *ASC*, 1041.

79. *ASC* 'E', 1050, 'D', 1051; see Chapter 11 below.

80. For the possible reintroduction of the heregeld between 1051 and 1066, see Pamela Nightingale, 'The Ora, the Mark and the Mancus: Weight-standards and the Coinage in Eleventh-century England', *Numismatic Chronicle*, 144 (1984), 245.

81. *ASC*, 1017.

82. IV Edgar, 15 (Chapter 7 above).

83. Keynes, 'Cnut's Earls', p. 81; Lawson, *Cnut*, p. 184.

84. See IV Edgar, 15, where Oslac of Northumbria is 'earl', while Æthelwine of East Anglia and Ælfhere of Mercia are 'ealdormen'.

85. Godwine in the east and Æthelweard in the west; an Earl Sired, who attests in 1019 and 1023 (S. 954, 960), may have had authority in Kent (Keynes, 'Cnut's earls', pp. 67–74, 76), but see below, note 108. For Æthelwine, see Hart, 'Athelstan "Half-king" and his Family', pp. 133–7.

86. Williams, '"Cockles amongst the wheat"', pp. 6–11; Keynes, 'Cnut's Earls', pp. 54–78.

87. S. 891; see also S. 932 (1014) and 1459 (between 1014 and 1016) and Chapter 9 above.

88. S. 1384.

89. The Evesham Chronicle associates the murder of Northman with the killing of Eadric Streona 'and with him also many of his *milites*' (*Chron Evesham*, p. 84).

90. *HC* i, p. 274.

91. For Leofric, see S. 1423, 1460 (Robertson, *Anglo-Saxon Charters*, nos. 81, 83), S. 991 (Harmer *Anglo-Saxon Writs*, no. 48 and note 93 below). For Edwin, see S. 1462 (Robertson, *Anglo-Saxon Charters*, no. 78), and *ASC* 'C', 1039, 'E' 1052, which record his death at the battle of Rhyd y Groes, at the head of the English levies. The fourth of Leofwine's sons, Godwine, seems not to have held any official position.

92. Godric, who attests a charter of 1022 as ealdorman (*dux*) might be one of them, and another possibility is Earl Sihtric, who appears in the late 1020s; Godric is associated with Norfolk and Sihtric with Hertfordshire (Keynes, 'Cnut's earls', pp. 65, 77–8, 86).

93. S. 985, 987–8, 991; Harmer, *Anglo-Saxon Writs*, nos. 26, 29–30, 48. The first three come from the archive of Christ Church, Canterbury; S. 985 is addressed to Æthelwine *scirman* (who also attests S. 1461, a private memorandum) and Æthelric; S. 987–8 are addressed to Æthelric, with no title, but the text of S. 987 refers to Æthelric as *gerefa*. S. 991 (Harmer, *Anglo-Saxon Writs*, no. 48) exists only as a Latin translation of dubious authority,

addressed to Bishop Leofsige (of Worcester), Earl Hakon, and Leofric the sheriff (*vicecomes*).

94. Robin Fleming, *Kings and Lords in Conquest England* (Cambridge, 1991), pp. 21–52.
95. *JnW* ii, pp. 510–1, 540–1; *HC* i, pp. 251–2. Her father was *Wyrtgeorn*, king of the Wends and her mother possibly *Santslave*, Cnut's sister, commemorated in the *Liber Vitae* of Hyde Abbey (Keynes, 'Cnut's earls', pp. 64–5). After Hakon's death in 1030 (see note 97 below), she married Earl Harald, who attests a Worcester lease of 1042 (S. 1396; Williams, '"Cockles Amongst the Wheat"', pp. 9–11).
96. Lund, 'Cnut's Danish kingdom', pp. 27–8.
97. Eric of Lade is not heard of after 1023; his son Hakon was drowned in 1030 (*ASC*, 1030, which calls him 'the gallant (*dohtiga*) earl'). Eilaf may have survived until the end of Cnut's reign, but is said to have returned to Scandinavia when Cnut died (Williams, '"Cockles Amongst the Wheat"', pp. 6–11).
98. Robin Fleming, 'Domesday Estates of the King and the Godwinesons: a Study in Late Saxon Politics', *Speculum*, 58 (1983), 987–1007; D. G. Raraty, 'Earl Godwine of Wessex: the Origins of his Power and his Political Affiliations', *History*, 74 (1989), 3–19; Keynes, 'Cnut's earls', pp. 70–4, 84–8.
99. *ASC*, 1009. It is the 'F' text, written at Canterbury after 1066, which identifies Wulfnoth as Godwine's father.
100. He may have been portreeve of Canterbury, and his estate of over 200 hides made him one of the richest of King Edward's thegns (Williams, 'Lost Worlds: Kentish Society in the Eleventh Century', forthcoming).
101. On the eve of the Norman Conquest, Godwine's family possessed about a third of the taxable land in Sussex, much of which was probably their patrimony (Williams, 'Land and Power in the Eleventh Century: the Estates of Harold Godwineson', pp. 176–7).
102. *JnW* ii, pp. 460–1. Stenton says Wulfnoth 'seduced the crews of twenty ships from their allegiance, and took to piracy along the south coast' (*ASE*, p. 382); Allen Brown describes him as a 'turncoat' (*The Normans and the Norman Conquest*, p. 66). Brihtric himself vanishes from sight after 1009 (Keynes, *Diplomas of Æthelred*, p. 216).
103. *JnW* ii, pp. 460–1; John's identification of Godwine's father as Eadric Streona's nephew is impossible on chronological grounds. For Sigeferth and Morcar, see Chapter 8 above.
104. S. 1503; *GDB* ff. 24, 34.
105. *ASC*, 1020 and note 85 above.
106. Barlow (ed.), *Vita Edwardi*, pp. 5–6.
107. Keynes, 'Cnut's earls', pp. 73–4.
108. Archbishop Æthelnoth (1020–38) held the third penny (the earl's share) of Kent's revenues, which was transferred to Godwine only in the time of his successor Eadsige (Brooks, *The Early History of the Church of Canterbury*, p. 301).
109. S. 970, dated 1033; *GDB* fo. 47.
110. Kelly, *Charters of St Augustine's Abbey*, p. xxxi; *GDB* fo. 9v.

111. Tim Tatton-Brown, 'Churches of the Canterbury Diocese', in Blair (ed.), *Minsters and Parish Churches*, p. 110. See also S. 1472 (Robertson, *Anglo-Saxon Charters*, pp. 190–1), dated to the early 1040s, in which Godwine brokered an agreement between St Augustine's and Leofwine, priest of Dover (Ann Williams, 'The Anglo-Norman abbey' in Richard Gem (ed.), *St Augustine's Abbey, Canterbury* (London, 1997), p. 62). Harold, Godwine's heir, had some interest in the lands of the church (*GDB*, fo. 2).

112. Eadsige became a monk of Christ Church in 1035, and was almost immediately promoted as Æthelnoth's assistant (*chorepiscopus*); it is clear that he was being groomed, at the king's instance, as Æthelnoth's successor (Brooks, *The Early History of the Church of Canterbury*, pp. 295–6).

113. Brooks, *The Early History of the Church of Canterbury*, pp. 300–1.

114. Keynes, 'Cnut's earls', pp. 74–5, 77–8.

115. Leofwine received lands in Warwickshire in 998 (S. 892), and in Herefordshire in 1014 (S. 932); his son Northman held an estate at Hampton, Worcs, later claimed by Evesham Abbey (S. 873; *Chron Evesham*, p. 84).

116. *Chron Ramsey*, p. 146; *GDB* ff. 138, 205v, 207; Ann Williams, *The English and the Norman Conquest* (Woodbridge, 1995), pp. 54–5. It may have been Northman who gave Twywell, Northants, to Thorney Abbey (S. 931; *ECEE*, pp. 193–8; *GDB* fo. 222v), and Leofwine was commemorated as a benefactor at Peterborough, a house ruled between 1052 and 1066 by his great-nephew, Abbot Leofric (W. T. Mellows (ed.), *The Chronicle of Hugh Candidus* (Oxford, 1948), p. 68). Hugh Candidus is the only authority to record the name of Leofwine's father Ælfwine.

117. Williams, 'The Spoliation of Worcester', pp. 382–408, esp. 386–8. Æfic, prior of Evesham (d. 1037/8), became confessor to Leofric and his wife Godgifu (*Chron Evesham*, p. 84).

118. King, 'Ealdred, archbishop of York: the Worcester years', pp. 125–7.

119. Williams, '"Cockles Amongst the Wheat"', p. 8. The first witness to an Evesham lease of 1016–23 is 'the Lady Ælfgifu, who governs the monastery'; this is always assumed to be Emma, who took the name Ælfgifu on her marriage to Æthelred II, but I see no reason why it should not refer to Ælfgifu of Northampton (S. 1432; Robertson, *Anglo-Saxon Charters*, no. 81, pp. 156–7).

120. Sawyer, *Charters of Burton*, pp. xli–xliii. Two of Ælfgar's and Ælfgifu's children were named Ealdgyth and Morcar.

121. See Chapter 8 above.

122. William E. Kapelle, *The Norman Conquest of the North* (London, 1979), pp. 27–49.

123. Harmer, *Anglo-Saxon Writs*, no. 121; for the problems of its date and authorship, see Phythian-Adams, *loc.cit.*, pp. 174–81.

124. Phythian-Adams, *Land of the Cumbrians*, pp. 132–3; *ASC* 'C', 'D', 1054. As in Harold's Welsh campaign of 1063 (Chapter 8 above), Siward employed both land- and sea-forces, as had Athelstan in 934 (*ASC*).

125. Phythian-Adams, *Land of the Cumbrians*, pp. 138–52.

126. *HR*, p. 191 (1070); Lewis, 'An Introduction to the Lancashire Domesday', pp. 5–7 (the estates appear in the Yorkshire folios, see Chapter 9, note 25 above); *ASC*, 1092.

11   Authority and Ambition, 1042–66

1. The major accounts are Barlow, *Edward the Confessor*; H. R. Loyn, *Harold Son of Godwin*, The Historical Association, Hastings and Bexhill branch, no. 2 (1966), reprinted in *Society and Peoples: Studies in the History of England and Wales, c. 600–1200*, pp. 299–321; Ian W. Walker, *Harold, the Last Anglo-Saxon King* (Stroud, 1997).

2. Notably Allen Brown, *The Normans and the Norman Conquest*, pp. 51–93; see also Fleming, *Kings and Lords in Conquest England*, pp. 53–103.

3. For Harold's Welsh campaign, see Chapter 8 above, and for Siward's authority in Cumbria, Chapter 10 above. The most detailed description of Stamford Bridge (25 September 1066) is in *ASC* 'C', which ends with Harold II's triumphant rout of the Norwegians; for a modern study of the battle, see F. W. Brooks, *The Battle of Stamford Bridge*, East Yorkshire Historical Society local history series no. 6 (1956).

4. See Chapter 10, note 5 above.

5. For the dating of its composition (1065–6 for Book I, 1067–70 for Book II), see Barlow (ed.), *Vita Edwardi*, pp. xxv–xxx.

6. Adam of Bremen and William of Jumieges, see Chapter 10 above. William of Poitiers, see Foreville (ed.), *Guillaume de Poitiers*; a partial English translation is available in R. Allen Brown, *The Norman Conquest* (London, 1984), pp. 15–41. The Tapestry, see David Wilson, *The Bayeux Tapestry* (London, 1985) and F. M. Stenton, *The Bayeux Tapestry* rev. ed. (London, 1965).

7. The voluminous literature on Domesday is surveyed (up to 1986) in David Bates, *A Bibliography of Domesday Book* (Woodbridge, 1986); for subsequent work, see especially David Roffe, 'The making of Domesday Book reconsidered', *Haskins Soc. J.*, 6 (1994), 152–66; Fleming, 'Oral testimony and the Domesday Inquest', pp. 101–22.

8. Keynes, 'The Æthelings in Normandy', pp. 173–205.

9. Including Robert of Jumieges (Barlow (ed.), *Vita Edwardi*, p. 17) and his nephew Ralph (*Chron Ramsey*, p. 171). Barlow (*Vita Edwardi*, p. 17, note 1 and *Edward the Confessor*, p. 50) adds Leofric, later bishop of Exeter, and Herman, later bishop of Ramsbury, but both had been Harthacnut's clerks (Keynes, *An Atlas of Attestations in Anglo-Saxon Charters*, table LXVIII and see Chapter 10 above).

10. C. P. Lewis, 'The French in England before the Norman Conquest'. *ANS*, 17 (1995), 123–44.

11. Ralph called his son Harold, while Robert's son was called Swein; it may not be coincidental that these were the names of Godwine's eldest sons. Richard fitzScrob, Robert's son-in-law, chose the more neutral Osbern, used on both sides of the channel, for his son and heir.

12. Foreville (ed.), *Gesta Guillielmi*, pp. 169–70; Lewis, 'The French in England before the Norman Conquest', pp. 128–9, 136–7.

13. George Garnett, '"*Franci et Angli*": the Legal Distinctions between Peoples after the Conquest', *ANS*, 8 (1986), 118, 121.

14. Ælfweard, bishop of London, died on 25 July 1044; for Robert's attestations as bishop, see Keynes, *An Atlas of Attestations in Anglo-Saxon Charters*, table LXXII.

15. *ASC* 'C' (1049), describes it as 'a bad appointment' and 'D' says 'he did nothing like a bishop in it, so much so that we are ashamed to say anything more about it'. 'E' says that Ulf was nearly deposed at the papal council of Vercelli (September 1050), maintaining his see only by bribery.
16. Williams, 'The King's Nephew: the Family and Career of Ralph, Earl of Hereford', pp. 327–43.
17. S. 1020.
18. Keynes, *An Atlas of Attestations in Anglo-Saxon Charters*, table LXXV(I). For Robert's castle, see *ASC* 'E', 1052 and R. Allen Brown, *Castles from the Air* (Cambridge, 1989), pp. 90–1. Robert attests S. 1000 and 1002, dated 1043 and 1044 respectively, but both are forgeries, and the witness-lists are inconsistent with the alleged dates.
19. *ASC*, 1043.
20. S. 998 (1042) and S. 1005 (1044), both to Ordgar of Devon; S. 999 (1043), to Ælfstan; S. 1004 (1044), to Urk of Abbotsbury; S. 1010 (1045), to Thorð; S. 1014 (1046), to Athelstan; S. 1017 (1048), to Tofig *comes*; S. 1018 (1049) to Ælfwine *militaris*; S. 1018 (1049), to Eadulf. At least some of these men (Ordgar, Urk and perhaps Thorð) can be shown to have been thegns of Cnut and Harthacnut.
21. Brooks, *The Early History of the Church of Canterbury*, pp. 295–303.
22. Barlow (ed.), *Vita Edwardi*, pp. 18–9.
23. Spearhafoc is said to have robbed both the king and his bishopric (*Chron Abingdon* i, p. 463). Rothulf had been in the service of the Norwegian kings and is perhaps identical with the Hrodolfr who spent 19 years as a bishop in Iceland (Abrams, 'The Anglo-Saxons and the Christianization of Scandinavia', pp. 223–4; Lewis, 'The French in England before the Norman Conquest', p. 127).
24. Ælfric *puttoc* died in 1051 (*ASC* 'C', 1050, 'D', 1051). Cynesige's accession is mentioned only by John of Worcester (*JnW* ii, pp. 556–7).
25. Only 'D' and 'E' give a complete account of the year 1051.
26. He married Edward's full sister Godgifu, after the death in 1035 of her first husband Drogo, count of Amiens and the Vexin (Earl Ralph's father). Godgifu was dead by 1049, when Eustace remarried (David Bates, 'Lord Sudeley's Ancestors: the Family of the Counts of Amiens, Valois and the Vexin in France and England During the Eleventh Century', in Robert Smith (ed.), *The Sudeleys, Lords of Toddington* (London, 1987), pp. 36–9).
27. Thus committing *hamsocn*, attack on a man in his own house (see above, Chapter 7).
28. See Chapter 10, note 111 above.
29. The post-Conquest castle, like those at Hastings and Pevensey, incorporates the pre-Conquest church (A. J. Taylor, 'Evidence for a Pre-Conquest Origin for the Chapels in Hastings and Pevensey Castles' *Chateau Gaillard*, 3 (1969), 144–51). William of Poitiers records Earl Harold's promise, in 1064, to fortify a castle at Dover for the duke, and his account of the Norman attack of 1066 refers to a *castellum*, 'sited on a cliff whose natural steepness has been everywhere artificially scarped, rising like a wall sheer out of the sea as high as an arrow can be shot'; he adds, however, that the Conqueror spent eight days at Dover, 'adding those fortifications (*firmamenta*) which it lacked' (Foreville

(ed.), *Gesta Guillielmi*, pp. 104–5, 211–12). It was this castle which Eustace attempted to seize in 1067 (Williams, *The English and the Norman Conquest*, pp. 15–6).

30. *ASC* 'E', 1052; Osbern Pentecost held some comital land in Herefords during the exile of Godwine and Harold (*GDB* fo. 186). 'Pentecost's castle' has been identified with Ewias Harold, held after 1066 by Osbern's nephew, Alvred of Marlborough, but see Lewis, 'An Introduction to the Herefordshire Domesday', p. 11. See also notes 44–5 below.

31. See note 18 above.

32. The 'D' *Chronicle* presents Tostig and Judith as already married when the family fled to Bruges in late September 1051 but the *Vita Edwardi* (Barlow (ed.), pp. 24–5) makes Godwine arrive in Bruges just after his son's wedding-feast. For Eustace and Baldwin, see Heather Tanner, 'The Expansion of the Power and Influence of the Counts of Boulogne under Eustace II', *ANS*, 14 (1992), 251–86.

33. For Odda, see Williams, *Land, Power and Politics: the Family and Career of Odda of Deerhurst*.

34. He seems to have gone direct from Bruges on his barefoot pilgrimage to Jerusalem, dying on the return journey at Constantinople (where he was buried) at Michaelmas (29 September) 1052 (*ASC* 'C', 1052).

35. *ASC* 'D', 1051: 'the king sent Bishop Ealdred from London with a force and they were to intercept [Harold]...but they could not – or would not'. Ealdred's activities seem confined to his diocese in 1051–2 (King, 'Ealdred, Archbishop of York: the Worcester Years', pp. 127, 134).

36. Fleming, *Kings and Lords in Conquest England*, pp. 53–103, especially Table 3,1 (p. 59).

37. *ASC*, 'D', E', 1052.

38. *ASC* 'C', 'D', 1052. For the *butsecarles*, see below.

39. We are not told the size of Godwine's fleet but Harold brought nine ships from Ireland.

40. *ASC* 'C,' 'D', 1052 (see also the chapter heading above).

41. *ASC* 'C,' 'D', 1052; 'E', the Canterbury text, specifically mentions the outlawry of Archbishop Robert, for whom it has a particular animus.

42. Stigand is given the leading role in the negotiations both in the 'E' *Chronicle* and in the *Vita Edwardi*. For his connection with Emma, see *ASC* 'C', 1043.

43. Brother of Duke William's most trusted friend, William fitzOsbern, later earl of Hereford.

44. *JnW* ii, pp. 572–3; Osbern was accompanied by one Hugh, otherwise unknown, who had yielded up a second, unnamed castle.

45. *JnW* ii, pp. 570–1; he includes Alvred the king's marshall and Ansfrid *Ceocesfot* (cocksfoot) among the 'survivors'. Alvred the marshall was perhaps Alvred of Marlborough, nephew of Osbern Pentecost (see previous note), who after 1066 received some of his uncle's land (Williams, *The English and the Norman Conquest*, pp. 10–11, 16).

46. *ASC* 'C' 1050, 'E' 1051; Barlow, *Edward the Confessor*, p. 102; Campbell, 'Some Agents and Agencies of the Late Anglo-Saxon State', p. 204. Beorn Estrithson had probably been commander of the lithesmen, who recovered his body for burial (*ASC* 'E', 1049).

47. *ASC* 'E' distinguishes the two royal ships (*þæs cynges ii scipum*), commanded by Earl Harold and his brother Tostig respectively, from the 42 ships of the *landesmenn*, under the overall command of Godwine. 'C' mentions the Mercians, but gives no figures.

48. In Scandinavian sources the *snekkja* is smaller than the great *drekkar*, 'dragons', but both are longships, built for size and speed (Rodger, 'Cnut's Geld and the Size of Danish Ships', pp. 394–5).

49. *ASC* 'E', 1052.

50. *ASC* 'D', 1051, 'C', 1063.

51. *GDB*, fo. 162.

52. *LDB*, fo. 48.

53. *GDB* ff. 238, 64v; *LDB* fo. 107. For the post-Conquest ship-sokes of Warwickshire, see Hooper, 'Some Observations on the Navy in Late Anglo-Saxon England', p. 211.

54. *GDB* ff. 26, 230. Ship-service was also due from Exeter and the other Devon towns, and from Bedford (*GDB* ff. 100, 209).

55. Hooper, 'Some Observations on the Navy in Late Anglo-Saxon England', pp. 206–8.

56. *GDB* ff. 1, 3, 4v, 10v.

57. The *butsecarles* of Hastings and 'the sea-coasts' are recorded in *ASC* 'C', 1052, while 'E' names the ports from which Godwine and Harold recruited ships; for the *butsecarles* of Sandwich, see *ASC* 'C', 1066. In 1049, the 'men of Hastings' captured two of Earl Swein's ships and took them to the king at Sandwich (*ASC* 'D', 1049).

58. *ASC*, 1066; 'C' tells of the enforced participation of the *butsecarles* of Sandwich, and 'E' of their later desertion.

59. *ASC* 'C', 1066: 'all that summer and autumn'. See also Chapter 9, note 110 above.

60. *ASC* 'D', 1051. Heregeld is contrasted with 'every other render' (*eghwilc oðer gaful*) in a writ, which, since it is addressed to Ælfgar as earl of Essex, may date from 1051–2 (S. 1075, Harmer, *Anglo-Saxon Writs*, no. 15). Geld is also distinguished from danegeld in a spurious writ forged at Westminster Abbey (S. 1137).

61. *HC* i, pp. 77–8 (see Chapter 9, note 78 above); *GDB* fo. 336v.

62. *GDB* fo. 30.

63. *GDB* fo. 336v; the other dues were heriot, personal forfeitures and pursuit of thieves.

64. *GDB* fo. 132 (Esgar the staller; Aki).

65. *GDB* fo. 56v.

66. Ditchford, Gloucs, was assessed at 1½ hides to the service of the lord (the bishop of Worcester) but discharged its dues as one hide 'at the king's summons' (S.1409, Robertson, *Anglo-Saxon Charters*, pp. 208–9); see also R. Welldon Finn, *Domesday Studies: the Liber Exoniensis* (London, 1964), pp. 111–4.

67. Sally Harvey, 'Domesday Book and Anglo-Norman Governance', *TRHS* 5th series, 25 (1975), 175–93; but see Clanchy, *From Memory to Written Record*, pp. 29–31. In the south-west, *only* the pre-Conquest hidages are recorded.

68. The titles are modern and there is no evidence that geld assessments or accounts were in fact kept in the form of rolls.

69. For V. H. Galbraith (*The Making of Domesday Book* (Oxford, 1961), p. 96), the Northamptonshire Geld Roll 'appears as the typical and ordinary form of these documents', as opposed to the south-western rolls, which 'stand out as the record of some exceptional, even unprecedented enquiry', i.e., the Domesday inquest. But they may simply be different kinds of documents.

70. Robertson, *Anglo-Saxon Charters*, pp. 230–7.

71. Robertson translates *gewered* as '[lands which] have paid geld', but it is more likely to mean 'assessed' (John Brand, *The Exchequer in the Later Twelfth Century*, unpublished PhD thesis, London, 1989, p. 44 and note 130, p. 72). The figures for 'waste' are 'arrived at by totting up the hidage figures for the land which gelded, the inland and the exempt estates, and subtracting the amount from the total hidage currently attributed to the hundred' (Cyril Hart, *The Hidation of Northamptonshire* (Leicester, 1970), p. 17). The shire was probably over-assessed.

72. The south-western Rolls are discussed in Galbraith, *The Making of Domesday Book*, pp. 87–101; Welldon Finn, *Domesday Studies: the Liber Exoniensis*, pp. 97–123. The Wiltshire rolls are edited by R. R. Darlington, *VCH Wiltshire* ii, 169–77; those for Dorset by Williams, *VCH Dorset* iii, 115–23.

73. The first or second Monday after Easter (hocktide, hockeday) was commonly used for the payment of rent (C. R. Cheney, *A Handbook of Dates for Students of English History* (London, 1970), p. 40; Ronald Hutton, *The Stations of the Sun: a History of the Ritual Year in Britain* (Oxford, 1996), pp. 202, 207–9). The 'feast of St Mary' is the Annunciation (Lady Day), 25 March; the autumnal feasts (the Assumption, 15 August and the Nativity, 18 September) were also used for dating in this period (*ASC*, 1051, 1069).

74. Galbraith assumed four to each hundred (*The Making of Domesday Book*, p. 88), Welldon Finn four to each shire (*Domesday Studies: the Liber Exoniensis*, p. 98, note 2).

75. Welldon Finn, *Domesday Studies: the Liber Exoniensis*, p. 101; *GDB* fo. 72v. The name elements *-wig* and *-wine* are often confused by the Domesday scribe, and both names are rare in the eleventh century.

76. Harmer, *Anglo-Saxon writs*, p. 440; Welldon Finn, *Domesday Studies: the Liber Exoniensis*, pp. 97, 100 and note 3.

77. OE *fegan*, 'to join, unite, bring together'; cf the *congregatores* 'bringers together, gatherers' of Wiltshire and Dorset.

78. *Domesday Book* iv, p. 489.

79. *Domesday Book* iv, p. 65; *GDB* ff. 113v–114v (Ralph de la Pommeraye), 117v (William *hostiarius*). William also had land in Notts (*GDB*, fo. 292) and Ralph in Somerset (*GDB* fo. 96v).

80. Galbraith, *The Making of Domesday Book*, p. 88. For the collectors' accounts, see Uggescombe Hundred, Dorset, where '3s.6d were found in their lists (*indicis eorum*) above the number of hides' (*VCH Dorset* iii, p. 126). At Bradenham (Norfolk), the annual rent was paid *in thesauro regis* and a written account (*brevis*) is mentioned (*LDB* fo. 276v).

81. *ASC* 'C', 1035 (Harold I's seizure from Emma of the treasure that had belonged to Cnut); *ASC* 'C' 'E', 1043 (Edward's seizure of treasure from Emma 'because she had withheld it too firmly from him'). The use of Easter as one of the terms for geld-payments may be connected with the holding of

royal assemblies at Winchester at that season (Barlow, *Edward the Confessor*, p. 186; Martin Biddle, 'Seasonal Festivals and Residence: Winchester, Westminster and Gloucester in the Tenth to Twelfth Centuries', *ANS*, 8 (1986), 51–72).

82. *ASC*, 1006; Martin Biddle, '*Felix urbs Winthonie*', David Parsons (ed.), *Tenth-century studies*, (London and Chichester, 1975), pp. 123–40; Martin Biddle (ed.), *Winchester in the Early Middle Ages*, Winchester Studies I (Oxford, 1976), pp. 289–92, 448–69.

83. *GDB*, ff. 49v-50v, 63v, 73–74v, 84–5 (Williams, *The English and the Norman Conquest*, pp. 109–17); *Winton Domesday* Survey 'A' (*c.* 1110), see Biddle (ed), *Winchester in the Early Middle Ages*, pp. 390–1.

84. Compare the heriot of the 'median thegn' in II Cnut 71,2 (a horse and its trappings and his weapons) with the heriot (*relevamentum*) of the *tainus vel miles regis* in Berkshire: his weapons and two horses, one saddled and one unsaddled, and his hounds and hawks if the king wanted them (*GDB* fo. 56v).

85. Henry and Theodoric appear in the *Winton Domesday* (Biddle (ed.), *Winchester in the Early Middle Ages*, p. 59) and the rest in Domesday Book (see note 83 above). For Oda, see note 93 below; his by-name is recorded only in Exon Domesday (the circuit return for the south-west) and other *taini* who held before 1066 may also have been royal officials of some kind.

86. *ASC* 'C', 1053; *JnW* ii, pp. 572–3.

87. The *Vita Edwardi*, gives the 'parts' of a palace, the *aula* or hall (Barlow (ed.), pp. 7, 29), the *thalamum* or chamber (pp. 14, 28, 29) and the *oratorium* or chapel (p. 63); see also Barlow, *The English Church, 1000–1066*, p. 119.

88. Barlow, *The English Church, 1000–1066*, p. 123.

89. Keynes, 'Regenbald the Chancellor (*sic*)', pp. 206–7; *GDB* ff. 63, 157, 208, 23. He died a violent death, and was buried at Westminster Abbey, of which he was a benefactor (Barlow, *Edward the Confessor*, pp. 165–6).

90. *Chron Ramsey*, pp. 170–1; see also Chapter 9, note 54 above.

91. V. H. Galbraith, *Studies in the Public Records* (London, 1948), p. 45; D. M. Metcalf, 'Continuity and Change in English Monetary History, *c.* 973–1086', *BNJ*, 50 (1980), 20–49, at p. 24(I owe this reference to Dr John Brand).

92. Charles Johnson (ed.), *Richard fitz Nigel, The Dialogue of the Exchequer* (London, 1950), pp. 8–13. See especially the duties of the Treasurer's clerk (pp. 8–9), who counts, packs and records the sums received and issues receipts (tallies) for them; Richard fitzNigel remarks elsewhere (p. 7), that the Exchequer had once been known as 'The Tallies'.

93. Biddle (ed.), *Winchester in the Early Middle Ages*, p. 59 (no. 184); Caroline and Frank Thorn (eds), *Domesday Book: Dorset* (Chichester, 1983), no. 1,21. For Cnut's 'treasurer', Henry, see Chapter 10, note 24 above.

94. For Ralph the staller, see Williams, *The English and the Norman Conquest*, pp. 60–2.

95. Keynes, 'Regenbald the Chancellor (*sic*)', pp. 185–222; *idem*, 'Giso, Bishop of Wells', p. 209.

96. S. 1088, 1105, 1140.

97. T. A. Heslop, 'English seals from the mid ninth century to 1100', *Journal of the British Archaeological Association*, 133 (1980), 1–16. Compare the portrayal

of Harold II, crowned and enthroned, on the Bayeux Tapestry (Wilson, *The Bayeux Tapestry*, plate 31). For the connection with 'crown-wearings', see Michael Hare, 'Kings, Crowns and Festivals: the Origins of Gloucester as Royal Ceremonial Centre', *Transactions of the Bristol and Gloucestershire Archaeological Society* 115 (1997), 41–78, at p. 52.

98. Florence E. Harmer, 'The English Contribution to the Epistolary Usages of the Early Scandinavian Kings', *Saga-Book of the Viking Society*, 33 (1950), 127–8, 139–41; Harmer, *Anglo-Saxon Writs*, pp. 17–8, 99–101.

99. It is of interest that when the northerners rose against William I in 1069–70, they chose as king, not Swein of Denmark, nor one of their own number, but the last West Saxon ætheling, Edgar (Williams, *The English and the Norman Conquest*, pp. 32–3).

100. *JnW* ii, pp. 598–9; *ASC* 'D', 'E', 1065. The heriots 'among the Danes' are noticeably lighter than those in Wessex, Mercia and East Anglia (II Cnut, 71).

101. Barlow (ed.), *Vita Edwardi*, pp. 51–5. The *Vita Edwardi* gives details which are in no other source (see Barlow, *Edward the Confessor*, pp. 233–9); the account in the 'C' *Chronicle* differs from that in the 'D' and 'E' texts, and both from the fuller version of John of Worcester.

102. Barlow, *Edward the Confessor*, p. 236; Kapelle, *The Norman Conquest of the North*, p. 101.

103. Peter A. Clarke, *The English Nobility Under Edward the Confessor* (Oxford, 1994), pp. 214–5, 216–7; see Chapter 10, note 120 above. Their father Ælfgar may have had similar ambitions (Chapter 8 above).

104. *The Witenagemot in the Reign of Edward the Confessor*, p. 1.

105. *Kings and Earls in Conquest England*, pp. 53, 103.

106. *Edward the Confessor*, pp. 197, 189.

107. *ASC* 'C', 1065. The poem is in 'D' also, but not in 'E', the text most sympathetic to Godwine and his family.

108. Barlow, *Edward the Confessor*, pp. 243–4; see Chapter 8 above.

109. See above, note 59. For an appreciation, wholly favourable, of Harold's abilities as a king, see *JnW* ii, pp. 600–1.

110. R. R. Darlington (ed.), *Vita Wulfstani*, Camden Society third series, 40 (1928), pp. 22–3; Emma Mason, *St Wulfstan of Worcester, c. 1008–1095* (Oxford, 1990), pp. 102–4.

111. The exception which proves the rule, Gospatric's charter for 'the lands which were Cumbrian' relates to an area recently acquired and not yet brought under English administration (Harmer, *Anglo-Saxon Writs*, no. 121 and see Chapter 10 above).

112. This was the earl's 'third penny', frequently mentioned in Domesday Book; the king's 'two pennies' were administered by the local sheriff.

113. Robertson, *Anglo-Saxon Charters*, no. 105, pp. 200–3, 447–9. For Odda see Williams, *Land, Power and Politics: the Family and Career of Odda of Deerhurst*, especially pp. 3–7, 14; for Ordgar, see Finberg, 'The house of Ordgar and the foundation of Tavistock Abbey', pp. 190–201.

114. *GDB* ff. 1, 1v; Williams, 'Lost Worlds: Kentish Society in the Eleventh Century', forthcoming.

115. Brown, *The Norman Conquest*, p. 37. Compare the Worcester description of the year 1016 as the time when 'the kingdom was in turmoil and not yet stabilized under the rule of a single king' (*HC* i, p. 277).
116. Downer (ed.), *Leges Henrici Primi*, cl. 6, 2a (pp. 96–7).

BIBLIOGRAPHY

Only works used and cited generally are included below; single references to specific topics will be found in the notes. The main sources for each section are discussed and the references given towards the beginning of each chapter.

1   General Works

Campbell, J., *Essays in Anglo-Saxon History* (London, 1986).
Campbell, J. (ed.), *The Anglo-Saxons* (Oxford, 1982).
John, E., *Reassessing Anglo-Saxon England* (Manchester, 1996).
Sawyer, P. H., *Kings and Vikings* (London, 1982).
Sawyer, P. H., *From Roman Britain to Norman England* (London, 1978).
Stenton, F. M., *Anglo-Saxon England*, 3rd edn (Oxford, 1971).
Welch, M., *Anglo-Saxon England* (London, 1992).
Whitelock, D. (ed.), *English Historical Documents, i, 500–1042* (London, 1955).
Wood, I. N. and Lund, N. (eds), *People and Places in Northern Europe, 500–1600* (Woodbridge, 1991).
Wormald, P., Bullough, D. and Collins, R. (eds), *Ideal and Reality in Frankish and Anglo-Saxon Society* (Oxford, 1993).

2   From the Adventus to Alfred

Arnold, C. J., *The Archaeology of Early Anglo-Saxon England* (London & New York, 1988).
Bassett, S., 'In Search of the Origins of Anglo-Saxon Kingdoms', in S. Bassett (1989) (ed.), *Origins*, pp. 3–27.
Bassett, S. (ed.), *The Origins of Anglo-Saxon Kingdoms* (Leicester, 1989).
Esmonde Cleary, A. S., *The Ending of Roman Britain* (London, 1989).
Dumville, D. N., 'The Treaty of Alfred and Guthrum', D. M. Dumville (1992), in *Wessex and England from Alfred to Edgar*, pp. 1–27.
Keynes, S., 'England, 700–900', in R. McKitterick (ed.), *The New Cambridge Medieval History, ii, c. 700–900* (Cambridge, 1995).
Keynes, S. and Lapidge, M., *Alfred the Great* (Harmondsworth, 1983).
Kirby, D. P., *The Earliest English Kings* (London, 1991).

Nelson, J. L., '"A King across the sea": Alfred in Continental Perspective', *TRHS* 5th series, 36 (1986), pp. 45–68.

Smyth, A. P., *Alfred the Great* (Oxford, 1995).

Wood, I. N., 'The Franks and Sutton Hoo', in I. N. Wood and N. Lund (1991) (eds), *People and Places in Northern Europe*, pp. 1–14.

Wood, I. N., 'Frankish Hegemony in England', in M. Carver (1992) (ed.), *The Age of Sutton Hoo*, pp. 235–41.

Yorke, B., *Kings and Kingdoms of Early Anglo-Saxon England* (London, 1990).

3   The Late Old English Kingdom

Allen Brown, R., *The Norman Conquest* (London, 1984).

Allen Brown, R., *The Normans and the Norman Conquest* 2nd edn (Woodbridge, 1985).

Barlow, F., *Edward the Confessor* (London, 1970).

Cooper J. (ed.), *The Battle of Maldon* (London, 1991).

Dumville, D. N., 'Between Alfred the Great and Edgar the Peaceable: Æthelstan, First King of England', in D. N. Dumville (1992), *Wessex and England from Alfred to Edgar*, pp. 141–72.

Dumville, D. N., *Wessex and England from Alfred to Edgar* (Woodbridge, 1992).

Fleming, R., *Kings and Lords in Conquest England* (Cambridge, 1991).

Harper-Bill, C., Holdsworth, C. and Nelson, J. L. (eds), *Studies in Medieval History presented to R. Allen Brown* (Woodbridge, 1989).

Hill, D. (ed.), *Ethelred the Unready: Papers from the Millenniary Conference*, BAR British series, 59 (1978).

Holt, J. C. (ed.), *Domesday Studies: Papers read at the Novocentenary Conference* (Woodbridge, 1987).

Keynes, S., *The Diplomas of King Æthelred, 'the Unready', 978–1016* (Cambridge, 1980).

Keynes, S., 'A Tale of two Kings: Alfred the Great and Æthelred the Unready', *TRHS* 5th series, 36 (1986), pp. 195–217.

Keynes, S., 'The Æthelings in Normandy', *ANS*, 13 (1991), pp. 193–205.

Keynes, S., 'The Historical Context of the Battle of Maldon', in D. Scragg (1991) (ed.), *The Battle of Maldon*, pp. 81–113.

Lawson, M. K., *Cnut: The Danes in England in the Early Eleventh Century* (London, 1993).

Lund, N., 'Cnut's Danish Kingdom', in A. Rumble (1994) (ed.), *The Reign of Cnut*, pp. 27–42.

Rumble, A. (ed.), *The Reign of Cnut: King of England, Denmark and Norway* (Leicester, 1994).

Scragg, D. (ed.), *The Battle of Maldon, AD 991* (Oxford, 1991).

Stafford, P., *Unification and Conquest: A Political and Social History of England in the Ninth and Tenth Centuries* (London, 1989).

Whitelock, D., *History, Law and Literature in Tenth- and Eleventh-century England* (London, 1981).

Williams, A., *The English and the Norman Conquest* (Woodbridge, 1995).

4   Sources and Source Criticism

(a)   Narrative Sources

Blake, E. O., (ed.), *Liber Eliensis*, Camden Society third series, 92 (1962).

Dumville, D. N., 'Sub-Roman Britain: History and Legend', *History*, 62 (1977), pp. 173–92.

Dumville, D. N., 'The Historical Value of the Historia Brittonum', *Arthurian Literature*, 6 (1986), pp. 1–59.

Jackson, K., 'On the Northern British Section in Nennius', in N. K. Chadwick (ed.), *Celt and Saxon* (Cambridge, 1964), pp. 20–62.

Keynes, S., 'The Declining Reputation of Æthelred the Unready', in D. Hill (1978) (ed.), *Ethelred the Unready*, pp. 227–53.

Keynes, S., 'On the Authenticity of Asser's *Life of King Alfred*', *Journal of Ecclesiastical History*, 47 (1996), pp. 529–51.

Lapidge, M. and Herren, M. (eds), *Aldhelm: The Prose Works* (Ipswich, 1979).

Sims-Williams, P., 'The Settlement of England in Bede and the Chronicle', *ASE*, 12 (1983), pp. 1–41.

Wallace-Hadrill, J. M., *Bede's Ecclesiastical History of the English People: A Historical Commentary* (Oxford, 1993).

Wormald, P., 'Bede, the *Bretwaldas* and the Origins of the *Gens Anglorum*', in P. Wormald *et al.* (1993) (eds), *Ideal and Reality in Frankish and Anglo-Saxon England*, pp. 99–129.

(b)   Charters, Writs and Literacy

Campbell, A., *Charters of Rochester* (Oxford, 1973).

Chaplais, P., 'The Origin and Authenticity of the Royal Anglo-Saxon Diploma'; 'Who Introduced Charters into England: The Case for St Augustine', in F. Ranger (ed.), *Prisca munimenta* (London, 1973), pp. 28–42; 88–107.

Harmer, F. E., *Select English Historical Documents of the Ninth and Tenth Centuries* (Cambridge, 1914).

Harmer, F. E., *Anglo-Saxon Writs* (Manchester, 1952).

Kelly, S., 'Anglo-Saxon Lay Society and the Use of the Written Word', in R. McKitterick (1990) (ed.), *The Uses of Literacy*, pp. 36–62.

Kelly, S., *Charters of St Augustine's Abbey, Canterbury and Minster-in-Thanet* (Oxford, 1995).

Kelly, S., *Charters of Shaftesbury Abbey* (Oxford, 1996).

Keynes, S., 'Royal Government and the Written Word in Late Anglo-Saxon England', in R. McKitterick (1990) (ed.), *The Uses of Literacy*, pp. 226–57.

Keynes, S., 'A Lost Cartulary of St Alban's Abbey', *ASE*, 22 (1993), pp. 253–79.

Keynes, S., 'The West Saxon Charters of King Æthelwulf and his Sons', *EHR*, 111 (1994), pp. 1109–49.

Keynes, S., *An Atlas of Attestations in Anglo-Saxon Charters, c. 670–1066* (Cambridge, 1995).

McKitterick, R. (ed.), *The Uses of Literacy in Early Medieval Europe* (Cambridge, 1990).

O'Donovan, M.-A., *Charters of Sherborne* (Oxford, 1988).
Robertson, A. J., *Anglo-Saxon Charters*, 2nd edn (Cambridge, 1955).
Sawyer, P. H., *Charters of Burton Abbey* (Cambridge, 1979).
Stenton, F. M., *The Latin Charters of the Anglo-Saxon Period* (Oxford, 1955).
Wormald, P., *Bede and the Conversion of England: The Charter Evidence*, Jarrow Lecture (Jarrow, 1984).

(c)   Law

Attenborough, F. L., *The Laws of the Earliest English Kings* (Cambridge, 1922, reprinted New York, 1963).
Kennedy, A. G., 'Disputes about *Bocland*: The Forum for their Adjudication', *ASE*, 14 (1985), pp. 175–95.
Lawson, M. K., 'Archbishop Wulfstan and the Homiletic Element in the Laws of Æthelred and Cnut', in A. Rumble (1994) (ed.), *The Reign of Cnut*, pp. 141–64.
Robertson, A. J., *Laws of the Kings of England from Edmund to Henry I* (Cambridge, 1925, reprinted New York, 1974).
Wormald, P., 'Æthelred the Lawmaker', in D. Hill (1978) (ed.), *Ethelred the Unready*, pp. 47–80.
Wormald, P., 'Charters, Law and the Settlement of Disputes in Anglo-Saxon England', in W. Davies and P. Fouracre (eds), *The Settlement of Disputes in Early Medieval Europe* (Cambridge, 1986) pp. 149–68.

(d)   Genealogies

Dumville, D. N., 'The Anglian Collection of Royal Genealogies and Regnal Lists', *ASE*, 5 (1976), pp. 23–50.
Dumville, D. N., 'Kingship, Genealogies and Regnal Lists', in P. H. Sawyer and I. N. Wood (1977) (eds), *Early medieval kingship*, pp. 72–104.
Dumville, D. N., 'The West Saxon Genealogical Regnal List and the Chronology of Early Wessex', *Peritia*, 4 (1985), pp. 21–66.

(e)   Numismatics

Blackburn, M. (ed.), *Anglo-Saxon Monetary History* (Leicester, 1986).
Blackburn, M., 'Æthelred's Coinage and the Payment of Tribute', in D. Scragg (1991) (ed.), *The Battle of Maldon, AD 991*, pp. 156–69.
Blunt, C. E., 'The Coinage of Offa', in R. H. M. Dolley (ed.), *Anglo-Saxon Coins, Studies Presented to Sir Frank Stenton* (London, 1961), pp. 39–62.
Blunt, C. E., Lyons, C. S. S. and Stewart, B. H. I. H., 'The Coinage of Southern England, 796–840', *BNJ*, 32 (1964), pp. 1–74.
Blunt, C. E., Stewart, B. H. I. H. and Lyons, C. S. S., *Coinage in Tenth-century England* (London, 1989).
Metcalf, D. M., 'Monetary Affairs in Mercia in the Time of Æthelbald (716–757)', in A. Dornier (1977) (ed.), *Mercian Studies*, pp. 84–106.
Metcalf, D. M., (ed.), *Coinage in Ninth-century Northumbria*, BAR British series 180 (1987).

Pagan, H., 'Coinage in Southern England, 796–874', in M. Blackburn (1986) (ed.), *Anglo-Saxon Monetary History*, pp. 45–65.

Stewart, I., 'The London Mint and the Coinage of Offa', in M. Blackburn (1986) (ed.), *Anglo-Saxon Monetary History*, pp. 27–43.

Talvio, T., 'Harold I's and Harthacnut's *Jewel Cross* type Re-considered', in M. Blackburn (1986) (ed.), *Anglo-Saxon Monetary History*, pp. 273–90.

5   Specific Topics

(a)   Kings and Kingship

Campbell, J., 'Bede's *Reges* and *Principes*', in J. Campbell (1986), *Essays in Anglo-Saxon History*, pp. 85–98.

Nelson, J. L., *Politics and Ritual in Early Medieval Europe* (London, 1986).

Sawyer, P. H. and Wood, I. N. (eds), *Early Medieval Kingship* (Leeds, 1977).

Wallace-Hadrill, J. M., *Early Germanic Kingship in England and on the Continent* (Oxford, 1971).

(b)   Society and Institutions

Brooks, N., 'The Administrative Background of the Burghal Hidage', in D. Hill and A. R. Rumble (1996) (eds), *The Defence of Wessex*, pp. 128–50.

Campbell, J., 'Some Agents and Agencies of the Late Anglo-Saxon State', in J. C. Holt (1987) (ed.), *Domesday Studies*, pp. 201–18.

Chadwick, H. M., *Studies on Anglo-Saxon Institutions* (Cambridge, 1905, reprinted New York, 1963).

Chaplais, P., 'The Anglo-Saxon Chancery: From the Diploma to the Writ', in F. Ranger (1973) (ed.), *Prisca Munimenta*, pp. 43–62.

Chaplais, P., 'The Royal Anglo-Saxon "Chancery" of the Tenth Century Re-visited', in H. Mayr-Harting and R. I. Moore (eds), *Studies in Medieval History Presented to R. H. C. Davis* (London, 1985), pp. 41–51.

Clanchy, M. T., *From Memory to Written Record: England, 1066–1307*, 2nd edn (London, 1993).

Davies, W. and Vierck, H., 'The Contexts of the Tribal Hidage: Social Aggregates and Settlement Patterns', *Frümittelaltliche Studien*, 8 (1979), pp. 223–93.

Dumville, D. N., 'The Tribal Hidage: An Introduction to its Texts and their History', in S. Bassett (1989) (ed.), *Origins*, pp. 225–30.

Finberg, H. P. R., 'The House of Ordgar and the Foundation of Tavistock Abbey', *EHR*, 58 (1943), pp. 190–201.

Fleming, R., 'Oral Testimony and the Domesday Inquest', *ANS*, 17 (1994), pp. 101–22.

Finn, R. W., *Domesday Studies: The Liber Exoniensis* (London, 1964).

Fleming, R., 'Domesday Estates of the King and the Godwinesons: A Study in Late Saxon Politics', *Speculum*, 58 (1983), pp. 987–1007.

Galbraith, V. H., *The Making of Domesday Book* (Oxford, 1961).

Hart, C. R., 'Athelstan "Half-king" and his Family', *ASE*, 2 (1973), pp. 115–44.

Hart, C. R., 'The Kingdom of Mercia', in A. Dornier (1977) (ed.), *Mercian Studies*, pp. 43–61.

Hill, D. and Rumble, A. R. (eds), *The Defence of Wessex: The Burghal Hidage and Anglo-Saxon Fortifications* (Manchester, 1996).

Keynes, S., 'Regenbald the Chancellor (*sic*)', *ANS*, 10 (1988), pp. 185–222.

Keynes, S., 'Cnut's Earls', in A. Rumble (1994) (ed.), *The Reign of Cnut*, pp. 43–88.

Keynes, S., 'Giso, Bishop of Wells (1061–88)', *ANS*, 19 (1997), pp. 203–71.

King, V. J., 'Ealdred, Archbishop of York: The Worcester Years', *ANS*, 18 (1996), pp. 123–37.

Larson, L. M., *The King's Household in England before the Norman Conquest* (Madison, Wisconsin, 1904).

Lewis, C. P., 'The French in England before the Norman Conquest', *ANS*, 17 (1995), pp. 123–44.

Loyn, H. R., 'The Hundred in England in the Tenth and Eleventh Centuries', in H. Hearder and H. R. Loyn (eds), *British Government and Administration* (Cardiff, 1974) pp. 1–15; reprinted in *Society and Peoples* (London, 1992), pp. 111–34.

Loyn, H. R., *The Governance of Anglo-Saxon England, 500–1087* (London, 1984).

Oleson, T. J., *The Witenagemot in the Reign of Edward the Confessor* (Oxford, 1955).

Raraty, D. G., 'Earl Godwine of Wessex: The Origins of his Power and his Political Affiliations', *History*, 74 (1989), pp. 3–19.

Reynolds, S., *Fiefs and Vassals* (Oxford, 1994).

Thacker, A., 'Some Terms for Noblemen in Anglo-Saxon England, *c.* 650–900', *ASSAH*, 2 (1981), pp. 201–36.

Williams, A., 'Land and Power in the Eleventh Century: The Estates of Harold Godwineson', *ANS*, 3 (1981), pp. 171–87.

Williams, A., '*Princeps Merciorum Gentis*: The Family, Career and Connections of Ælfhere, Ealdorman of Mercia, 956–83', *ASE*, 10 (1982), pp. 143–72.

Williams, A., '"Cockles amongst the Wheat": Danes and English in the West Midlands in the First Half of the Eleventh Century', *Midland History*, 11 (1986), pp. 1–22.

Williams, A., 'The King's Nephew: The Family and Career of Ralph, Earl of Hereford', in C. Harper-Bill *et al.* (1989) (eds), *Studies in Medieval History Presented to R. Allen Brown*, pp. 327–43.

Williams, A., *Land, Power and Politics: The Family and Career of Odda of Deerhurst* (Deerhurst, 1997).

Williams, A., 'Lost Worlds: Kentish Society in the Eleventh Century', *Medieval Prosopography*, forthcoming.

(c) Towns, Trade and Economics

Campbell, J., 'The Sale of Land and the Economics of Power in Early England: Problems and Possibilities', *Haskins Society J.*, 1 (1989), pp. 23–37.

Clarke, H. and Ambrosiani, B. (eds), *Towns in the Viking Age* (Leicester, 1991).

Hodges, R., *Dark Age Economics: The Origins of Towns and Trade, AD 600–1000* (London, 1982).
Sawyer, P. H., 'Kings and Merchants', in P. H. Sawyer and I. N. Wood (1977) (eds), *Early Medieval Kingship*, pp. 139–58.

(d) Military

Abels, R. P., *Lordship and Military Obligation in Anglo-Saxon England* (Berkeley, Los Angeles & London, 1988).
Abels, R., 'Tactics, Strategy and Military Organization', in D. Scragg (1991) (ed.), *The Battle of Maldon, AD 991*, pp. 143–55.
Brooks, N., 'The Development of Military Obligations in Eighth- and Ninth-century England', in K. Hughes and P. Clemoes (eds), *England before the Conquest* (Cambridge, 1971), pp. 69–84.
Hawkes, S. C. (ed.), *Weapons and Warfare in Anglo-Saxon England* (Oxford, 1989).
Hooper, N., 'The Housecarls in England in the Eleventh Century', *ANS*, 7 (1985), pp. 161–76.
Hooper, N., 'Some Observations on the Navy in Late Anglo-Saxon England', in C. Harper-Bill *et al.* (1989) (eds), *Studies in Medieval History Presented to R. Allen Brown*, pp. 203–13.
Hooper, N., 'Military Developments in the Reign of Cnut', in A. Rumble (1994) (ed.), *The Reign of Cnut*, pp. 89–100.
Lund, N., 'The Armies of Swein Forkbeard and Cnut: *Leding* or *lið*?', *ASE*, 15 (1986), pp. 105–18.
Rodger, N. A. M., 'Cnut's Geld and the Size of Danish Ships', *EHR*, 119 (1995), pp. 392–403.

(e) Place-names and Settlements

Campbell, J., 'Bede's Words for Places', in J. Campbell (1986), *Essays in Anglo-Saxon History*, pp. 99–119.
Gelling, M., *Signposts to the Past* (London, 1978).
Hill, D., *An Atlas of Anglo-Saxon England* (Oxford, 1981).

(f) Ecclesiastical

Barlow, F., *The English Church, 1000–1066* (London, 1963).
Blair, J. (ed.), *Minsters and Parish Churches: The Local Church in Transition, 950–1200* (Oxford, 1988).
Campbell, J., 'Observations on the Conversion of England', in J. Campbell (1986), *Essays in Anglo-Saxon History*, pp. 69–84.
Dornier, A., 'The Anglo-Saxon Monastery of Breedon-on-the-Hill', in A. Dornier (1977) (ed.), *Mercian Studies*, pp. 155–68.
Rollason, D., 'The Cults of Murdered Royal Saints in Anglo-Saxon England', *ASE*, 11 (1983), pp. 1–22.
Rollason, D., *Saints and Relics in Anglo-Saxon England* (Oxford, 1989).

6   Local Studies

Anderson, A. O., *Early Sources of Scottish History, 500–1286*, 2v, reprinted (Stamford, 1990).
Anderson, M. O., *Kings and Kingship in Early Scotland* (Edinburgh, 1973).
Bailey, K., 'The Middle Saxons', in S. Bassett (1989) (ed.), *Origins*, pp. 108–22.
Blair, J., 'Frithuwold's Kingdom and the Origins of Surrey', in S. Bassett (1989) (ed.), *Origins*, pp. 97–107.
Blair, J., *Early Medieval Surrey* (Stroud, 1991).
Blair, J., *Anglo-Saxon Oxfordshire* (Stroud, 1994).
Brooks, N., *The Early History of the Church of Canterbury* (Leicester, 1984).
Brooks, N., 'The Creation and Early Structure of the Kingdom of Kent', in S. Bassett (1989) (ed.), *Origins*, pp. 55–74.
Brooks, N., 'The Formation of the Mercian Kingdom', in S. Bassett (1989) (ed.), *Origins*, pp. 159–70.
Carver, M., (ed.), *The Age of Sutton Hoo* (Woodbridge, 1992).
Cunliffe, B., *Wessex to AD 1000* (London, 1993).
Davies, W., *Wales in the Early Middle Ages* (Leicester, 1982).
Dornier, A. (ed.), *Mercian Studies* (Leicester, 1977).
Drewett, P., Rudling, D. and Gardiner, M., *The South-east to AD 1000* (London, 1988).
Dumville, D. N., 'Essex, Middle Anglia and the Expansion of Mercia in the South-east Midlands', in S. Bassett (1989) (ed.), *Origins*, pp. 123–40.
Dumville, D. N., 'The Origins of Northumbria: Some Aspects of the British Background', in S. Bassett (1989) (ed.), *Origins*, pp. 213–22.
Eagles, B., 'Lindsey', in S. Bassett (1989) (ed.), *Origins*, pp. 202–12.
Gelling, M., 'The Early History of Western Mercia', in S. Bassett (1989) (ed.), *Origins*, pp. 184–201.
Hall, R. A., 'Sources for Pre-Conquest York', in I. N. Wood and N. Lund (1991) (eds), *People and Places in Northern Europe*, pp. 83–94.
Hall, R. A. (ed.), *Viking-age York and the North*, CBA Research Report no. 27 (1978).
Hart, C. R., *The Danelaw* (London, 1992).
Higham, N., *The Northern Counties to AD 1000* (London & New York, 1986).
Kapelle, W. E., *The Norman Conquest of the North* (London, 1979).
Keynes, S., 'The Control of Kent in the Ninth Century', *Early Medieval Europe*, 2 (1993), pp. 111–31.
Lewis, C. P., 'An Introduction to the Herefordshire Domesday', in A. Williams and R. W. H. Erskine (eds), *The Herefordshire Domesday* (London, 1988).
Phythian-Adams, C., *Land of the Cumbrians: A Study in British Provincial Origins* (Aldershot, 1996).
Pretty, K., 'Defining the Magonsæte', in S. Bassett (1989) (ed.), *Origins*, pp. 171–83.
Roffe, D., 'The Origins of Derbyshire', *Derbyshire Archaeological Journal*, 106 (1986), pp. 102–22.
Roffe, D., 'An Introdction to the Lincolnshire Domesday' and 'Hundreds and Wapentakes', in A. Williams and G. H. Martin (eds), *The Lincolnshire Domesday* (London, 1992).

Scull, C. J., 'Before Sutton Hoo: Structures of Power and Society in Early East Anglia', in M. Carver (1992) (ed.), *The Age of Sutton Hoo*, pp. 3–23.

Sims-Williams, P., *Religion and Literature in Western England, 600–800* (Oxford, 1990).

Smyth, A. P., *Scandinavian York and Dublin*, 2 vols (Dublin, 1975–9).

Smyth, A. P., *Warlords and Holy Men: Scotland, AD 80–1000* (London, 1984).

Stafford, P., *The East Midlands in the Early Middle Ages* (Leicester, 1985).

Tatton-Brown, T., 'The Towns of Kent', in J. Haslam (ed.), *Anglo-Saxon Towns in Southern England* (Chichester, 1984), pp. 1–36.

Vince, A., *Saxon London: An Archaeological Investigation* (London, 1990).

Wainwright, F. T., *Scandinavian England* (Chichester, 1975).

Whitelock, D., 'The Dealing of the Kings of England with Northumbria', in P. Clemoes (ed), *The Anglo-Saxons* (London, 1959), pp. 70–88, reprinted in D. Whitelock (1981) *History, Law and Literature in Tenth- and Eleventh-century England*.

Williams, A., 'An Introduction to the Worcestershire Domesday', in A. Williams and R. W. H. Erskine (eds), *The Worcestershire Domesday* (London, 1988).

Williams, A., 'The Vikings in Essex', *Essex Archaeology and History*, 27 (1996), pp. 92–101.

Yorke, B., 'The Jutes of Hampshire and Wight and the Origins of Wessex', in S. Bassett (1989) (ed.), *Origins*, pp. 84–96.

Yorke, B., 'The Kingdom of the East Saxons', *ASE*, 14 (1985), pp. 1–36.

Yorke, B., 'Lindsey: The Lost Kingdom Found?', in A. Vince (ed.), *Pre-Viking Lindsey* (Lincoln, 1993), pp. 141–40.

Yorke, B., *Wessex in the Early Middle Ages* (Leicester, 1995).

INDEX

231